The Cambridge Companion to Samuel Johnson provides a unique introduction to the works and intellectual life of one of the most challenging and wide-ranging writers in English literary history. Compiler of the first great English dictionary, editor of Shakespeare, biographer and critic of the English poets, author both of the influential journal *The Rambler* and the popular fiction *Rasselas*, and one of the most engaging conversationalists in literary culture, Johnson is here illuminatingly discussed from different points of view. Essays on his main works are complemented by thematic discussion of his views on the experience of women in the eighteenth century, politics, imperialism, religion, and travel, as well as by chapters covering his life, conversation, letters, and critical reception. Useful reference features include a chronology and guide to further reading. The keynote to the volume is the seamlessness of Johnson's life and writing, and the extraordinary humane intelligence he brought to all his activities. Accessibly written by a distinguished group of international scholars, this volume supplies a stimulating range of approaches, making Johnson newly relevant for our time.

CAMBRIDGE COMPANIONS TO LITERATURE

THE CAMBRIDGE
COMPANION TO
SAMUEL JOHNSON

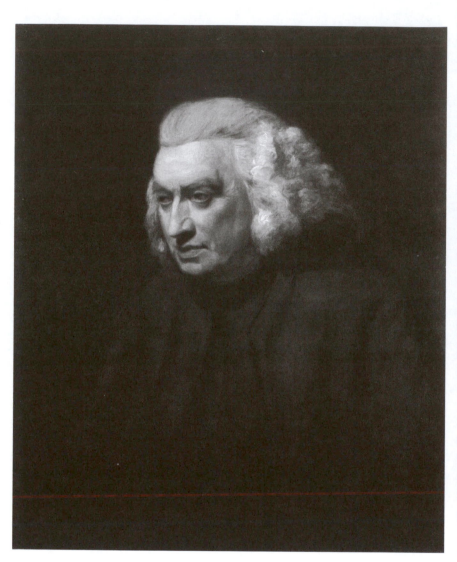

Samuel Johnson (1784) by John Opie

THE CAMBRIDGE COMPANION TO

SAMUEL JOHNSON

EDITED BY

GREG CLINGHAM

National Endowment for the Humanities Chair in the Humanities
Bucknell University

CAMBRIDGE
UNIVERSITY PRESS

PUBLISHED BY THE PRESS SYNDICATE OF THE UNIVERSITY OF CAMBRIDGE
The Pitt Building, Trumpington Street, Cambridge CB2 1RP, United Kingdom

CAMBRIDGE UNIVERSITY PRESS
The Edinburgh Building, Cambridge CB2 2RU, United Kingdom
40 West 20th Street, New York, NY 10011–4211, USA
10 Stamford Road, Oakleigh, Melbourne 3166, Australia

First published 1997

Printed in the United Kingdom at the University Press, Cambridge

Typeset in 10/13 Monotype Sabon by SE

A catalogue record for this book is available from the British Library

Library of Congress cataloguing in publication data

The Cambridge companion to Samuel Johnson / edited by Greg Clingham.
p.   cm. – (Cambridge companions to literature)
Includes bibliographical references and index.
ISBN 0 521 55411 X (hardback). – ISBN 0 521 55625 2 (paperback)
1. Johnson, Samuel, 1709–84 – Criticism and interpretation.
I. Clingham, Greg.   II. Series.
PR3534.C34   1997
828'.609–dc21   95–51162 CIP

ISBN 0 521 55411 X hardback
ISBN 0 521 55625 2 paperback

CONTENTS

ILLUSTRATIONS

NOTES ON CONTRIBUTORS

PHILIP DAVIS, Reader in the English Department, University of Liverpool, is the author of *In Mind of Johnson: Study of Johnson the Rambler* (1989), as well as four other books: *Memory and Writing, Experience of Reading, Malamud's People*, and *Sudden Shakespeare*.

CATHERINE N. PARKE is Professor of English and Women's Studies at the University of Missouri–Columbia. She writes on British and American literature, on biography and autobiography, and is a poet. Her recent books are *Samuel Johnson and Biographical Thinking* (1991), *In the Shadow of Parnassus: Zoé Atkins's Essays on American Poetry*, and a collection of her own poems, *Other People's Lives*. Forthcoming is a historical–critical study of life writing, *Biography: Writing Lives*.

HOWARD D. WEINBROT is Vilas and Quintana Research Professor at the University of Wisconsin, Madison. He has written widely on Samuel Johnson, eighteenth-century intellectual and literary history, and on Anglo-classical and Anglo-French relations. His latest book is *Britannia's Issue: the Rise of British Literature from Dryden to Ossian* (1994).

PAUL J. KORSHIN, Professor of English at the University of Pennsylvania, is editor of *The Age of Johnson: A Scholarly Annual*, and author of scores of essays on Johnson. His contribution is taken from his forthcoming book, *Samuel Johnson at Mid Century: A Study of "The Rambler."*

EITHNE HENSON teaches English part-time at Durham University. Her publications include *"The Fictions of Romantic Chivalry": Samuel Johnson and Romance* (1992), and critical and biographical studies on women writers of the Romantic period in *The Feminist Companion to Literature in English*. She has continuing research interests in gender and landscape in nineteenth-century novels.

ROBERT DEMARIA, JR. is the Henry Noble Macracken Professor of English Literature at Vassar College. He is the author of *Johnson's Dictionary and the Language of Learning* (1986), *The Life of Samuel Johnson* (1993), and the forthcoming *Samuel Johnson and the Life of Reading*. With Gwin Kolb, Mr. DeMaria is editing Johnson's writings on language for *The Yale Edition of the Works of Samuel Johnson*.

ROBERT FOLKENFLIK, Professor of English and Comparative Literature at the University of California, Irvine, is the author of *Samuel Johnson, Biographer* (1978) and other books. One of his numerous articles on Johnson will appear in the next edition of the *Encyclopaedia Britannica*.

CLEMENT HAWES is Associate Professor of English at Southern Illinois University at Carbondale. He is the author of *Mania and Literary Style: The Rhetoric of Enthusiasm from the Ranters to Christopher Smart* (1996), as well as articles on Jonathan Swift, Laurence Sterne, Christopher Smart, and "Ranter" Abiezer Coppe.

FRED PARKER lectures on English literature at Cambridge University and is a Fellow of Clare College, Cambridge. He is the author of *Johnson's Shakespeare* (1989) and is currently working on a study of skepticism in eighteenth-century literature.

PHILIP SMALLWOOD is Head of the School of English and Professor of English Literature at the University of Central England in Birmingham. His publications include a commentary on Johnson's *Preface to Shakespeare* (1985), and a study of modern criticism, *Modern Critics in Practice: Critical Portraits of British Literary Critics* (1990). He is currently working on aspects of the relations between literary criticism and philosophy.

GREG CLINGHAM holds the National Endowment for the Humanities Chair in the Humanities at Bucknell University, where he is also director of the University Press. His publications include *James Boswell: The Life of Johnson* (1992), the edited *New Light on Boswell* (1991), and the co-authored *Literary Transmission and Authority: Dryden and Other Writers* (1993). His *Writing Memory: Textuality, Authority, and Johnson's "Lives of the Poets"* is forthcoming.

MICHAEL SUAREZ, SJ has been a Marshall Scholar and winner of the Matthew Arnold Prize for literary criticism at Oxford. Suarez is the first person in the history of Oxford University to win both the Newdigate Poetry Prize and the Chancellor's Essay Prize in the same year. He has published scholarly articles and reviews in *The Age of Johnson* and other journals, and is a Junior Research Fellow at St. John's College, Oxford.

JOHN WILTSHIRE is a Reader in the School of English, La Trobe University, Australia, where he specializes in "literature and medicine." His *Samuel Johnson in the Medical World: The Doctor and the Patient* was published in 1991. His most recent book, with Paul A. Komesaroff, is *Drugs in the Health Marketplace: Experiments in Knowledge, Culture and Communication* (1995).

TOM KEYMER is a Fellow and Tutor in English at St. Anne's College, Oxford, and a Lecturer of the university. His publications include *Clarissa and the Eighteenth-Century Reader* (1992), an edition of Fielding's *Journal of a Voyage to Lisbon* (1996), and articles on Pope, Smart, and Sterne.

STEVEN LYNN is a Professor in the English Department at the University of South Carolina. He is the author of *Samuel Johnson after Deconstruction: Rhetoric and*

"*The Rambler*" (1992) and *Texts and Contexts: Writing about Literature with Critical Theory* (1994). In addition to Johnson and eighteenth-century literature, his interests include critical theory, the history of rhetoric, the teaching of writing, and science fiction. He has two projects forthcoming, *The Briefest Guide to Writing* and *Introduction to Reading, Writing, and Literature*. Mr. Lynn is currently completing a history of eighteenth-century rhetoric.

1709   Samuel Johnson born 7 September 1709 (18 September, "new style," after the introduction of the Georgian calendar in 1752), Lichfield, Staffordshire.

1712   Taken to London by Michael Johnson (father) to be touched by Queen Anne for scrofula, a disease of the lymph glands known as the "King's evil" because it could supposedly be cured by the royal touch.

1717   Enters Lichfield Grammar School.

1726   Visits his cousin, Rev. Cornelius Ford, at Stourbridge and attends school there.

1728   Goes up to Pembroke College, Oxford in October; leaves in December 1729 without a degree.

1731   Michael Johnson dies.

1732   Teaches at Market Bosworth.

1733   In Birmingham; translates Father Jerome Lobo's *Voyage to Abyssinia* (1735).

1735   Marries Elizabeth Jervis (the widow of Harry Porter).

1736   Opens a school at Edial, near Lichfield. Begins writing *Irene*.

1737   Nathanial Johnson (brother) dies. Moves to London with David Garrick in March.

1738   Begins writing for the *Gentleman's Magazine*. Publishes *London* and the "Life of Sarpi"; begins translation of Sarpi's *History of the Council of Trent* (later abandoned).

1739   *Marmor Norfolciense, Vindication of the Licensers of the Stage* (anti-government pamphlets); "Life of Boerhaave"; translation of Crousaz's *Commentary on Pope's Essay on Man*.

1740   Lives of Admiral Robert Blake, Sir Francis Drake, and Jean-Philippe Barretier.

1741   For the next four years contributes biographies to Robert James's *Medicinal Dictionary*; "Life of Sydenham"; contributions to the *Harleian Miscellany* and the catalogue of the Harleian Library (with Thomas Birch); *Parliamentary Debates* and many articles for the *Gentleman's Magazine*.

1745   Proposals for an edition of Shakespeare (later abandoned); *Miscellaneous Observations on Macbeth*.

1746   Contract for the *Dictionary*; drafts *Plan for an English Dictionary*, dedicated to Lord Chesterfield (published 1747).

1749   *Vanity of Human Wishes*; *Irene* performed and published.

1750   Begins *The Rambler* (to 1752).

1752   Elizabeth Johnson (wife) dies.

1753   Contributes to *The Adventurer* (to 1754), edited by John Hawksworth.

1755   *Dictionary of the English Language*; awarded honorary Master's degree by Oxford University.

1756   Edits the *Literary Magazine*; proposals for an edition of Shakespeare.

1758   Begins *The Idler* (to 1760).

1759   Sarah Johnson (mother) dies; *Rasselas*.

1762   Awarded annual pension of £300 by the prime minister, Lord Bute.

1763   Meets Boswell in Tom Davies's bookshop.

1764   The Literary Club formed – Johnson, Reynolds, Burke, Nugent, Beauclerk, Langton, Goldsmith, Chamier, and Hawkins meet weekly for conversation at the Turk's Head, Soho.

1765   Publishes edition of Shakespeare; meets Henry Thrale and Hester Lynch Thrale; awarded an honorary LL D by Trinity College, Dublin.

1766   Assists Robert Chambers with Vinerian lectures on the law at Oxford; severe depression.

1770   *The False Alarm.*

1771   *Thoughts on Falkland's Islands.*

1773   4th, revised edition of the *Dictionary* and revised edition of Shakespeare; tours Scotland with Boswell (August to November).

1774   Tours Wales with the Thrales; *The Patriot.*

1775   *Journey to the Western Islands of Scotland*; *Taxation No Tyranny*; awarded honorary DCL by Oxford; visits France with the Thrales.

1777   Agreement to write prefaces to the lives and works of the English poets (*The Lives of the Poets*); unsuccessful campaign to reprieve Rev. William Dodd, condemned to death for forgery.

1779   First four volumes of *Prefaces, Biographical and Critical to the Works of the English Poets.*

1781   Henry Thrale dies; last six volumes of *Prefaces, Biographical and Critical.*

1782   "On the Death of Dr. Robert Levet."

1783   Suffers a stroke and loss of speech; recovers; suffers illness and depression during winter 1783–84.

1784   Undergoes religious "conversion"; Dedication to Charles Burney's
        Account of Commemoration of Handel; dies 13 December; buried
        in Westminster Abbey, 20 December.

1785   James Boswell's *Journal of a Tour to the Hebrides with Samuel
        Johnson, LL.D.*

1786   Hester Thrale Piozzi's *Anecdotes of Samuel Johnson, LL.D.*

1787   Sir John Hawkins's *The Life of Samuel Johnson, LL.D.*

1791   James Boswell's *Life of Samuel Johnson, LL.D.*

1793   2nd edition of Boswell's *Life of Johnson*.

SHORT TITLES AND ABBREVIATIONS

THE YALE EDITION OF THE WORKS OF SAMUEL JOHNSON
General Editor: John H. Middendorf
(New Haven and London: Yale University Press, 1958–).

Diaries	*Diaries, Prayers, and Annals*, ed. E. L. McAdam, with Donald and Mary Hyde (1958).
Idler	*The Idler* and *The Adventurer*, ed. W. J. Bate, John M. Bullitt, and L. F. Powell (1963).
Adventurer	*The Idler* and *The Adventurer*, ed. W. J. Bate, John M. Bullitt, and L. F. Powell (1963).
Poems	*Poems*, ed. E. L. McAdam, Jr., with George Milne (1964).
Rambler iii–v	*The Rambler*, ed. W. J. Bate and Albrecht B. Strauss, 3 vols. (1969).
Shakespeare	*Johnson on Shakespeare*, ed. Arthur Sherbo, introduction by Bertrand H. Bronson, 2 vols. (1969).
Journey	*A Journey to the Western Islands of Scotland*, ed. Mary Lascelles (1971).
Politics	*Political Writings*, ed. Donald J. Greene (1977).
Sermons	*Sermons*, ed. Jean Hagstrum and James Gray (1978).
Abyssinia	*A Voyage to Abyssinia*, ed. Joel J. Gold (1985).
Rasselas	*Rasselas and Other Tales*, ed. Gwin J. Kolb (1990).
Works	*The Works of Samuel Johnson*, ed. Arthur Murphy, 15 vols. (Edinburgh, 1806).
Lives	*Lives of the English Poets*, ed. G. B. Hill, 3 vols. (Oxford: Clarendon Press, 1905).

Letters	*The Letters of Samuel Johnson.* The Hyde Edition, ed. Bruce Redford, 5 vols. (Princeton University Press and Oxford: Clarendon Press, 1992–94).
JM	*Johnsonian Miscellanies*, ed. G. B. Hill, 2 vols. (Oxford: Clarendon Press, 1897).
Life	James Boswell, *The Life of Samuel Johnson, LL.D., with a Journal of a Tour to the Hebrides*, ed. G. B. Hill, rev. L.F. Powell, 6 vols. (Oxford: Clarendon Press, 1934–64).
Hawkins	Sir John Hawkins, *The Life of Samuel Johnson, LL.D.* (London, 1787).
CH	*Johnson: The Critical Heritage*, ed. James T. Boulton (London: Routledge and Kegan Paul, 1971).
Savage	*Life of Savage*, ed. Clarence Tracy (Oxford: Clarendon Press, 1971).
Early Lives	*Early Biographical Writings of Dr. Johnson*, ed. J. D. Fleeman (Farnborough: Gregg International, 1973).
Early Biographies	*The Early Biographies of Samuel Johnson*, ed. O M Brack, Jr. and Robert E. Kelley (University of Iowa Press, 1974).
Greene	*Samuel Johnson.* The Oxford Authors. ed. Donald Greene (Oxford and New York: Oxford University Press, 1984).
AJ	*The Age of Johnson: A Scholarly Annual*
CQ	*The Cambridge Quarterly*
ECL	*Eighteenth-Century Life*
ECS	*Eighteenth-Century Studies*
ELH	*English Literary History*
JHI	*Journal of the History of Ideas*
LRB	*London Review of Books*
MLQ	*Modern Language Quarterly*
MLR	*Modern Language Review*
MLS	*Modern Language Studies*
MP	*Modern Philology*

NQ	*Notes and Queries*
PMLA	*Publications of the Modern Language Association of America*
PQ	*Philological Quarterly*
RES	*Review of English Studies*
TLS	*Times Literary Supplement*

GREG CLINGHAM

Introduction

"He has made a chasm, which not only nothing can fill up, but which nothing has a tendency to fill up. – Johnson is dead. – Let us go to the next best: – there is nobody; – no man can be said to put you in mind of Johnson." Thus the words of William Hamilton as reported by James Boswell at the end of his *Life of Johnson* (1791). In a sense Johnson scholarship has always been concerned with filling up the space left by Johnson's death in 1784; at the same time it has also been aware of the impossibility of that effort. Since Boswell's *Life* and the review of John Croker's edition of that work by Thomas Babington Macaulay in 1831 readers have internalized a certain set of physiological images and style of speech that have come to identify Johnson in the popular and even the academic mind. Perhaps more than any other English writer, including Shakespeare, Johnson's words have been quoted and misquoted in almost every form of public discourse, and his works have been interpreted and misinterpreted, not only by eighteenth-century scholars but by specialists in other areas. Johnson has been fair game for all. The attention he has received is the mark of many things: it is a sign that his personality continues to fascinate, that his works continue to speak to the experience of modern people, and that he and his works represent a complex cultural authority that provide some readers with deep, intelligent instances of moral, social, and literary insight, while symbolizing for others the worst excesses of absolutist and ethnocentric rationalism produced by the Enlightenment.

For these reasons, and for the sheer breadth and complexity of Johnson's work, the publication of new introductory essays to Johnson is no simple task. No collection or monograph on Johnson can claim or expect to be comprehensive, to satisfy all expectations and perspectives. This book is no different from others on Johnson in its hope of having done *some* justice to the nuances and the depths of its subject, while knowing that its very focus and strengths will inevitably bring to mind its omissions and weaknesses. But as Johnson says in the Preface to his *Dictionary*, "In this work, when it shall be found that much is omitted, let it not be forgotten that much likewise is performed."

Not all introductory books introduce in the same way. This one does not aim to cover all aspects of Johnson's large *œuvre* nor does it have much to say about Johnson's life as it was independent of his works. Johnson is a great English writer and it is for his writings that this book is written. These essays by British, American, and Australian scholars treat all of Johnson's major works and some lesser-known ones; and since those works are so rich in language and experience, the essays are designed to approach single works and general themes in Johnson's thinking from a number of different yet complementary perspectives. For example, *Rasselas* (a book that ought to be on every humanities syllabus) is discussed by Fred Parker under the headings of skepticism and (in)conclusiveness and by Clement Hawes under that of imperialism and political authority, while also featuring strategically in Eithne Henson's essay on the condition of women in the eighteenth century, John Wiltshire's on travel, Catherine Parke's on conversation, Michael Suarez's on religion, and Philip Davis's opening life of Johnson. Similarly, Johnson's religious consciousness is located by Michael Suarez in the tradition of Anglican apologetics, while other forms of Johnson's spiritual sensibility – the charity that is part of but goes beyond Christian dogmatics – are identified by Robert Folkenflik as underlying Johnson's politics, by Fred Parker as informing Johnson's skeptical grasp of experience, by myself as quintessential to the imaginative structure of the *Lives of the Poets*, and by Philip Davis as permeating almost all aspects of Johnson's day-to-day living. This multidimensional and critically varied approach by several contributors to single texts – to the *Rambler*, the poems, the letters, and the *Dictionary* as well as to the *Lives of the Poets*, *Rasselas*, and the political prose – and to various aspects of Johnson's political, social, philosophical, and literary interests, enables the volume to convey some sense of the seamlessness and the complexity of Johnson's writing, and the damage that is done to its fineness by arbitrarily imposing defining generic, theoretical, and historical categories. The book thereby amounts to more than the sum of its parts, and Pope's advice (endorsed by Johnson) to "survey the whole" as a touchstone for good critical reading applies here.

Contributors have avoided oversimplification, expecting the student and the scholar alike to welcome the rigors of critical engagement with the text. The essays work mostly by treating of things known so as to suggest things unknown, returning repeatedly to the powerful exploration in Johnson works of how the limits and the strengths of the human mind are inextricably linked with one another, and doing so by appealing to that fictive yet quite real entity that Johnson called the common reader: as he wrote of Gray's *Elegy Written in a Country Churchyard*, "by the common sense of readers uncorrupted with literary prejudices, after all the refinements of subtlety and the dogmatism of learning, must be finally decided all claim to poetical honours." Academic practice of the 1990s sometimes suggests that there is no such thing as a common reader, and that no critical position comes without "literary prejudice." The post-modern or postcolonial tenet that all critical and historical knowledge is linguistically constructed and culturally conditioned has been used by such eminent eighteenth-century scholars as John Bender to identify Johnson as a literary and political conservative, representative of the Enlightenment's rationalist resistance to difference, heterogeneity, and liminality, all of which compel attention today.[1] While the *Cambridge Companion to Johnson* does not engage in theoretical disputation, it offers sufficient appreciation of Johnson's critical and skeptical handling of totalizing systems and of the binarism that is a preoccupation of the modern critic to suggest the error of classifying his writings within Enlightenment stereotypes. Of perhaps more enduring importance, however, is the testimony in these essays of (as Christopher Ricks points out in another context) that intelligence in Johnson "of which an important function is the discernment of exactly what, and how much, we feel in any given situation."[2]

This book, then, has as its goal the stimulation of intelligent reading of Johnson and of the intelligent critical thinking (and feeling) that could follow. People always (rightly) read as moderns; but if read as if one *were* a common reader, Johnson's writings demonstrate the need not only for difference but for commonality in our attempts at cultural- and self-definition. It is in the various, intelligent combinations of those two powerful human discourses – difference and commonality – that Johnson is most modern even as he is most of the eighteenth century. And it is in his unfailing and intelligent commitment to all forms of truth and civility that his difficulty and his pleasure lie for us today.

NOTES

1 See John Bender, "A New History of the Enlightenment?," in *The Profession of Eighteenth-Century Literature: Reflections on an Institution*, ed. Leo Damrosch (Madison: University of Wisconsin Press, 1992), pp. 62–83.
2 Christopher Ricks, "Literary Principles as Against Theory," in *Essays in Appreciation* (Oxford: Clarendon Press, 1996), p. 314. The quotation is Eliot's and is used by Ricks of Johnson and others.

I

PHILIP DAVIS

Extraordinarily ordinary: the life of Samuel Johnson

When the painter William Hogarth visited the novelist Samuel Richardson one day, "he perceived a person standing at a window in the room, shaking his head and rolling himself about in a strange ridiculous manner. He concluded that he was an ideot, whom his relations had put under the care of Mr. Richardson, as a very good man." Yet suddenly the retard began to talk. Such was the power of his eloquence that Hogarth then looked at him with astonishment "and actually imagined that this ideot had been at the moment inspired" (*Life*, I, 146–47). This was Samuel Johnson, a great man who looked like an idiot. External appearances may not matter, but there is something symbolic here. For Johnson was indeed a man ever beset by a sense of discrepancy and paradox.

Here is another snapshot. In the early years, in Birmingham, a mercer's wife, one Mrs. Elizabeth Porter, had encountered a strange young man whose "convulsive starts and odd gesticulations tended to excite at once surprize and ridicule." His face was pock-marked, the result of the scrofula; blind in one eye, he blinked repeatedly, rolled his body about oddly, performing strange, nervous movements with his feet and his hands. But Mrs. Porter was so struck by his conversation that she "overlooked all these external disadvantages." Instead of thinking that this was a divine idiot, she said to her daughter, "This is the most sensible man I ever saw in my life" (*Life*, I, 95).

Huge, ill-dressed, and uncouth, Johnson looked almost subnormal; but he had extraordinary powers. Those extraordinary powers he committed, nonetheless, to the purposes of ordinary life. How to endure; how to enjoy; how to spend time; how to balance the mind: these are his emphatically practical subjects. We hear much of Augustanism or Anglicanism as concerned with the middle way, the classic balancing mean between extremes. This idea comes to real life in the case of Johnson: in some respects he was superior to ordinary life, in others he felt himself barely up to it. Between the two, the living of ordinary life was a constant challenge to Samuel Johnson, for Johnson's life, like his appearance, did not resemble that of the conventional great hero. Barely a year after meeting him, Elizabeth Porter, suddenly a widow, married this sensible yet hopelessly unat-

Plate 1 Samuel Johnson in his late thirties, by George Zobel

tractive figure, twenty years her junior (see plate 1). Johnson, who later said he had never thought of the possibility of his being able to please anybody till he was past thirty, always insisted that it was a love match. But people would laugh at the ludicrous alliance between a large-bosomed widow and a twitching youth. Yet reading the first issues of *The Rambler* in 1751, his wife paid Johnson the compliment that went deepest with him: "I thought very well of you before; but I did not imagine you could have written any thing equal to this" (*Life*, 1, 210).

By this time, however, Tetty, as his wife was known, had given herself over increasingly to drink and opiates, as she lay reading romances in a bed she had long since refused to share with her husband. They were half-separated. Yet when Tetty died, Johnson was distraught with remorse. A man of strong sexual passions, Johnson hated loneliness, but though he considered remarrying, he never did so. Instead he surrounded himself with poor dependents – a blind spinster, a black servant, a rough doctor; Anna Williams, Frank Barber, Dr. Robert Levet – yet their quarrelling often made his home a misery to him.

In the face of such untidy and undignified incongruities one is tempted to adopt Johnson's own conclusion in *Rambler* 14: "A man writes much better than he lives."

Johnson was a man who fought constantly with contradictions. One of the most intelligent men ever to commit himself to the sanity of sheer common sense, all his life Johnson had an irrational and uncommon fear of madness. He feared solitude and depression, and needed to try to escape from himself by late hours and company. Humanely charitable to the poor, even when their condition was the result of their own fault, he nonetheless lashed out violently in conversation, acting like a bull or bear in his hatred of cant and his love of mastery. Although he wrote of the need for habit and regularity, he himself could bear to work only in fits and starts, when the time-pressure of deadlines created a sense of necessity that otherwise he found lacking in the ever-passing arbitrariness of daily life. He always felt that unless he could keep himself distracted or busy, he would fall into some dark hole, some vacuum, at the very center of life.

Insanity, says Boswell, "was the object of his most dismal apprehension; and he fancied himself seized by it, or approaching to it, *at the very time* when he was giving proofs of a more than ordinary soundness and vigor of judgement" (*Life*, I, 66). Johnson knew how much he depended upon his mind in order to distinguish and defend himself. But the mind, in both its power of imagination and its skeptical undermining of certain knowledge, could be as much his enemy as his friend. Moreover, Johnson feared that he had inherited a dangerous tendency to severe depression from his father.

Johnson's father, Michael, was an impecunious Lichfield bookseller who in the end would scrupulously lock the front door of his business even after its back wall had fallen down. *This*, said his son, was madness (*JM*, I, 148). The failure of the father's business also meant that Johnson himself had no chance of staying on at Oxford after his first year there, but had to leave and come sullenly back home without a degree in 1729. This defeat frequently drove the unemployed young Johnson to tread the sixteen miles from Lichfield to Birmingham and back again in a day, in an effort to walk off the resulting depression. It was a characteristic attempt to give himself at least the semblance of keeping going, if not actually getting anywhere in life.

But this ill-fated beginning at Oxford meant that it took Johnson years of frustrated struggle and gutter-poverty to establish himself in the literary world of London, to which he set out in 1737. "SLOW RISES WORTH, BY POVERTY OPPREST" he wrote, in large letters, in his poem *London*. Johnson never forgot that success had not come easily to him; he saw something of himself in the fate of his friend, the rake and poet Richard Savage:

> On a Bulk, in a Cellar, or in a Glass-house among Thieves and Beggars, was to be found the Author of the *Wanderer*, the Man of exalted Sentiments, extensive Views and curious Observations; the Man whose Remarks on Life might have assisted the Statesman, whose Ideas of Virtue might have enlightened the Moralist, whose Eloquence might have influenced Senates, and whose Delicacy might have polished Courts.
> (*Savage*, p. 97)

"Might, might, might," with "the man" repeatedly left hanging: one can feel from those early days in London a bitter sense of the unjust waste. All his life Johnson remained stubbornly on the side of the neglected, rejected, and underprivileged because he had known more of life at the bottom of the pile than most successful people who had reached the top. In his sixties, Johnson told Boswell that he still wished he had become a lawyer, but had been prevented by lack of funds and a degree. Yet when someone else added that this was greatly to be regretted since he could well have become Lord Chancellor of Great Britain, Johnson became much agitated and exclaimed in an angry tone, "Why will you vex me by suggesting this, when it is too late?" (*Life*, III, 310).

Why was Johnson vexed? His own curriculum vitae seems monumentally impressive. Between his birth in 1709 and his death in 1784, this man dominated the English literary world. He composed two major poems, *London* (1738) and *The Vanity of Human Wishes* (1749), the latter in particular written with great rapidity of genius – seventy lines of it composed and held in his head in a single day before he ever put pen to paper. He wrote a fine biography, *The Life of Savage*, in the white heat of bereaved friendship in 1744, recasting the last forty-eight pages in a single all-night session; and he produced a great didactic novel, *Rasselas*, in the evenings of just one week in 1759 to help pay for his mother's funeral. Emphatically Johnson's is one of the swiftest and largest minds in English literature. Moreover, Johnson was not just a master of the quick, short work. It took him nine years of dull but scholarly labor to complete his *Dictionary of the English Language*, finally published in 1755. In the meantime between 1750 and 1752, in order to relieve his mind from the drudgery of his dictionary work, he committed his spare time to composing two essays a week until he had written over two hundred moral and intellectually exploratory essays known as *The Rambler*. *The Adventurer* (1753–54) and *The Idler* (1758–60) yield over a hundred further occasional essays. And there is more still: an edition of

Shakespeare completed after eight years work in 1765, a narrative of his *Journey to the Western Islands of Scotland* in 1775, the fifty-two *Lives of the Poets* from 1779 to 1781; besides a vast number of distinguished sermons, reviews, prayers, letters, political tracts, scientific treatises, and occasional poems in both Latin and English.

Yet, behind these outward scenes of success, there remained another, inner side to the story. Johnson did not feel like a great writer or like a great man: he felt like a failure.

Even in his lifetime his friends and admirers were startled to learn that Johnson thought his life a failure and that he feared damnation for wasting his God-given talents. When, says Hannah More, his friends spoke comfortingly of the value of his writings in defense of virtue and religion, Johnson replied, "Admitting all you urge to be true, how can I tell when I have done *enough*."[1]

Modern criticism has taught us to concentrate on the achieved works themselves, the autonomous texts, rather than the life of the person who wrote them – as though literature and biography were entirely separate entities. Yet Boswell wrote his great biography that we might know more of Johnson, day by day, "than any man who ever lived" (*Life*, I, 30). So, what *is* the point of studying the life of Samuel Johnson? Especially if it seems to teach us no more than the reductive lessons of disillusion – the great writer as idiot, as ludicrous husband, depressive hack, or neurotic self-doubter:

> Those whom the appearance of virtue, or the evidence of genius, have tempted to a nearer knowledge of the writer in whose performances they may be found, have indeed had frequent reason to repent their curiosity; the bubble that sparkled before them has become common water at the touch; the phantom of perfection has vanished when they wished to press it to their bosom. (*Rambler* 14, III, 74)

The thought that every idol has feet of clay would not have disillusioned Johnson himself. As he makes Imlac say, "The teachers of morality . . . discourse like angels, but they live like men" (*Rasselas*, p. 74). Johnson's commitment to down-to-earth experience always means that a thought which at its first appearance might shock a young and inexperienced idealist such as Rasselas (or Boswell), in Johnson has been already integrated into a firm acceptance of the realities of life.

To those who knew him and wrote about him, and to those who still read him with care, Johnson's writings offer a strong, personally embodied attitude to life. There is an abiding sense of something residually and intrinsically vital and memorable about Johnson himself. It lay behind his work, and it came out abundantly in his talk and in the robust force of his being. And yet this sense of power over and above whatever it is concentrated in also points to something redundant or underachieved about Johnson. All the extra significance *is*, in a deep sense, Johnson's *life*. Many of Johnson's contemporaries, in particular Sir John

Hawkins, Hester Thrale Piozzi, and James Boswell, wrote accounts of that life. They did so not only because of Johnson's memorable impressiveness but as if there was something vitally left-over in him that demanded to be saved and converted into writing, even if Johnson did not do the writing himself. These biographies are a tribute to Johnson and his strength as a human being. And yet, notwithstanding Johnson's exemplary self-knowledge, they also connect with his own sense of personal weakness and waste. "How can I tell when I have done enough?"

Johnson lived for seventy-five years, but often he thought in vain of the time he had wasted and of how small a proportion of his life he had spent in the act of real artistic creation:

> It is said by modern philosophers, that not only the great globes of matter are thinly scattered thro' the universe, but the hardest bodies are so porous, that, if all matter were compressed to perfect solidity, it might be contained in a cube of a few feet. In like manner, if all the employment of life were crowded into the time which it really occupied, perhaps a few weeks, days, or hours, would be sufficient for its accomplishment, so far as the mind was engaged in the performance.
>
> (*Rambler* 8, III, 41)

Seventy-five years may have consisted of really no more than a few intense minutes of true thinking to purpose. The remaining time was spent in the impatient labor of composition, or in merely filling up time. But the sheer force of Johnson's summative language is like that of a man trying to marshal and compress together an otherwise diffused or wasted experience. Whole years' worth of experience goes into a single massy sentence; but equally, one occasional sentence may be the sole apparent result of those years. Johnson had failed to write a magnum opus – the definitively great work that incorporated all that he knew and believed. He felt he had been too like a part-time writer: "On this day little has been done and this is now the last hour. In life little has been done, and life is very far advanced" (*Diaries*, p. 152). To Johnson life is no more than a matter of one brief day after another, a series of little things passing thus gradually and insidiously without their seeming separately important. Johnson was a big man conscious of living in a world of little things: again, instead of merely lamenting the discrepancy, he tried to apply largeness of purpose to everyday life.

Thus, on one side of Johnson, publicly, there are the great moral essays and lay sermons of his strength:

> Nothing but daily experience could make it credible, that we should see the daily descent into the grave of those whom we love or fear, admire or detest; that we should see one generation past, and another passing, see possessions daily changing their owners, and the world, at very short intervals, altering its appearance, and yet should want to be reminded that life is short. (*Sermons* 15, p. 160)

"Men more frequently require to be reminded than informed," says Johnson in *Rambler* 3 (III, 14). But how could we ever forget what is so serious? why do we keep on lapsing back into living unconsciously?

In time what is important becomes taken for granted and effectively forgotten. This, Johnson feared, is how we lose our very minds. Thus Johnson writes in his diaries:

> APR. 14 GOOD FRIDAY 1775 . . . 10.30 p.m. . . . . When I find that so much of my life has stolen unprofitably away, and that I can descry by retrospection scarcely a few single days properly and vigorously employed, why do I yet try to resolve again? I try because Reformation is necessary and despair is criminal. I try in humble hope of the help of God.
> *(Diaries, p. 225)*

Emphatically, this kind of deeply personal and spiritual reflection lay behind the public texts. Their strength and their success came out of Johnson's sense of weakness and failure. And the more we read of those public texts, the more we begin to register the underlying private dimension felt, in translation, beneath them.

In the diaries, in the solitude he hated, Johnson found not so much human privacy as confrontation with the thought of God. The basic underlying weakness in him is disclosed in his constant recordings of apparently fruitless prayer and humiliatingly desperate little resolutions – to get up earlier, to study the Bible, to work harder. Aged fifty-five, sixty, sixty-five, and still "nothing, but resolutions without effect, and self-reproach without reformation" (*Sermons* 15, p. 164). Nothing but *daily* experience could make it credible – 14 April, 1 January, or 18 September, year after year, marked only by unavailing reminders on holy days, anniversaries, and birthdays.

"A man writes much better than he lives." When, therefore, we look at the public and private sides of Johnson – his writing and living, success and failure, strength and weakness, sanity and the fear of madness – what are we to conclude?

That he was a hypocrite? Johnson never denied that hypocrisy might apply in any particular case. In the last year of his life, he told Sir John Hawkins that he feared he had written as a philosopher but not lived like one: "Shall I, who have been a teacher of others, myself be a castaway?"[2] But equally in his pillar-to-post argument with himself, he denied that, in general, hypocrisy was necessarily all to which the contradictions amounted: "Nothing is more unjust, however common, than to charge with hypocrisy him that expresses zeal for those virtues, which he neglects to practise; since he may be sincerely convinced of the advantages of conquering his passions, without having yet obtained the victory" (*Rambler* 14, III, 76). A man *may* "honestly" preach what he does not practice; terrifyingly, he may be utterly in favor of what he quite fails to perform; even *because* of that commitment, rather than despite it, he may "sincerely" urge upon others what he fails to do himself. In such clauses Johnson accepts and maintains life's imbalances with a paradoxically firm authorial balance of mind. *Nihil humanum alienum a me.* There are different levels in a human life.

But if not personal hypocrisy, is it due to Augustan decorum that the public and the private should seem thus separate? John Wain, arguably the best of Johnson's modern biographers, stresses Johnson's deliberately counter-autobio-graphical stance as a commitment to disinterested reason:

> The fact that his parents were incompatible did not prevent him from marrying in his turn. Even the fact that he had been unjustly beaten at school did not lead him to maintain that schoolboys should not be beaten. And here, already, we see a pattern that was to persist. Johnson, as an individual, was highly independent and unbiddable. He did not fit smoothly into any system. Intellectually, on the other hand, he approved of systems. Free of any starry-eyed notion of the natural good-ness of man, he insisted on the need to keep up the outward forms and conventions that act as some check on man's natural lawlessness because he felt its power in his own anarchic impulses.
>
> In this we see something of Johnson's generous self-forgetfulness, his power to reach intellectual conclusions on impersonal grounds. Most people are entirely lacking in this quality.[3]

We need to understand the terms of Johnson's relation to himself. Unlike Boswell, Johnson did not believe in singularity or explicitly personal auto-biography. Instead he kept memory repressed as a power *behind* his writing and thinking. Thus what Wain calls self-forgetfulness is actually transmuted auto-biography – Johnson externally checking the lawlessness or resisting the unhappiness which he found inside himself. For Johnson could do for others what often he could not do for himself. In that way only, by looking steadily outward, could Johnson help himself precisely by not thinking of so doing. In his youth, mourning for the loss of Oxford and given only hack translation work to do, a depressed Johnson could only be roused to work when "Mr Hector, who knew that a motive of humanity would be the most prevailing argument with his friend, went to Johnson, and represented to him, that the printer could have no other employment till this undertaking was finished, and that the poor man and his family were suffering. Johnson upon this exerted the powers of his mind, though his body was relaxed" (*Life*, 1, 87). Similarly, Johnson's impersonal writing is not self-forgetfulness so much as autobiographical self-recall put into a general language. In that general language the personal is raised to a level wherein it can reflect back on itself as though from outside-in.

Thus, when we read the warnings and reminders in Johnson's essays and sermons, only to find Johnson in his journals conscious of still disobeying them, it is not that the two realms are merely separate. The essays and sermons are in linguistically transmuted memory of the particular failings and re-failings. And conversely those failings and re-failings are themselves an example of what came back to Johnson's mind even as he kept on writing. Tacitly the most autobiographical of all writers, Johnson preached from the text of his own errors: that is where his paradoxical greatness comes from. For Johnson made his own limitations and "failures" and the general limitations and "failures" of the human mind his subject-matter. Self-checkingly, the very difference between writing and living was a thought always included within the holding and testing ground of Johnson's writing itself.

Those private inner autobiographical echoes in Johnson are his private version of what he wanted his readers to be reminded of in themselves. The memory of their own private autobiographies was to be triggered, just as his had been, on the other side of the big, public words of powerful commonalty. Johnson's language creates on the page a general human meeting-point which exists at once to repress *and* to recall personal meanings in writer and reader alike.

"Self-reproach without reformation" is one such characteristic formulation. There are so many like it – the opening of the Preface to the *Dictionary*, on those whose fate it is "to be rather driven by the fear of evil than attracted by the prospect of good; to be exposed to censure, without hope of praise" (Greene, p. 307); or the "Life of Collins," on "that depression of mind which enchains the faculties without destroying them, and leaves reason the knowledge of right without the power of pursuing it" (*Lives*, III, 338). These phrases in the power of their formal and general meaning tacitly appeal for a *context* for themselves within a reader's own particular, private and informal understanding. Put the words together, or rather – in these overlapping combinations of one thing "without" another – find the distinctions and dilemmas between them, and the words seem like solid mental objects, making readers recall in themselves the meaning of what language stands for.

In the old romances, Johnson complained in *Rambler* 4: "the reader was in very little danger of making any applications to himself . . . he amused himself with heroes and with traitors, deliverers and persecutors, as with beings of another species, whose actions were regulated upon motives of their own, and who had neither faults nor excellencies in common with himself" (*Rambler* 4, III, 21). What Johnson wants is writings which are not "safe" or remote from daily life, not enclosed in their own autonomous fictionality, nor fantasies of another species of being; but real and open representations of life, "in danger from every common reader" (*Rambler* 4, III, 20). Like "practical," "common" is always for Johnson, as later for Wordsworth, an affirming word. His generalizations are not pomposities but dangerous risks, literary formulations in search of common, practical, and personally lived applications outside literature. The appeal is always "open . . . to nature" (*Shakespeare*, I, 67): open to be both influential upon and criticizable by everyone's ordinary experience of existence.

At one level, therefore, Johnson brought his colossal literary intellect down to earth to deal in common matters of ordinary life: "'Books,' said Bacon, 'can never teach the use of books.' The student must learn by commerce with mankind to reduce his speculations to practice, and accommodate his knowledge to the purposes of life" (*Rambler* 137, IV, 363). At the same time as undertaking this "reduction," Johnson raised matters of ordinary life to extraordinary levels of thought and expression – as Boswell explains: "he delighted to express familiar thoughts in philosophical language; being in this the reverse of Socrates, who, it was said, reduced philosophy to the simplicity of common life" (*Life*, I, 217–18). In his "Life of Watts" Johnson admired the way that Isaac Watts made a "voluntary descent," laying aside high scholarship in order usefully to teach little children. In Johnson the double movement of a "voluntary descent" to a level of the ordinary which is then raised to philosophic heights derives from a central paradox in the man himself, itself a characteristic mix in him of strength and weakness, of humility and pride. For Johnson's commitment to ordinary practical life has, on the other side of it, his sense of not having become the extraordinary man he half-presumptuously, half-guiltily, thought he should have been. "Nature sets her gifts on the right hand and on the left" (*Rasselas*, p. 110): in every act of choice there is a corresponding disadvantage, a loss one way as well as a gain another. When friends asked Johnson why he consistently offered charity to neglected people, he replied that it was precisely because of that neglect. He identified with the forgotten and the marginalized, a failed and lonely widower who could afford to take other failures in.

At other times, like the deranged astronomer in *Rasselas*, Johnson almost believed he could have been an intellectual superman, a new Renaissance universal mind bringing together all fields of knowledge. But too often his intelligence only served to show him what he could not know. What he said of the difficulty of definition in the *Dictionary* is true of the difficulty of thinking itself for Johnson: "kindred senses may be so interwoven that the perplexity cannot be disentangled, nor any reason assigned why one should be ranged before the other. When the radical idea branches out into parallel ramifications, how can a consecutive series be formed of senses in their nature collateral" (Greene, pp. 316–17). There were too many possible thoughts, too many considerations branching out at the same time, for any one train of consecutive reasoning wholly to contain the truth. Only an acute sense of life's unbearable and impossible complexity gave Johnson a license for recourse to the reductions of the relatively simple, for sane and practical purposes. This is where Johnson's powerful tolerance came from – a tough recognition that in a fallen world he had lived long enough not to expect "to find any action of which the original motive and all the parts were good" and yet, precisely on that basis, could still find that human beings behaved better than one might have expected: "As I know more of mankind I expect less of them, and am ready now to call a man a *good man* upon easier terms than I was formerly" (*Life*, IV, 239).[4] Nonetheless, near the end of the otherwise indignant demolition of Soame Jenyns's attempt (in *A Free Inquiry into the Nature and Origin of Evil* [1757]) to rationalize away all the evils of the universe, there is no mistaking Johnson's sense of self-disappointment and guilt:

> I do not mean to reproach this author for not knowing what is equally hidden from learning and from ignorance. The shame is to impose words for ideas upon ourselves or others. To imagine that we are going forward when we are only turning round. To think that there is any difference between him that gives no reason, and him that gives a reason, which by his own confession cannot be conceived.
>
> (Greene, 534)

Jenyns would have been both more humane *and* more religious, had he stayed as silent in the face of the mystery of human suffering as Johnson himself did. It was easy for Johnson to demolish Jenyns's system. But in place of that system he offers no alternative but silence. The fundamental silence at the heart of Johnson marks his inability to construct an equivalent magnum opus, to raise a transcendent temple containing a completed and final account of life's purpose. Yet even whilst at one level he blamed himself for this "failure," at another Johnson was resigned to being an occasional writer – at least insofar as he did *not* want to be a man who lived wholly on paper or who thought only on the page. Writing was to be something that let life and the thought of life in, however untidily or inconveniently. It was not to be a closed and complete system all on its own.

Johnson knew too much to have certainty. Standing in the circle of his own consciousness, what he knew was that he knew too little, and that "Men will submit to any rule, by which they may be exempted from the tyranny of caprice and chance" (*Life*, I, 365). It was a nervous relief to be dogmatically singleminded in the lively momentariness of conversation. But back in the study Johnson could not write about ultimate things with certainty, but only about those secondary defenses and defiances which take place when intellectual and moral greatness, on the rebound from its own limitations, recommits itself to having to live within the second-rate, the small, and the ordinary. He stuck with that. To the stoic argument in favor of opting out of emotional commitment, he responds: "is it not like advice, not to walk lest we stumble?" (*Rambler* 32, III, 179). If Johnson could not fly, he walked, stumbled, carried on walking again, as a human being.

Opposed to the hermit's retirement or the scholar's withdrawal, Johnson is constantly committed to going back to normal life. "It is as unreasonable for a man to go into a Carthusian convent for fear of being immoral, as for a man to cut off his hands for fear he should steal" (*Life*, II, 434–5). Though often tempted to do so, Johnson never went into retreat, religious or otherwise. He was a committed lay Anglican: his religion lay not in withdrawal from the world but, down to earth, was rooted in the everyday life of his country and related in his mind with all other aspects of common existence. "Return from the contracted views of solitude to the proper duties of a relative and dependent being" (*Rambler* 44, III, 242).

In committing himself to that return, Johnson is, in both senses of the phrase, a great failure – a *great* failure. This paradox may be more important than the conventional view of success. The man of enormous talents feared he had gravely disappointed God through his inability to be anything more than generally commonsensical. But equally, by another of God's strange sacrificial plans, it may have been his calling precisely to have been that equivocal great failure – writing supremely well about still falling short, like a bigger version of our struggling selves.

Yet Johnson himself was utterly silent about this second, secretly compensating possibility: namely, that his failure was also his vocation. And he was silent about it for two reasons. First, because for Johnson to embody himself in the ordinary was as much a result of involuntary inadequacy – the habit of idleness, the fear of solitude, the failure of knowledge – as of deliberate commitment. And without the involuntariness, to pride himself upon the vocation of shared ordinariness would be precisely to de-authenticate it. Second, because, either way, it made no difference: Johnson still remained in his own terms a failure, whether in that he were fulfilling or letting down some plan of God's. We can say, however, that Johnson's greatness is not to transcend normality, as he might have ambitiously wished, but to embody it in a larger and more articulate form of being. But Johnson could not claim so much for himself. With him there are always thoughts which cannot really *be* thought, thoughts at the very limits of mortal being. In his downright world there was no difference, as he says of Jenyns, "between him that gives no reason, and him that gives a reason, which by his own confession cannot be conceived." So Johnson kept silent about the possible reasons for his relative failure. Any secret justification of himself as the great representative common person was, if not inconceivable, at any rate unspeakable – so plausible was it that it might still be mere excuse or delusion.

Paradoxically Johnson writes best when he is at the very bounds of mortal sense, on the verge of silence. When he reviewed Jenyns, or when in the "Life of Waller" he wrote of the point at which religious poetry must give way to silent prayer, Johnson was almost beyond himself. So it was too when, with typical compassion, Johnson composed a final sermon of repentance for the clergyman Dr. Dodd on the eve of his being executed for forgery. That a clergyman should be a felon, that he should seem to repent only after being caught and in imminent danger of God's judgment after execution, laid Dodd so open to the imputation of hypocrisy that he could hardly find words with which to presume to speak on his own behalf. Instead Johnson himself speaks for Dodd: "The shortness of the time which is before us, gives little power, even to ourselves, of distinguishing the effects of terrour from those of conviction; of deciding, whether our present sorrow for sin proceeds from abhorrence of guilt, or dread of punishment" (*Sermons* 28, p. 307).

"Even to ourselves," even *in extremis*, as mere creatures we cannot be sure of our own sincerity. Near tongue-tied through circularity, Dodd looks as though he were defeated twice over – made to repent, and because *made* to repent, also made to doubt the true value of such a repentance. Johnson must have felt similarly, if less dramatically, doubly bound when what he wrote as a philosopher, comprehended the limitations which he knew he would still practice and still suffer from a moment later. Johnson's Dodd, like Johnson, is "almost afraid" to renew his dubious resolutions, but like Johnson himself is made to return to ordinarily doing so. There is no new, no extra, no higher thing he can do but continue to repent, while doubting it. But through Johnson's textual intervention, like a second fallen Adam, Dodd was given language on the very edge of silence, so that such a double defeat might be turned into the voice of true repentance. The paradox here is that people may be most authentic when seeming to themselves least so. In his "Life of Cowley" Johnson said that the metaphysical poets viewed life as external "beholders" rather than as common "partakers" (*Lives*, 1, 20). For Johnson, however, we are always partakers, insiders, unable to get outside life and to take a clear view of ourselves: in life's double-binds it is the human way that a good person should be one who did not know himself or herself certainly to be so, that a great person became so precisely because of, as well as despite, a sense of failure.

Boswell once asked Johnson what he should think of a person who was accustomed to using the Latin tag *non est tanti* – that is to say, "it is not worth while," why should I be bothered? Johnson answered with an aggressive trenchancy of speech directly proportional to all he could not sufficiently rationalize in writing: "'That he's a stupid fellow, Sir . . . What would these *tanti* men be doing the while?' When I, in a low-spirited fit, was talking to him with indifference of the pursuits which generally engage us in a course of action, and inquiring a *reason* for taking so much trouble; 'Sir, (said he in an animated tone) it is driving on the system of life'" (*Life*, IV, 112). In the midst of the Age of Reason, Johnson could offer no extra transcendental *reason* for keeping life in motion. "We proceed, because we have begun; we complete our design, that the labor spent may not be vain" (*Rambler* 207, V, 311). We carry on – why? – because we have already started. There is finally, in this man of robust common sense, doggedly going on with life, more intimation of mystery than in many a more Romantic proclamation of life's mysteriousness. In the system of life you stumbled but still walked; you could not always justify what you did but you *lived* it, short of knowledge, in silent faith, hope, and obedience. That is Johnson's extraordinary commitment to ordinariness.

In the last year of his life Johnson went back to Uttoxeter, a market town, close to his birthplace in Lichfield. Over fifty years earlier, Michael Johnson, poor, ailing, and unable to get to Uttoxeter market and tend his bookstall, asked his scholarly son to go in his stead. Depressed at having to leave Oxford, the bookish son, who regularly walked as far as Birmingham and back as therapy, refused to go and trade in nearby Uttoxeter. In a few months his father was dead. In 1784 Samuel Johnson stood for an hour on the spot where his father's stall had been, a bare-headed penitent, oblivious to onlookers, silent in the rain (*Life*, IV, 373).

This was the sort of private life and personal thinking that went on before, after, and behind Johnson's writings, pressing them beyond and outside themselves. Precisely because the whole of his meaning was never contained in a single great work, Johnson stands for the life that always lies outside literature as well as within it. In that way, by refusing to make great writing separate from efforts at ordinary living, Johnson is the finest of human encouragers:

> To strive with difficulties, and to conquer them, is the highest human felicity; the next, is to strive, and deserve to conquer: but he whose life has passed without a contest, and who can boast neither success nor merit, can survey himself only as a useless filler of existence; and if he is content with his own character, must owe his satisfaction to insensibility.   (*Adventurer* 11, p. 455).

There may not be complete success, and even the idea of such success may be a dangerous fantasy. But equally, at the other end of the scale, there must not be no effort toward human victory, for all the likelihood of partial failure. Through the sharing of a powerful common language, Johnson at the least offers his fellow-creatures, in the midst of life, the sober courage of striving and deserving, albeit short of fully attaining. He is unashamed of such practicality.

NOTES

1 See William Roberts, *Memoirs of the Life and Correspondence of Mrs Hannah More*, 2nd edn. (London, 1834), p. 376.
2 Hawkins, p. 564.
3 John Wain, *Samuel Johnson* (London: Macmillan, 1974), pp. 45–46.
4 See also *Life*, III, 236 and *JM*, I, 208–9.

2

CATHERINE N. PARKE

Johnson and the arts of conversation

> It is observed by Bacon, that "reading makes a full man, conversation a ready man, and writing an exact man." (*Adventurer* 85)

Conversation is so central to and representative of Samuel Johnson's work and life that by assembling and examining his writings on conversation, dialogue written for his fictional and factual characters, accounts of Johnson talking, and the meanings and performance of conversation in Johnson's England, a metonymic biography of this man could be written, one which Johnson, I suspect, might not be sorry to see undertaken or even, perhaps, to have written himself. An essay cannot, of course, be a full-fledged biography. But my aim in the pages that follow is to provide biographical insight by taking something like a core sample of Johnson through the strata of his ideas about and practice of conversation. Johnson experienced personally and wrote about the values of conversation as one of the greatest pleasures and improving exercises of human life. He was alert to risks endemic to conversation, directly proportional to its entertaining and instructive possibilities. After his death, Johnson became admired and valued increasingly for spoken words attributed to him, sometimes even more than for his published work. Memorable (though apocryphal) quotes include the familiar "'Sir, a woman's preaching is like a dog's walking on his hinder legs. It is not done well; but you are surprised to find it done at all'"; "'No man but a blockhead ever wrote, except for money'"; and "'Depend upon it, Sir, when a man knows he is to be hanged in a fortnight, it concentrates his mind wonderfully'" (*Life*, I, 463; III, 19, 167). Johnson's audience took their cue for valuing his reported talk so highly from an understanding, or misunderstanding, of James Boswell's emphasis on the oral tradition of Johnson's greatness in the *Life of Johnson* and from subsequent attenuated caricatures, Thomas Babington Macaulay's among the best known and probably the most damaging. Thus a trend began of appropriating Johnson as either compelling personality or eccentric character, talking sage or pompous orator, rather than as professional writer whose writings should be reckoned with first as substance of his reputation.

Scholars, beginning in the early twentieth century, shifted focus back onto Johnson's production as professional writer. Critiquing and reversing Boswell's and other biographers' emphasis on personality, these scholars identified limitations and deformations of such an approach. They encouraged readers not to mistake the experience of reading Boswell's Johnson for an encounter with Johnson in his own published words. But since there can be no second beginning with any writer, Johnson the talker, of popular tradition, and Johnson the writer, of scholarly tradition, both having substantial texts to validate their existence, will both figure in this essay.[1]

I

Perhaps the best place to begin examining Johnson's writings on conversation is *Rambler* 14, where Johnson surveys factors accounting for the "manifest and striking contrariety" so often observed between writers' lives, particularly their reported talk, and their writings. This manifest discrepancy, which has proved disappointing to readers and writers alike, has an obvious, if often elusive, explanation; namely, that people are unwilling to admit that theory is easier to propose than practice, and that pure reason may prove difficult to apply in the improvisational context of circumstance. This explanation is elusive not because it is intricate or difficult, but because human beings are unwilling to accept its implications for constraints on human possibility.

Writers are typically poor conversationalists in direct proportion to their early investment of time and energy required to become good writers. In addition, writers are habituated by their profession to rely on defenses of prepared texts, like the theorist's dream of pure reason untested by circumstance. Finally, their published work sets standards by which their conversation is, in turn, judged, rightly or wrongly, by others. Hence, like "oriental monarchs" who "hide themselves in gardens and palaces, to avoid the conversation of mankind, and [are] known to their subjects only by their edicts" (*Rambler*, III, 74–75), writers often prefer to avoid impromptu tests of conversation where they can neither control the subjects introduced nor revise the performance text. Monarchs of pen and palace alike have so much at stake in the contest of improvisation that they often choose simply not to enter.

Johnson examines this ego-threatening anxiety, which often results from measuring achieved practice against hoped-for possibility, by exploring the material bases of how people learn to talk and write ably. He identifies both activities as "graces" to indicate how each pleases to the degree that it appears artless and easy. Graceful practice of a skill or discipline requires long training begun early. The grace of writing requires years of solitary study, while conversational grace requires practice in company. The distinctive material conditions essential to learning each grace makes cultivating the other virtually impossible. Those who prefer to imagine the possibility of cultivating both may be trapped in greedy indecision and thus fail to undertake seriously the study of either.

Although Johnson is explicitly skeptical about the possibility of equally thorough training in writing and conversation, he cites John Milton, whose conversation reportedly lived up to his writing, as an anomalous instance of success. Milton, he continues, took great satisfaction in "the consciousness of being found equal to his own character, and having preserved in a private and familiar interview that reputation which his works had procured him" (*Rambler*, III, 74), proportionate to the difficulty and improbability of this achievement. Writers, Johnson admits with disarming frankness through his Rambler persona, are anxious to measure up to the test of conversation, the indispensable province of common social pleasure and comfort. Good conversationalists do not, presumably, feel similar anxiety about writing well.

Johnson reintroduces these issues in *Rambler* 89 (22 January 1751), an extended endorsement of John Locke's advice on the importance of conversation as counterbalancing corrective for those whose "business is to think." People who think for a living and must thereby spend much time alone are especially susceptible to "regaling [their] mind[s]" with the "secret prodigality" of "airy gratifications." They must protect themselves against insidious dangers of the "invisible riot of the mind" by educating their sympathy and other arts of imaginative connection ("social pleasures and amicable communication" [*Rambler*, IV, 107]). The "most eligible amusement of a rational being," Johnson continues, "seems to be that interchange of thoughts which is practised in free and easy conversation; where suspicion is banished by experience, and emulation by benevolence; where every man speaks with no other restraint than unwillingness to offend, and hears with no other disposition than desire to be pleased" (*Rambler*, IV, 108). Johnson details dramatic confrontations between wholesome social pleasures of reason and delusory, autistic siren songs of unreason, demonstrating how each makes distinctive appeals to imagination and appetite. He neither resolves this contest sanctimoniously on the side of reason and the therapeutic efficacy of conversation, nor overemphasizes the melodramatic attraction of unreason. Rather he underscores the oddness of the fact that these two logically incompatible impulses evidently do coexist regularly in the imagination, proof of the mind's often curiously successful, profoundly disturbing capacity to accept indiscriminate contents.

Rambler 98 (23 February 1751), published a month after number 89, adopts an epistolary persona, Eutropius, to advise the Rambler on his responsibility to "descend to the minuter duties of social beings, and enforce the observance of those little civilities and ceremonious delicacies," conversation chief among them, which contribute strategically to the knowledge and practice of the daily art of living, *savoir vivre*. Eutropius identifies *savoir vivre* as an indispensable rational notion, informed by the principle "that no man should give any preference to himself" or engage in the tyranny of "unnecessarily obtrud[ing] unpleasing ideas" (*Rambler*, IV, 162, 164). This directive extends the operation of etiquette into the province of ethical assertion. By cooperating in the daily art of living one may reasonably hope "not to give pain" (*Rambler*, IV, 161), though not always to give positive pleasure. This aim may be humble, but scarcely unnoteworthy, since its benevolent effects are so reliable.

To apply this principle rationally is one thing, to recognize, in advance, the stakes involved quite another. Such recognition involves more than reason alone; it requires intuitive foresight to imagine what one does not already know. Like sickness interrupting good health, which goes unnoticed until interruption brings discomfort, conversational incivilities by which freedom "degenerates to rudeness," self-esteem "swells into insolence," and a person's behavior betrays neglect, may similarly damage the reliable rhythm of social pleasure (*Rambler*, IV, 161).

In *Rambler* 126 (1 June 1751), appearing just over three months after *Rambler* 98, Johnson reintroduces the subject of conversation in a yet broader context, again using a fictional correspondent. Thraso opens his letter to the author, by observing: "Among other topics of conversation which your papers supply, I was lately engaged in a discussion of the character given by Tranquilla of her lover Venustulus, whom, notwithstanding the severity of his mistress, the greater number seemed inclined to acquit of unmanly or culpable timidity" (*Rambler*, IV, 306). This remark about a periodical essay series providing "topics of conversation" was familiar to Johnson's contemporary audience. In the tradition popularly associated with Addison's and Steele's early eighteenth-century *Tatler* and *Spectator* series, the bi-weekly periodical essay is conceived as entering practically into readers' lives. Essay topics become the subjects of conversation among family, friends, and acquaintances, translated from the silent, single-authored fixity of print into the participatory improvisational scene of domestic talk.

In addition, the eighteenth-century familiar letter was understood to be the written equivalent of conversation, hence typically written as a performance text, with the understanding that it would be read aloud, often in a group setting, when it arrived. Thus the fact that Johnson's remark on the *Rambler*'s providing topics of conversation occurs within a fictional letter from a reader underscores this written–oral circuit of meaning. Thraso's report of discussion of an earlier *Rambler* essay, number 119, another fictional letter, exemplifies the *Rambler*'s relevance to real life, a follow-up on the issue introduced in *Rambler* 98. And by referring to Tranquilla's earlier letter, which also depicts conversation between two fictional correspondents with the Rambler, Thraso identifies one function of the bi-weekly series as serving as a readers' exchange.

In one of his *Adventurer* essays, just over two years later, Johnson returns to the topic of conversation in the lives of those who think for a living. *Rambler* 89 had focused on the mental health of professional thinkers, prescribing regular conversation as a tonic corrective to unhealthy solitude. *Adventurer* 85 examines a related aspect of conversation in their lives, the responsibility of the learned "most widely [to] diffuse and most agreeably impart" their knowledge. Citing Francis Bacon's advice that "reading makes a full man, conversation a ready man, and writing an exact man," Johnson discusses each element, devoting most attention to how to communicate useful and pleasurable knowledge successfully. The reclusive "man of study" is often ill-equipped to communicate his knowledge for reasons directly related to conditions necessary for the work, which, in turn, make him potentially so valuable to others. He may love his own ideas too dearly, "indulge [them] too long without suspicion," and thus become carelessly naive or positively thoughtless about the fear and difficulty others may experience when first encountering the ideas he knows so well (*Adventurer*, p. 415).

Several of Johnson's contemporaries noted that he expressed similar sentiments in life and behaved accordingly. "When he saw a person eminent for literature, though wholly unconversable," Hester Lynch Piozzi remarks in her *Anecdotes of Samuel Johnson*, "it fretted him" (*JM*, I, 126). Boswell reports the following remark: "Depend upon it, Sir, it is when you come close to a man in conversation that you discover what his real abilities are" (*Life*, IV, 179). Johnson believed in the public, educational responsibilities associated with the scholarly and literary professional life. He was also actively curious about how the mind works and believed that much can be learned with pleasure, often with little conscious effort, by conversing with well-informed people, not necessarily scholars or intellectuals in the narrow sense. Of minds whose work he admired, Johnson's curiosity often fastened first on qualities of their conversation, matters to which I will return in the second half of this essay.

When, six years later, Johnson began writing *Rasselas* (1759), he had already thought long and substantially about conversation in relation to education, health of mind, and ethical responsibility. In *Rasselas* he applies conversation to reexamine these issues by embodying them in sustained dramatic narrative. What he had found out by writing on the subject of conversation and creating epistolary dialogue for characters in his periodical essays he now tested more cohesively and passionately in *Rasselas* as subject-matter and as a metaphor for social behavior.[2]

Prince Rasselas, like the oriental monarchs in *Rambler* 14, who protect themselves from accidental scrutiny by issuing prepared edicts and never speaking impromptu before their subjects, lives in a pleasure garden, the happy valley. For Rasselas, however, unlike these monarchs in *Rambler* 14, the happy valley's pleasures, protections, and allied constraints seem worth giving up for an opportunity to see the world. The prince plans an escape with Imlac, the poet, who also becomes his teacher. Imlac has lived in the world and recently retired to the protection and supposed pleasures of the happy valley. But he soon feels unhappy and bored because none of the inhabitants takes interest in his experience and knowledge. Imlac's resources remain disappointingly useless until Rasselas approaches him with curiosity born of his own boredom. Joined by Nekayah, the prince's sister, and Pekuah, her maid, the prince and Imlac escape from their prison of tedious pleasure. The group plans to see the world, interview people in various walks of life, and choose, based on collected evidence, the happiest occupation for each member.

Beginning with the prince's fascination with Imlac's story of his life, the conversation that initiates their acquaintance, and continuing through the young travelers' interviews with people they meet on their journey, the drama of knowledge as ongoing conversation becomes the theme of and motive for their actions. As the narrative progresses and conversation comes to be understood implicitly by all participants as an essential circuitry of relationship, in which the key is to keep lines of communication open, the challenge of how to maintain fruitful, trustworthy exchanges increasingly engages their attention and concern. Johnson's fourth definition of *conversation* in the *Dictionary* (1755) – "behaviour; manner of acting in common life" – is directly relevant to the widening, deepening significance of dialogue as the narrative unfolds. The journey's meanings and aims configure around the challenge of acknowledging the crucial importance of establishing safe, ongoing conversation and living out the practical implications of this recognition.

Even within this intimate, generally well-intentioned group, temptations to self-aggrandizement, self-pity, self-delusion, inaccuracy, selfishness, and short-sightedness threaten the delicate, essential weave of trustworthy communication indispensable to human survival. Moments of high drama, when characters become each other's and their own worst enemies, include Rasselas's aggressively condescending criticism of his sister's report on her inquiry into married life: the princess discovers equally compelling evidence on both sides of the question of whether to marry or not to marry, and if yes, whether to marry early or late in life. Rasselas identifies the contradiction in Nekayah's findings: "Both conditions may be bad, but they cannot both be worst," and concludes with smug superiority: "Thus it happens when wrong opinions are entertained, that they mutually destroy each other, and leave the mind open to truth" (*Rasselas*, p. 104). Nekayah, who is more largely committed to keeping the conversation going than merely rebutting her brother or defending herself, replies: "I did not expect to hear that imputed to falshood which is the consequence only of frailty. To the mind, as to the eye, it is difficult to compare with exactness objects vast in their extent, and various in their parts . . . We differ from ourselves just as we differ from each other, when we see only part of the question" (*Rasselas*, pp. 104–5).

The princess reframes the issue non-defensively, non-aggressively, in such a way that, while acknowledging hurt feelings, she effectively places short-term interests of personal emotions in second place behind long-term interests of cooperative inquiry. Nekayah makes neither self-deprecating concessions nor stereotypically feminine apologetic conciliations. She demonstrates maturity and models behavior which Rasselas, to his credit, imitates in his final remark: "Let us not add to the other evils of life, the bitterness of controversy, nor endeavour to vie with each other in subtilties of argument. We are employed in a search, of which both are equally to enjoy the success, or suffer by the miscarriage. It is therefore fit that we assist each other" (*Rasselas*, pp. 105–6). The prince's transformed behavior exhibits new recognition of the essential collaborative interdependency of human life.

Another episode examining related aspects of this drama of conversation involves Nekayah, Pekuah, and a brilliant but emotionally disturbed astronomer who believes he controls the weather and thus feels responsible for the entire earth's well being. The two young women, sympathetic to the astronomer's painful delusion that combines the perceptions of responsibility and the inherent impossibility of the task, invent a plan to help him. They will masquerade as travelers in distress, gain his confidence, and through the tonic sociability of conversation restore this tortured, decent, solitary man's common sense. The benevolent logic of their plan seems to embody the narrative's theme of collaborative interdependency. Rasselas, however, sees the serious flaw in their scheme for conversational therapy. He advises against their well-intentioned but essentially duplicitous strategy – "treason," he calls it – warning the women against making "any man's virtues the means of deceiving him." When the prince concludes by observing gravely that "all imposture weakens confidence and chills benevolence," he expresses, in the form of a sober warning, the fundamental insight revealed through the travelers' journey (*Rasselas*, p. 158).

In keeping with his career-long belief in the values and importance of conversation, Johnson brought this interest to the *Lives of the Poets* (1779–81), his final project. Knowing conversation's pervasive significance in human relations, if measured by the pleasure factor alone in relation to life's unavoidable unhappiness, he was not snobbish or elitist about conversation in general. Yet in the *Lives* he does lament the loss of some people's conversation over others'. He remarks with active curiosity and regret, in the "Life of Pope" (1781), for instance, that "so near [Pope's] time, so much should be known of what he has written, and so little of what he has said:"

> Traditional memory retains no sallies of raillery nor sentences of observation; nothing either pointed or solid, either wise or merry. One apophthegm only stands upon record. When an objection raised against his inscription for Shakespeare was

defended by the authority of Patrick, he replies – horresco referens – that "he would allow the publisher of a Dictionary to know the meaning of a single word, but not of two words put together."
                                                                (*Lives*, III, 201)

Johnson salves this regret by speculating that Pope "may be said to have resembled Dryden, as being not one that was distinguished by vivacity in company" (III, 296). Nonetheless, this passage demonstrates how Johnson's biographical curiosity was frustrated by lack of recorded conversation of so great a writer. Boswell gives additional positive evidence of such curiosity in reporting Johnson's May 1779 visit to Lord Marchmont, Pope's contemporary and friend. Johnson's first question to Marchmont was, "What kind of man was Mr. Pope in his conversation?" (*Life*, III, 392).

In writing the life of Richard Savage, the only author included in the *Lives* whom Johnson had known personally and whose biography he had written in 1744, he brought firsthand knowledge of and acute insight into how conversation functioned in Savage's life:

> He had the peculiar felicity that his attention never deserted him: he was present to every object, and regardful of the most trifling occurrences. He had the art of escaping from his own reflections, and accommodating himself to every new scene.
>
> To this quality is to be imputed the extent of his knowledge, compared with the small time which he spent in visible endeavours to acquire it. He mingled in cursory conversation with the steadiness of attention as others apply to a lecture; and, amidst the appearance of thoughtless gaiety, lost no new idea that was started, nor any hint that could be improved. He had therefore made in coffee-houses the same proficiency as others in their closets; and it is remarkable that the writings of a man of little education and little reading have an air of learning scarcely to be found in any other performances, but which perhaps as often obscures as embellishes them.
>   (*Lives*, II, 429–30)

Johnson is here insightfully alert to Savage's acute capacity to listen, often the forgotten or undervalued half of conversation, within the larger context of analyzing how, for Savage, conversation was simultaneously a superb talent, a rich resource, and a self-destructive escape from serious application and self-examination.

Johnson was often praised by his contemporaries for similar conversational talents of good talking combined with good listening, "the art," as Thomas Tyers remarks, "for which Locke was famous of leading people to talk on their favourite subjects, and on what they knew best. By this [Johnson] acquired a great deal of information. What he once heard he rarely forgot. They gave him their best conversation, and he generally made them pleased with themselves, for endeavouring to please him."[3] Johnson's delight in conversation manifested itself in various forms throughout his London years, beginning in mid-century. He belonged to two men's clubs, whose members met for good talk and good food:

the Ivy Lane Club, which he founded in 1749, and the larger, more famous Literary Club, begun in the early 1760s. He was a guest particularly sought after for *conversation-assemblies*, evening conversation parties, or *conversaziones*, which flourished in London from the 1750s into the 1780s, and which Johnson attended during the last fifteen years of his life. Hosted by well-educated women of social position, the so-called *Blue Stockings* (Elizabeth Montagu, Mrs. Agmondesham Vesey, Mrs. Walsingham, Lady Rothes, Lady Crewe, Mrs. Ord, Miss Monckton, Hester Thrale [later Piozzi], among them), these conversations were conceived "as a counter-attraction to the popular and omnipresent card-table" and an opportunity for "ladies" to demonstrate that "being learned [is] no fault," nor a liability to marriage.[4]

Johnson's well-known conversational talents, a touchstone for his social reputation during the second half of his life, became an equally significant touchstone for representations of his life, the subject to which I now turn.

II

James Boswell in his *Life of Samuel Johnson, LL.D.* (1791) identifies conversation as the most valuable and important element for depicting Johnson. "The peculiar value" of this biography, the characteristic distinguishing it from all competitors, is, Boswell asserts, the "quantity" it contains of Johnson's actual spoken words. The biographer makes his assertion of quantity nearly synonymous with the claim for quality by noting general agreement that, whenever a celebrated man exerts himself in conversation, these spoken words will be "eminently instructive and entertaining" and will also "best display his character" (*Life*, I, 31). Boswell adds nuances to this claim by observing that Johnson's wit and wisdom preserved in the *Life* are not a "particular selection from his general conversation" but "merely his occasional talk at such times as [Boswell] had the good fortune to be in his company" (*Life*, I, 11). Thus into the realm of this biographer's planning and shaping enters the element of random opportunity which, Boswell observes, is proof positive of Johnson's authentic genius.

The story is more complicated than Boswell's diffidence in this passage might suggest, since he also depicts himself as Johnson's interviewer, who often asks questions directly, arranges meetings between Johnson and others, and sometimes goes to elaborate rhetorical lengths to set the stage for Johnson's talk. The biographer announces at the outset that "instead of melting down [his] materials into one mass," he has traced "the chronological series of Johnson's life," producing "his own minutes, letters or conversation," furnishing narrative only when "necessary to explain, connect, and supply" (*Life*, I, 29). Thus even when Boswell is not literally posing a question to Johnson, he stage-manages the rhetorical scene, if not the actual event, in such a way that his life of Johnson has many qualities of a long interview with its subject. Boswell arguably invents the genre of the literary interview, a form of rapidly growing popularity over the next two centuries.

Boswell's introduction of long dramatic conversations, Bertram H. Davis comments, marked "the final step in the development of Johnsonian biography" by Johnson's contemporaries whose work preceded Boswell's and to whom he was indebted (Thomas Tyers, William Cooke, Isaac Reed, George Steevens, William Shaw, Hester Thrale Piozzi, Sir John Hawkins, among the most important).[5] Boswell recorded "more of Johnson's conversation" than all of his predecessors combined. And "whereas," Davis continues, "others had generally recorded isolated statements," Boswell reconstructed "whole conversations in the form of dramatic dialogue."[6]

Boswell performs as interviewer in an impressive variety of ways, which cumulatively simulate ongoing, if not uninterrupted, conversation between Johnson and himself – conversation which Boswell apparently controls. Sometimes the biographer introduces a topic, makes an assertion, or questions Johnson to elicit response. Sometimes he assembles Johnson's comments on a particular issue gathered over time, or by others from whom he solicited materials or who themselves volunteered materials to the biographer. Occasionally Boswell plays an even more active, constructivist role, as in the extraordinary dinner party meeting and extended conversation between Johnson and a flamboyant adversary, John Wilkes, republican politician, writer, and notorious debauchee, arranged by Boswell, on Wednesday, 15 May 1776, (*Life*, III, 64–79). Boswell so actively conceives, organizes, observes, and recounts this meeting that the episode might be called more aptly an *invent*. These two men probably never would have met if Boswell had not elaborately arranged this chancy meeting, uncannily predictive, in its melodramatic, adrenaline-pumping, humorous riskiness, of late twentieth-century talk-show confrontations between potentially volatile antagonists.[7]

Whatever Boswell's methods and rhetorical techniques, his aim is consistent: to suggest the dramatic, transactional nature of Johnson's performance in spoken language, thought, and feeling. Energy and spontaneity are consistently evoked rhetorically by Boswell to help readers imagine Johnson as a living person talking and his biographer as an active, inquiring interviewer, not merely a secretary transcribing language after the fact – though he also claims to be a very good secretary whose greatest asset is his discipline in writing down what he heard at the time, or very close to the time, he heard it. Gertrude Stein, one of the greatest twentieth-century theorists and practitioners of biography, attributed her education in this genre to Boswell. From him, she acknowledges in *Narration* (1935), she learned that authentic life-writing is not naive transcription, nor transparent representation of preexisting reality; neither does it attempt to replace the biographical subject. To fulfill the genre, biography must be a language event in the continuous present that authorizes itself independently of, but not in annihilating competition with its subject.[8]

While Boswell's recounting of Johnson's talk asserts the substantive importance of the speaker's utterance, it also implies the counter-assertion that the value of a particular conversational episode lies in the existential moment (of the past), which is to say in the listener's having been in Johnson's presence. Johnson's body, the sound of his voice, even his silences seem sometimes to signify more than his reported words. Thus this biography, in creating a simulacrum of Johnsonian moments, places equal emphasis on how much readers have missed. The final sentence of the *Life*, advising readers that "the more [Johnson's] character is considered, the more he will be regarded by the present age, and by posterity, with admiration and reverence" (*Life*, IV, 430), compensates for this lack to some degree by assigning all future readers the duty of being silent interviewers. Their responsibility and pleasure become henceforth perennial meditation on the august figure of Johnson, presumably with indispensable help from Boswell's text.

Boswell's accuracy and his motives for creating the character, "Johnson the great talker," have sometimes been called into question by scholars and critics. He has been faulted for dramatizing a stodgy, unappealing, conservative bigmouth and for inventing things.[9] But none has succeeded in arguing that conversation is not at the heart of the *Life*, nor apparently yet convinced readers that Johnson's conversation is uninteresting.

In the light of subsequent biographical developments, Boswell was perhaps too successful at creating personality through conversation. Virginia Woolf comments that "the personality which Boswell's genius set free was hampered and distorted" by nineteenth-century biographers.[10] Macaulay, who in his 1831 review of John Croker's edition of Boswell's *Life* and his subsequent longer biographical–critical essay, "Samuel Johnson" (1856), praised Johnson's talk far above his writing, was perhaps the most notorious of these distorters: "The influence exercised by his conversation, directly upon those with whom he lived, and indirectly on the whole literary world," Macaulay remarks, "was altogether without parallel. His colloquial talents were indeed of the highest order . . . As respected style, he spoke far better than he wrote . . . [I]n his talk there were no pompous triads."[11] Boswell, even in his wildest dreams, or nightmares, of success for the *Life*, could scarcely have predicted that this reordering of priorities would result from his high valuing of Johnson's conversation.

Yet even before Macaulay cartoonishly appropriated Boswell's image of Johnson, the great talker, and deflected attention from his writings additionally by emphasizing physical appearance – "his brown coat with the metal buttons and the shirt which ought to be at wash, blinking, puffing, rolling his head, drumming with his fingers, tearing his meat like a tiger, and swallowing his tea in oceans" (Macaulay, "Samuel Johnson," p. 578) – others had placed greater emphasis on Johnson's spoken words than his published works. In her *Anecdotes* (1786), Hester Lynch Piozzi gives the following reasons for her emphasis on Johnson's conversation:

> To recollect, however, and to repeat the sayings of Dr. Johnson, is almost all that can be done by the writers of his life; as his life, at least since my acquaintance with him [Johnson and Piozzi (then Thrale) met in 1765], *consisted in little else than talking, when he was not absolutely employed in some serious piece of work; and whatever work he did, seemed so much below his powers of performance*, that he appeared the idlest of human beings; ever musing till he was called out to converse, and conversing till the fatigue of his friends, or the promptitude of his own temper to take offence, consigned him back again to silent meditation.
>
> (*JM*, I, 160 – my emphasis)

Piozzi justifies this emphasis on her subject's spoken words based on both the amount and quality of talk in Johnson's later life. In so doing, she also identifies, if indirectly, the greatest challenges facing biographers of writers. Unlike biographers of military heroes, politicians, or other public figures whose achievements occur in the exteriorized world of visible action, directly convertible into episodic plot, literary biographers depict subjects who typically do most of their work in solitude. Hence literary biographers must gather exteriorized dramatic materials chiefly in places other than the scene of writing. In the case of Johnson, this scene is frequently an episode of conversation, which his biographers relate back to his writings in a variety of ways, a technique which, in turn, gives several retrospective rationales for reporting his talk: his conversation, so the argument of Johnson's biographers goes, was better than his writing, at least as good as his writing, a relief from the solitude of writing, proof that he lived out the ideas in his writing (or that he sometimes contradicted them), an essential supplement to his writings for depicting the man's character.

No simple, single portrait of Johnson talking can be assembled from accounts by his contemporaries, whose own variety, in combination with Johnson's complexity, must have influenced what they heard and how they reported it.[12] By Piozzi's account Johnson commented that he most loved "conversation without effort" (*JM*, I, 273). Boswell attributes to Johnson a similar sentiment that in "the happiest conversation" there is "no competition, no vanity, but a calm interchange of sentiments," where nothing is distinctly remembered but a general effect of pleasing impression," (*Life*, II, 359; IV, 50). Yet Johnson also liked what he called "solid conversation," in which people "differ in opinion" (III, 57). And he greatly enjoyed "animated conversation," driven by love of contest and impulse for superiority (II, 444).

Boswell was assiduous in exposing errors in portraits of Johnson by his chief rivals, Hawkins (whose *The Life of Samuel Johnson, LL.D.* appeared in 1787) and Piozzi. All three biographers had much at stake in supporting their respective claims of definitive accuracy, authority, proximity, interpretive finesse, and taste, on the one hand, and in questioning the rival's similar claims, on the other. Since Boswell's full-length work was published after the other two (a second edition of the *Life* appeared in 1793), he had the last word in the eighteenth-century debate over what Johnson actually said and intended. Boswell criticizes Hawkins for the mistaken tone of his life as a whole – "the dark uncharitable cast of the whole, by which the most unfavourable construction is put upon almost every circumstance in the character and conduct of my illustrious friend" (*Life*, 1, 28). Boswell similarly criticizes Piozzi's book overall. "By its very nature and form" her anecdotes convey a "mistaken notion of Johnson's character." The author's brevity, Boswell continues, compresses twenty years' acquaintance into two hours of reading which expand erroneously to fill the reader's mind with a portrait of Johnson's "whole conversation" (IV, 340–41).

Boswell focuses with yet more aggressive particularity on several instances of Piozzi's inaccuracy, in each case identifying her error and then providing what he offers as the "genuine" anecdote. It is beyond the scope of these final pages to discuss each variant. But one familiar instance must serve to exemplify the issue and identify some of the problems involved in determining what Johnson said, what he intended, how his spoken words were represented, and what difference the reporter might make.[13] "When I one day," Mrs. Piozzi recounts, "lamented the loss of a first cousin in America," Johnson replied: "'Prithee, my dear (said he), have done with canting: how would the world be worse for it, I may ask, if all your relations were at once spitted like larks, and roasted for Presto's supper?' Presto was the dog that lay under the table while we talked" (*JM*, 1, 189–90). Piozzi reports Johnson's remark as evidence of two characteristics: first, that "he was no gentler" with her than with others less intimate "whom he treated with roughness"; and second, that he did not necessarily hate or despise those "whom he drove from him by apparent scorn."

Boswell sets out to correct the record by noting the "evident tendency" of Piozzi's anecdote "to represent Dr. Johnson as extremely deficient in affection, tenderness, or even common civility." While allowing that Johnson "made her an angry speech," Boswell cites the account of Joseph Baretti, who was present, to "let the circumstances fairly appear":

> Mrs. Thrale, while supping very heartily upon larks, laid down her knife and fork, and abruptly exclaimed, "O, my dear Mr. Johnson, do you know what has happened? The last letters from abroad have brought us an account that our poor cousin's head was taken off by a cannon-ball." Johnson, who was shocked both at the fact, and her light unfeeling manner of mentioning it, replied, "Madam, it

would give you very little concern if all your relations were spitted like those larks, and drest for Presto's supper." (*Life*, IV, 347)

There is much to be discussed regarding these two accounts: Piozzi was the object of Johnson's anger, not, like Baretti, a mere spectator to the exchange, so doubtless she experienced the event differently; Boswell was not present at the exchange; his account was secondhand; and finally Boswell could scarcely have been predisposed to disbelieve Baretti since this informant's correction of Piozzi supported Boswell's claim to superior authenticity.

Johnson's contemporary biographers, despite their often highly charged disagreement about what Johnson said, how he intended it, what his conversation reveals about his personality, and whether or not it was appropriate to take notes on his conversation while he was speaking,[14] do agree on several key points: first, that his spoken words were worth recording; second, that he rarely initiated a topic; third, that he did not "much delight in that kind of conversation which consists in telling stories" (*JM*, I, 265); fourth, that he spent a great deal of time talking with friends, when he was not writing or otherwise occupied, beginning in mid-1760s; and fifth, that his friends "were eager for the advantage and reputation of his conversation" (Tyers, "Biographical Sketch," p. 72).

For twentieth-century Johnsonians this writer's published words have become the main subject of interest and study. His reported conversation, with all its complexity of variant accounts, does not come into focus for us as an edifying, entertaining collection of wit and wisdom, though it remains a handy repository of apt quotations for journalists and other popular writers; but rather appears as pieces of a puzzle, the solution to which does not represent a life but figures forth the problem of literary representation.[15]

For latterday readers, Johnson, the personality, will always be a missing person in the several senses described above, and we seem, all in all, to have settled for this absence. For Johnson's friends and acquaintances the man's death was a palpable loss, his spoken words no small part of what they missed so greatly. For Johnson's contemporaries, most of whom believed his writings would interest future readers perennially, loss of this man – body, talk, being – was the reality, opening a "chasm, which not only nothing can fill up, but which nothing has tendency to fill up" (*Life*, IV, 420).

Some authentic, useful insight may derive from contemplating such palpable grief, to which we are not party, and from imagining Johnson in the act of conversation, if not to trust implicitly any single report of his spoken words. The logic of this usefulness is formulated well by Johnson himself in his deep valuing of biography, the attempt to report accurately and configure intelligibly, imaginatively, sympathetically, and usefully the life of another: "I have often thought that there has rarely passed a life of which a judicious and faithful narrative would not be useful" (*Rambler* 60, IV, 320). To imagine Johnson in conversation, in addition to reading his writings on this subject, is to reckon with one who was once living, a creative agent impelled and constrained by materials, motives, and drives of the physical and psychological worlds, who produced a substantial body of varied writings, whose life has been and continues to be an object of admiration, ridicule, and affection, whose value to us will be, we may hope, more than the mere sum of our projections of him.

NOTES

1 See Bertrand H. Bronson, "The Double Tradition of Dr. Johnson," in *Johnson Agonistes and Other Essays* (Berkeley: University of California Press, 1965), pp. 156–76.

2 See my *Samuel Johnson and Biographical Thinking* (Columbia: University of Missouri Press, 1991), chapter 4, "The Conversation of History: *Rasselas.*"

3 Thomas Tyers, "A Biographical Sketch of Dr. Samuel Johnson," in *Early Biographies*, p. 79.

4 For the Blue Stockings see M. G. Jones, *Hannah More* (Cambridge University Press, 1952), chapter 3, "The Literati."

5 See *Early Biographies* and *JM*.

6 Bertram H. Davis, *Johnson Before Boswell: A Study of Sir John Hawkins* (New Haven: Yale University Press, 1957), pp. 178, 179.

7 For a full analysis of the Wilkes episode see Greg Clingham, *James Boswell: The Life of Johnson* (Cambridge University Press, 1992), pp. 61–78.

8 Gertrude Stein, *Narration: Four Lectures by Gertrude Stein* (University of Chicago Press, 1935), p. 60.

9 See, for example, Donald Greene, "The World's Worst Biography," *The American Scholar*, 62 (1993), 365–82.

10 Virginia Woolf, "The New Biography" (1927), in *The Essays of Virginia Woolf*, ed. Andrew McNeillie, 4 vols. (London: Hogarth Press, 1994), IV, 474.

11 Thomas Babington Macaulay, "Samuel Johnson," in *Macaulay Prose and Poetry*, ed. G. M. Young (Cambridge, MA: Harvard University Press, 1952), p. 567.

12 Mary Hyde (among others) discusses the different, even irreconcilable, accounts of Johnson given by Boswell and Thrale (Piozzi) in *The Impossible Friendship: Boswell and Mrs Thrale* (Cambridge, MA: Harvard University Press, 1972).

13 Compare both accounts with those in James Prior, *Life of Edmond Malone* (London, 1860), p. 368. See also Piozzi's account of Johnson's reply to Hannah More's flattery (*JM*, I, 273) and Boswell's *Life*, IV, 341; Piozzi's account of Johnson's rebuff of Mr. Cholmondeley (*JM*, I, 318–19) and *Life*, IV, 345–46; Piozzi's citation of Johnson's "unprofitable chat" (*JM*, I, 278) and *Life*, II, 194; Piozzi's account of a quarrel between Johnson and Pepys (*JM*, I, 244–45); and Burney, *Diary and Letters of Madame D'Arblay*, 7 vols. (London, 1854), II, 30–35 and *Life*, IV, 65, n.1.

14 Piozzi criticizes Boswell's reputed habit of scribbling down Johnson's words as he spoke, when she recounts that once she "begged [Johnson's] leave to write down directly" a particularly interesting remark "before any thing could intervene that might make me forget the force of expressions," but that she found this practice in general to be "so ill-bred, and so inclining to treachery . . . that were it commonly

adopted, all confidence would soon be exiled from society, and a conversation assembly-room would become . . . as a court of justice" (*JM*, I, 175).

15 See, for example, Fredric V. Bogel, "'Did you once see Johnson plain?': Reflections on Boswell's *Life* and the State of Eighteenth-Century Studies," in *Boswell's "Life of Johnson": New Questions, New Answers*, ed. John A. Vance (Athens: University of Georgia Press, 1985), pp. 73–93.

3

HOWARD D. WEINBROT

Johnson's poetry

Samuel Johnson's preeminence rests upon the extraordinary intellectual and moral achievements within his prose. That truth universally acknowledged nonetheless admits a complementary truth – Johnson is a great prose writer in part because he is a great poet. Johnson wrote poetry throughout his life. Even after a stroke and, later, upon his deathbed he turned to prayer in Latin verse. He wrote a blank-verse tragedy, translations, adaptations of classical poems, satires, love poems, poems warning of the dangers of love, elegies, epitaphs, comic parodies, serious prayers, odes, sonnets, meditations on his inner psychological and spiritual being, and, in the nature of things, poems that combined several of these genres. Johnson correctly said that at Pembroke College, Oxford his group of student-poets was a "nest of singing birds" (*Life*, I, 75). However naturally artful, Johnson's poetic production is small in comparison with other great poets, but several of his poems nonetheless are major and minor masterpieces. They include many devices that make his prose memorable, for his prose is memorable in part because it is so poetic. I begin this chapter by exploring some of his characteristic modes of proceeding.

I

Johnson's dramatically figurative prose reflects and creates insight. In the Preface to his edition of Shakespeare (1765), for example, Johnson repudiates the largely modern French neo-classical orthodoxies regarding the three unities. We require unity of action; but advocates of the unities of time and place wrongly assume that we think the actors real and the stage really Rome. Johnson reinforces his perception with a startling simile based on the realities of maternal love and fear: "If there be any fallacy, it is not that we fancy the players, but that we fancy ourselves unhappy for a moment; but we rather lament the possibility than suppose the presence of misery, as a mother weeps over her babe, when she remembers that death may take it from her" (*Shakespeare*, I, 78). Johnson's more extensive metaphor characterizes the difference between Shakespeare's copious dramas and classicized French or Addisonian drama:

[theirs] is a garden accurately formed and diligently planted, varied with shades, and scented with flowers; the composition of Shakespeare is a forest in which oaks extend their branches, and pines tower in the air, interspersed sometimes with weeds and brambles, and sometimes giving shelter to myrtles and to roses; filling the eye with awful pomp, and gratifying the mind with endless diversity.

(*Shakespeare*, I, 84).

Such images from Johnson's prose could appear in the best poetry. Each encapsulates a complex human activity or response, makes it comprehensible and attractive, and enhances perception or response.[1]

Response is indeed what Johnson seeks both from us and with us. As a benevolent guide he is a companion in inquiry. He knows that we follow our own paths to the place he wishes to guide us, and that he can best help us by offering general guidelines which we as readers particularize. In so proceeding, Johnson follows John Locke in the *Essay concerning Human Understanding* (1690), a portion of which appears in the *Dictionary*'s (1755) third illustrative quotation for the adjective "general": "A *general* idea is an idea in the mind, considered there as separated from time and place, and so capable to represent any particular being that is conformable to it." Such particularizing of the general was a principle of eighteenth-century psychological and aesthetic theory. In the *Spectator* 512 (1712) Addison argues that the enjoyable fable allows the reader to apply "Characters and Circumstances, and is in this respect both a Reader and a Composer." In 1788 Sir Joshua Reynolds praises Gainsborough's "undetermined" portrait manner; his "general effect" reminds "the spectator of the original; the imagination supplies the rest, and perhaps more satisfactorily, if not more exactly, than the artist, with all his care, could possibly have done."[2]

The intimate relationship between the general and the particular, the author and the reader, informs much of Johnson's literary theory and poetic practice. He uses a rich image that suggests two of his *Dictionary* definitions of "conception" – both birth and knowledge – in order to criticize Cowley's excessively detailed description of the archangel Gabriel in *Davideis* (1656): a general idea allows us to "improve the idea in our different proportions of conception" ("Life of Cowley," *Lives*, I, 53). Hence in *The Vanity of Human Wishes* (1749) Johnson invokes History to "tell where rival Kings command, / And dubious Title shakes the madded Land." In such a case, "Statutes glean the Refuse of the Sword" and we learn "How much more safe the Vassal than the Lord" (29–32). This general statement evokes readers' particular associations: it can apply to ancient Roman civil wars, numerous English dynastic conflicts, the English revolution of the 1640s, the Jacobite rebellions of 1715 and 1745–46, or other comparable situations that readers recognize as conformable to the general statement.

Johnson also uses questions pleasurably to involve us in his poems and in our own education – that is, as his *Dictionary* defines the term, in our nurture and instruction. In 1738 he argues that questions give "the reader the satisfaction of adding something that he may call his own, and thus engage his attention by flattering his vanity" (*Politics*, p. 9).[3] Questions encourage personal involvement and one's "different faculties of memory, judgment, and imagination." In the *Dictionary* Johnson uses an illuminating quotation from Bacon's essay "Of Discourses" to illustrate the verb "to question": "He that *questioneth* much shall learn much, and content much; but especially if he apply questions to the skill of the persons whom he asketh." In a sentence Johnson does not quote, Bacon adds that "he shall give them occasion to please themselves in Speaking, and himself shall continually gather Knowledge."[4] Each side profits from the process of questioning and asking. To be sure, as poetic narrator Johnson normally is the superior questioner, but so long as we also learn, engage various intellectual faculties, and are variously pleased, our dialogues with Johnson, with ourselves, and with our culture proceed generously – as we shall see in the "Drury Lane Prologue" (1747) and in *The Vanity of Human Wishes*. Johnson ably uses two other poetic devices in both his prose and his poetry. One device insists on empiricism that urges us to look around us, see reality as it is, gather a large sample from our observation, and draw the appropriate inferences that books and precepts cannot supply.

Johnson's poems frequently exhort us to examine, look, mark, observe, remark, see, survey, and then apply the fruits of discovery to our actual lives. He thus often includes varied known tribulations, as in his satire *London*, that includes images of danger familiar to the modern urban dweller, who also understands that "*Slow rises Worth, by Poverty deprest*" (177):

> Here Malice, Rapine, Accident, conspire,
> And now a Rabble rages, now a Fire;
> Their Ambush here relentless Ruffians lay,
> And here the fell Attorney prowls for Prey. (13–16)

Such lines also make clear that Johnson figuratively embodies his empiricism. Personification turns things, abstractions, or emotions into persons. Internal concepts become allegorical actors when empiricism looks inward and through art becomes an observable part of human life. Johnson makes his well-populated poetry visual by means of externalized emotions as well as by "real" individuals in action. That is why in *London* Malice, Rapine, and Accident "conspire" to attack the poor and innocent Londoner. That also is why the opening of the *Vanity* includes both personification and empiricism. "Observation with extensive View" widely surveys the world's strife, remarks, watches, and can "Then say how Hope and Fear, Desire and Hate, / O'erspread with Snares the clouded Maze of Fate" (1, 5–6).

One aspect of Johnson's inner and outer empirical world was its Christianity that so improved classical paganism. Johnson and the small, male, educated classes in the eighteenth century were gratefully to have been instructed by Greek and especially Roman literature. Numerous students and their teachers nonetheless shared Milton's familiar assessment in *Paradise Lost* (1667): classical knowledge was "Vain wisdom all, and false Philosophie!" (II.565). Johnson's Preface to Dodsley's *Preceptor* (1748) provides an appropriate syllabus for young men. He warns his reader to avoid "vitiating his *habits*, and depraving his *sentiments*" and recommends three helpful texts, "two of which were of the highest authority in the ancient Pagan world. But at this he is not to rest; for if he expects to be wise and happy, he must diligently study the Scriptures of God."[5]

Samuel Johnson himself so studied and so refused to rest on ancient authority. Hence his striking "Upon the Feast of St. Simon and St. Jude" (1726) begins with a characteristic denigration of martial heroism and those who sing "Fields with dead bestrew'd around, / And Cities smoaking on the ground" (1–2). His own "nobler themes" and "nobler subjects" (7–8) will concern the proselytizing martyr saints. They are motivated by heaven not by this world, by God's love not human hate, by God's concern for humanity not for individual acclaim at others' expense, by desire to "raise them from their fall" (30) not to push them into a grave. Johnson demonstrates the benevolence of divine victory:

> When Christ had conquer'd Hell and fate
> And rais'd us from our wreched state,
>   O prodigy of Love!
> Ascending to the skies he shone
> Refulgent on his starry throne
>   Among the Saints above.   (19–24)

Johnson's poems, then, often include some of the best traits of his prose, as his prose includes some of the best traits of his poems. They can be at once figurative and realistic, general and particular, empirical and concrete, and personified and apparently abstract. They often engage readers in their own education and encourage response and partnership with a humane, experienced guide. He urges us toward a specific moral end while also recognizing variations in the path we may choose to take. That path, though often bordered with classical flowers, is British and Christian. A fuller examination of several of his poems suggests how well Johnson uses those poetic devices. I shall look first at some of his elegies, prologues, and a splendid poem advising "Stella" how to navigate in the shoals of sexual attraction.

II

Johnson wrote excellent poems honoring the dead. His "Epitaph on Claudy Phillips, a Musician" (1740) responds to David Garrick's reading of Richard

Wilkes's roughly comparable six-line epitaph. Johnson said that he would do better and soon recited his own version:

> Phillips, whose touch harmonious could remove
> The pangs of guilty pow'r, and hapless love,
> Rest here distress'd by poverty no more,
> Find here that calm, thou gav'st so oft before.
> Sleep, undisturb'd, within this peaceful shrine,
> Till angels wake thee, with a note like thine.

Johnson names his subject, celebrates his skills as musician and musical psychologist, and contrasts his rewards in death with his poverty in life. Those rewards are functions both of Phillips's own and of divine goodness. His music removed personal misery; the angels' reciprocating music removes his misery. He gave calm and rest; he receives calm and rest in a temporary sleep before eternal harmony. Johnson's concrete six lines about an obscure musician affirm a profound and general religious system that we also can apply to our lives. One part of that application is awareness that ultimate worth depends more upon inner decency made overt than on grander accomplishments.

"On the Death of Dr. Robert Levet" includes several similar qualities but is longer, more moving, and more personal. Levet was one of the impoverished residents Johnson supported in his home. He especially admired Levet, who, though not a licensed physician, had some medical training and walked long distances to help London's yet more indigent families. His peaceful death on 17 January 1782 evoked this poem published in August of 1783, when Johnson knew that his own end was slowly approaching. Johnson honors Levet, records his response to loss, and helps to make that response significant for others.

Hence as "Levet" begins Johnson writes that "we" are all condemned to a daily life in penal mines, and that as we age "Our social comforts drop away" (4). He particularizes the soon-named Levet as one of his social comforts. He is more. Levet medically comforts the poor and, we as readers know, like Johnson himself is "Of ev'ry friendless name the friend" (8). He worked "In misery's darkest caverns," among the lonely and hopeless whom he respected and aided (17). Though these virtues may be ignored by the powerful world, they are seen by the more powerful God. Johnson strikingly reverses the Parable of the Talents in Matthew 25: 13–30. There the bad servant is eternally punished for burying rather than investing his absent master's gift of a single talent – a sum of money. Here Johnson knows that God will reward his friend who handsomely used God's humble but essential gift:

> His virtues walk'd their narrow round,
> Nor made a pause, nor left a void;
> And sure th' Eternal Master found
> The single talent well employed. (25–28)

Levet's earthly rewards are awareness of a life well spent, a healthy old age, a peaceful rapid death, and a consequent freedom from temporal prison. As the allusion to Matthew denotes, the Eternal Master also rewards Levet: "Death broke at once the vital chain, / And free'd his soul the nearest way" (35–36) – nearer to God, who welcomes Levet as a good and faithful servant who has entered the far country that is Heaven. Johnson's secular poem spiritually comforts the poet and the poet's readers. As Johnson says in his prologue to Oliver Goldsmith's *The Good Natured Man* (1768), "social sorrow loses half its pain" (4).

Johnson's insistence on exchange with readers, on sympathetic questioning that leads to education, extends to some of his five prologues as well. Both the prologues to the new performance of Milton's *Comus* (1750) and to the revival of Hugh Kelly's *A Word to the Wise* (1777), for example, are designed to win audience support for distressed surviving family members. The prologue to Goldsmith's *The Good Natured Man* has a comparable function, for Johnson there lends his authority to his nervous friend's first comedy. As we expect from a form that requires direct address, the prologues also share Johnson's insistence on the author's responsibility to engage the audience in moral or at least in wise aesthetic decisions. The prologue to *Comus* ends with "Yours is the Charge, ye Fair, ye Wise, ye Brave! / 'Tis yours to crown Desert – beyond the Grave" (37–38). He tells the auditors at *The Good Natured Man* that "confident of praise, if praise be due, / [Goldsmith] Trusts without fear, to merit, and to you" (29–30). The very title of Kelly's *A Word to the Wise* allows Johnson to compliment the audience and urge it to exercise "liberal pity" and "bounty" (22, 24).

The best of Johnson's prologues illustrates his view of the reciprocal relationship between author and audience. The full title suggests how well Johnson adapted his poem to the occasion: "Prologue Spoken by Mr. Garrick at the Opening of the Theatre in Drury-Lane, 1747." As new partner and actor–manager Johnson's former student had begun to reform British acting, theatrical business, the stage, and its canon now friendlier to Shakespeare. Though illness kept Garrick from acting, on 15 September 1747 the redecorated Drury Lane theatre opened to a performance of *The Merchant of Venice*. Johnson's prologue blends the presence of Shakespeare and of renewal with insistence upon the auditors' role in making a healthy stage. This sophisticated but comprehensible prologue and progress-poem also encapsulates English drama from the late sixteenth to the mid-eighteenth century, and does so with the dominant metaphors of warfare and of the extent of a ruler's kingdom. Johnson knows that improvement is a battle. He also knows that the local stage suggests the world beyond its borders and influences and reflects the larger world of real action.

We hear about personified Learning who triumphs "o'er her barb'rous Foes."

The triumph allows peace, and the military event becomes an emblem of maternal nurture and national identity: when this triumph "First rear'd the Stage, immortal Shakespear rose" (1–2). Like other children, he liked to draw imaginative pictures; but his were plays that ignored the unities of time and place:

> Each Change of many-colour'd Life he drew,
> Exhausted Worlds, and then imagin'd new:
> Existence saw him spurn her bounded Reign,
> And panting Time toil'd after him in vain. (3–6)

When Johnson returns to the martial image Shakespeare becomes the benevolent warrior who drafts – impresses – Truth into his army and uses his play to conquer an audience: "His pow'rful Strokes presiding Truth impress'd, / And unresisted Passion storm'd the Breast" (7–8). Immortal Shakespeare is subject to neither time nor space and lives now as he lived then, in our hearts energized by Passion.

The next three stanzas reorient earlier devices and initiate the poem's "progress." The admired but laborious Ben Jonson is "instructed from the School" and associated with a neatly ordered tentatively advancing European army. He "By regular Approach essay'd the Heart" and can only win the bays from "Cold Approbation." Johnson's regnal image is the finite triangular tomb of an ancient nation: "A Mortal born he met the general Doom, / But left, like *Egypt*'s Kings, a lasting Tomb" (9–16). Thereafter, the intellectually and morally slothful Restoration wits look inward and find obscenity all too appropriate for their mirror images in the audience. "They pleas'd their Age, and did not aim to mend," but they nonetheless "proudly hop'd to pimp in future Days" (22, 24). The grand martial and regnal images in the first two stanzas dwindle to a skirmish and a dynasty in which slavery to mean passions is overthrown by human decency: "Shame regain'd the Post that Sense betray'd, / And Virtue call'd Oblivion to her Aid" (27–28). The fourth stanza evokes a world of tired elders snoozing to drama crushed by rules, refined into weakness, frigidly cautious, loudly declamatory, and passionless. Though virtue and philosophy remained in this unnatural world, Tragedy was "forc'd at length her antient Reign to quit" (35). Folly, pantomime, and raucous song replaced her.

Johnson brings us to the immediate moment, freezes hitherto rapidly moving time, and requires a decision regarding the future. What will be the direction of Drury Lane, and of British theatre in general? Will Lear and Hamlet be replaced by Behn and Durfey? Will boxers, stage farce, flashy machinery, and exotic rope-dancers entertain "distant Times" (41)? Johnson's brilliant turn makes plain that the audience no longer merely may listen. It must act and decide what it wishes to see. Having already banished the pseudo-Aristotelian rules, Johnson announces the source of theatrical law – the boxes, pit, and gallery now listening to the call for renewal. Law givers must be just, wise, and responsible:

> Ah! let not Censure term our Fate our Choice,
> The Stage but echoes back the publick Voice.
> The Drama's Laws the Drama's Patrons give,
> For we that live to please, must please to live. (51–54)

Johnson's symbolic transfer of the audience to the stage allows him unthreatening incrimination and benevolent return to healthy origins: "Then prompt no more the Follies you decry, / As Tyrants doom their Tools of Guilt to die" (55–56). With correct prompting on a corrected stage, Drury Lane can recreate the genius portrayed in the first stanza. We recall its use of Nature, Truth, and Learning's triumph over barbarism that immediately rears the stage and evokes Shakespeare. With Garrick's Shakespearean emphasis and the audience's reformed moral state, a new reign in the British theatre can begin with an enlightened people's conscious decision:

> 'Tis yours this Night to bid the Reign commence
> Of rescu'd Nature, and reviving Sense;
> To chase the Charms of Sound, the Pomp of Show,
> For useful Mirth, and salutary Woe;
> Bid scenic Virtue form the rising Age,
> And Truth diffuse her Radiance from the Stage. (57–62)

The "Drury Lane Prologue" is a significant achievement. It harmonizes metaphors, theories of causation, chronological movement, narrative elegance, audience response, and trust in its ultimate intelligence.

Johnson, then, characteristically intrudes upon his poems, making plain that as human beings adrift in a dangerous world we need the guide he is willing to be until revelation replaces reason. Being a moral guide, though, denotes good intentions but not necessarily good poetry. One test of whether the moral also is the poetic is whether the poem persuades and pleases, often in appropriately figurative language. Johnson's best-known poetry handsomely passes such a test. Another of his short poems does so as well and should be better known.

The poem's short action is based upon its long title: "To Miss —— On Her Playing Upon the Harpsichord in a Room Hung with some Flower-Pieces of Her Own Painting" (1738–39?). The woman is both artist and subject of art, and is pleasingly threatened by an aggressively amorous but charming young man. In this hot-house environment, "Stella's" music imitates the sounds of spring as her painting imitates the flowering sights of spring. Johnson as guide, however, warns her that she is not art but nature, and as such is a tasty meal in a predatory sexual world:

> Ah! think not, in the dang'rous hour,
> The Nymph fictitious as the Flower;
> But shun, rash Youth, the gay Alcove,
> Nor tempt the Snares of wily Love. (7–10)

The charms of sense, the hopes of conquest, and the vanity of desire accompany her music as she fantasizes that her "unerring Art" will enchain the approaching youth and ameliorate his hunt (17). Johnson sets his moral song against her amorous song, and his poet's voice of truth against her suitor's voice of hormones-as-love. If she listens, "*Instruction* with her Flowers might spring, / And *Wisdom* warble from her String" (23–24). Johnson does not refrigerate warm love; he encourages the vulnerable woman to "Mark . . . Mark," properly to see the dangerous world (25, 29, 26), and to balance passion with restraint. Whether in prose or in poetry Johnson hopes to guide us toward a problem's solution. Nature here is the normal passions of men and women in a sensuous, perhaps sensual, spring-time environment that for human beings should include desire and limits. Johnson's paradigm for such amiable conflict is the ancient concept of *concordia discors*, of a benevolent God making a world from reconciled opposites. Johnson engages the art of music as a friendly check upon the art of love: notice "How Passion's well-accorded Strife / Gives all the Harmony of Life" (31–32). Let energetic nature learn from the already taught lessons of Stella's music and art. Be sufficiently beautiful beautifully to attract; but be sufficiently artful artfully to restrain attraction and thus to restrain danger. Good courtship is like good art, at once free and controlled.

> Thy Pictures shall thy Conduct frame,
> Consistent still, tho' not the same;
> Thy Musick teach the nobler Art,
> To tune the regulated Heart.   (33–36)

We know that Johnson's own heart was not as regulated as he hoped Stella's would be and that his public and private personae do not always cohere. Johnson the public poet alerts us to the world's dangers and difficulties and helps us to cope with them while we prepare ourselves for a better place. He is a companionate guide who asks questions, urges us to ask improving questions, and continues to help us find answers and options rather than despair and death.

Johnson earned this public posture. He himself had at least three episodes of what psychiatrists call severe agitated depression. He understood the human potential for darkness and the physical and spiritual danger surrender to it entailed. Some of his private poems without a guiding benevolent narrator embody that danger. Johnson wrote and recited "An extempore Elegy" (1778?) with Mrs. Thrale and Frances Burney, and both the assignment of parts and of the stanzas' order are uncertain. The grimly realistic poem was not designed for publication; it nevertheless both skillfully explores some of modern life's dangers for an isolated poor woman and forces the reader to ponder apparent truths.

The poem begins with a flippant dismissal of a prostitute presumably known in her small community. She is "as Dead as any Nail!" and perhaps in an unmarked pauper's grave (2). Her natural and coltish youth colors the description of her body plump as a cherry, her cheeks rosy as a pear, and her "Rump" nubile and sexual: it "made the Neighbours stare" (5–8). Her guilty success soon evokes its own failure and reorients the animal imagery. She does poorly "Till Purse and Carcase both were low" (12) and a country squire removes her from urban squalor to his rural seat. The final stanza forces us to rethink our response to the beginning of the tale:

> Black her eye with many a Blow,
> Hot her breath with many a Dram,
> Now she lies exceeding low,
> And as quiet as a Lamb. (17–20)

The senseless piece of driven metal becomes a lamb led to slaughter – by her own vain youth, ignorance, and misplaced ambition, by the neighbors who saw and feared her animal attraction; by "her friends and sire" (15) who allowed her to be seduced away, and by the larger culture that ignores the brute who apparently beat her to death. Johnson and his admired female colleagues need not overtly homilize. The poem offers an intense inversion, a rapid movement from amused distant observation regarding a dead nail to a theory of causation that makes us potential accomplices. The woman's demonstrably guilty life is replaced by the squire's demonstrably guilty life. Only she pays. If we do not berate him and his context, the guilt is ours. No one else cares enough to mourn her and to mark her perhaps non-existent stone. Do you?

Two other even darker poems also suggest the difference between Johnson the public and the private poet. One is Johnson's Latin poem "Post Lexicon Anglicanum Auctum et Emendatum" (1772). Johnson often would write in Latin, a language that allowed him to hide sensitive thoughts from some others while exploring those thoughts himself. In "Post Lexicon Anglicanum" Johnson records his emotional exhaustion after revising the *Dictionary* for its fourth folio edition (1773).

The episode ignited firestorms of self-examination and self-recrimination. Johnson wonders whether he used his talents well, whether his intellectual and moral life has meaning, and whether he can indeed survive his postpartum depression. From 1755 on, he was known as "Dictionary Johnson," Britain's most distinguished man of letters, and a serious competitor to the best of continental Europe's best. Is that enough? Is it all? Is that what he is designed for? Is it true? Where does he go from here? Is there anywhere *to* go?

Johnson begins his sad meditation by likening himself to Joseph Justus Scaliger (1540–1609), who upon finishing his own dictionary regarded lexicography as a form of punishment. Yes, Johnson says, no doubt thinking of himself,

Scaliger was fit for more exalted tasks. Johnson laments that he cannot match Scaliger's achievements or his extensive and deserved applause. With the revisions finished, Johnson now sees nothing but gloomy idleness, sleeplessness, bouncing from late noisy dinners to solitude, from wanting the night to fearing the day, and perpetual seeking of the unachievable, a superior life. Whatever he does and wherever he is taken, his financial and intellectual limits arrest his efforts. Johnson finds solace neither in nature nor in supernature, neither in his achievements nor in his potential. He sees only vast silent nocturnal expanses haunted by flitting ghostly shapes.

Like *The Vanity of Human Wishes* the riveting "Post Lexicon Anglicanum" ends with a series of questions – but without answers. The first recalls a pitiful outburst that begins a work written in prison, John Bunyan's *Pilgrim's Progress* (1678). There Christian dreams of seeing a ragged man, "*a Book in his hand, and a great burden upon his Back.*" He opens the book, reads, weeps, trembles, "and not being able longer to contain, he brake out with a lamentable cry; saying, *what shall I do?*"[6] Johnson the public writer tries to answer that question; Johnson the private writer only raises it. Paradoxically, even in his isolation he asks what Bunyan's Christian and so many others seeking counsel ask – "Quid faciam?" What shall I do? The Latin below is Johnson's; the English is Arthur Murphy's translation for his *Essay on the Life and Genius of Samuel Johnson* (1792):

> Quid faciam? tenebrisne pigram damnare senectam
> Restat? an accingar studiis gravioribus audax?
> Aut, hoc si nimium est, tandem nova lexica poscam? (52–54)

> What then remains? Must I in slow decline
> To mute inglorious ease old age resign?
> Or, bold ambition kindling in my breast,
> Attempt some arduous task? Or, were it best
> Brooding o'er lexicons to pass the day,
> And in that labour drudge my life away?   (*Poems*, p. 274)

Johnson understands our concerns because they are his own.

He also knows that such concerns must be met by individual responsibility within a larger community. Failure to meet obligations, to use one's talent, endangers ourselves and those who depend upon us. Johnson's more overheated youthful political poems excepted, his public voice generally mutes anger. In private he lets us know how he feels – as in the manuscript poem he sent to Mrs. Thrale with a request that she not show it to others.

"Long-Expected One and Twenty" (1780) also is called "A Short Song of Congratulation" for the Thrales' profligate nephew Sir John Lade, who at twenty-one assumes the ancient family estate. The normally optimistic birthday poem regards the day as one among many such happy events. The poem to Sir John rejects that pattern because as a tragic Tony Lumpkin Sir John rejects his communal obligations in favor of sordid personal pleasures.

Sir John now eliminates the voice of parents, guardians, and ancestors, for whom he substitutes "the Bettys, Kates, and Jennys / Ev'ry name that laughs at Care" (9–10) – that is, at guardianship. In so doing, Sir John transforms himself from responsible human male who helps others, to hunted animal on the food chain. Delighted gamblers, money lenders, and assorted Bettys see their meal out of the covert: "All that prey on vice and folly / Joy to see their quarry fly" (13–14). They so joy because Sir John fails to understand his true role – he is not owner but steward for what his ancestors have given to him and what he should give to his posterity. Sir John regards adulthood as pomp, pleasure, pride, profligacy, and transience. He is "Wild as wind, and light as feather"; he wastes his "Grandsire's guineas"; and his wealth wanders (7, 11, 17–18). The consequences are as grave for his inheritance as they are for him: "What are acres? what are houses?" Johnson asks, mimicking and then answering for Sir John: "Only dirt, or wet or dry" (23–24). For Sir John, the busy-body filial guides are too dim to recognize his brave new world. For Johnson, such a path leads to the grave: "Scorn their counsel and their pother, / You can hang or drown at last" (27–28). Johnson reduces the cheery birthday poem to a potential deathday poem – for the celebrant, his chronologically extended family, and the estate he will reduce to dirt. Johnson denigrates this violation of duty and failure to carry a burden that is also a privilege. He expresses his anger in the private poem, whereas in a public poem, as indeed in public when he met and at first scolded Sir John, he is more likely to instruct than to blame.

III

London and *The Vanity of Human Wishes* are Johnson's longest non-dramatic public poems. Each falls into that rich eighteenth-century genre called the "imitation," in which an earlier or even contemporary poem is adapted to modern or different circumstances. Often in the imitation the specific lines adapted are printed on the bottom of the page, on the facing page, or alluded to with their line references. In other cases an author may assume general knowledge of the poem imitated.

As the *Lives* of Pope and West make plain, Johnson later disapproved of the genre of imitation because it required knowledge of the parent-poem fully to engage its audience. This is partially true, since as a form imitation asks us to move between poets, poems, cultures, and centuries. A skillful poet, though, can make the modern work valuable in its own right, however much greater knowledge enhances our pleasure.

Johnson's *London* imitates Juvenal's (60–140?) third satire, a poem in which Umbricius tells his friend that he must leave degenerate un-Roman Rome for the country, where he can find old Roman values. For Juvenal, Rome crumbles through the weight of voracious foreigners, corruption, and crowded urban life. Johnson's adaptation was part of his early, and thereafter repudiated, political opposition to the controversial administration of Sir Robert Walpole. It regards the collapse of London as an emblem of the larger collapse of the nation, laments French influence and British political decay, and portrays its speaker Thales as having to vacate the morally un-British city. In so writing, Johnson well exploits Juvenal's reputation as the chronicler of Roman decline. Johnson's imitation implies that the government of King George II and of Sir Robert Walpole was doing to Britain what, say, Nero and Domitian had done to Rome.

In the process, Johnson's familiar opposition tactics praise Queen Elizabeth for defeating Spain and blame Walpole for allowing Spain to threaten British trade. The poem is vigorous, vibrant, and often urgent in its youthful anger and characterization of urban danger: "Some frolick Drunkard, reeling from a Feast, / Provokes a Broil, and stabs you for a Jest" (228–29). Unlike Pope's imitations, however, *London* lacks a necessary part of successful satire – a speaker, unlike "injur'd Thales" and "Indignant Thales" (2, 34) whom we like and whose judgment we trust. Johnson's rural "elegant Retreat" (212) is standard political opposition praise of the country at the expense of Walpole's commercial London, but it lacks the attractive specificity that Pope supplies for Twickenham's squirearchic alternative in *An Epistle to Dr. Arbuthnot* (1735). *London* is better at outrage than at providing a demonstrable political norm. After all, Johnson claims that Britons are too clumsy to be good liars and cheats, rather than that they refuse lying and cheating (144–51). *London* is well worth reading, but *The Vanity of Human Wishes* is one of the great poems in the English language. It follows the outline of Juvenal's tenth satire, embraces some of what Johnson thought of as its "sublimity," but also uses it as a touchstone rather than an argument on authority.

The two opening paragraphs of the *Vanity* depict a dark, misty, dangerous world in which Johnson asks us to observe, survey, remark, watch, and only "Then say" how ominous is the world before and within us (5). The first paragraph ends with "restless Fire precipitates on Death" (20). The second paragraph ends with "The Dangers gather as the Treasures rise" (28). This world and its actors need correction – if possible, for the poem's title tells us that we are dealing with inherent human nature.

Johnson, however, characteristically provides a theory of causation and, at the least, palliation. We see "wav'ring Man, betrayed by vent'rous Pride, / To tread the dreary Paths without a Guide" (7–8), and observe "How rarely Reason guides the stubborn Choice, / Rules the bold Hand, or prompts the suppliant Voice" (11–12). Johnson as narrator hopes to become a guide we will trust and follow.

He takes several approaches within his poem. He unifies different portraits through a common denominator of vain human wishes and through interlocking metaphors, like collapsing buildings and life as a battle. The portraits include several classes of human activity, as with the invading general who takes life and the birthing mother who gives life. As this example suggests, Johnson contrasts those portraits, so that the doting and dying old men Marlborough and Swift precede the pregnant and optimistic young mother, and the withdrawn scholar anxious for acclaim in the enclosed academic world appears just before the public celebration for a general's foreign victory. Such breadth and contrast suggest broad induction and a wide variety of human wishes. As guide, Johnson uses a plural pronoun to suggest that he shares our human weakness. The rejected statesman evokes our amused contempt: "now no more we trace in ev'ry Line / Heroic Worth, Benevolence Divine" (87–88). When Johnson invokes the laughing philosopher Democritus (49–72) to mock eternal folly in the human farce, he reminds us of the importance of continuing our search before we draw inferences: "How just that Scorn ere yet thy Voice declare, / Search every State, and canvass ev'ry Pray'r" (71–72).

Johnson shows his skill in human and moral psychology in several of the character portraits. Cardinal Wolsey rose so high that he seemed to threaten his monarch. He is cast down, takes refuge in a monastery, "And his last Sighs reproach the Faith of Kings" (120) – not religious but secular faith still so important to the prince of the Church. The ambitious Oxford scholar, surely like Johnson himself, must "pause awhile from Letters to be wise" (158). The old man "Hides from himself his State, and shuns to know, / That Life protracted is protracted Woe" (257–58).

The portrait of Charles XII of Sweden (1682–1718) is deservedly famous. He was the overreaching monarch and general whose bold but finally fatal attacks terrorized much of Europe. The passage skillfully includes many of Johnson's familiar themes – repulsion with slaughter that aggrandizes one man and kills and impoverishes thousands, understanding of the human need to glorify heroes, and subtle contrast with the classical parent-poem and its inadequate moral vision. Characteristic poetic devices include the metaphor of the insecure building, personifications that energize the poem with externalized emotions, questions that further involve the reader, a shocking rapid reversal, and an inference drawn from what we have just seen. Johnson knows that pompous martial glory and its rewards "With Force resistless o'er the Brave prevail" (178) as it does for us as admirers of the apparent national success in which we safely share. Yet this is irrational, for nations may die to celebrate one man, grandchildren may be impoverished to pay for their ancestors' triumphs, and conquerors wreaths will "rust on Medals, or on Stones decay" (190). In that case, "On what Foundation stands the Warrior's Pride?" (191) – let us look at Swedish Charles.

He is fearless, tireless, immune to female temptation, and defeats king after king. "Peace courts his Hand, but spreads her Charms in vain" (201), we hear, not surprised by Charles's indifference to feminized peace in favor of masculine, possessive war and the first person singular that thinks nothing his until "all be Mine beneath the Polar Sky" (204). He enjoys only advance and victory until, in a brilliant couplet that encapsulates the brevity of fame, "He comes, nor Want nor Cold his Course delay; – / Hide, blushing Glory, hide *Pultowa's* Day" (209–10). Defeat by Peter the Great leads to collapse, exile, loss of royal authority, and dependence upon hitherto irrelevant women to help him. Johnson anticipates our response, a series of questions that show how we cherish our myths. Surely he could not die ignobly:

> But did not Chance at length her Error mend?
> Did no subverted Empire mark his End?
> Did rival Monarchs give the fatal Wound?
> Or hostile Millions press him to the Ground? (215–18)

No. He died in obscurity, at an insignificant battle, and perhaps by his own soldiers' hands. The powerful life that once extended over thousands of miles and men now requires the space of a grave. He leaves only "the Name, at which the World grew pale, / To point a Moral, or adorn a Tale" (221–22). The once terrible warrior now is contained in a homily.

Johnson's ultimate target and audience is the human situation – hence he includes Juvenal and his parochial treatment of the North African Hannibal, Juvenal's original of Swedish Charles. When reading the *Vanity* our response includes pity for Charles, for Europe, and for ourselves. In contrast, Juvenal enjoys the barbarian lunatic's death and miniaturization into Roman schoolboys' declamation. The great empire perpetually triumphs over and torments the elephant-driving one-eyed alien who humiliated republican Rome at Cannae (Satire 10: 164–66). Johnson is cosmopolitan; Juvenal is local. Johnson is sympathetic; Juvenal is vengeful. Like Democritus, Juvenal is an inadequate guide for the Christian empiricist. The conclusion to the poem further illustrates its moral and poetic grandeur, and satisfies a key expectation of formal verse satire – praise of the virtue opposed to the vice attacked.

The final portrait before the *Vanity's* conclusion exploits that most enduring and endearing emblem of human renewal – the birth of a child. After all, what parent does not wish to have an attractive child? That child, alas, becomes a prisoner of the dangerous, cloudy, snare-encrusted world of Johnson's first paragraph, but now with special reference to female fragility. He transfers the martial imagery of earlier passages to a siege image in the battle of and within the sexes:

"Against your Fame with Fondness Hate combines, / The Rival batters, and the Lover mines" (331–32). The young woman "falls betray'd, despis'd, distress'd, / And hissing Infamy proclaims the rest" (341–42).

By now the reader has been with Johnson on a long journey. He began by urging us to look carefully at the world and "Then say how Hope and Fear, Desire and Hate" (5) confuse, disorient, and generally lead to failure or death. Enough, we now say. Human desire is indigenous to fallen humanity. If even the wish for a pretty daughter is vain and useless, what are we to do? The reader virtually breaks into the poem, repeats some of the earlier key words in this new context, proclaims several questions, and gives Johnson the opportunity to reorient our vision:

> Where then shall Hope and Fear their Objects find?
> Must dull Suspence corrupt the stagnant Mind?
> Must helpless Man, in Ignorance sedate,
> Roll darkling down the Torrent of his Fate?
> Must no Dislike alarm, no Wishes rise,
> No Cries attempt the Mercies of the Skies?
> Enquirer, cease, Petitions yet remain,
> Which Heav'n may hear, nor deem Religion vain.
> Still raise for Good the supplicating Voice,
> But leave to Heav'n the Measure and the Choice.
> Safe in his Pow'r, whose Eyes discern afar
> The secret Ambush of a specious Pray'r. (343–54)[7]

The antidote for vain human wishes is non-vain spiritual wishes; the antidote for an unreliable monarch is a reliable God; the antidote for overreaching is trust in God's knowledge of what is best for us. For Juvenal god is anthropomorphic; since we create him, we also can create our own improvement. For Johnson, God is the creator to whom we turn to help us control our passions, restlessness, impatience, and anger. "Ill" in this world can never be eliminated; but it can be "transmuted" if we pray for God's "Love, which scarce collective Man can fill," and "For faith, that panting for a happier Seat, / Counts Death kind Nature's Signal of Retreat" (361–64). The poem's final couplet returns us to one of Johnson's key images – the empiricist who looks at the world and draws appropriate inferences. Now, however, that empiricist no longer is the lonely human searcher. Personified "celestial Wisdom" also searches and also sees our misery. She can look up, rather than look only to human beings, and so "calms the Mind, / And makes the Happiness she does not find" (367–68). As Johnson says in his Sermon 12, on Ecclesiastes 1: 14, earthly vanity does not infect "religious practices, or . . . any actions immediately commanded by God, or directly referred to him" (*Sermons*, p. 130). Revelation removes earthly vanity.

Here is Johnson's alternative to his first paragraph that ends with death and his penultimate paragraph that ends with infamy: find celestial wisdom and you make happiness. Look in the proper celestial direction and the restless mind can be calmed. *The Vanity of Human Wishes* was published in 1749, but it includes many of the moral and poetic traits that permeate the best of Johnson's public poetry in English. It answers the darkness in his private poetry in English and Latin, and it does so with a narrator and guide who urges "Love, which scarce collective Man can fill." We can say of Johnson as a poet and as a man what Johnson said in his "Epitaph on William Hogarth":

> If Genius warm thee, Reader, stay,
> If Merit touch thee, shed a tear,
> Be Vice and Dulness far away
> Great [Johnson's] honour'd Dust is here. (5–8)

NOTES

1 I quote Johnson's poetry from the excellent old-spelling edition by J. D. Fleeman, *Samuel Johnson: The Complete English Poems* (Harmondsworth: Penguin, 1971). The Yale Edition, edited by E. L. McAdam, Jr. with George Milne (1964), is a fine modernized version, from which I quote Arthur Murphy's translation of Johnson's "Post Lexicon Anglicanum."

2 Addison, *The Spectator*, ed. Donald F. Bond (Oxford: Clarendon Press, 1965), IV, 318. Reynolds, *Discourses on Art*, ed. Robert R. Wark (New Haven: Yale University Press for the Paul Mellon Centre, 1975), p. 259.

3 The quotation comes from "Examination of a Question Proposed in the [Gentelman's] Magazine of June, p. 310."

4 See Bacon, *The Essays of Francis Lo. Verulam* (London, 1625), p. 196.

5 *Preceptor*, in *Works* II, 253.

6 Bunyan, *The Pilgrim's Progress from this World to That which is to Come*, ed. James Blanton Wharey and Roger Sharrock, 2nd edn. (Oxford: Clarendon Press, 1967), p. 8.

7 I prefer the Yale edition's reading of line 348 in *Vanity*: "attempt" not "invoke" (as Fleeman has) Heaven's mercies.

4

PAUL J. KORSHIN

Johnson, the essay, and *The Rambler*

Johnson started *The Rambler* almost at the midpoint of his most productive literary and scholarly decade (1745–55). In 1745, with his *Observations on Macbeth*, he laid the groundwork for his largest editorial project; in the first months of 1746, as he finished his "Short Scheme of an English Dictionary" (dated 30 April 1746), he set forth on his immense lexicographical labors. He was already well acquainted with large, ambitious undertakings, as we know from his parliamentary reporting. His *Debates in Parliament*, as the publishers of the first collected edition (1787) called them, form his first major literary project, although Johnson obviously did not undertake that task, which ran from November 1740 to February 1743, with a final collection in mind. *The Rambler* is different. As the centerpiece of this decade of immense literary activity, Johnson saw it from the beginning as an entrepreneurial undertaking that would rival the other great collections of English essays, Bacon's *Essays Civil and Moral* and Addison and Steele's *The Spectator*. Every collection is a miscellany, but Johnson, even before he started *The Rambler*, understood the opportunity for his new project to rival if not supersede his famous predecessors. His edition of Shakespeare and his preparations for the dictionary were long-term projects, but a series of periodical essays, as an active participant in contemporary letters like Johnson knew, could create a following and, through publication in a collected version, widen an author's reputation. Johnson's choice of title seems almost accidental and, if we recall one contemporary meaning of "ramble," may seem somewhat adventurous bordering on the *risqué* (Lord Rochester's obscene "A Ramble in St. James's Park" illustrates this aspect of the name). But the subjects that Johnson had planned for the first few months show how much he expected his collection to differ from what are loosely called his models, whether classical, Renaissance, or English.

I

The tendency of twentieth-century readers of *The Rambler* is to insist on the work's incidental qualities, since we assume that Johnson wrote his essays hastily and with little advance preparation to obey the summons of the press. This assessment overlooks Johnson's original intention, which his contemporaries clearly understood. Johnson's original audience, the purchasers of the 500 copies that appeared twice weekly from March 1750 to March 1752, were supplemented after the first few months of the periodical's existence by readers who saw individual numbers that various provincial newspapers began – piratically – to reprint. Complete sets of the original 208 issues are very rare, but this fact does not mean that the work lacked a serious following. Missing numbers in an eighteenth-century work published in series usually indicate that the work was so popular that it was literally read until the copies fell apart. Moreover, enterprising booksellers began to publish the first collected volumes of *The Rambler* within six months of its beginning; Johnson himself was at work on the first volume of the two-volume folio edition before the work was a year old. The usual format for collected editions of *The Rambler* independent of Johnson's collected works was a four-volume octavo; Johnson extensively revised his original for the 1756 edition, which remained his final version, substantially unchanged for the rest of his life.

Most eighteenth-century readers of *The Rambler* first made an acquaintance with the work as a complete collection. In Johnson's own century, this audience was large and influential. By 1759, Goldsmith, in his essay in *The Bee* on the "fame machine," implies that Johnson's reputation was greater for his series of essays than for the *Dictionary*.[1] Besides the original run of the 208 essays, there were more than twenty reprintings of the entire work by 1800 and, in the nineteenth century, there were another three dozen separate editions of the work plus twenty more reprintings in editions of Johnson's works. Nineteenth-century editions have a larger press run than those of the eighteenth century and are on cheaper paper, so they cost less than the earlier collections. Thus we can be sure that Johnson's periodical writings reached an even wider audience in the century after his death than they did during his lifetime.

The perceptions of *The Rambler*'s second, larger audience clearly differed from those of his primary readers. First, these later readers did not encounter the essays as a periodical or an interrupted series. Rather, this second audience saw it as a coherent literary work, with translations of the Greek and Latin mottoes and other quotations from the classics and a table of contents (added by one of Johnson's publishers, so it has no authorial mandate). Later readers would readily have seen the interconnections among various essays that have similar subjects; doubtless, too, this audience would have been misled by the thumbnail descriptions in the table of contents, which are often amusingly different from the subject of the essays they purport to describe. For example, number 134, one of Johnson's few statements on his method of composition, the table of contents describes thus: "Idleness an anxious and miserable state." Number 114,

Johnson's famous attack on capital punishment, in the table of contents is blandly announced as "the necessity of apportioning punishments to crimes." *Rambler* 90, the first in Johnson's original study of Milton's versification, the contents calls "the pauses in English poetry adjusted." Readers of *The Rambler* in these collected editions must inevitably have wondered why Johnson gave his essays such inaccurate titles or why he wandered so far from his announced topics. However, *The Rambler*, until the first complete edition of the twentieth century, the Yale edition of Johnson's works (3 vols., 1969), has received little or no annotation, which means that Johnson's eighteenth- and nineteenth-century readers had the benefit of his thoughts without the interjection of editorial opinions.

Beginning also in the eighteenth century, and continuing until the present day, there is yet another kind of audience of *The Rambler*. This group, which is probably the largest, consists of readers who have become acquainted with Johnson through the pages of an anthology. The first collections of British essays date from the 1780s, and the first anthologizers began to publish at about the same time. These people were often schoolmasters or others (to use Lady Bracknell's phrase) "remotely connected with education"; often they were respectable minor writers like Vicesimus Knox and W. F. Mavor. Knox, Mavor, and their associates plundered the entire field of eighteenth-century periodical literature to assemble their collections. In an age with only a modest idea of the nature of literary property, the essay was an ideal subject for the anthologizer and, as we would expect, the favorites included *The Spectator* and *The Rambler*. The two series are more or less equally represented in contemporary anthologies; since *The Spectator* contains 635 numbers, this parity shows that Johnson's work, which was less than one-third as long, was already more popular than that of Addison, Steele, and their collaborators. The early anthologies had an immense audience; some of them survive in dozens of editions. Knox's *Elegant Extracts in Verse and Prose* was still appearing in new editions in the 1830s. The many editions of Knox's collection include a number of essays from *The Rambler* printed without abridgment save for the removal of the Greek and Latin mottoes and most of the quotations in the texts themselves. By the middle of the nineteenth century, several hundred editions of a number of different anthologies had reprinted about a quarter of *The Rambler* as individual essays in an untold number of copies. The first selection devoted solely to Johnson's essays, G. B. Hill's *Select Essays of Dr. Johnson* (1899) prints seventy-seven of Johnson's essays, including about a quarter of *The Rambler*. The formation of modern departments of English in the late nineteenth century created a further need for collections of the classics of English literature and here *The Rambler* outstrips any other series of eighteenth-century literary essays in popularity.

Johnson tells us that he designed *The Rambler* for the largest possible audience in number 106, an essay on the vanity of the hopes of authors for fame:

There are, indeed, few kinds of composition from which an author, however learned or ingenious, can hope a long continuance of fame. He who has carefully studied human nature, and can well describe it, may with most reason flatter his ambition. Bacon, among all his pretensions to the regard of posterity, seems to have pleased himself mainly with his essays, "which come home to mens business and bosoms," and of which, therefore, he declares his expectation, that they "will live as long as books last." (IV, 204)

The Rambler was, by number 106, already appearing in book form, so when Johnson tells his original and secondary audiences that Bacon prized his essays above all his works, it is a declaration that he hoped people would compare him not to other eighteenth-century series of essays but to the inventor of the essay in English.[2]

II

Perhaps among the most frequently anthologized essays from *The Rambler* since Hill's collection of 1899 have been two of Johnson's many contributions to literary criticism, numbers 4 (on prose fiction) and 60 (on biography). Those interested in Johnson's literary criticism, however, are more likely to turn to his famous critical prefaces – to the *Dictionary* and to Shakespeare – and to his *Lives of the Poets* than to his periodical essays. Yet it seems clear that Johnson took as one of his regular topics the explication of themes from the world of letters, a sign that he expected his original audience not just to understand these subjects but to have an appetite for learning more about them. Johnson was aware that literary criticism was often motivated by envy, a vice which he deplored. In *Rambler* 183, for instance, he devotes most of an essay to the subject. This essay contains a collection of maxims on envy, but the essay is a rare original for Johnson, since none of the essayists he modeled himself on, from Plutarch and Seneca to Addison, had written on it. "Envy," he writes, "is mere unmixed and genuine evil; it pursues a hateful end by despicable means, and desires not so much its own happiness as another's misery" (V, 200). The frequency of envy, Johnson makes clear, means that we encounter it in the world of letters as well as in everyday life: "The genius, even when he endeavours only to entertain or instruct, yet suffers persecution from innumerable cricks, whose acrimony is excited merely by the pain of seeing others pleased, and of hearing applauses which another enjoys" (V, 199). *Rambler* 183 is therefore a reference point for the other literary essays in the series, since Johnson comments, throughout the 1740s and 1750s, on questions of the morality of authors.

In *Rambler* 4, for example, Johnson worries about the moral effect of the rapidly expanding genre of prose fiction, books which he believed were "written chiefly to the young, the ignorant, and the idle, to whom they serve as lectures of conduct, and introductions into life" (III, 21). Consequently the authors of novels, Johnson believes, cannot themselves be ignorant of the moral impact of fiction:

> Vice, for vice is necessary to be shewn, should always disgust; nor should the graces of gaiety, or the dignity of courage, be so united with it, as to reconcile it to the mind. Wherever it appears, it should raise hatred by the malignity of its practices, and contempt by the meanness of its stratagems; for while it is supported by either parts or spirit, it will be seldom heartily abhorred. (III, 24)

This essay is Johnson's contribution to a larger debate about novels as different as Richardson's *Clarissa* (1748) and Fielding's *Tom Jones* (1749). But in terms of the literary-critical essays in *The Rambler*, number 4 is also about the old Renaissance critical commonplace of whether an author had to be a good man writing good things. Johnson returns to this problem often in *The Rambler*, for it is clear that in the 1740s and 1750s he was not certain of its solution. Barely six years before, Johnson dealt with this problem in *The Life of Savage* (1744), a man whom no form of reasoning could permit Johnson to see as a good or a moral person, yet Johnson had to acknowledge Savage's literary merits.[3] The statement of *Rambler* 4 is almost uncompromising. Yet barely four months later he changes his attitude. This change comes in *Rambler*s 36 and 37, on pastoral poetry. Later in his life, in his "Life of Milton," Johnson would declare his aversion for pastoral, with "Lycidas" as his example of what can go wrong with this genre. But in 1751, while Johnson insists that "the range of pastoral is indeed narrow," he concedes that every now and then someone has augmented the stock of pastoral poetry with a new idea (III, 197–98). Moreover, the classical writers of pastoral sometimes made a fresh and original contribution; the absurdity of the genre consists in having people so remote from state affairs as shepherds discuss "errors in the church, and corruptions in the government" (III, 205). Pastoral writers are not wicked, then, as are the authors of novels that exalt vice; they are simply misguided.

Biographers are another matter entirely, as we know from Johnson's *Rambler* 60, perhaps his best-known critical essay, which the table of contents describes as "The dignity and usefulness of biography." Traditionally, critics have seen this essay as praise of the genre to which Johnson had already contributed a number of short studies and to which he would later make his most important contributions in *The Lives of the Poets*. It is easy to overlook the fact that Johnson had already written one substantial biography, of Richard Savage. Although in *Rambler* 4 Johnson had insisted that the writer of prose fiction must always reprehend vice, he himself had written with understanding of vice in the *Life of Savage*, for his friend Savage was plainly addicted to vice, a fact which Johnson does not try to deny, although he does palliate it. Hence in *Rambler* 60, Johnson can hardly rule out the depiction of vice, since biography must inevitably deal with human wickedness:

> I have often thought that there has rarely passed a life of which a judicious and faithful narrative would not be useful. For, not only every man has, in the mighty mass of the world, great numbers in the same condition with himself, to whom his mistakes and miscarriages, escapes and expedients, would be of apparent and immediate use; but there is such an uniformity in the state of man, considered apart from adventitious and separable decorations and disguises, that there is scare any possibility of good or ill, but is common to human kind. (III, 320)

It is no longer necessary, in other words, for vice to disgust and, in fact, one of Johnson's best examples in *Rambler* 60 on the truth of biography in describing the human condition is Sallust's description of Catiline: "Thus Salust, the great master of nature, has not forgot, in his account of Catiline, to remark that 'his walk was now quick and again slow,' as an indication of a mind revolving something with violent commotion" (III, 321). Whether Sallust's characterization is accurate is not the point; what matters is that we can scarcely describe the arch-conspirator and traitor Catiline as a figure of virtue. Thus the subject of biography does not have to be a good person.

The genre of biography had evolved, in Johnson's lifetime, from the hagiography of Izaak Walton to a form which could accommodate all shades of moral behavior; significantly for Johnson, literary criticism of biography had to reflect reality. One of Johnson's greatest improvements to the genre, in distinction to writers like Walton or classical figures like Plutarch, is immediacy; the biographer has to form his or her work while the clay of human life is still malleable. He writes in *Rambler* 60: "If a life [i.e., a biography] be delayed till interest and envy are at an end, we may hope for impartiality, but must expect little intelligence; for the incidents which give excellence to biography are of a volatile and evanescent kind, such as soon escape the memory, and are rarely transmitted by tradition" (III, 323). Thus biography, in order to be successful, actually has to take account of "political" interest, a vice, and envy, the most reprehensible vice of all. In *Rambler* 93, Johnson readily concedes that critics, "like all the rest of mankind, are very frequently misled by interest" (IV, 132). Furthermore, critics are subject to the dreadful vice of envy: "Criticism has so often given occasion to the envious and ill-natured of gratifying their malignity, that some have thought it necessary to recommend the virtue of candour without restriction, and to preclude all future liberty of censure" (IV, 133). The only way that the critic can avoid envy, Johnson continues, is "to hold out the light of reason, whatever it may discover" (IV, 134). Determinations of vice are up to the audience: the literary critic, like the biographer, simply must describe everything, whether beauties or faults, without envy, interest, or censure. The permissiveness of this

view is striking, for it shows that even as early as the 1750s Johnson's conceptions of literary criticism are not monolithic, but evolve in *The Rambler* as he
applied his craft to practical situations, to actual writings.

The most extended practical criticism in *The Rambler* is the seven essays
Johnson devotes to Milton, five on his versification (numbers 86, 88, 90, 92, and
94) and two on *Samson Agonistes* (numbers 139–40). Johnson's great attention
to Milton at this time may represent an effort to surpass Addison, the first
periodical essayist to write about Milton;[4] it may also serve as an atonement of
sorts for his role in the affair of the duplicitous Lauder. The Scottish writer
William Lauder in 1749 alleged that Milton had plagiarized portions of *Paradise
Lost*; Johnson at first accepted Lauder's argument but later, when he learned that
Lauder had lied, urged him to admit the truth, and actually helped him to draft
his recantation.[5] Milton's reputation at the time of *The Rambler* was considerable but Johnson, while he acknowledges his greatness, nevertheless has reservations, chiefly about Milton's personal and political views. One reason for writing
five critical essays on Milton's versification, essays which specialists on Johnson's
criticism usually ignore, is to compete with Addison, "the illustrious writer [on
Milton] who has so long dictated to the commonwealth of learning" (IV, 88) but
on a topic that Addison had overlooked. The same desire would later lead him
to write about *Samson*, the work of Milton's most ignored in the eighteenth
century. Aware of the danger of using abstruse technical terms, and that
versification is a topic for which "the dialect of grammarians" is available,
Johnson recognizes "that offence which is always given by unusual words" (IV,
89). To be sure, some "hard words" intrude, but the progress of these essays is
clearly to take Johnson's audience from Milton's techniques (numbers 86, 88, 90)
through classical methods (number 92) to contemporary English practice
(number 94). Just as Addison had done forty years before, Johnson finds himself
in the role of educating the taste of a contemporary audience for a style of verse
that was unfamiliar to the bulk of his readers. "The imitator treads a beaten
walk," Johnson notes in *Rambler* 86 (IV, 88); hence his unorthodox choice of
subject underscores his search here, as elsewhere in *The Rambler*, for originality.

This impulse recurs in another notable series of critical essays, numbers 152,
154, 156, and 158, which, like those on Milton, shows how carefully he planned
The Rambler. We find the theme of originality again, in number 154: "No man
ever yet became great by imitation" (V, 59). These four essays are also related.
Number 152 is entirely original, since it is the first modern critical comment on
the art of letter writing. What Johnson, as the author of the most famous letter
in the English language (that of February 1755 to Lord Chesterfield), has to say
about everyday epistles is worth reading, for he believes that the usual rules of
composition do not apply to so varied a genre as letters (V, 45). Number 154 is
about another modern intellectual problem, the search for originality through

study, for Johnson believes that eminence is possible in every age. He continues his search for greatness in number 156, focusing this time on authority and the so-called rules of literature, making the important distinction between "laws of nature" and "accidental prescriptions of authority" (v, 66). In literary criticism, as in politics, Johnson rejects "despotick antiquity" and "rules which no literary dictator had authority to enact" (v, 67, 70). In the final essay in this series, number 158, Johnson turns again to the rules of composition and asks whether there are rules for literary criticism, for lyric poetry, even for essays (v, 76–77). With the examples of Montaigne and Addison before him, Johnson can find no reason for thinking that an essayist need follow rules:

> A writer of later times has, by the vivacity of his essays, reconciled mankind to the same licentiousness [as we find in lyric poetry] in short dissertations; and he therefore who wants skill to form a plan, or diligence to pursue it, needs only entitle his performance an essay, to acquire the right of heaping together the collections of half his life, without order, coherence, or propriety.　　　　(v, 77)

There is no shortage of irony here, as we may often note in Johnson's comments about his own achievements, but his chief concern is that the rules of a given genre must come from reason and nature instead of from authorial caprice. The literary criticism in *The Rambler*, as these four essays show, is highly practical: Johnson is not simply telling his audience what to prefer, he is setting standards for the authors of his own generation to follow and offering evidence against which he hoped people would judge his writings.

III

Johnson did not plan for *The Rambler* to be a collection of political essays; there was hardly a need for another political voice in the miscellaneous publications of mid-century England. Inevitably, however, the language which he uses to discuss the world of literature – the "despotick authority" of critics, "the commonwealth of letters," the "tyranny" of previous example – is often the language of contemporary politics. And, since one of his habitual modes of expression in *The Rambler* is allegorical, occasionally we see that some essays which appear to be on apolitical subjects have direct political implications. With rare exceptions, *The Rambler* eschews subjects of contemporary topical interest; one of the outstanding exceptions, in fact, is *Rambler* 114, which deals directly with the severity of English criminal law and the frequent use of the death penalty.[6] Early in 1751, Henry Fielding had called for an increase in the frequency of capital punishment in his *Enquiry into the Causes of the Late Increase of Robbers*; in number 114, Johnson specifically addresses England's wide application of the death penalty and finds it an inadequate deterrent of the spread of crime, precisely the reverse of Fielding's position. In the parliamentary debate on relaxing the breadth of capital punishment in 1818, one of the harbingers of its eventual abolition, Sir Samuel Romilly, would introduce the text of *Rambler* 114 into Hansard; it remains one of Johnson's most powerful political writings.

A second strongly political essay is *Rambler* 148, which, as the table of contents describes it, is ostensibly about "The cruelty of parental tyranny." This essay does, indeed, speak about capricious behavior by parents, especially fathers, a frequent topic in *The Rambler*, but at the start Johnson says bluntly, "The robber may be seized, and the invader repelled wherever they are found" (V, 22), which describes how the Jacobite invasion of 1745–46 was crushed. Throughout *Rambler* 148, Johnson urges that arbitrary, "capricious" power in the hands of a parent or a sovereign is detestable; this view is consistent with Johnson's dislike of tyranny, but it also shows how he inserts this issue into the current political debate on Jacobitism. The tyrannical family, of course, in the rhetoric of Stuart kingship, was widely understood to represent the tyrannical state, so Johnson here unmistakably expresses his revulsion with the recent Jacobite invasion and with Jacobitism itself. In his essay against capital punishment, Johnson appeals to the authority of Sir Thomas More for political support; in *Rambler* 148, he appeals to Aristotle's *Politica*, which Johnson cites to support his claim that the family analogizes the state. None of the other *Ramblers* on tyrannical parents employs allegory to represent the state in this way, so Johnson must be referring here to another topical issue. The events of the Jacobite invasion may have seemed remote by 1751, but Jacobite incursions and plots and state executions of malefactors continued long after the fateful Battle of Culloden (16 April 1746), into the 1750s. It is possible that Johnson alludes to the execution of the Jacobite Paul Tierney, who recruited for the French army, which attracted much national attention in 1751; nearly half of the issues of *The Rambler* for August and September 1751 touch on issues ancillary to politics. These essays are contemporaneous with the intensive debate about establishing arrangements for a regency if George II were to die before the eleven-year-old Prince George reached the age of eighteen (the death of the Prince of Wales, Frederick Louis, in March 1751, was the immediate catalyst for this discussion). Evidently, Johnson's discussions of parental tyranny in *The Rambler* have more than one focus outside the family.

There is a remarkable similarity among the many "family" essays in *The Rambler*, especially those which purport to be written by young people about family difficulties. Anthologizers of Johnson have generally ignored them. Almost all of these essays deal with adolescence, youth, and early adulthood; the imaginary authors more than half the time are women. The question of authority is always present, whether it is the tyrannical authority of an aging parent, the abused or usurped authority of a guardian or relative, or the insolence of an older person who has some kind of power over the author of the letter. A particularly insidious subgroup of this category are the essays where Johnson talks about the dependence of a weaker, younger, poorer person on someone older, often a patron of some sort. The male patrons in *The Rambler* are usually aristocrats or prominent people in civil affairs with the power to bestow places or to open other avenues to success; his female patrons usually are women who introduce younger female correspondents to polite society (Johnson presents no cases of men patronizing young women or women patronizing young men). Johnson's family tyrants, a word he often uses in this context, exercise their powers arbitrarily. Myrtilla in *Rambler* 84, for example, appears to most readers as a silly child who wants more than her years entitle her to have (she closes her letter with the memorable postscript, "Remember I am past sixteen" – IV, 81), but her opening is very different: "SIR, You seem in all your papers to be an enemy to tyranny . . . I shall therefore lay my case before you, and hope by your decision to be set free from unreasonable restraints" (IV, 76–77). Myrtilla's oppressor is her guardian, an aunt who objects to her wasting time with idle things like intelligent conversation and books, and the presentation is political, dealing with usurped authority, power mishandled, the refusal of the governor to consider the wishes of the governed.

The character of Squire Bluster, the rural tyrant of *Rambler* 142, typifies a number of similar people whom Johnson sketches, for he has a special purpose in presenting village and domestic despotism. While he never says anything to suggest that one can overthrow the political power of the family unit, Johnson is dissatisfied with the damage that ill-natured rich people can cause in the social order. Insolent patrons may be able to tyrannize over their dependants; Johnson does not believe that such despotism should escape censure. "The general story of mankind will evince, that lawful and settled authority is very seldom resisted when it is well employed," he writes in *Rambler* 50, an essay on the complaints of old men about the state of the world. This theme is the obverse of the topic of political abuse, which runs through several dozen essays, and is Johnson's best statement in *The Rambler* on the proper use of authority. Yet we find many more complaints about "despotick and dictatorial power" (*Rambler* 61, III, 326) exercised by people in every walk of life. We hear Ruricola complaining about Mr. Frolick's usurpation of the power to prescribe taste to his rustic neighbors simply because he has lived in London; in *Rambler* 176 we learn of Bishop Vida's skill in "the politicks of literature" to thwart the "arrogance and brutality" of his critics. In many ways, *The Rambler*, despite its non-political view of the world, is Johnson's best contribution to the wars of truth.

IV

Just as *The Rambler* shows Johnson's progress in his ideas about literature and politics, so it reveals his changing attitude toward women. The work contains about three dozen essays on the problems that eighteenth-century women, almost always of the middle and upper classes, face in society and everyday life. These essays are known mainly to readers of the complete text, for the anthologizers of more than two centuries have seldom considered Johnson's thoughts on women worthy of being reprinted.[7] Johnson evidently did not at first expect that *The Rambler* would appeal to a feminine audience, for he makes a concession to this effect at the start of number 34: "I have been censured for having hitherto dedicated so few of my speculations to the ladies; and indeed the moralist, whose instructions are accommodated only to one half of the human species, must be confessed not sufficiently to have extended his views" (III, 184). A year before, the "extensive view" of *The Vanity of Human Wishes* had encompassed "mankind" alone; hence Johnson's self-rebuke in number 34 is an important advance for him. It is noteworthy that, in *The Rambler*, we may see Johnson's progress from Misellus (the successful young male author of number 16) to Misella (the prostitute to whose story Johnson devotes numbers 170–71). The complaint of Misellus, whose literary success has led to a fame greater than he wants, was a traditionally masculine subject, but literary fame is beyond the reach of the average woman. Hence the essays about women deal less with the world of intellect than with the lack of preparation English society gives them for more than "the most servile employments," Misella, herself the daughter of a good family, points out (V, 145). In an early essay on marriage, Johnson comments on the tradition of blaming women for the woes of the married state: "As the faculty of writing has been chiefly a masculine endowment, the reproach of making the world miserable has been always thrown upon the women" (*Rambler* 18, III, 98). Hence, he continues, "I sometimes venture to consider this universal grievance, having endeavoured to divest my heart of all partiality, and place myself as a kind of neutral being between the sexes."

The Misella essays, like many others in *The Rambler*, are nominally the work of a correspondent; indeed, Johnson employs the device of the fictional letter-writer often in his essays about women. All journalistic enterprises receive letters from readers; many earlier eighteenth-century essay collections actually had published a fair number of such writings. Johnson often mentions correspondence from his audience, but the only epistles in *The Rambler* are those of his own authorship, over the signature of a large array of Greek and Latin appellations. Johnson uses this device often in his essays about women. Evidently he found the feminine persona a convenient way to represent the less public sphere that eighteenth-century women occupied, but the fictional correspondent is just as frequently an inexperienced young male whose unworldliness we can especially remark. Hymenaeus on marriage (numbers 113 and 115), for example, discusses his growing awareness of marital life and Ruricola (number 61) ridicules the hauteur of those who think their residence in London exalts them over their former associates back in the shires. In the same way, Zosima (number 12) discusses the trials of a young gentlewoman's search for a place as a servant and Myrtilla (number 84) tells us of her discovery of domestic tyranny. The letter from an invented correspondent was a common eighteenth-century political and satiric approach to contemporary social problems. In Johnson's many adept applications of this method, we can see yet another way in which *The Rambler* broadens the appeal of topics that have rather narrow applications; he seems always to be reaching for the wider audience.

For an eighteenth-century male writer, indeed, Johnson goes much further than most in treating women as the intellectual equals of men, but his idea of a "neutral being" is not androgyny; rather, he tries to show that men as well as women are capable of shallowness and trifling. The essays on women who waste their time playing cards (e.g., number 15), then, are balanced by essays on the wastefulness of masculine dissipation (as in number 197, the story of Captator, the legacy-hunter). So many essays comment on marriage that, if one collected them separately, they would show Johnson to be one of the most copious male writers of his age on the subject. His view is not always compassionate, but it is often aphoristic, as in the proverbial view of remarriage: "It is not likely that the married state is eminently miserable, since we see such numbers, whom the death of their partners has set free from it, entering it again" (number 45, III, 245). Johnson is in favor of education for women; the essays consisting of letters from women often speak of the need for women – women of good families, to be sure – to read widely and converse intelligently. But Johnson's thoughts on the education of women in *The Rambler*, as distinct from other works, are quite limited. In *Rambler* 85, for example, he writes, "I have always admired the wisdom of those by whom our female education was instituted, for having contrived, that every woman of whatever condition should be taught some arts of manufacture . . . whenever chance brings within my observation a knot of misses busy at their needles, I consider myself as in the school of virtue" (IV, 85–86).

Johnson tends, perhaps inevitably, given his century and education, to associate women with housework. Cornelia, who in number 51 tells the story of Lady Bustle, whose life is devoted to pickles and conserves, represents the extreme of this attitude. There is much similar evidence in *The Rambler* to support Johnson's treatment of women as primarily involved with housework and child-rearing. As he notes in number 112, "When female minds are imbittered by age or solitude, their malignity is generally exerted in a rigorous and spiteful superintendance of domestic trifles" (IV, 234). Often, however, essays about women rise above domesticity. One of the most common themes of eighteenth-century moralism is the need to accommodate oneself to loss – of health, wealth, and youth – and Johnson is at his best in writing about such topics. So the story of Melissa in *Rambler* 75 is a parable about the abrupt loss of riches ("My endless train of lovers immediately withdrew," she tells us, when news of her relative poverty spreads [IV, 31]); she learns to live without the perpetual masquerade of wealth. *Rambler*s 130 and 133 tell the story of the incomparable beauty of Victoria both before and after she catches and recovers from smallpox: the lesson is that when we live with adversity, we learn to value the good things that we have. The essays on women in *The Rambler*, however neglected they have been, are consistent with the central message of Johnson's periodical essays.[8]

V

The Rambler contains a number of thematic clusters, some of them the result of Johnson's careful planning, as with many of those on literary topics, some the result of his response to current issues, and others part of typical views on subjects of general moral interest. His dislike of tyranny and arbitrary power, which we find in his political pamphlets, appears persistently in various contexts, and his allegorical, personifying approach to morality is as common in the periodical essays as it is elsewhere in his writings. Johnson's essays are not indebted only to the colloquial tradition of Montaigne, Bacon, and Addison and the classical tradition of Plutarch, Cicero, and Seneca. As a Christian moralist, he learned much from the methodology of the great English homileticists; hence his remark to John Wilkes, "Sermons make a considerable branch of English literature" (*Life*, IV, 105). The argumentative method of a typical essay in *The Rambler* is sermonlike, beginning with a quotation from or an allusion to a well-known author, and following with homiletic exposition, development, and didactic conclusion. But Johnson's purpose is different from a preacher's (his audience is invisible, for one thing, and entirely voluntary), since he does not mean to inculcate lessons and teachings that are simply Christian. Rather, he wishes to reach general themes above sectarian belief; this is one reason why he cites Scripture much less frequently than he alludes to classical and secular authors. For a Christian moralist, Johnson actually refers to specifically Christian topics rather seldom. In number 81 he speaks of "the divine author of our religion" in the context of a discussion of doing unto others as we would have others do unto us (IV, 61, 64; [25 December 1750]). In *Rambler* 185 (24 December 1751) Johnson meditates on the birth of "our Redeemer" in order to propose that forgiveness is the highest of virtues: "On this great duty eternity is suspended, and to him that refuses to practise it, the throne of mercy is inaccessible, and the Saviour of the world has been born in vain" (V, 210). Yet these specifically Christian topics have a seasonal context; Johnson does not follow them with other essays in which his presentation imitates that of a sermon.

A more usual approach for *The Rambler* is that of number 77, extensively rewritten for the several editions revised by Johnson.[9] Ostensibly, number 77 is about the unjustified neglect of learning and of the learned, a favorite Johnsonian topic, but in reality the question that concerns Johnson is whether the neglect of learning is ever justified. Here he introduces the notion of the worthless guide: "The vicious moralist may be considered as a taper, by which we are lighted through the labyrinth of complicated passions; he extends his radiance farther than his heat, and guides all those within view, but burns only those who make too near approaches" (IV, 41). The theme is that of Luke 12: 48, "Of him, to whom much is given, much shall be required," and Johnson's application is to the perverted man of genius: "The wickedness of a loose or profane author is more atrocious than that of the giddy libertine, or drunken ravisher" (IV, 43). By broadening his topic from the specifically religious context of the biblical text, Johnson translates the moral approach of the sermon to that of the essay. A vicious author is not un-Christian – Johnson does not even imply that – but is rather a civil criminal of a sort, one guilty of fraud: "Whoever commits a fraud is guilty not only of the particular injury to him whom he deceives, but of the diminution of that confidence which constitutes not only the ease but the existence of society" (*Rambler* 79, IV, 55). *Rambler* 180 (the other essay extensively revised) is also about the problems of learning and the responsibilities of the author. Johnson commonly finds fault with the conduct of "the scholastick race" (V, 184); here, as he does in other essays about learning, he criticizes scholars who focus their attentions on fashionable topics instead of upon "the permanent lustre of moral and religious truth" (V, 186).

Similarly, Johnson devotes a number of essays to ridiculing, not always gently, pointless collecting, as in numbers 82 and 83, with the story of the collections of Quisquilius, or wasted learning, as in number 106, with its often-quoted lament about libraries: "No place affords a more striking conviction of the vanity of human hopes, than a publick library, for who can see the wall crouded on every side by mighty volumes, the works of laborious meditation, and accurate enquiry, now scarcely known but by the catalogue . . . without considering how many hours have been wasted in vain endeavours" (IV, 200). It is difficult to generalize about those *Rambler*s that anthologizers have tended to choose as Johnson's "moral" writings, but one of the most frequent themes is the unwelcome difference between appearance and reality in human behavior. The conclusion of *Rambler* 14 illustrates this attitude as well as any essay:

> A transition from an author's books to his conversation, is too often like an entrance into a large city, after a distant prospect. Remotely, we see nothing but

spires of temples, and turrets of palaces, and imagine it the residence of splendor, grandeur, and magnificence; but, when we have passed the gates, we find it perplexed with narrow passages, disgraced with despicable cottages, embarrassed with obstructions, and clouded with smoke. (III, 79–80)

Here, as so often in *The Rambler*, we see Johnson as moral commentator on the world of learning, a subject to which he turns scores of times in the two hundred-plus essays that constitute his major contribution to the eighteenth-century essay.

Johnson had written essays before *The Rambler* – mainly reviews and brief lives – and he would continue to favor the genre afterwards, as his pieces in Hawkesworth's *The Adventurer* (1753–54) and his authorship of *The Idler* (1758–60) show. Our memory of the great landmarks of the periodical essay may, however, obscure an important truth about this form. It is that, save for the eight or ten most famous collections, the periodical essays of the eighteenth century, even in the golden age of essay writing, from 1710 to 1775, did not last beyond their first appearance. After 1775, save for the few most famous collections, like those of Johnson, Addison, and Goldsmith, the changing taste of England's literary audience leads to a lessening of demand for separate collections of essays. The form becomes steadily more confined to ephemeral publications like weeklies and monthlies or, in other words, moves closer to what we would now call journalism. Thus while the contemporary periodical essay gradually becomes more journalistic, the outstanding examples of the genre acquire the status of classics. *The Rambler* and the other classics of eighteenth-century periodical writing have a wide circulation as part of entire sets of books, as in Alexander Chalmers's enormous series, Bell's English Essayists (1802–10). In the first third of the nineteenth century, when the market for Johnson's writings, in collections of his works, appears to decline, when the most popular collections, like those of William Hazlitt and Charles Lamb, were no longer part of a titled series, his periodical essays reached the widest reading public they have ever enjoyed.

NOTES

1 *The Works of Oliver Goldsmith*, ed. Arthur Friedman, 5 vols. (Oxford: Clarendon Press, 1965), I, 447–48.
2 Johnson is also, perhaps audaciously, suggesting that his collection might rival Bacon's in audience. See Paul J. Korshin, "Johnson's *Rambler* and its Audiences," in *Essays on the Essay: Redefining the Genre*, ed. Alexander J. Butrym (Athens: University of Georgia Press, 1989), pp. 92–105.
3 See Aaron Stavisky, "Johnson and the Noble Savage," *AJ*, 6 (1994), 165–203.
4 Addison's discussion of *Paradise Lost* occurs in *Spectator* numbers 267, 273, 279, 285, 291, 297, 303, 309, 315, 321 (extending from 5 January 1712 to 8 March 1712).
5 See James L. Clifford, "Johnson and Lauder," *PQ*, 54 (1975), 342–56.

6 There is a full discussion of *Rambler* 114 in my "Johnson and . . . : Conceptions of Literary Relationship," in *Greene Centennial Studies*, ed. Paul J. Korshin and Robert R. Allen (Charlottesville: University Press of Virginia, 1984), pp. 299–301.

7 See James G. Basker, "Dancing Dogs, Women Preachers, and the Myth of Johnson's Misogyny," *AJ*, 3 (1990), 63–90.

8 For a full discussion of Johnson on women's education see Kathleen Kemmerer, *"A Neutral Being Between the Sexes": Samuel Johnson's Sexual Politics* (Lewisburg: Bucknell University Press, 1998).

9 According to the Yale editors, Johnson made more than a hundred revisions to *Rambler* 77; in only one other case (number 180) did he make so many alterations in a single issue.

5

EITHNE HENSON

Johnson and the condition of women

Samuel Johnson would have enjoyed the truly Quixotic irony that, however scholars tilt at the windmill of the Johnson myth, it stubbornly persists. His misogyny is as firmly established in the public mind as his "amorous propensities" behind the scenes of Garrick's theatre. At best, he is seen as patronizing the "pretty dears." The most familiar pronouncement seems to say it all: "Sir, a woman's preaching is like a dog's walking on his hinder legs. It is not done well; but you are surprized to find it done at all" (*Life*, I, 463). Less well known but certainly more representative is Johnson's assertion that "Men know that women are an over-match for them, and therefore they choose the weakest or most ignorant. If they did not think so, they never could be afraid of women knowing as much as themselves" (V, 226). Unsurprisingly, Johnson does share with his contemporaries firm ideas on the demarcation between the genders, but he demonstrates in his writing an extraordinary sympathy with women. Showing the limitations imposed on them by social conditions, he consistently advocates their education, and places a supreme value on "female" qualities of tenderness, gentleness, and emotional responsibility, for both men and women. For Johnson, the domestic sphere, marriage and family life, rather than the traditional public world of male action, is where the human being becomes most profoundly her or his full moral self. In the writing of his forties – *The Vanity of Human Wishes*, the periodical essays, *Rasselas* – Johnson offers a great variety of representations of women – society ladies, adolescents, "good housewives," and wage-earners, and above all, gives women a dramatized voice.[1]

Addison's *Spectator* essays established women as an audience for facetious and patronizing treatments of fashionable life. In *Rambler* 23, Johnson foregrounds this view: he has been censured, he says, for failing "to take the ladies under his protection, and give them rules for the just opposition of colours, and the proper dimensions of ruffles and pinners" (III, 129). He rejects this advice – an author "selects those subjects which he is best qualified to treat," and on the whole, he also avoids Addison's tone, although many *Rambler*s are similarly set in fashionable urban society. More seriously, in *Rambler* 34, he counters objections that he does not devote enough space to women, arguing that because men's lives and experiences are more varied, men need more varieties of moral teaching, whether theoretical or narrative, than women. This is why "the peculiar virtues or faults of women fill but a small part" of moral writing, "perhaps generally too small, for so much of our domestic happiness is in their hands, and their influence is so great upon our earliest years, that the universal interest of the world requires them to be well instructed in their province" (III, 185). This observation resembles the traditional division of the world into male and female spheres, where the most powerful arguments for socializing and educating women would be to make them better housewives and mothers for "us," the implied male readers. This would indeed be normal thinking: revolutionary feminists like Mary Wollstonecraft were still using this argument for women's education in the 1790s. But time and again, Johnson calls into question this instrumental role.

I

How does Johnson define gender characteristics? He reminds readers that gender roles are culturally specific, illustrating that "national manners are formed by chance" in *Idler* 87 with two extremes of female behavior – man-hating Amazons, and Indian widows' self-immolation, contrasted with European women, who will neither "dye with husbands" nor "live without them" (pp. 270–72). In *Rambler* 18, the speaker tries, he says, to place himself as "a kind of neutral being between the sexes": the received wisdom has been overwhelmingly male originated and transmitted, and, since "the faculty of writing has been chiefly a masculine endowment, the reproach of making the world miserable has been always thrown upon the women" (III, 98). Johnson often challenges literary and philosophical tradition, and often in favor of women, but here, women prevail against "the venerable testimonies of philosophers, historians and poets" by "the sighs of softness, and the tears of beauty." We would expect to find women characterized in these terms: throughout Johnson's writing, beauty, elegance, delicacy, and vulnerability are common attributes of the feminine. Elsewhere he shows how this idealized currency can be debased in the marriage market, and here the Rambler's brave attempt at neutrality appears limited by such partial readings of women.

How are women shown as vulnerable? In *Rambler* 39, it is clear that Johnson sees women as condemned to physical suffering. Evidently, he subscribed to the contemporary medical view that females are sick insofar as they diverged from the male norm of human physiology: "The condition of the female sex has been frequently the subject of compassion to medical writers, because their constitution of body is such, that every state of life brings its peculiar diseases." Whether single or married, women must expect "sickness, misery, and death." The Rambler goes on to wish that such "natural infelicity" should not be increased by social attitudes, questioning, as culturally imposed, the "prescription" of marriage as women's natural destiny. Women are again clearly defined as other – "beings whose beauty we cannot behold without admiration, and whose delicacy we cannot contemplate without tenderness," and whose suffering the writer therefore wishes to "alleviate" (III, 211). One definition of "delicate" in Johnson's *Dictionary* is "soft; effeminate; unable to bear hardships," while "delicacy" bears the idea of female weakness as "softness; feminine beauty." It is a conditioned view, evidently – whatever uncontrolled childbirth did to women, Johnson knew and wrote about healthy women of all classes, and, conversely, about sickly men. Perhaps Johnson's passion for romances of chivalry helped to commend this stereotype of passive, suffering beauties, which exists alongside many very different representations of women in his writing.[2]

Transgressions of gender boundaries produce characters perceived by narrators of both sexes as either monstrous or pathetic. In *Rambler* 115, for instance, Camilla despises women as frivolous and empty-headed, and will not follow the social customs of female society. She wants to be one of the boys, and praises "the noble sentiment of Plato, who rejoiced that he was born a man rather than a woman." She enjoys other women's hatred, imagining mistakenly that men will welcome her "generous advances to the borders of virility." Predictably, they reject her, including Hymeneus, the impersonated writer, who is seeking a wife: "novelty soon gave way to detestation, for nothing out of the common order of nature can be long borne." Although Johnson has a keen sense that "the order of nature" is a social construct and not necessarily a universal, Camilla falls outside Hymeneus's acceptable boundaries, having "the ruggedness of man without his force, and the ignorance of woman without her softness" (IV, 249–50). In *Rambler* 113, Hymeneus describes Ferocula, of whom he approves because she has wit, spirit, assurance, and such courage that he feels her naturally free from the "weakness and timidity of female minds"; another candidate is "a lady of great eminence for learning and philosophy" (IV, 238–39), who will only accept an intellectual superior. Paradoxically, "unnatural" courage and learning are shown as attractions: instead, the women are rejected for, respectively, meanness and doubtful fidelity. Johnson recognized that feminine cowardice was culturally fostered: in *Irene*, learned Aspasia argues that women are "Instructed from our infant Years to court / With counterfeited Fears the Aid of Man" (II.ii.27–28), although she sees women's essential courage as "passive Fortitude" (II.viii.44), not Amazonian aggressiveness (*Poems*, pp. 300, 323).[3]

Johnson often allows a female voice to answer attacks by male "correspondents." In *Rambler* 119, Tranquilla counters Hymeneus with an account of her many rejected male lovers. Johnson spells out the injustice that although she too is unmarried by choice, only spinsters suffer the cruelty and mockery of society. She first falls for spoilt, "beautiful" Venustulus, bred to the "softness of effeminacy," but rejects him because he has "the cowardice as well as elegance of a female." Hymeneus scorns affectedly cowardly women, but Tranquilla clearly condemns Venustulus's failure in gender terms: "Women naturally expect defence and protection from a lover or a husband." Flosculus, too, is a narcissistic fop, "rather a rival than an admirer" (IV, 272–74). When definitions of gender are in question, roles must be complementary, but significantly, the faults for which Hymeneus and Tranquilla reject possible partners – affectation, selfishness, avarice, stupidity, above all failures in sympathy and benevolence – are more often those common to either sex, and carry a much greater weight of moral condemnation.

A recurring topic in all Johnson's writing is the upbringing and conditioning of young adults, in the care of unsatisfactory guardians who mislead them by false models and try to limit their development. Girls grow up in female society, so those who wield such power over them are also women, but Johnson repeatedly aligns himself with the disempowered – the young as against the old, the female as against the male – to promote the full intellectual and moral development of the human being. A surprising number of "correspondents" in the periodical essays are young girls, whose passage into the adult freedoms of society tests the advice and models they have been given, often proving them inadequate. In *Rambler* 191, Bellaria, aged fifteen and a half, has been sent mixed signals by her mother and aunts who, once "celebrated for wit and beauty" in fashionable society, now counsel sense and prudence. Moralists universally insist that as women's beauty will fade, they need something solid to fall back on – Clarissa, in Pope's *The Rape of the Lock*, questions: if beauty did not fade, "who would learn one earthly thing of use?" (V.22). Johnson, however, wants women to be both useful and educated, whether young or old, plain or beautiful.

Bellaria is sensibly taught that

> nothing but knowledge could make me an agreeable companion to men of sense, or qualify me to distinguish the superficial glitter of vanity from the solid merit of understanding; and that a habit of reading would enable me to fill up the vacuities of life without the help of silly or dangerous amusements, and preserve me from the snares of idleness and the inroads of temptation. (V, 235)

Good Johnsonian advice, but not the view of the glamorous men and women who attract adolescents in Bellaria's world: Mr. Trip hates "hard words," and "ladies" only read play-bills, and talk about fashion. For them learning is counter-productive in society's marriage market. Bellaria's elders have tried to impress on her that men are dangerous, but because the young are attractively ingenuous, she takes the beaux' devotion at face value, and exults, unconscious of danger, that an "old man" has invited her to his country house "that we may try by ourselves who can conquer" at cards (v, 234–38).

The disparity between prudent adult advice and the world young girls encounter is soberly treated in *Rambler* 66, where Johnson shows how society rewards women for "an unreasonable regard for trifling accomplishments," and that, instead of condemning, we need to "consider how much we have countenanced or promoted" women's attention to hairdressing or cosmetics:

> We recommend the care of their nobler part, and tell them how little addition is made by all their arts to the graces of the mind. But when was it known that female goodness or knowledge was able to attract that officiousness, or inspire that ardour which beauty produces whenever it appears? And with what hope can we endeavour to persuade the ladies, that the time spent at the toilet is lost in vanity, when they have every moment some new conviction, that their interest is more effectually promoted by a ribband well disposed, than by the brightest act of heroick virtue? (III, 352–53)

Clearly, Johnson believes women capable of "heroick virtue," as well as "goodness" and "knowledge": Irene, the flawed heroine of his play, is still a forceful speaker for women's heroic potential. Combating the Emperor Mahomet's assertion that women lack souls, she charms and persuades him by a powerful claim to equality. Adopting, Irene says, "the boastful arrogance of man," she asks

> Do not we share the comprehensive Thought,
> Th' enlivening Wit, the penetrating Reason?
> Beats not the female Breast with gen'rous Passions,
> The Thirst of Empire, and the Love of Glory?"
> (II.vii.55–58; *Poems*, p. 311).

The desire for terrestrial "empire" and "glory" leads men to cruelty and treachery in the play, but here the audience is intended to assent to women's capacity for "masculine" greatness. Aspasia demonstrates both learning and heroic virtue, encouraging a stoic acceptance of death rather than apostasy, but such virtues, however appropriate to tragedy, are irrelevant to most women's interest in the narrow arena of age and gender specifications that is the marriage market in the eighteenth century.

Johnson gives surprisingly sympathetic treatment to young girls misled by false models, even when they seem at first sight to be merely silly. In *Ramblers* 42 and 46, fashionably bred Euphelia has been persuaded by "a studious lady" reading her pastoral poetry, that the country is paradise. She is bored to death there, in a female society obsessed with genealogy. Engagingly admitting that she has no mental resources, she attacks the (male) succession of writers of pastorals who just copy lies about the country from "old authors perhaps as ignorant and careless as yourselves." She claims her equal right, although young, unlearned, and female, to be heard as a critic "on a question in which women are supposed to have very little interest." Her criterion for literary judgement – often Johnson's own – is truth to experience, and she has proved the falsehood of pastorals through a summer's boredom: "As I read, I have a right to judge, as I am injured, I have a right to complain; and these privileges, which I have purchased at so dear a rate, I shall not easily be persuaded to resign" (III, 229, 249).

Adults should warn girls against the particular world they will encounter, and Johnson often joins Bellaria's aunts in attacking frivolous town society, the license of masquerades, the emptiness of cards, dress, and dancing. The story of the Beauty in *The Vanity of Human Wishes* (323–42) is a cautionary tale of town life, where the mother's prayer for beauty exposes her daughter to the treachery of a woman friend and the insidious attack of a seducer, and where the loss of virginity means cruel disgrace, when "hissing Infamy proclaims the rest." *The Fountains*, the fairy story Johnson wrote for Anna Williams's *Miscellanies in Verse and Prose* (1768), is an expanded version of many of the vain wishes in the *Vanity*, here applied to a young girl. It details the problems met in fashionable society by Floretta, to whom a fairy grants her wishes for, successively, beauty, wit, wealth, and long life. There, wit in a woman ("the powers of the mind; the intellects," as Johnson defines "wit" in the *Dictionary*) is particularly feared and attacked; unfortunately it leads Floretta to criticize with unaccommodating frankness, and she is also "censured as too free of favours, because she [is] not afraid to talk with men," as an intellectual equal (*Rasselas*, p. 246). A simple moral tale against women's unsuitable desires? Frances Burney recalls Johnson coming specially to reassure her about a satire in which her name appeared. He "bid me not repine at my success, but think of Floretta, in the Fairy Tale, who found sweetness and consolation in her wit sufficient to counterbalance her scoffers and libellers!"[4] Johnson was really an outstanding promoter of female "intellects."

If town life for women is selfish and shallow, surely Johnson must recommend the life of the good housewife, hard-working, thrifty, and provident? Not so. In *Rambler* 51, educated Cornelia visits from town, and finds Lady Bustle, who excels in preserving the fruits of nature: it is an idyllic Laura Ashley picture of the eighteenth-century housewife, but her daughters' only education is in trivial household tasks, "to which," says Cornelia, "the early hours of life are sacrificed, and in which that time is passing away which never shall return." Lady Bustle disapproves of books, which only teach girls "hard words; she bred up her daughters to understand a house." Cornelia asks the Rambler if she should give up her serious reading for "the *Lady's closet opened*, the *Compleat servant-maid*, and the *Court cook*, and resign all curiosity after right and wrong," and instead, preserve plums and mushrooms. Lady Bustle herself finds by experience the vanity of human wishes, since "Her conserves mould, her wines sour, and pickles mother [go moldy]; and, like all the rest of mankind, she is every day mortified with the defeat of her schemes, and the disappointment of her hopes." (This delightful use of weighty language for trivial purposes will reappear in Jane Austen's writing.) "With regard to vice and virtue she seems a kind of neutral being. She has no crime but luxury, nor any virtue but chastity" (III, 276, 278–79). Lady Bustle is one of many well-intentioned but culpably limited female guardians who try to fit their charges for marriage, supposedly their only destiny.

In *Rambler* 138, a squire's widow becomes a capable farmer, doing a man's job, but is condemned because she neglects her sons and daughters, "whom she has taught nothing but the lowest houshold duties" (IV, 369). *Idler*s 13 and 35 caricature other versions of the good housewife. In number 13, for example, a husband complains of his wife, who seems a model: "The house was always clean, the servants were active and regular, dinner was on the table every day at the same minute," but as before, the education of the daughters is sacrificed, this time to sitting in an emblematically windowless garret, doing useless needle-work. For their mother, "any business is better than idleness," but they are not taught to read or write, and are ignorant of the Bible, of geography, mathematics, and history (pp. 43, 45).

By contrast, in *Rambler* 84, the speaker is Myrtilla, aged sixteen and a half, who says with tactless honesty that reading the *Rambler* bores her. She has been brought up to "all the common rules of decent behaviour, and standing maxims of domestick prudence; and might have grown up by degrees to a country gentle-woman," but Flavia comes down from town and Myrtilla feels an attraction almost sexual, "a new confusion of love and admiration." The young girl can only evaluate her own, like other people's, behavior according to "common rules" or gender models: "I know not how others are affected on such occasions, but I found myself irresistibly allured to friendship and intimacy." Flavia, universally civil, hypocritical, subverts Myrtilla's trust in her guardian aunt's judgment and worth. Her erudition in "subjects of learning" frightens off all the gentlemen but the vicar, who dusts off his old Homer. Myrtilla, however, is delighted to read what she recommends, seeing "new worlds hourly bursting upon my mind," and is "enraptured at the prospect of diversifying life with endless entertainment." Myrtilla, consequently, revolts against her aunt, who "seemed . . . to look upon Flavia as seducing me." The language expressing Myrtilla's desire is remarkable, and the conflict is not simply between virtuous country housewifery and attractive town frivolity. Flavia is well read, and the aunt's values cannot be the reader's, since her match for Myrtilla is "young Mr. Surly," whose only interest is cock-fighting, and who is deterred by Myrtilla's new learning. Nor can we agree with the aunt that "the consequence of female study" is that "girls grow too wise to be advised, and too stubborn to be commanded." Myrtilla consults the Rambler as to what duty she owes, ending disarmingly "P.S. Remember I am past sixteen" (IV, 76–81). Raising questions of young women's spontaneous pleasure in learning, and of autonomy, rather than submissive obedience to the ideal of the good housewife, the essay's effect is to enlarge the boundaries of the woman's "province." Although we smile at Myrtilla, as we do at the other young women, Johnson is far from offering them as mere objects of moral narrative: he is giving a voice to a silenced group, exploring a tentatively developing female subjectivity, and expressing powerful female desires.

What, then, does Johnson think about women's education? Boswell points out how unusual Johnson's attitude is: in 1769, he "maintained to me, contrary to the common notion, that a woman would not be the worse wife for being learned; in which, from all that I have observed of *Artemisias* [learned women], I humbly differed from him" (*Life*, II, 76; see *Life*, V, 226). In essay after essay, Johnson makes it clear that women should be intelligent, well read, capable of serious conversation and moral reasoning, but he also shows how difficult learning can make life for women. (Ironically, Frances Burney would not dare to admit knowing the Latin he taught her.) In *Idler* 39, the speaker suggests that women's education is markedly improved. In a light-hearted, and partly ironic, discussion of the fashion for wearing miniature portraits on bracelets, he remarks that

> This addition of art to luxury is one of the innumerable proofs that might be given of the late increase of female erudition; and I have often congratulated myself that my life has happened at a time when those, on whom so much of human felicity depends, have learned to think as well as speak, and when respect takes possession of the ear, while love is entering at the eye. (p. 122)

Thirty years later Burney reports Johnson as commenting, without irony, on "the amazing progress made of late years in literature by the women. He said he was himself astonished at it, and told them he well remembered when a woman who could spell a common letter was regarded as all accomplished; but now they vied with the men in everything" (*Diary*, I, 207).

In *Rasselas*, education, not gender, determines ability: it is Nekayah who proposes and organizes the inquiry into "the choice of life," and analyzes its results. She is consistently represented as her brother's equal, and is given language as weighty and generalizations no less valid than his, although the siblings may tease each other over some grandiose conclusions. Nekayah, who is at home in the "male" world of intelligent conversation, finds women confined in the harem inadequate as companions: she plays with them as with "inoffensive animals," and finds "their thoughts narrow, their wishes low, and their merriment often artificial" (*Rasselas*, p. 92). Nekayah's intelligence and open-mindedness clearly indicate that Johnson believes women are not necessarily confined to the narrow social and intellectual life of the harem and of fashionable London. Furthermore, for Johnson, "wish" has a powerful meaning: the *Vanity* deals not with passing fancies, but with all the abiding human passions. To have "low" wishes is to fail to fulfill your human potential.

Pekuah, Nekayah's companion, is kidnapped by an Arab, and she too paints a picture of entirely uneducated child–women, charming only as lambs or birds, who can have no knowledge of anything but the harem, because they cannot read. As so often in eighteenth-century discussions of women's education, the loss is not perceived as theirs, but as their master's: for him, "their talk could take nothing from the tediousness of life." (Johnson, however, condemns Milton's "Turkish contempt of females as subordinate and inferior beings," shown in the "mean and penurious education" of his daughters, simply as a violation of justice [*Lives*, I, 157].) Pekuah studies astronomy with the Arab, who is unwilling to give her up for ransom: as Imlac asks, "How could a mind, hungry for knowledge, be willing, in an intellectual famine, to lose such a banquet as Pekuah's conversation?" (*Rasselas*, p. 140). When, on her return, Imlac cannot believe she will be "a very capable auditress" of the astronomer's teaching, she answers that her "knowledge is, perhaps, more than you imagine it, and by concurring always with his opinions I shall make him think it greater than it is." Her learning, as well as her knowledge of male psychology, triumphs, and this wise and learned man, finding her "a prodigy of genius," urges her to continue her studies (pp. 159–60). It is significant that at the end of the story, both women's dreams are concerned with ruling autonomous female communities: Pekuah imagines being prioress of a convent, while Nekayah's final dream is to promote women's education: "The princess thought, that of all sublunary things, knowledge was the best: She desired first to learn all sciences, and then purposed to found a college of learned women, in which she would preside" (p. 175). A women's college was still an exorbitant dream in 1759, in spite of the efforts of earlier feminists like Mary Astell and Bathsua Makin. Nekayah's ambition to "learn all sciences" is as excessive as Imlac's claims for poetry, and she knows it cannot be realized, but the text does not otherwise condemn it. Boswell records Johnson's offering a strong, and surprising, moral argument that women's education resulted in "prudence" and "piety": "He praised the ladies of the present age, insisting that they were more faithful to their husbands, and more virtuous in every respect, than in former times, because their understandings were better cultivated" (*Life*, III, 3; see III, 353–54).

II

One of the most familiar lines from *Rasselas* is Nekayah's gloomy conclusion that "'marriage has many pains, but celibacy has no pleasures'" (p. 99). How does Johnson represent marriage for women? Certainly marriage, not learning, was the aim of most women in the eighteenth century; Perdita, an *Adventurer* "correspondent," tells us sarcastically that "As the great end of female education is to get a husband, this likewise is the general subject of female advice." As a girl Perdita is conditioned to be submissive to the sage advice of older women, and profits by being left a fortune. She therefore decides "to continue the same passive attention, since I found myself so powerfully recommended by it to kindness and esteem." "Passive attention" to elders and to men would usually be seen as entirely suitable for young females, but here as elsewhere Johnson shows its pitfalls. As so often, those in authority are motivated by greed or snobbery, and "wrinkled wisdom" lands Perdita in a miserable marriage in pursuit of wealth and position (*Adventurer*, pp. 296–97). In *Rambler* 130, Victoria, a young beauty, is educated by her mother to catch a husband, learning only to dance, to dress, to play the harpsichord, to play cards. She has no conversation, and her suitor chooses her better-educated rival. Victoria's beauty is destroyed by smallpox and she is out of the marriage market. In *Rambler* 133, a wise woman friend rouses her from despair: "Consider yourself, my Victoria, as a being born to know, to reason, and to act" (IV, 345). She is successfully recalled from depression and female passivity to the universal human condition, though, as Johnson shows us, knowledge, reason, and action are all problematic for women in these social and political conditions. In taking on this wider selfhood, however, she will no longer define herself only by her success in relation to men or to rivals, but in terms of her own developing human potential.

In *Rasselas*, Nekayah sets her brother to research the male world of "'command and authority,'" and herself investigates marriage, and the pros and cons of "'domestick peace'" (p. 89). Seen in the eighteenth century as the woman's sphere, for Johnson the domestic realm is where human beings play out the real moral drama of the self. In *Rambler* 60, on biography, he rejects "vulgar greatness," the public, male world of battles and politics, as a way to define human interest: the biographer should deal with "domestick privacies," and "the minute details of daily life, where exterior appendages are cast aside, and men excel each other only by prudence and by virtue" (III, 321), that is, where the demands on men and women are identical. Most people, Johnson writes in *Rambler* 68, "pass the chief part of their time in familiar and domestick scenes," and he makes the remarkable claim that "To be happy at home is the ultimate result of all ambition, the end to which every enterprise and labour tends, and of which every desire prompts the prosecution" (III, 360).

In *Rambler* 39, Johnson recognizes the arbitrariness of conventional attitudes to marriage: "the custom of the world," rather than nature, conspires to make women's choices painful. Though spinsterhood promises the happiness of freedom from control, yet women do their best to escape it, and married ladies condemn "the heroines who endeavour to assert the natural dignity of their sex." (The context here suggests mockery of feminist rhetoric, although much of Johnson's writing about women does in fact assert women's dignity.) In practice, spinsters are seen as "the refuse of the world," yet marriage has "many disadvantages, that take away much from the pleasure which society promises, and might afford, if pleasures and pains were honestly shared, and mutual confidence inviolably preserved" (III, 211–13). Johnson is consistent in defending women against parental tyranny: Boswell and other biographers record several occasions when "he maintained that a father had no right to control the inclinations of his daughters in marriage" (*Life*, III, 377). In his essays, he recognizes that verbal or actual violence, economic or emotional pressure, influencing a woman's choice of husband: "The miseries, indeed, which many ladies suffer under conjugal vexations, are to be considered with great pity, because their husbands are often not taken by them as objects of affection, but forced upon them by authority and violence, or by persuasion and importunity, equally resistless when urged by those whom they have been always accustomed to reverence and obey" (*Rambler* 39, III, 213). Here again, the submission required of women is seen as leading them to suffering (see plate 2).

Rambler 35 dramatizes this suffering. An eligible young heir goes into country society: "I saw not without indignation, the eagerness with which the daughters, wherever I came, were set out to show; nor could I consider them in a state much different from prostitution," when they are made to show off their accomplishments. He sees the irony that marketing girls in this way deprives them, in their own valuation, of just that romantic distance, the pedestal of unstained virtue, necessary to the sale: "I could not but look with pity on young persons condemned to be set to auction, and made cheap by injudicious commendations; for how could they know themselves offered and rejected a hundred times, without some loss of that soft elevation, and maiden dignity, so necessary to the completion of female excellence?" (III, 192–93). Several perspectives are present here: while attacking the material reality of the marriage market (akin to slavery and to organized prostitution), Johnson himself endorses a romanticized construction of the feminine, akin to the ideal *princesse lointaine* of chivalric romance; yet this feminine ideal is at once undermined by the mutually reliant economic reality of the marriage market.

Most of Johnson's candidates for marriage are freer agents than these "prostituted" daughters. As Rasselas optimistically argues, nature dictates marriage: "'men and women were made to be companions of each other,'" therefore marriage must be "'one of the means of happiness'" (*Rasselas*, pp. 103–4). Nekayah's definition of a solitary life is central to Johnson's thinking about what is essential to any human relationship: "'To live without feeling or exciting sympathy, to be fortunate without adding to the felicity of others, or afflicted

Plate 2 William Hogarth, *Marriage à la Mode: The Marriage Contract*, 1745. Fathers settle their children's marriage, the nobleman finding the merchants' wealth "a sufficient compensation for deficient ancestry" (*Adventurer* 74, p. 298).

without tasting the balm of pity, is a state more gloomy than solitude: it is not retreat but exclusion from mankind'" (p. 98). Johnson frequently affirms the value of sensitive response to the emotional needs of others. *Rambler* 60 opens with a most important statement about the psychology of empathy: "All joy or sorrow for the happiness or calamities of others is produced by an act of the imagination . . . placing us, for a time, in the condition of him whose fortune we contemplate; so that we feel, while the deception lasts, whatever motions would be excited by the same good or evil happening to ourselves" (III, 318–19). Johnson's *Dictionary* definition of "sympathy" is "Fellow-feeling; mutual sensibility; the quality of being affected by the affection of another," and he illustrates it by a powerful quotation from Robert South's *Sermons*: "There never was any man truly great and generous, that was not also tender and compassionate; it is this noble quality that makes men to be all of one kind." This sympathy, especially in his dealings with women, marks Johnson out from many contemporaries. As he shifts the theatre for significant moral responsibility from the outside world to the domestic, from the "male" sphere of action into the "female" world of relationships and feeling, he demands from men and women alike qualities traditionally seen as particularly characteristic of women.

Perhaps the most positive prospect for marriage in Johnson's writings is that of Hymeneus and Tranquilla, who come together with realistic expectations. In *Rambler* 119, Tranquilla had defined her position on the gender war: "As . . . men and women must at last pass their lives together, I have never therefore thought those writers friends to human happiness, who endeavour to excite in either sex a general contempt or suspicion of the other" (IV, 270). In *Rambler* 167, Hymeneus and Tranquilla have no romantic delusions: they know that even with "confederate intellects and auxiliar virtues," they will sometimes disagree. However, since both have "amused [their] leisure with books" of history and classical learning, they will have plenty to talk about, and will enjoy "that suitable disagreement which is always necessary to intellectual harmony." It is significant that this mature and considered marriage is one of intellectual equals, entailing absolute openness – "the most solemn league of perpetual friendship, a state from which artifice and concealment are to be banished for ever" (V, 121–24). This scenario is very different from the artifices of gender role-playing implied in so many accounts of male-female relationships, in either Johnson's writing or that of his contemporaries.

But Johnson does not only write about those who can choose marriage, or live without it. He gives a dramatized voice to women in all social strata. Whether they are reduced gentlewomen or educated village girls, looking for work can be humiliating and dangerous, and once found, conditions can be harsh. Here, power relations are overtly unequal, and such power is mainly misused by other women. In *Idlers* 26 and 29, charity-school pupil Betty Broom, whose voice and perspective are the subject of these essays, is encouraged to read but finds that she cannot get work. Many employers, she finds, believe that "They who are born to poverty . . . are born to ignorance, and will work the harder the less they know" (pp. 80–81). Johnson was no advocate of social equality, but he consistently defended the right of the poor of both sexes to education. Betty draws a vivid picture of different conditions of domestic work for women in the 1740s; tyrannical women – mistresses and fellow-servants – threatened by her knowledge, are generally the targets of Johnson's attacks. Left £500, Betty still plans a country school to teach poor girls to read and write. Women's role as teachers of the young was thoroughly approved and recognized, and it is always one of the most powerful arguments for women's education, even from conservatives, that they have this duty to their (husband's) children. Johnson, then, demonstrates the powerlessness of women who lack economic and social advantage, in spite of education, and unquestionably supports their empowerment. His range of working – or would-be working – women includes several forced by sudden poverty onto a suspicious labor market, or working wives of city tradesmen, dependent on their husbands' behavior for the success of their joint enterprises. But these women, however difficult their circumstances, still remain within the boundaries of "respectable" society.

III

"The woman's a whore, and there's an end on't" (*Life*, II, 247). Boswell seems purposely to provoke Johnson into intransigently defending the double standard of sexual morality, blaming wives for their husbands' infidelity, and concerned for the legitimate transmission of property and family names. Even for a woman trapped in a brutal and loveless marriage, he will hear no excuse. When Boswell asks him if one sexual lapse "'should so absolutely ruin a young woman,'" Johnson is adamant: with illegitimate sex "'she has given up every notion of female honour and virtue, which are all included in chastity'" (II, 55–56). Patently, this is nonsense, and, as we have seen, Johnson constantly celebrates examples of women's honor and virtue quite unrelated to chastity, and his practice, like his writing, shows a very different attitude. For example, Boswell records, amazed, how Johnson brought a "wretched female" (Poll Carmichael) home one night, and instead of "harshly upbraiding her," took her into his household, where Boswell unwittingly met her in 1778 (*Life*, IV, 321; II, 215). How, then, does Johnson represent those "fallen" women in his writing? In *Rambler* 107, a foundling hospital leads Amicus to think about unmarried mothers, who progress from "deluded virtue" to "hopeless wretchedness." He pleads for prostitutes, "those forlorn creatures . . . whose misery here, might satisfy the most rigorous censor, and whose participation of our common nature might surely induce us to endeavour, at least, their preservation from eternal punishment." He bitterly attacks the privileged males who have seduced them, and graphically describes prostitutes who must work "or perish in the streets with nakedness and hunger." Their seducers ignore "these miserable females, covered with rags, shivering with cold, and pining with hunger" and go on to ruin others. "But surely [these women] . . . have some claim to compassion, from beings equally frail and fallible with themselves" (see plate 3). It is a powerful and audacious demand, that the readership of the *Rambler* should identify itself with women whom they would normally see as barely human, and as justly suffering (the more so that they were women) for their "crimes." Johnson goes further – echoing Christ and the woman taken in adultery: "Nor will they long groan in their present afflictions, if none were to refuse them relief, but those that owe their exemption from the same distress only to their wisdom and their virtue." An outrageous appeal by the standards of eighteenth-century "civilized" society, specifically to respectable women readers, to say that there, but for the grace of God, *they* might have gone – kept pure only by circumstances, not by moral strength (IV, 207–9).

However, even these women are nameless and distanced, objects of our compassion. Johnson goes further: the prostitute Misella, seduced and abandoned by a guardian, speaks in her own voice in *Ramblers* 170 and 171, and shows how middle-class women could find themselves in her position. She introduces herself as "one whom the rigour of virtuous indignation dooms to suffer without complaint, and perish without regard; and whom I myself have formerly insulted in the pride of reputation and security of innocence." She points out that women do not necessarily fall to amorous blandishments. More realistic and less flattering motives lead to men's success: some women have been afraid of "losing benefits which were never intended, or of incurring resentment which they could not escape; some have been frighted by masters, and some awed by guardians into ruin" (V, 135, 139). Destitute, Misella is forced into prostitution, and her final plea is Swiftian in its unflinching horror: if prosperous people

> could visit for an hour the dismal receptacles to which the prostitute retires from
> her nocturnal excursions, and see the wretches that lie crowded together, mad with
> intemperance, ghastly with famine, nauseous with filth, and noisome with disease;
> it would not be easy for any degree of abhorrence to harden them against compas-
> sion, or to repress the desire which they must immediately feel to rescue such
> numbers of human beings from a state so dreadful.   (*Rambler* 172, V, 144–45)

The stress is again on the shared humanity of the women. Prostitution is "infamy," worthy of "shame," but the blame is far more severe and contemptuous for the libertines who cause and profit from it. There is striking passion in these narrations, and Johnson's compassion is consistent with the very high

Plate 3 William Hogarth, *Garret Scene*, 1730(?). This study of a ragged prostitute, perhaps suffering from "the diseases of incontinence" (*Rambler* 107, II, 209).

value he placed on the "female" virtues of sympathy and tenderness, and demonstrates a capacity to identify with women, even women as improbable as prostitutes like Misella.

IV

"Down with her Burney! . . . you are a rising wit, and she is at the top; and when I was beginning the world, and was nothing and nobody, the joy of my life was to fire at all the established wits" (Burney, *Diary*, I, 80). Johnson's playful incitement of the young novelist Frances Burney to attack Elizabeth Montagu, the established scholar and patron, is engaging evidence of the sympathetic identification which led him to help and encourage women writers all his life.[5] Boswell's male-directed *Life* tells us relatively little of Johnson's relations with women.[6] For this knowledge, we must read Hester Thrale, Frances Reynolds, Hannah More and Frances Burney, and above all, Johnson's own letters, constructive, affectionate, and respectful. His comments on individual women bear out his sense of an explosion of female learning – at Elizabeth Montagu's house he might dine with half a dozen women whose writing he praised and actively promoted – Elizabeth Carter, Hester Chapone, Reynolds, More, Burney, Thrale. Although he complained that Montagu flattered him – they exchanged hyperbolical compliments until they quarreled over his "Life of Lyttleton" (1781) – his praise of her remains consistent (provided, as Burney says, "others do not praise her improperly"). Joining Hester Thrale in praising her learning, he concluded that "She diffuses more knowledge in her conversation than any woman I know, or, indeed, almost any man" (Burney, *Diary*, I, 90).

To Elizabeth Carter, the classical scholar who contributed numbers 44 and 100 to *The Rambler*, he wrote in 1756 that he had hesitated to write to her, "deterred by the fear of your understanding," and signed himself "with respect which I neither owe nor pay to any other" (*Letters*, I, 126). He was soliciting subscriptions for poems by Anna Williams, the blind poet and scientist whom he took into his household: writing to Richardson in 1754, probably about Williams's project for a dictionary of scientific terms, he praised her knowledge of "these subjects, which indeed she appears to me to understand better than any person that I have ever known," adding that she was "certainly qualified for her work, as much as any one that will ever undertake it, as she understands chimistry and many other arts with which Ladies are seldom acquainted" (*Letters*, I, 79). Another friend and literary protegée was Charlotte Lennox, for whom he wrote a chapter of *The Female Quixote*, and many dedications. Johnson sat for the painter Frances Reynolds, whose *Enquiry Concerning the Principles of Taste*, he wrote, demonstrated "such force of comprehension and such nicety of observation as Locke or Pascal ought to be proud of" (*Letters*, III, 355). The highest praise he could give a woman writer is that she might compete with the greatest men, and this brief sample ends with his "extraordinary" Burney, of whose *Evelina* he said he doubted if there was, or ever had been, "a man who could write such a book so young" (*Diary*, I, 207).

In conclusion, Johnson's wide-ranging and sympathetic representations of "the condition of women" recognize the social and economic limitations under which they suffer, and consistently argue for the development of their intellectual capacities. He opposes the oppressive authority of parents and guardians, the conditioning of young girls for society and the marriage market, and, more surprisingly, for the limited sphere of the "good housewife." But he refuses to promote gender warfare. He makes equal moral and emotional demands on men and women, and concludes that both are most fully human in "domestick privacy," in the benevolent companionship of moral and intellectual equals, whether enjoying the *concordia discors* of marriage, potentially, as Hymeneus says in *Rambler* 115, "the highest happiness decreed to our present state" (IV, 252), or in such affectionate, supportive friendship as Johnson enjoyed with intelligent women.

NOTES

1 See James G. Basker, "Dancing Dogs, Women Preachers and the Myth of Johnson's Misogyny," *AJ*, 3 (1990), 63–90 for Johnson's essays treating women.

2 See my *"The Fictions of Romantic Chivalry": Samuel Johnson and Romance* (London: Associated University Presses, 1992).

3 For a full discussion of *Irene* in the context of Johnson's thinking about women, see Kathleen Kemmerer, *"A Neutral Being Between the Sexes":Johnson's Sexual Politics* (Lewisburg: Bucknell University Press, 1998).

4 Frances Burney, *Diary and Letters of Madame D'Arblay*, ed. Charlotte Barrett, 3 vols. (London: Macmillan, 1904–5), I, 161.

5 See Isobel Grundy, "Samuel Johnson as Patron of Women," *AJ*, 1 (1987), 59–77.

6 For Boswell and misogyny see Felicity Nussbaum, *The Autobiographical Subject: Gender and Ideology in Eighteenth-Century England* (Baltimore: Johns Hopkins University Press, 1989), and Annette Wheeler Cafarelli, "Johnson and Women: Demasculinizing Literary History," *AJ*, 5 (1992), 61–114.

6

ROBERT DEMARIA, JR.

Johnson's *Dictionary*

So little is known about Johnson's activities and whereabouts in the year 1745 that enthusiasts have imagined him in Scotland serving Bonnie Prince Charlie until the Jacobite cause met its final end at the battle of Culloden. The truth about his activities in 1745 is probably much more mundane. In 1745 Johnson published his *Miscellaneous Observations on the Tragedy of Macbeth*, a sixty-four page specimen of what would eventually become his edition of Shakespeare's plays (1765). It has been suggested that Johnson was responsible for a bare-bones edition of Shakespeare, hastily assembled in 1745 under the auspices of London publishers eager to reclaim the copyright over his works seized by Oxford University Press with the edition of Thomas Hanmer in 1744.[1] This hack work would not be inconsistent with much that Johnson had done before for the London publishers. Moreover, it fits roughly into the particular kind of work Johnson was doing in the early 1740s and suggests a professional transition of the kind he made in the second half of the decade as part of the ongoing compromise in his life between the "dreams of a poet" and the fiscal realities of writing for a living in the eighteenth century.

Johnson's youthful dreams of becoming a great scholar and a neo-Latin poet in the European humanist tradition died slowly away as he realized he would have to make a living in a literary world of English readers and of booksellers concerned about finances. His whole career as a writer was a necessary process of compromise between his fantasy of a learned, polite life and the drudgery of a grubstreet hack. In the early 1740s Johnson collaborated with William Oldys on cataloguing the vast library of Lord Harley so that the purchaser, the relatively crude and rapacious Thomas Osborne, could maximize his profit. The job itself required learning, and Johnson and Oldys both wrote learned and sometimes curious descriptions of the books.[2] Osborne evidently objected to Johnson actually reading the books that he was cataloguing, and when he rebuked his employee, Johnson knocked him down with a large folio volume, or so the story goes, echoing an older tale in which the Italian humanist Poggio felled an opponent with a folio. But it is true that Johnson disliked Osborne and that he wanted to lift himself above mere bookselling of the kind his father did for a living. The kind of learning, bordering on antiquarianism, in which Johnson indulged while compiling the Harleian catalogue shows up also in *Observations on Macbeth*, and Johnson's work on both projects provided the intellectual orientation he exhibits in *A Dictionary of the English Language*.

Boswell reports that Johnson had considered the possibility of writing an English dictionary long before he signed his historic contract with Messers Knapton *et al.* in 1746 and that the project had "grown up in his mind insensibly" (*Life*, I, 182). To an extent, this internal gestation clashed with the expectations that polite literary society entertained about the function of a national dictionary. Ever since the foundation of the Royal Society in 1660 proposals had been afoot for correcting and improving the English language after the models laid down by the Académie Française and the Italian Academia della Crusca. The continental dictionaries had been published, after many years of work and contestation, and revised; there was a sense that England had fallen behind, and English literary society hoped Johnson would bring the nation level with its cultural rivals, particularly France. Johnson was sensitive to this expectation and he says explicitly in his Preface, "I have devoted this book, the labour of years, to the honour of my country, that we may no longer yield the palm of philology without a contest to the nations of the continent" (Greene, p. 327). However, the "palm of philology" meant something different for Johnson than for the Académie and for many of Johnson's countrymen. The *Dictionnaire* was principally concerned with correctness and refinement. It excluded technical terms of all kinds as coarse; it restricted its standards of usage to carefully chosen classics of literature; it did not stoop to quoting its sources, but instead, said authoritatively "On dit," before going on to give a (usually) made-up example of correct usage. This authoritarian and exclusivist way of proceeding was not unopposed in France (Antoine Furetière spent a great part of his life preparing the *Dictionnaire universel* on more inclusivist principles), and English dictionaries had long been including, even specializing in, technical terms. But Swift and Pope in the generation before Johnson and Lord Chesterfield in his own time had called for a work that would select, discriminate, and exclude; that would, like the *Dictionnaire*, establish standards and reflect only the best usage of the language. Although he had some sympathy with these aims, Johnson took a much broader view of language and lexicography.

During his work (with William Oldys) on the annotated catalogue of the great Harleian library in the 1740s, Johnson had an opportunity to look at virtually all of the great dictionaries ever produced by European scholarship; it is also likely that he acquired some of these books in partial payment for his work of cataloguing them. The great dictionaries in Harley's library, as well as the intellectual world that they represented, provided Johnson with models of lexicography that went well beyond the prescriptive work imagined by Swift, for example, in his *Proposal for Correcting, Improving, and Ascertaining the English Tongue* (1712). The works in the Harleian library that concerned English helped Johnson with etymologies, definitions, and eventually with the specimen texts in the "History of the English Language" that he included in his preliminary matter. They also drew him away from the polite world's rejection of the "gothic" in English; works like the Thesaurus of George Hickes confirmed that English was fundamentally a Germanic language and could not, as Chesterfield may have liked, be "latinised," despite the influence of the culturally superior tongue. The Latin–Latin dictionaries based on the work of Robert Estienne (known as Stephens) and those descended from the lexicon of Basilius Faber convinced Johnson that a serious dictionary, even if it was only in English, should have illustrative quotations and should break down each headword into several distinct senses, which are responsive to the varieties of meaning in the illustrations. These are both features that Johnson instituted in English lexicography and, to a large degree, in the lexicography of modern languages. They are the principal features that no discussion of the *Dictionary* should overlook. Johnson's particular use of illustrative quotations represents a clear break with the most "polite" wishes for lexicography by giving example, generally, rather than prescription the chief linguistic authority. In addition, the illustrative quotations give Johnson's book its encyclopedic quality; and they unite him with Furetière, and many other laborious "drudges," in opposition to the authoritative academicians who are content to say, "On dit."

Of course, laborious lexicography had its own fantasies of power and control; its dreams centered not on linguistic purity or superiority, however, but rather on encyclopedic inclusion. Johnson clearly expresses his investment in this scholarly fantasy in his Preface, even as he recognizes its impossibility:

> When first I engaged in this work, I resolved to leave neither words nor things unexamined, and pleased myself with a prospect of the hours which I should revel away in feasts of literature, the obscure recesses of northern learning, which I should enter and ransack, the treasures with which I expected every search into those neglected mines to reward my labour, and the triumph with which I should display my acquisitions to mankind. When I had thus enquired into the original of words, I resolved to show likewise my attention to things; to pierce deep into every science, to enquire the nature of every substance of which I inserted the name, to limit every idea by a definition strictly logical, and exhibit every production of art or nature in an accurate description, that my book might be in place of all other dictionaries whether appellative or technical. But these were the dreams of a poet doomed at last to wake a lexicographer. (Greene, pp. 321–22)

In the early editions of Faber and in Arabic–Latin dictionaries, including that of Joseph Scaliger, Johnson also saw the potential for moral and religious teaching in a book designed to be read by learners. Some of the early dictionaries of languages used in non-Christian countries are very explicit about religious teaching, and most of the great humanist lexicons acknowledge the moral responsibility of the lexicographer to his readers.[3] An early draft of the Preface to the *Dictionary* shows that Johnson had learners in mind when he planned his book, and his final product shows that, as usual, he felt a responsibility to educate learners in the essential matters of religion and morality. In discharging this responsibility, he was being true not only to his ethical beliefs but also to his scholarly identity.

The educational mission of the *Dictionary* was undoubtedly brought to the fore partly through the influence of Robert Dodsley, who made his fortune publishing Pope as well as his own successful writings. Many of these were educational in nature, including the two-volume *Preceptor* (1748), a work designed for home schooling and covering a broad curriculum in a dozen chapters contributed by various experts. Precisely how much Johnson helped Dodsley with this project is unknown, but he certainly supplied the introduction and one of the three moral fables appended to the academic portion of the book. Johnson's fable, "The Vision of Theodore, the Hermit of Teneriffe," is a composition on a traditional humanist theme: the goal of learning is piety because only religion can guide us to redemption. At the end of Johnson's allegory the pilgrims marching up the Mountain of Existence must depart from the guidance of Reason and find their direction only from Religion. Although the *Dictionary* is obviously a much larger and more diffuse work than this simple allegory, Johnson arranged things so that on many occasions his great book makes a similar point. There are a few bald examples of the *Dictionary*'s allegorical nature, such as Johnson's definition of "crossrow" as "Alphabet; so named because a cross was placed at the beginning, to show that the end of learning is piety" and his example of a brevier typeface. Whereas a modern dictionary tends to print a sentence like, "This sentence is in brevier type," Johnson prints, on one occasion, Raphael's advice to Adam in *Paradise Lost*, "Nor love thy life, nor hate, but what thou liv'st / Live well, how long or short, permit to Heav'n" (XI.553–54).

On these and other rare occasions Johnson made a moral point directly, but his scholarly and laborious method of composing the book limited those opportunities. Johnson was empirically minded enough to believe that the proper method of assembling a dictionary was to canvass the real, existing uses of words and make a record of them. Although he certainly made use of earlier dictionaries, especially Nathan Bailey's *Dictionarium Britannicum* (2nd edn., 1736), Johnson also sought words where they were employed by writers and determined their meanings on the basis of their real usage. This principle, taken to its logical extreme, leads to the ideal espoused by James A. H. Murray and the other "Men of Science," as he called them, who composed the *Oxford English Dictionary*.

Theoretically, according to such an ideal, every usage of a word counts as much as any other, and the lexicographer's task, like the natural historian's, is simply to catalogue what he finds in the world. Johnson did not wish to be totally empirical; he was not deaf to polite wishes for correctness and so he is selective about the language he examines; but there is a conflict between even his incomplete empiricism and his wish to make the *Dictionary* an encyclopedia with moral and religious overtones, just as there is a conflict between his empiricism and polite wishes for linguistic correctness.

Thirteen texts are known to exist in which Johnson marked out passages for inclusion in his *Dictionary*. These books along with numerous slips of paper with quotations on them (many of them in an interleaved copy of the *Dictionary* used for assembling the revised edition of 1773) reveal a great deal about Johnson's method of composition.[4] He read the collected works of authors like Shakespeare, Bacon, and Robert South, to name three of the thirteen, and put vertical lines around the passages he wanted to include and underlined the word that he wanted the passages to illustrate. He put the first letter of the word in the margin, where his amanuenses kept track of their progress in copying by crossing out the letters. At first Johnson may have had the secretaries copying the quotations right onto the sheets that he intended for the printer, with room left for him to enter the definitions and etymologies. This did not work, evidently, and the copy was further botched by being written on both sides of the sheet. At this point (sometime around 1749) Johnson seems to have detached the quotations from the copy-sheets, cutting them into slips of paper. This mobility increased Johnson's capacity to shape the work by arranging and selecting quotations, much as modern lexicographers do.

Just how many books Johnson himself read to do his research is unclear. His amanuenses may have done some of the work of finding quotations, and the slight inaccuracies in numerous quotations, especially of favorite authors like Shakespeare, the Bible, Pope, and William Law, suggest that Johnson entered a great many quotations from memory. In addition, he used other dictionaries and he made heavy use of several encyclopedias. There is one verified case of his using a kind of concordance – an index to the sentiments in Richardson's *Clarissa*[5] – rather than consulting the original text, and he used glossaries to editions of Spenser and Shakespeare. It is also possible that he used other shortcuts, like Cruden's concordance to the Bible, but it is impossible to be sure. Nevertheless, Johnson did a great deal of research in preparing his book, and it is likely that he marked up scores of other books in addition to the extant thirteen. Had he been truly empirical, however, Johnson would not have taken care in selecting the books from which he drew his examples of English. A random sample would have provided more purely empirical information. In the Preface Johnson described his collection of words and quotations as the result of "fortuitous and unguided excursions into books, and gleaned as industry should find, or chance should offer it, in the boundless chaos of a living speech" (Greene, p. 312). There are fortuitous elements in Johnson's *Dictionary*, to be sure: there are many books cited only once or twice that simply came to Johnson's hand. In 1753, to give just one example, Richardson published Jane Collier's *Essay on the Art of Tormenting*, a hilarious mock manners book. Johnson evidently read the book and gleaned two, but only two, illustrative quotations (s.v. "marital" and "prink"), which he probably inserted on the spot. This fortuitousness is the exception, however, and the rule is that Johnson concentrated his searches on certain authors; by selecting the domain of research, Johnson limited both the kind of English and the kind of knowledge his book could contain.

Many of Johnson's choices are highly predictable and would have been the choices of most well-educated Englishmen from 1746 to 1755. In fact, Johnson obtained a list of writers to be used from the estate of Alexander Pope, who made suggestions for such a project shortly before his death in 1744.[6] This was only two years before Johnson signed his agreement with the London publishers, including Pope's publisher Dodsley. In the *Plan* of the *Dictionary* (1747), Johnson refers to his reliance on Pope, who had selected a list of prose writers and began a list of poets to be used as authorities in an English dictionary. The prose writers chosen that also appear in Johnson's *Dictionary* are Bacon, Hooker, Clarendon, Tillotson, Dryden, Temple, Locke, Sprat, Atterbury, Addison, and Swift. This is a fairly predictable list of writers acknowledged for their excellence as stylists and, by and large, for their widely accepted, mainstream political and religious views. Nevertheless, some early critics of Johnson's *Dictionary*, including Thomas Edwards, complained that Johnson had made his book a vehicle for high-church, or "high-flying," Tory sentiments. Edwards was not unjustified, but he would have had the same complaint had Pope, or almost any other prominent literary figure of the day, executed the project. For the most part, Johnson was not expressing his personal political views in his choice of sources; he was doing the predictable and the expected, the largely unexceptional. Johnson was very far from reflecting all of British society or all English-speakers in his book, but he tried for a broad range of literate, educated society, and he further attempted to avoid controversy by excluding living writers and by deferring to a recently deceased acknowledged literary luminary.

However, Johnson excluded three writers from Pope's list – Thomas Hobbes, Isaac Barrow, and Lord Bolingbroke – and he naturally added many more. (When he wrote the Preface to the *Dictionary* in 1755 Johnson made no mention of Pope's list.) Johnson conscientiously excluded Hobbes, and said so, because he believed that his writings promoted immorality: his vision of human life as naturally "nasty, brutal, and short" may have hit the mark for Johnson in his melancholy moods, but he did not believe in transmitting such a message to his audience, especially when that audience included young people. Hobbes's determinism was also troubling to Johnson. Not only did Johnson deny Hobbes the opportunity to appear in the *Dictionary*, he also quoted on numerous occasions his chief opponent on the matter of determinism, John Bramhall. Like Milton's encyclopedia of values, *Paradise Lost*, Johnson's lexicon of beliefs is insistent upon the importance of freedom to the existence of morality. Indeed, Johnson frequently quotes Milton to illustrate and moralize the meanings of "freedom" and "free." He also, though infrequently, paused in the midst of his lexicographical activity to make the point about freedom explicit in his own voice. After tracing the etymology of "caitiff" to the Italian word *cattivo* and the Latin word *fur*, both of which have the same double meaning of "slave and scoundrel," he cites a verse from the *Greek Anthology* meaning that the loss of freedom destroys the better half of virtue. Moments like this are rare in the *Dictionary*, but they represent more widespread attempts on Johnson's part to shape the field of knowledge presented in his book, and to give it a moral and religious bent that he felt was appropriate for the instruction of students.

Johnson's exclusion of Bolingbroke from the *Dictionary* is similarly tendentious, but it is not total. Johnson mentions him a few times and he actually quotes him occasionally from letters he wrote to Pope included in the available editions of Pope's letters. (Given the general exclusion of Bolingbroke, these inclusions may have been the work of amanuenses scanning for quotations.) Johnson objected to Bolingbroke's English, which he found Frenchified and corrupt. He makes this clear under sense number 5 in his treatment of the verb "to owe":

> A practice has long prevailed among writers, to use *owing*, the active participle of *owe*, in a passive sense, for owed or due. Of this impropriety Bolinbroke was aware, and, having no quick sense of the force of English words, has used *due* in the sense of consequence or imputation, which by other writers is only used of debt. We say, the money is *due* to me; Bolinbroke says, the effect is *due* to the cause.

But Johnson censures almost all of his sources on occasion (including favorites like Dryden and Shakespeare), and the grounds for excluding Bolingbroke are ideological rather than linguistic. Bolingbroke's politics weave their way in and out of positions that Johnson shared; Johnson disapproved of Bolingbroke's manner of personal and political behavior; but the real problem is his complacent religious optimism. Johnson was critical of this attitude as it appears in Pope's *Essay on Man* (*Lives*, III, 242–44), but in its pure form in the patrician Bolingbroke it made him angry. This anger comes out in Johnson's definition of "irony": "A mode of speech in which the meaning is contrary to the words: as, *Bolinbroke was a* pious *man*." Printing records show that Johnson composed this part of the *Dictionary* very shortly after Bolingbroke's death in 1751, but the old adage of *Nihil nisi bonum* (Speak only good about the dead) could not restrain him from taking a shot at the deistic philosopher.

It is unclear why Johnson excluded Barrow, the Cambridge mathematician and divine, nor why he reinstated Sir Walter Raleigh when Pope had specifically rejected him. It may be that Johnson owned a copy of Raleigh and not one of Barrow; there may be deeper reasons, but Johnson's researches were sometimes "fortuitous and unguided," and it would be incorrect to see fixed policy in all of his inclusions and exclusions. This is especially true of the poets. Johnson extensively quoted all of those on Pope's list: Spenser, Shakespeare, Waller, Butler, Milton, Dryden, Prior, Swift. There are implicit ideological commitments in his selections, to be sure, and Johnson is partly responsible for establishing the cannon of English writers that has undergone severe scrutiny in recent years. Johnson does not include many women writers. Although there are fragments of Charlotte Lennox, Jane Barker, Elizabeth Carter, Hester Mulso, and a few others, their presence is not significant. Working-class writers are also underrepresented, and some other classes of society, including radicals, get relatively little attention. In most cases, however, this is not solely the result of Johnson's personal predilections but also of his wish to create a mainstream *Dictionary*, where "mainstream" means, among other things, those who could afford the £4–10 that the book would cost when it arrived before the public on 15 April 1755.

Whatever their politics, however, many of Johnson's choices of texts reveal his encyclopedic and pious educational design. For example, he took a great many quotations from the so-called physico-theologists. These were "philosophic," or scientific, writers who set out to show that study of the natural world should increase admiration of God and Providence, rather than pose a rationalistic doubt of God's existence. Robert Boyle, for example, made the motto of his collected works a statement of this credo: "to rise from study of secondary causes to contemplation of the first Cause." He also established a trust to support in perpetuity a series of lectures on this theme. Richard Bentley was the first Boyle lecturer, and Johnson quotes him heavily, as he does many of his successors. These books are perfect for providing the combination of religious and moral instruction that Johnson believed a book for learners should contain.[7]

Basic educational works likewise attracted Johnson's notice because he saw them as akin to his own work; taking quotations from them naturally makes his book educational in the same way. Locke's educational treatise is heavily quoted, as are two books by his occasionally critical disciple Isaac Watts, *Logic* and *The Improvement of the Mind*. Milton's essay "Of Education" is the only one of his prose works that finds its way into the *Dictionary*. Clearly, Johnson objected to Milton's politics, but there are parts of *Areopagitica*, the divorce tracts, or the historical writings that would have been unobjectionable. Johnson knew

Milton's prose from his youth, but he settled on the essay on education because it furthered his ends. Ascham's *Schoolmaster* (1570) is another telling choice because it predates the boundary of "Sidney's work" (1590s) that Johnson set in the Preface for his idea of the "wells of English undefiled." There are many more examples, including George Cheyne's *Philosophical Principles of Religion: Natural and Revealed*, written "for the Use of Younger Students of Philosophy, who while they were taught the most probable acount of the Appearances of Nature from the Modern Discoveries, might thereby have the Principles of Natural Religion insensibly instilled into them at the same time" (Preface to 2nd edn. [1715]). These educational works are conspicuous when one considers that a very large proportion of the quotations in the *Dictionary* come from a core list of books that was, as it were, inevitable – on Pope's list and most educated eighteenth-century people. Using the work of cataloguing done by Lewis Freed, I estimate that about 75 percent of the quotations in the *Dictionary* come from the basic list plus a small additional group of well-known sermon writers.[8] Another large proportion of quotations comes from encyclopedias and specialized books of knowledge; hence, the educational texts are prominent among the works that comprise Johnson's more special choices, and they must be weighed heavily in determining the nature of his attempts to shape the field of knowledge in the *Dictionary*.

In addition to selecting certain texts (and excluding a few, like Hobbes), Johnson shapes the meaning of his book by excerpting quotations from the chosen books in particular ways. He seemed to look for the individual poems and passages of chosen authors that would best transmit his educational message. For example, Matthew Prior's "Solomon on the Vanity of the World" provided Johnson with many opportunities to present pithy statements of the underlying meaning of the *Dictionary*; he also frequently quoted Prior's youthful paraphrase of Exodus 3: 14. In every case, Johnson's recognition of his opportunities to express his major themes seems unfailing. To give just one example: under the word "definer," where his own activity and that of his readers was itself being defined, Johnson produced from Prior:

> Your God, forsooth, is found
> Incomprehensible and infinite;
> But is he therefore found? Vain searcher! no:
> Let your imperfect definition show,
> That nothing you, the weak *definer*, know.
> ("On Exodus 3.14," 21–25)

This is one of many instances in which the *Dictionary* reminds its readers of the vanity of human learning even as it pursues learning. Johnson is excellent at snatching such germane fragments of poetry from longer works, especially where they comment on his general educational purpose, and his particular lexicographical activity. He thus makes many words with irrelevant meanings contribute to the presentation of his overall theme. To give another example, he has Congreve say to author and reader alike under the apparently irrelevant word "pincushion," "Thou art a retailer of phrases, and dost deal in remnants of remnants, like a maker of pincushions." This quotation is from *Incognita*, a play which Johnson said, in the "Life of Congreve," that he would rather praise than read (II, 214). But Johnson could turn his reading to his purposes, even when he was bored. Johnson also does a fine job with Richard Corbet, naturally finding much advice for the young in "To his Son, Vincent Corbet." Because of the proverbial quality of his verse, George Herbert seems to have attracted Johnson more than other metaphysical poets, though he quotes several others from time to time.

One cannot prove that Johnson excerpted Shakespeare and other heavily quoted authors in a particular way that emphasized his program.[9] Proportionally, *As You Like It* is the most heavily quoted play; that may be suggestive, as may be the fact that *Love's Labours Lost* is well represented. Despite the sense that Johnson looked in Shakespeare, as in other writers, for his major themes, I must acknowledge that Johnson's survey of Shakespeare might also be described as "fortuitous and unguided." But there is at least one quotation of Shakespeare in which Johnson clearly manipulated his text to make it express his educational purpose. Under the key word "to learn" we hear Caliban say:

> You taught me language, and my profit on't
> Is, I know not how to curse: the red plague rid you
> For *learning* me your language. (*The Tempest*, I.ii.365–67)

Johnson did not find the interpolated "not" in any edition that he used for the play, nor did he again interpolate it or mention it as a possibility when he edited the plays in 1765. This interpretation seems to be merely designed to comment on Johnson's own attempts at instruction.

Such examples of bowdlerization are rare. Johnson often seemed to select his quotations for his teaching purposes but rarely did he tailor them to make them fit his educational scheme. He frequently abridged, and as he says in the Preface: "it may sometimes happen, by hasty detruncation, that the general tendency of the sentence may be changed: the divine may desert his tenets, or the philosopher his system" (Greene, p. 319). Mostly, however, this accidental or creative falsification does not happen. Johnson sometimes "detruncates" his sources so that their remarks are more pointed, and when he resorts to this measure, the position is sometimes rendered closer to one that he takes in his book overall. To give just one example, under "incurably" Johnson quotes Locke: "We cannot know it is or is not, being incurably ignorant." That we are "incurably ignorant" and must rely on revealed religion for true knowledge is essential to the meaning of the *Dictionary*, but all Locke actually wrote was "how can we be sure that this or that quality is in *Gold*, when we know not what is or is not *Gold*? . . . being incurably ignorant, whether it has or has not that which makes anything to be called *Gold*, i.e. that real Essence of *Gold* whereof we have no *Idea* at all."[10] Although such creative abridgment is rare (Johnson omits forty-eight words in the quote), it contributes to Johnson's overall shaping of his book into a pious encyclopedia with a religious message for learners.

Some of the educational texts from which Johnson took his quotations deal, like his own book, with language. Sometimes quotations from these books present self-portraits of the *Dictionary* itself. In the Preface Johnson says that he has printed many illustrative quotations which "may relieve the labour of verbal searches, and intersperse with verdure and flowers the dusty desarts of barren philology" (Greene, p. 318). Johnson is here quoting William Walker, *English Examples of the Latine Syntaxis* (1683), and he uses the passage again in illustrating "philology." Johnson provides plenty of relief to those looking up words, but it must be remembered that the *Dictionary*, like Walker's *Syntaxis*, is mainly a word book, and, in the sense of the metaphor from Walker, mainly desert. Moreover, Johnson's whole presentation of the encyclopedia is filtered through language. It is good Lockean theory. Despite Johnson's famous remark that he was "not yet so lost in lexicography, as to forget that *words are the daughters of earth, and that things are the sons of heaven*" (Greene, p. 310), he thought, like Locke, that there was a practical, if shifting and relative, correspondence between the order of words and the order of things, because only in words, he believed, can we retain and express our knowledge of things.

The single most important and innovative way that Johnson arranges the order of words is by breaking each headword into a train of numbered senses. Johnson set out with definite ideas about how he was going to accomplish this task. In the first draft of the *Plan*, "A Scheme of an English Dictionary," he contemplated making all of his headwords "primitives," or words not derived from other words. One reader of the scheme objected that this would oblige readers of the *Dictionary* to know the language well enough to know the etymologies of the words they were looking up, thus spoiling sales to learners and foreigners. But in the *Plan* Johnson retained a firm notion of how he might distinguish "primitive" from "accidental" meaning:

> In explaining the general and popular language, it seems necessary to sort the several senses of each word, and to exhibit first its natural and primitive signification, as "To *arrive*, to reach the shore in a voyage: he *arrived* at a safe harbour." Then to give its consequential meaning, "*to arrive*, to reach any place whether by land or sea; as, he *arrived* at his country seat." Then its metaphorical sense, "to obtain any thing desired; as, he *arrived* at a peerage". . . Then follows the

accidental or consequential signification . . . Then the remoter or metaphorical signification . . . After having gone through the natural and figurative senses, it will be proper to subjoin the poetical sense of each word, where it differs from that which is in common use; as, *wanton* applied to any thing of which the motion is irregular without terror, as

In wanton ringlets curl'd her hair.

To the poetical sense may succeed the familiar; as of *toast*, used to imply the person whose health is drunk . . . The familiar may be followed by the burlesque; as of *mellow*, applied to good fellowship . . . And lastly, may be produced the peculiar sense, in which a word is found in any great author. (*Works*, II, 21–22)

However, by the time he wrote the Preface Johnson had to admit of his scheme,

This is specious, but not always practicable; kindred senses may be so interwoven, that the perplexity cannot be disentangled, nor any reason be assigned why one should be ranged before the other. When the radical idea branches out into parallel ramifications, how can a consecutive series be formed of senses in their nature collateral? The shades of meaning sometimes pass imperceptibly into each other . . . and sometimes there is such a confusion of acceptations, that discernment is wearied, and distinction puzzled, and perseverance herself hurries to an end, by crouding together what she cannot separate. (Greene, pp. 316–17)

Despite acknowledging that he has failed to organize the language on regular principles and has capitulated to its irrational and irregular ways, Johnson tries throughout the *Dictionary* to keep his scheme in order. If he could have succeeded or even felt that he had succeeded, Johnson would have become a more idealistic philologer than, for the most part, he is. His critics in the next generation, the more idealistic linguists Charles Richardson, Horne Tooke, and Noah Webster, criticized Johnson for interpreting contexts rather than words. Johnson did indeed believe that the "solution of all difficulties, and the supply of all defects [in his definitions] must be sought in the examples, subjoined to the various senses of each word" (Greene, p. 318) and that it was his job "not [to] form, but register the language . . . not [to] teach men how they should think, but relate how they have hitherto expressed their thoughts" (Greene, p. 322). However, he did not regard the situation with complete equanimity; he gave in to the superior strength of experience, and he knew that was his duty as a laborious, empirically minded drudge, but also had his dreams of scholarly control and order.

Throughout the *Dictionary*, in various ways, Johnson can be seen struggling with the empirical facts of language and trying to make them obey a rational order. The way he orders the senses of each word provides the most widespread evidence. He does what in the *Plan* he says he must do with "ardour": the first definition is "Heat," which recapitulates the etymology, "ardor, Lat. heat." Johnson provides no evidence that the English word was ever used in this sense;

the definition is there only to maintain the integrity of the word as an ideal organization of meanings. Johnson writes the second definition with this ideal order in mind: "Heat of affection, as love, desire, courage." Happily, at least one of Johnson's illustrative quotations properly supports his etymological sense of the word: in Robert South's sermons he found the sentence, "Joy, like a ray of the sun, reflects with a greater ardour and quickness, when it rebounds upon a man from the breast of his friend." Of course, it was just such "philosophical" (i.e. Latinate) language that attracted Johnson to many of the authors cited in the *Dictionary*; as well as providing examples of the wisdom of God manifest in the creation, these writers tended to bind words to their Latin origins. The third and last definition of "ardour" reflects the peculiar usage of a single author: "The person ardent or bright. This is used only by Milton . . . 'celestial ardours [angels].'" This usage is set aside from the chain anchored to the primitive or etymological sense, though it is not all that different.

Johnson is more assiduous about keeping his concatenations in order for Latin words, even when this means introducing an unreal, unemployed meaning. To give just one more example of many, his first definition of the noun "ruin" follows the meaning of the common Latin word *ruo* (to fall): "The fall or destruction of cities or edifices." He has no illustrative quotation to offer. The second meaning, for which there are several illustrations, is "The remains of a building demolished." In his definitions of the related words, however, Johnson keeps coming back to the etymological sense of "falling": the intransitive verb "to ruin" is "1. To fall in ruins," and "ruinous" is "Fallen to ruin; dilapidated; demolished." For the transitive verb "to ruin" Johnson resorts to a Latinate definition, "To subvert; to demolish." This very much follows the less common transitive meaning of the Latin verb, which is "to level; to pull down," according to Robert Ainsworth's *Thesaurus*, the Latin dictionary that Johnson used while writing his *Dictionary*. In fact one of Ainsworth's definitions for "subvert" in the English–Latin part of his *Thesaurus* is *diruo*, an intensified form of *ruo*. Examples of etymological meanings that strain fidelity to usage are easy to find. The first sense of "candid" is "White," although Johnson notes, "This sense is very rare." "Trivial" is not only "Vile; worthless; vulgar" but also "such as may be picked up in the highway" (Latin, *via*). A "terrier" is a dog that "follows his game under ground" (Latin, *terra*). A "seminary" is a "place of education, from whence scholars are transplanted [like seeds, Latin, *semines*] to life."

Johnson also tries to keep what he calls "Teutonick" words close to their roots, but here idealist linguistic motives are less separable from the goal of historical presentation. For example, the first sense of "to doom" is the etymologically accurate "To judge" (Old English, *dom*). The illustration comes from Milton, who often displays linguistic idealism of this kind: "Him . . . thou did'st not doom / So strictly" (*Paradise Lost*, III.401–2). Also for idealist reasons "strong" comes into Johnson's definition of "stark" and the first definition of "starve" is "to die," although the illustration, as in the case of the lines from Milton under "to doom," may be self-consciously archaic. Still, in all these instances Johnson is historically accurate, so he is arguably empirical. In fact, his arrangement of senses looks like what one finds in the more historical and empirical *Oxford English Dictionary (OED)*.

In many cases, Johnson's definitions of Germanic words display little sense of etymological concatenation as they move along, but sometimes in the end he seems to remember his ideals and to tie up the loose ends of his definition in a concluding remark. These remarks provide statements that define the middle ground between the idealism of the *Plan* and the move toward experience represented by the Preface eight years later. For example, after detailing sixty-four transitive and intransitive senses of the verb "to break" Johnson looks back over the tangle and sees an organizing principle: "It is to be observed of this extensive and perplexed verb, that, in all its significations . . . it has some reference to its primitive meaning by implying either detriment, suddenness, or violence." In the *OED* Murray was less sanguine; he began his treatment of "break" with the remark, "Many of the uses of this verb are so contextual, that it is difficult, if not impossible, to find places for them in a general scheme of its signification." A few letters on, under the sixty-fourth sense of "to fall" Johnson has capitulated a bit further: "This is one of those general words of which it is very difficult to ascertain or detail the full signification. It retains in most of its senses some part of its primitive meaning, and implies either literally or figuratively descent, violence, or suddenness." After cataloguing the eighty-eight different senses of "to set," Johnson has no comment. His silence is a kind of capitulation to usage, but perhaps more telling is his extraordinary list of thirty-six quotations under the second sense, including six consecutive quotations from Dryden. The entry dances out an image of usage overwhelming the powers of distinction and rational concatenation.

Despite some evidence to the contrary, in the bulk of his definitions Johnson is worrying more about usage than ideal meaning. For the most part, he follows the advice of Jeremy Collier that he prints in illustration of the word "etymology": "When words are restrained, by common usage, to a particular sense, to run up to *etymology*, and construe them by dictionary, is wretchedly ridiculous." Collier implies that dictionary definitions are etymological definitions; Johnson's dictionary definitions are partly that and partly descriptions of usage. Those of his definitions that are most responsive to usage try to suggest the broad sense of common words with numerous strokes of synonyms and antonyms. "Sluggish," for example, is "Dull; drowzy; lazy; slothful; idle; insipid; slow; inactive; inert," and "mild" is "Kind; tender; good; indulgent; merciful; compassionate; clement; soft; not severe; not cruel." In these cases, Johnson is reacting to the word, rather than analyzing it or anchoring it to a primitive meaning. His work here is almost impressionistic, although, as in his literary criticism, he presents his impressions in a formal pattern.

The indications that Johnson gradually surrendered his idealist notions of language to the superior power of usage are clear in the differences between the *Plan* and the Preface. They also appear in numerous ways throughout the *Dictionary*. Perhaps the single best example is in Johnson's discussion of the word "latter." Johnson says, "This is the comparative of *late*, though universally written with *tt*, contrary to analogy, and to our own practice in the superlative *latest*. When the thing of which the comparison is made is mentioned, we use *later*: as, this fruit is *later* than the rest; but *latter* when no comparison is expressed: as those are *latter* fruits." As if to say, "this doesn't really make sense, but that's the way it is," Johnson adds a quotation from Horace: "Volet usus / Quem penes arbitrium est, et vis, et norma loquendi" (*Ars poetica*, 72–73) ("if so willed by usage, which is the proper rule of judgment, both the strength and the standard of speaking"). Johnson does not always throw up his hands so easily. He is often willing to do battle with usage. For example, under "to dissever" Johnson says, "In this word the particle *dis* makes no change in the signification, and therefore the word, though supported by great authorities, ought to be ejected from our language." Ejection, however, is prevented by Johnson's faithful recording of illustrative quotations from Sidney, Raleigh, Shakespeare, and Pope.

In the event, looking ahead to the influence of Johnson's *Dictionary* on the future of language study, the record of quotations speaks more loudly than Johnson's strictures. James Murray had a copy of Johnson's *Dictionary* handy when he compiled the *OED*, and it is far more likely that he used it to supplement his collections of quotations than to follow its advice on propriety. In the late 1930s Philip Gove, the editor of Webster's III, directed a team of WPA (Workers Progress Administration) workers to copy all of the quotations in Johnson's *Dictionary* onto three-by-five cards and alphabetize them by author. This resource returned the *Dictionary* to the state it was in before Johnson's authorial intervention and reduced it to a record of usage before reemploying it in twentieth-century lexicography.[11] Such a legacy is not what Lord Chesterfield had in mind when he encouraged Johnson to undertake the work and declared to the world, "I will not only obey him, like an old Roman, as my dictator, but like a modern Roman, I will implicitly believe in him as my pope, and hold him to be infallible while in the chair."[12] But even before the "celebrated letter," as Boswell called it, in which Johnson rejected Chesterfield's tardy offer of patronage,[13] Johnson's allegiance to historical accuracy was stronger than it was to linguistic ideas or dictatorial reform. He fashioned that commitment to history in his early days of scholarship as he tried to make himself into a Renaissance humanist in the mold of great scholars like Joseph Scaliger. Perhaps the key element of their work was an increased respect for the historical fact, even when this meant rejecting pleasing myths of national origin or pleasing, harmonious systems of scholastic thought. Johnson refined his commitment to historical study as he worked on the catalogue of the Harleian library in the early 1740s, and he brought this commitment to his work on Shakespeare, which he began the year before he signed the contract to write the *Dictionary*.

Johnson is not thoroughly and purely historical in this great work. He believed his book should contain moral and religious teaching. Hence he gives shape and meaning to the field of knowledge that he presents in the *Dictionary*; indeed, he does more of this than Ephraim Chambers, whose *Cyclopedia* is Johnson's reference book of first resort. Although he clung to some idealist wishes for the rational improvement of language, Johnson's overall presentation of language is historical, and the effect of this presentation is, generally, to historicize knowledge too. As Allen Reddick has demonstrated in *The Making of Johnson's Dictionary*, when Johnson revised his book for the fourth edition of 1773, he trimmed some of the long passages of encyclopedias to make room, presumably, for more material of a moral nature. He added material from some favorite writers, mostly those, like William Law, who would amplify his moral message. It may be that by this time, Johnson had shed some of his historical and antiquarian zeal. His research program for the *Lives of the Poets* (1779–81) was not strenuous. But both in the *Lives* and in the revised *Dictionary*, Johnson's interest in historical accuracy remains strong. He tends to explode false beliefs about English authors in the *Lives*, and he reveals a similar interest in the revised *Dictionary*. Despite his increased attention to the moral argument of his work, Johnson also tried to improve its factual accuracy. He repositioned and renumbered thousands of quotations, often for reasons of historical accuracy, and he made an effort to change his treatment of terms so that they would be better understood in 1773 than they were in 1755. After quoting his earlier explanation from Quincy, Johnson remarks, "Such was the account given a few years ago of electricity; but the industry of the present age . . . has discovered in electricity a multitude of philosophical wonders." In naming a few of them, Johnson shows that his own interest in the facts of the natural world is undiminished. Even in 1784, when he was nearing death, Johnson remained interested in experimental knowledge. He had his own chemistry laboratory, and in his diaries he recorded the results of trials he made on his own vitality: determining how quickly his hair would grow back after being shaven or how well he could lift the bucket from a deep well at Mrs. Thrale's house. Despite its attempts to present knowledge with moral and religious overtones, and in spite of its attempts to make language more ideal, the *Dictionary* must also be seen as an expression of Johnson's lifelong interest in empirical, historically verifiable truth.

NOTES

1 See Bernice Kliman, "Samuel Johnson, 1745 Annotator?," *Analytical and Enumerative Bibliography*, n.s. 6 (1992), 185–207.

2 See O M Brack, Jr., *Bred a Bookseller: Samuel Johnson on Vellum Books* (Los Angeles: Samuel Johnson Society of Southern California, 1990).

3 See Paul J. Korshin, "Johnson and the Renaissance Dictionary," *JHI*, 35 (1974), 300–12.

4 See James Sledd and Gwin Kolb, *Dr. Johnson's Dictionary: Essays in the Biography of a Book* (University of Chicago Press, 1955), and Allen Reddick, *The Making of Johnson's Dictionary 1746–1773* (Cambridge University Press, 1990).

5 See W. R. Keast, "The Two Clarissas in Johnson's *Dictionary*," *Studies in Philology*, 54 (1957), 429–39.

6 See Joseph Spence, *Observations, Anecdotes, and Characters of Books and Men*, ed. James M. Osborn, 2 vols. (Oxford: Clarendon Press, 1966), I, 170–1 and 374–75.

7 See William K. Wimsatt, *Philosophic Words* (New Haven: Yale University Press, 1948).

8 "The Sources of Johnson's Dictionary," unpublished Cornell University Ph.D. dissertation (1939).

9 For an analysis of how Johnson excerpted Shakespeare and the other thirteen authors of the extant marked books, see E. J. Thomas, "A Bibliographical and Critical Analysis of Johnson's Dictionary," unpublished Ph.D. dissertation, University College of Wales at Aberystwyth (1974).

10 *An Essay Concerning Human Understanding*, ed. Peter H. Nidditch (Oxford: Clarendon Press, 1975), p. 581.

11 The file which was preserved and reorganized by Herman Liebert, and became known as the Gove–Liebert file, is now in my possession. It has been superseded as a resource for scholars by the CD-ROM version of Johnson's *Dictionary*, ed. Anne McDermott (Cambridge University Press, 1996).

12 *The World*, 4 vols. (1755), III, 267 (no. 100).

13 The letter of 7 February 1755, *Letters*, I, 94–97.

7

ROBERT FOLKENFLIK

Johnson's politics

I

Scholars writing about Johnson like to point out, correctly, that he wrote more on politics than most readers suppose. In a broad sense it can be argued that all writing implies a politics, but Johnson's engagement with politics in one way or another is coterminous with his professional life as a writer. Writers were less specialized in the eighteenth century than they have become, and "literature" had a broader signification. Apart from Johnson's late work as political pamphleteer, whether as journalist, satirist, essayist, lexicographer, book reviewer, sermon-writer, biographer, throughout his career many of Johnson's writings directly engage politics and others touch upon politics in a range of ways. This essay will trace the broad outline of Johnson's political opinions and make particular observations on some of his political writings.

Even those writings that do not seem political as such sometimes had political implications. In the 1740s his biographies of the English admirals Blake and Drake of earlier centuries were designed to encourage a nation dishonored by Walpole's pacific policies, as Johnson then saw it, to go to war. This particular example brings up another important point. In later years Johnson was one of the most thoroughgoing opponents of wars, such as the Seven Years' War, and he came to respect Walpole. Not all of Johnson's positions remained static, and some cannot be predicted from assumptions about Johnson's Toryism.

Johnson was a self-identified Tory and was so identified by both friends and enemies. He "gloried in the name" according to the close friend of his later years, Hester Thrale. The difficulty here is to know just what a Tory was. It matters little whether or not Johnson was (in Boswell's phrase) "an infant Hercules of Toryism" and (a doubtful anecdote) a three-year-old adherent of Henry Sacheverell, the High Churchman whose attack on the Protestant dissenters was a *cause célèbre* in 1710, nor, to take a more serious question, whether his father Michael Johnson, clearly not a Nonjuror, was a Jacobite.

Johnson himself was neither a Nonjuror nor a Jacobite, though he was called both by some in his own day, and a number of twentieth-century scholars have revived the issue.[1] Following the "Glorious Revolution" of 1688, which led to James II's fleeing to France and the coming of William and Mary to the English throne, the Nonjurors were those who refused to take the Oath of Allegiance to the new rulers and their successors and the Oath of Abjuration (renunciation of James and his heirs), oaths required for degrees at Oxford and Cambridge, public office, and a range of professions (clergyman, professor, schoolteacher). Johnson clearly disliked the oaths, especially the oath of abjuration, and argued against them on moral and logical grounds, but there is no reason to believe he either refused to take them or that he avoided putting himself in a position where he would be required to take them. Although he respected those who did not take them – they suffered for their principles – he considered doing so "perverseness of integrity" ("Life of Fenton," *Lives*, II, 257). Refusal to take such an oath would debar them from occupations and make them more likely to be criminal. The reasoning seems drawn from natural law. Johnson admired the Nonjurors for their learning and piety, yet his statement that "I never knew a non-juror who could reason" is suggestive (*Life*, IV, 286 and n. 3). He asserted that he had never set foot in a Nonjuring meeting-house, the places of worship that those rejecting the church under William and Mary and their successors established as an alternative (*Life*, IV, 288).

The notion of Johnson as a Jacobite depends upon teasing out evidence for a treasonous and therefore secret commitment that carried the threat of hanging, but it founders on clear-cut positions. He was neither a supporter of the Catholic James II and the restoration of Stuart rule, nor a believer in the divine right of kings. And he knew too much about the history of England to take James as having an indefeasible right to the throne. Earlier usurpations had changed the line of kingship. He thought in the reign of George III that the Hanoverian kings had "as good a right" by succession "as the former family" (*Life*, II, 220). He believed in hereditary right by established possession. About a hundred years was sufficient to establish a continuing right to the throne (or the greatness of a poet).

In his writings Johnson describes the dethroning of James II as necessary, and James's "violence" against religion as the reason for it. He refers to "the dangerous bigotry of James" in *The False Alarm* and claims in his "Introduction to the Political State of Great-Britain" (1756) that James "thought rightly, that there is no happiness without religion; but he thought very erroneously and absurdly, that there is no religion without popery" (*Politics*, pp. 342, 142). He claims here that "the necessity of self-preservation . . . impelled the subjects of James to drive him from the throne" (p. 142). He told his friend Bennett Langton that "It was become impossible for him to reign any longer in this country" (*Life*, I, 430). In his Preface to the Index of the *Gentleman's Magazine* in 1753 he describes the Jacobite rebellion of 1745 as "not less contemptible in its beginning than threatening in its progress and consequences; but which, through the favour of Providence, was crushed at once." Those who doubt that Johnson wrote this passage have not pondered the quotation in his *Dictionary* (1755) chosen from Addison's *Freeholder* 55 to illustrate the word "crisis": "The undertaking . . . was entered upon in the very *crisis* of the late rebellion, when it was the duty of every Briton to contribute his utmost assistance to the government, in a manner suitable to his station and abilities." The quotation refers to the Jacobite rebellion of 1715. Johnson also satirized Jacobites and Whigs in *Idler* 10 (1759). There is no reason to think that Johnson had changed his mind from an earlier position, or that he lied about his beliefs.

His respect for and praise of Jacobites as individuals centered on some core principles that he shared with them but could be reduced to what he said in the Hebrides, "These people are not Whigs." When he shocked Bennett Langton's Tory father by saying to the old man's niece, "I hope, my dear, you are a Jacobite," he explained his "compliment" by a logical series:

> A Jacobite, Sir, believes in the divine right of Kings. He that believes in the divine right of Kings believes in a Divinity. A Jacobite believes in the divine right of Bishops. He that believes in the divine right of Bishops believes in the divine authority of the Christian religion. Therefore, Sir, a Jacobite is neither an Atheist nor a Deist. That cannot be said of a Whig; for *Whiggism is the negation of all principle.*
>
> (*Life*, I, 430–31)

The common ground is religious, not in terms of religious doctrine, but in terms of the relation of religion to the state. Johnson's definition of "Tory" in the *Dictionary* is tendentious, not merely descriptive but it was also what Johnson believed: "One who adheres to the ancient constitution of the state, and the apostolical hierarchy of the church of England, opposed to a Whig." When he claimed that "the first Whig was the Devil," he had in mind an opposition to religious and political authority (*Life*, III, 326).

Johnson clearly thought of himself as a Tory before he left Lichfield for Oxford; whether his father or the signs of destruction in Lichfield caused by the English Civil War contributed to the making of his political identity is not clear. Johnson may well have found his commitment to Toryism in his youthful disputes with the elderly Gilbert Walmsley, "a Whig, with all the virulence and malevolence of his party," whom Johnson nonetheless deeply respected and eulogized in his "Life of Smith" (*Lives*, II, 20). It was probably Walmsley of whom Johnson spoke to Boswell in the Hebrides when he said "There was a violent Whig, with whom I used to contend with great eagerness. After his death, I felt my Toryism much abated."

It has been argued, following the work of Lewis Namier on the House of Commons around 1760, that Whig and Tory meant little more than "In" and

"Out." There is certainly a great deal of truth in recognizing Tory identity as committing Johnson to an opposition politics throughout most of his life. But Namier's model was devised to explain the politics of members of the House of Commons. Even if it were to be fully credited, it would not necessarily be pertinent to explain the writings, positions, and acts of someone who never ran for office, and in all likelihood never voted. The voting franchise was limited to males, and among them to that small minority who met the property qualifications.

The meaning of "Tory" in the eighteenth century was subject to shifts over the course of Johnson's lifetime, and remains contested. The Tories as a party were proscribed from office in 1714 at the accession of George I, the first Hanoverian king, and they remained outsiders. Even after George III took the throne, power was held by a succession of powerful Whig alliances. No Tory was prime minister during Johnson's lifetime after Robert Harley, who lost office following the death of Queen Anne in 1714. This meant that until Johnson was in his fifties, his political writing took place as an opponent to government. Tory positions were not monolithic even in Parliament, and a number of those we think of as Tories would have considered themselves "Independents." They were sometimes identified as the "Country party," or the "country gentlemen."

A number of the Tory positions with which Johnson agreed are recognizably those of the "outs": desire for more frequent elections (triennial as opposed to septennial), attack on taxes (especially the "excise"), against standing armies (as needless expense and tool of government), against corruption and pensioners. These are issues that often led to distinct Whig–Tory divisions in the House of Commons. Yet they are also positions that would appeal to those who wanted a better government. The fact that politicians manipulate the populace with ideas that seem self-serving, hypocritical, or beside the point on closer examination does not mean that the ideology put forward is of little importance to their followers. The Tory party saw itself as popular. The Tories, not the Whigs, represented themselves as defenders of the poor and middling population. Even Johnson's humanitarianism, which is deeply connected to his religious thinking, is in keeping with certain strains of Tory ideology. A number of Tories during the eighteenth century were against slavery, and the Whigs, rather than the Tories, were strongly associated with imperial conquest.

Oxford was a Tory and even Jacobite stronghold, and Johnson's college, Pembroke, was more conservative than most. However, the key to Johnson's politics is his religious beliefs. A conversational statement makes the relative values clear. When Boswell laughingly said he had heard that Johnson claimed he "would stand before a battery of cannon, to restore the Convocation to its full powers," Johnson "thundered out" the accuracy of the remark (*Life*, I, 464). Johnson thought of Convocation, the assembly of clergy of the Church of

England, as one part of parliament, the "Lords spiritual," along with the Lords temporal and the Commons. Throughout most of Johnson's lifetime, Convocation was prevented from deliberating by the Whig government as a means of neutralizing the High Tory opposition that used theological controversy to mount pro-Stuart and anti-Hanoverian arguments.[2] Johnson believed that each nation should decide its single established religion. He also believed in the importance of the Test Act, which required subscription to the thirty-nine articles of the Church of England in order to hold office or matriculate at the universities. Although Church and monarchy (despite his low estimate of particular kings) were the twin pillars of Johnson's political beliefs, and although he refers in the "Life of Yalden" to "the party who had the honourable distinction of high-churchmen," he did not agree with a number of tenets associated with a "High Church" position by Boswell among others (*Lives*, II, 299).

As he saw it, subordination was necessary, but he did not believe that might makes right, or as he puts it, "that Right is the Consequence of Power" (*Savage*, p. 93). Johnson was a Tory in a broad ideological sense, on principles more than issues, though he was usually in agreement with the Tory side on parliamentary divisions. He has been well described as an "anti-Whig," one who opposed the governments of George I and II on a range of issues and who both temperamentally and ideologically stood against what the ministerial Whigs in general stood for.[3] He was for constitutional monarchy, not absolute monarchy. He did believe that the king was irresistible in the sense that the king-in-parliament is the ultimate authority, and that all government must have a final authority. He accepted without quibble the idea that tyrants could be overthrown. He did not follow the doctrine of passive obedience on the part of the governed put forward in such works as Sir Robert Filmer's *Patriarcha*. While Johnson did not ground his conception of Britain's government on theory, he recommends Hooker and Locke in his Introduction to *The Preceptor* and quotes them frequently in his *Dictionary*.

Johnson's London career puts some of his views in context. His first memorable poem, *London* (1738), allied him with the opposition, including such writers as Alexander Pope, who admired it. As Pope had imitated Horace in his anti-government satires, Johnson imitated Juvenal's third satire, applying what the Roman said of his own culture to the corruption of England emanating from its court and parliament, which he takes London to symbolize. In its attack on standing armies, the excise, pensions, the licensing act, the avoidance of a war with Spain, and other targets, it echoes the Opposition's side on parliamentary issues. These are mixed with more generalized attacks on looseness of morals, atheism, and criminality. While *London* contains a few direct jibes at George II, whose courtiers might "get a kick for awkward flattery" (131), most of the poem consists of the parting words of Thales, possibly based on Richard Savage, whom Johnson may or may not have met by this time, as he prepares to go into voluntary exile in Wales. That Johnson rejected the patriots praised in this poem and grew to love London should not lead readers to judge the poem weak or, even less appropriately, insincere. It is not Johnson's greatest poem, only because *The Vanity of Human Wishes* is better. Politically, he would give up the notion of the opposition Whigs as useful allies or virtuous men, but he continued to think of most of the issues (with the notable exception of the need for a war with Spain to restore besmirched honor) in the same way.

Johnson's criticism of the government and the House of Hanover continued in the Swiftian parodies, *Marmor Norfolciense* (1739) and *A Compleat Vindication of the Licensers of the Stage* (1739). *Marmor* may have led the government to hunt for Johnson. The fiction presents a scholar, a government sycophant, puzzling out the meaning of an ancient prophecy on a stone found in Norfolk. His antiquarian interests lead him to explain what does not need explaining, and in doing so to add unconsciously to the offensiveness of the prophecy. Explicating the poem's most daring line, "Kings change their laws, and kingdoms change their kings," the scholar alludes to James II's deposition but waives the question of whether this "prediction . . . portends any alteration of government in Carolina and Georgia" (*Politics*, p. 38), a hardly veiled reference to George II and his late queen.

The *Vindication* ironically justified the suppression of Henry Brooke's play *Gustavus Vasa* under the new Licensing Act of 1737.[4] Chesterfield had spoken eloquently against the Act in the House of Lords, but few if any joined him in voting against it. The "author" quickly identifies himself as a government hack and courtier who cannot understand why the opposition has "rejected all offers of places and preferments" (*Politics*, p. 56). He also cannot understand why such "Patriots" as Lyttelton and Pitt are so concerned for posterity. But he judges the "present poets" the foremost foes of the ministry and gives Brooke as his prime example. This spokesman for power makes the baldest defense of the licenser and the act: "Our intention was to invest him with new privileges, and to empower him to do that *without* reason, which *with* reason he could do before" (*Politics*, p. 63). Brooke's play, in which a Swedish hero overthrows a foreign usurper and his corrupt minister, actually struck too close to home for the government, but the vindicator goes through the play showing himself as inept as the scholar in *Marmor Norfolciense* in protesting the sentiments in favor of liberty and love of country. He looks forward to a day when "no politicks shall be read but that of the *Gazetteer*, nor any poetry but that of the Laureat" (*Politics*, p. 71). This sly, sustained ironic piece deserves to be better known. With its appeal to Magna Carta and "sacred, inalienable rights," and other Patriot watchwords, it would have been taken as the work of an opposition Whig. Johnson's later response to the topic of censorship was more complex, but his attitude toward the licenser remained clear, as his *Dictionary* definition attests: "A granter of permission; commonly a tool of power."

The government intended to crack down on the reporting of parliamentary debates in 1738 as a breech of privilege. Since these reports were one of the staples of the *Gentleman's Magazine* and other journals, the Swiftian expedient devised, very likely by Johnson, was to represent the series as reports by Lemuel Gulliver's grandson originally under the title "Debates in the Senate of Magna Lilliputia," and later as "Debates in the Senate of Lilliput." William Guthrie first wrote these speeches with Johnson's help, and Johnson took over this large assignment from 1741 to 1744. The speakers appeared under somewhat comical distortions of their actual names: Waleop, Ptit, Hafilax. While much of the reportage was dignified and significant, the framework did seem to diminish the institution of Parliament, and Johnson clearly had fun with such speakers as Sir William Yonge and Velters Cornewall extolling their regional ciders.

The debates early appeared in histories and other writings as the productions of their purported speakers, and Johnson even heard those he had written compared to the classical orators Demosthenes and Cicero by those who did not realize that they were his. They have gained most notoriety from Arthur Murphy's claim that Johnson said he "'took care that the WHIG DOGS should not have the best of it'" (*JM*, 1, 379). Since both the government supporters and most of the opposition were Whigs, it is not clear whom he had in mind, even if he were serious. Most scholars who have looked at his debates closely have been struck by the way in which the various speakers are enabled to put their points with dignity, especially Sir Robert Walpole at the time of the attack upon his conduct of the administration. A discernible bias against "Whigs" is not readily apparent in the debates, though one could argue that parliament as a whole is to some extent belittled by the Lilliputian fiction. Certainly when the "Patriot" Whigs gained power and showed themselves to be no different from their predecessors, Johnson found them worse than Walpole, whom he came to admire as one who kept his country from war, a war that Johnson had supported.

Though Johnson seems to have later had qualms about his role in recreating the speeches, there were signs early and late that they were not verbatim. A speech might be introduced with the notice that "Sir Wimgul Yegon spoke in Substance as follows." Such formulas ("spoke to this Effect," "spoke in the manner following," "spoke next to this Purpose") should have alerted the reader that the debates were being recreated rather than merely reported, an awareness perhaps enhanced by the fictional framework. Nevertheless, in his Preface to the *Literary Magazine* (1756) he explains that "The speeches inserted in other papers have been long known to be fictitious, and produced sometimes by men who never heard the debate, nor had any authentick information." While writing for the *Gentleman's Magazine*, he presumably had good information from those sent by Cave to report back on the debates, for the substance of a number of speeches tallies with independent reports. Johnson may have been in the House of Commons only on one occasion.

II

Johnson's work in the later 1740s can be read in part as political disillusionment following the downfall of Walpole and the decision of the "Patriots" to behave similarly to the minister whom they treated as the fount of corruption. His Preface to the 1743 volume of the *Gentleman's Magazine* complains "that the struggles of opposite parties have engrossed the attention of the publick, and that all subjects of conversation and all kinds of learning have given way to Politicks," and the next year he stopped writing the parliamentary debates. Certainly the *Vanity of Human Wishes* (1749) suggests in its Olympian perspective on human activities and desires that politics matters relatively little. As Johnson wrote in a couplet for Goldsmith's *The Traveller* (1764):

> How small of all that human hearts endure
> The part that laws or kings can cause or cure. (429–30)

This may be Johnson's way of indicating the ultimate limits on the importance of politics and stressing that those things that must be endured by humankind count for more than the littleness of the political state as such. Such a view was inflected in his parliamentary debates through the fiction that they came from Lilliput by way of Gulliver's grandson and the ludicrous encoding of names and titles. Many of Johnson's comments on the modern world in which he lived suggest a strong dissatisfaction with the politics of Britain. The "Patriots" whom he praised in passing in *London* are satirized and dismissed in the *Vanity of Human Wishes*:

> Our supple tribes repress their patriot throats,
> And ask no question but the price of votes:
> With weekly libels and septennial ale,
> Their wish is full to riot and to rail. (95–98)

The poem does not focus on contemporary English politics, though it does mordantly remark upon a range of political figures (including religious and military), mainly from the last century or so: Wolsey, Villiers, Harley, Strafford, Clarendon, Laud, Charles VII (the Holy Roman Emperor) and Charles XII of Sweden. His lines (191–222) on Charles XII of Sweden (a coded hero for the Jacobites, but not for Johnson) suggest an unsurpassed contempt for the would-be conqueror, a position clarified in *Adventurer* 99 (1753):

> I am far from intending to vindicate the sanguinary projects of heroes and conquerors, and would wish rather to diminish the reputation of their success, than the infamy of their miscarriages: for I cannot conceive, why he that has burnt cities,

and wasted nations, and filled the world with horror and desolation, should be more kindly regarded by mankind, than he that died in the rudiments of wickedness; why he that accomplished mischief should be glorious, and he that only endeavored it should be criminal: I would wish Caesar and Cataline, Xerxes and Alexander, Charles and Peter, huddled together in obscurity or detestation.

(*Adventurer*, p. 433)

Here is a nexus for his anti-war thinking and the limits to his interest in political history.

In 1756 at the outset of the Seven Years' War, Johnson became editor of and contributor to the *Literary Magazine*, thought to be a Pittite journal. His "Introduction to the Political State of Great-Britain," the first article in the new journal, set the tone and suggests, among other things, that he is extending his role as contemporary historian. He was undoubtedly engaged because he was good at savaging the government, though as Pitt shifted and came into office, Johnson's anti-war efforts must have rankled, and he was replaced as editor. Johnson considered the dispute between the English and French in the American colonies "only the quarrel of two robbers for the spoils of a passenger" ("Observations on the Present State of Affairs" [1756], *Politics*, p. 188).

George III's accession to the throne in 1760 and opening of his councils to a greater range of political opinion, along with Johnson's friendship with Henry Thrale, a Rockingham Whig elected to the House of Commons in 1765 as MP for Southwark, led Johnson to become a supporter of government positions. In the next decade there was talk of getting Johnson himself a seat in the House of Commons, but it came to nothing. He also agreed to help the Whig MP William Gerard Hamilton, who sought a scholar with classical learning and a knowledge of contemporary issues and law.

From 1767 to 1773 Robert Chambers delivered law lectures at Oxford as successor to Sir William Blackstone. Johnson secretly aided him to an extent not known but certainly significant.[5] These lectures substitute a more conservative conception of English government with an emphasis on duties of the subject for Blackstone's account of the status of the king and the importance of Magna Carta and individual rights. The passage in Chambers minimizing Magna Carta as the work of barons with "little foresight of the future," and "little knowledge of the past," most of whom could not write their own names, sounds very Johnsonian, as do many others, a shift from some of the Patriot emphases that he had used in lampooning the government in the late 1730s.

Johnson received a pension from the government in 1762, two years after the ascension of George III to the throne. Bute, the new prime minister, told him that it was given to him not "'for any thing you are to do, but for what you have done'" (*Life* I, 374). This is generally taken to mean for the importance of his writings, yet part of them were devoted to the Seven Years' War, and the new king like

Johnson opposed that war. Bute and George III may have intended to make Tories feel that they had a stake in the government by singling out such a stern oppositional writer for distinction. Johnson was uneasy about taking the £300 annual grant, given his definitions of "pension" and "pensioner" ("A slave of State hired by a stipend to obey his master") in the *Dictionary* and his fear of loss of independence.

When he was asked to aid government with his pen in 1763 he did not act, and he agonized about the possibility of returning the pension. But in the 1770s Johnson did write a series of four pro-government pamphlets: *The False Alarm*, *Thoughts on the Late Transactions Respecting Falkland's Islands*, *The Patriot*, and *Taxation No Tyranny*. Some of these have given the political Johnson a popular image as a reactionary. All can fairly be taken to represent his own views. For example, in dismissing the bellicose opposition response to the crisis with Spain over the Falkland Islands in 1771, Johnson turns a withering eye on the sources of colonial disputes, in this case the tussle for "tempest-beaten barrenness" (*Politics*, p. 358). A brief history gives way to the dismissal of patriotic claims that soldiers "*filled with England's glory, smile in death.*" In opposition to this image from Addison's "The Campaign" he drily notes that "The Life of a modern soldier is ill represented by heroick fiction" and goes on to describe memorably the actual effects of sickness and unnoticed death in war (*Politics*, p. 370). Johnson thinks there is little to gain except for those poised to profit from war, and he attacks vociferously "Junius," the pseudonymous gadfly, and the elder Pitt, now Earl of Chatham. Likewise, *The Patriot* (1774) distilled thirty years of scorn into Johnson's demystification of the term. His claim that "Patriotism is the last refuge of a scoundrel" is better known (*Life*, II, 348), but this essay, "Addressed to the Electors of Great Britain," is devoted to the exposure of what Johnson sees as interest and ambition masquerading as love of country.

One variety of false patriotism he attacks is "American usurpation," discussed at length in his last and longest pamphlet, *Taxation No Tyranny* (1775). His attitude toward the colonies brought him into conflict with his great friend and political opposite, Edmund Burke. He considers the taxation of the American colonists by Britain to pay for the cost of their defense in earlier years entirely valid. Their claims that they are unrepresented in parliament he rejects on the grounds that those who would have been able to vote for their representatives have voluntarily left and that most do not have the franchise to vote. Elsewhere he had claimed that "Liberty is, to the lowest rank of every nation, little more than the choice of working or starving" ("The Bravery of English Common Soldiers" [1760], *Politics*, p. 283). Here he asks "how is it that we hear the loudest yelps for liberty from the drivers of Negroes?" (*Politics*, p. 454). The question is not simply a rhetorical ploy. Johnson's anti-slavery views and anti-colonialism were intertwined from early on, the powerful outgrowth of his belief in merchantilist self-sufficiency and his humanitarianism. He finds that European "imaginary sovereignty" leads to "Rapine, Bloodshed and Desolation";[6] and he deplores the effect of colonialism upon both "the oppressed" and "the oppressers": "Happy had it then been for the oppressed, if the designs of Henry [the Navigator, of Portugal] had slept in his bosom, and surely more happy for the oppressors" (*Works*, II, 220).

Johnson, however, was proudest of his first pamphlet, *The False Alarm* (1770). He had no qualms about supporting the House of Commons' expulsion of the profligate John Wilkes, even when they went farther and ruled someone with fewer votes seated. He also approved of the use of general warrants to arrest Wilkes. Johnson's philosophical and historical argument takes the high ground and mentions Wilkes himself only with passing contempt as one currently jailed for "sedition and impiety." He thinks there is no constitutional issue at stake and gives a good brief account of his historical conception of British government:

> Governments formed by chance, and gradually improved by such expedients, as the successive discovery of their defects happened to suggest, are never to be tried by a regular theory. They are fabricks of dissimilar materials, raised by different architects, upon different plans. We must be content with them as they are; should we attempt to mend their disproportions, we might easily demolish, and difficultly rebuild them. (*Politics*, p. 328)

Despite his mentioning in the *Preceptor* the right of the Englishman, that "second legislator," to petition Parliament, he attacks the petitioning movement that supported Wilkes, and satirizes the activities of a typical election. The case had the important subsidiary effect of leading the House of Commons to condemn general warrants, though Johnson thought Wilkes and his case had very little to do with liberty. Wilkes, grown conservative, spent his later years shooting rioters in defense of the Bank of England and reprehending the French Revolution. Johnson's treatment of Wilkes's supporters reminds us that the same people with whom Johnson sympathized as the poor, were sometimes attacked by him as "the rabble." *The False Alarm* also attacks the Tories' "frigid neutrality," on the topic of general warrants, a rare public disagreement with the Tories in parliament.

While these are Johnson's main political works, other works, such as *Rasselas* (1759), *A Journey to the Western Islands of Scotland* (1775), and the *Lives of the Poets* (1779–81), exemplify a politics without having a political agenda. Any full scholarly account of Johnson's political thought would necessarily have to take them into account. Those discussed here challenge the idea of Johnson as a bundle of Tory tics who sometimes "talked for victory," and at others humorously overstated his position, the idea of Johnson derived mainly from Boswell's

Life. The political Johnson, however, was a trenchant opposition satirist and the most able political journalist of his day. He was grounded in the representation of all sides in parliamentary debate, and in the history of the laws and language of his country. Johnson's later politics was devoted to defending the government position, of which he approved, against perceived radical threats, internal and external, but seeing him as "opposing the tide of history" will only distort his views.[7] The Johnson who proclaimed that "A decent provision for the poor is the true test of civilization," and who struggled against capital punishment, slavery, and colonialism (which included the treatment of the Catholics of Ireland) was in advance of his age. But such a claim reinscribes the Whig view of history. To see Johnson's politics accurately and fairly, one must see it whole.

NOTES

1 The main accounts of Johnson's politics are those by Donald Greene, J. C. D. Clark, and John Cannon (see "Further reading"). A convenient account of the dispute about Johnson's putative Jacobitism can be found in the following essays in *AJ*, 7 (1996): Howard Erskine-Hill, "Johnson the Jacobite? A Response to the New Introduction to Donald Greene's *The Politics of Samuel Johnson*" (3–26); J. C. D. Clark, "The Politics of Samuel Johnson" (27–56); Donald Greene, "Johnson: The Jacobite Legend Exhumed. A Rejoinder to Howard Erskine-Hill and J. C. D. Clark" (57–136); Thomas M. Curley, "Johnson No Jacobite; or, Treason Not Yet Unmasked" (137–62); and Howard D. Weinbrot, "Johnson, Jacobitism, and the Historiography of Nostalgia" (163–212); and in the following essays in *AJ*, 8 (1997): Howard Erskine-Hill, "A Kind of Liking for Jacobitism" (3–14); J. C. D. Clark, "The Cultural Identity of Samuel Johnson" (15–70); Donald Greene, "Jonathan Clark and the Abominable Cultural Mind-Set" (71–88); Howard D. Weinbrot, "Johnson and Jacobitism Redux: Evidence, Interpretation, and Intellectual History" (89–126); and Thomas M. Curley, "Johnson No Jacobite; or, Treason Not Yet Unmasked Part II, a Quotable Rejoinder from A to C" (127–31).

2 See John Cannon, *Samuel Johnson and the Politics of Hanoverian England* (Oxford: Clarendon Press, 1994), pp. 122–23.

3 Cannon, *Samuel Johnson and the Politics of Hanoverian England*, p. 112.

4 See Donald J. Greene, *The Politics of Samuel Johnson* (New Haven: Yale University Press, 1960), pp. 99–105.

5 See Robert Chambers, *Course of Lectures on the English Law Delivered at Oxford 1767–1773*, ed. Thomas M. Curley, 2 vols. (Madison: University of Wisconsin Press, 1987).

6 "Appendix to Capt. Lemuel Gulliver's Account of the Famous Empire of Lilliput," *Gentlemen's Magazine*, 7 (June, 1738), 283–87, reprinted in Benjamin B. Hoover, *Samuel Johnson's Parliamentary Reporting: Debates in the Senate of Lilliput* (Berkeley: University of California Press, 1953), p. 176.

7 J. P. Hardy, Introduction, *The Political Writings of Dr. Johnson* (London: Routledge and Kegan Paul, 1968), p. xix.

8

CLEMENT HAWES

Johnson and imperialism

The most infamous evaluation of Samuel Johnson's literary *œuvre* is the broad attack launched by Thomas Babington Macaulay, in his *Encyclopedia Britannica* article of 1856. Macaulay's assessment stands soundly rejected today.[1] Yet what was really at stake in his attack – the discomfort of a Whig historiographer and colonial administrator with the universalist thought of Johnson – is seldom fully understood. Macaulay's views about Johnson's *Rasselas* thus bear quoting at some length:

> Rasselas and Imlac, Nekayah and Pekuah, are evidently meant to be Abyssinians of the eighteenth century; for the Europe which Imlac describes is the Europe of the eighteenth century: and the inmates of the Happy Valley talk familiarly of that law of gravitation which Newton discovered, and which was not fully received even at Cambridge until the eighteenth century. What a real company of Abyssinians would have been may be learned from Bruce's *Travels*. But Johnson, not content with turning filthy savages, ignorant of their letters and gorged with raw steaks cut from living cows, into philosophers as eloquent and enlightened as himself or his friend Burke, and into ladies as highly accomplished as Mrs. Lennox or Mrs. Sheridan, transferred the whole domestic system of England to Egypt.[2]

The object of Macaulay's attack here is quite pointedly Johnson's scandalous association of rationality with non-Europeans. Indeed, what most troubles Macaulay is Johnson's audacious universalism: what an older generation of scholars identified as "Enlightenment Uniformitarianism." Johnson's uniformitarian thought is simultaneously a product of the emancipatory potential of the eighteenth-century Enlightenment and refusal – almost in advance, as it were – of the Enlightenment's eventual rearticulation from within the exclusive and racial logic of an imperial Eurocentrism. It is Johnson's principled universalism that ultimately fails to harmonize with Macaulay's imperialist worldview. The purpose of this essay is precisely to recover in the writings of Johnson the emancipatory potential of uniformitarian thought: a critique of imperial ideology all the more telling precisely because it arises from within the Enlightenment.

Macaulay's criticism of Johnson belongs to a moment of violent revisionism that is still poorly understood: a moment beginning in the later eighteenth century during which an emergent racializing process, fueled by the simultaneous projects of nation- and empire-building, began to lead to quite drastic rewritings of political and cultural history. It was a process, during the era of "race thinking before racism," as Hannah Arendt puts it,[3] by which the past itself, in short, was colonized by the modern category of "race."[4] The well-known speculative historicism of the second half of the eighteenth century can thus be more polemically described as the beginning of a "Romantic-racialist" rewriting of history.[5] This evolutionary historicism, which began to view Europe as the fulfillment of a "westering" world-historical process, would eventually consolidate the emerging imperial binary of "the West and the rest" into a newly racialized version of the past.[6] Within such a logic, Europe's superior claim to rationality could be traced back, in the anachronistic terms of "race," to the "Greek miracle" of classical Athens. [7] Indeed, by the 1790s, the notion that Europeans enjoy an exclusive racial monopoly on the faculty of rationality began to escalate into the fabrication of the continuous history of a uniquely rational white "race" – now named, for the first time, either "Caucasians" or "Aryans."[8] This *recuperation* of the Enlightenment – this fateful diversion of its emancipatory energies into a program of race-based domination – continues to distort our understanding of Johnson's eighteenth-century moment.

Given that the theme of a uniquely civilized "race" was already surfacing by the 1750s,[9] Johnson's lifelong insistence on the uniformity of human nature is in fact much more than the expression of an admirably humane sensibility. For Johnson's views about human nature, though often understood as just another instance of his moral decency, inform one of his greatest achievements. In Johnson's earliest writing about Africa, the Preface to his translation of the Portuguese Jesuit Jerome Lobo's *A Voyage to Abyssinia* (1735), he writes "wherever human nature is to be found, there is a mixture of vice and virtue, a contest of passion and reason; and . . . the Creator doth not appear partial in his distributions" (*Abyssinia*, pp. 3–4). This spare universalism informs Johnson's subsequent efforts to envision the possibility of fair and friendly cross-cultural exchanges and also his scathing denunciations of the spurious universalism that was serving to underwrite imperialism. Indeed, what we find in Johnson's practice of uniformitarianism is nothing less than an alternative that transcends the debilitating choice between a phony universalism, on the one hand, and, on the other, a cheap and easy relativism that renounces all hope of finding common ground.[10] Johnson's uniformitarian ideal gains real force precisely because – unlike, say, the American revolutionary Thomas Jefferson – he refuses silently to accommodate its emancipatory potential to the racist agendas of slavery and settler-colonialism: a fatal contradiction of the American revolutionaries that Johnson registers in his famous observation that "the loudest yelps for liberty are

Plate 4 S. Diamantis, ink drawing from the Arabic translation of *Rasselas* by Kamel el Mohandes and Magdi Whaba (1959)

coming from the drivers of Negroes" (*Politics*, p. 454). Thus Johnson's uniformitarian ideals cannot be reduced to a mere stalking-horse for Eurocentrism. And it is he, rather than the relentlessly progress-oriented Macaulay, whose work now seems prescient and anticipatory.

The most telling example of the radical potential of Johnson's uniformitarian thought is *Rasselas* (1759). Although *Rasselas* is ostensibly an "oriental" tale, it is notable above all for the marked absence of a reifying local color. It seems likely, for example, that Johnson picked the setting of Coptic Christianity in the highlands of Ethiopia as a way of reminding his Protestant readers of Christianity's location, during its formative years, in the deserts of West Asia and North Africa. And one finds more emphasis in *Rasselas* on African engineers, philosophers, theologians, astronomers, architects, and poets than on exotic customs and animals. Even the harem in which Pekuah is temporarily confined disappoints all expectations of salacious "Oriental" excess: it is merely a dull prison.

Plate 5 S. Diamantis, ink drawing from the Arabic translation of *Rasselas* (1959)

Rasselas, moreover, exemplifies a remarkably sophisticated engagement with those older civilizations whose reputations were becoming increasingly vulnerable to imperial revisionism. Johnson has no difficulty during the book's Egyptian chapters in acknowledging the pyramids as (excepting the Great Wall of China), "the greatest work of man" (*Rasselas*, p. 117). In Imlac's words to Rasselas: "You are in a country famous among the earliest monarchies for the power and wisdom of its inhabitants; a country where the sciences first dawned that illuminate the world, and beyond which the arts cannot be traced of civil society or domestic life" (p. 111). Egyptians, in other words, are the originators of civilization. "The ruins of their architecture," Imlac goes on to say, "are the schools for modern builders" (p. 111). Johnson, furthermore, does not emphasize the pyramids' monumentality merely as a pretext for lamenting the terrible decline of present-day Egyptians from their ancient greatness, a favorite imperial theme. And it is precisely in the spirit of a wholehearted engagement with Egyptian civilization that Johnson's generous admiration does not preclude a criticism of what he considered to be its oppressive features. Thus he complicates our wonder at the pyramids by introducing a theme of slave-labor, reminding us that the great monuments were built by "thousands labouring without end" (p. 119). This insight, coming as it does at the end of a response to the whole of Egyptian civilization, cannot be taken as a mere gibe at "Oriental despotism." It is, rather, a deflation of the irrational pride and ennui typical of ruling classes everywhere – of a universal "hunger of imagination," as Imlac puts it (p. 118).

Even when *Rasselas* seemingly comes closest to incorporating the emergent Eurocentric narrative of the "westering of civilization" and its ubiquitous theme of evolutionary progress, the novella is redeemed by Johnson's scrupulous and overriding commitment to uniformitarian ideals. Thus, in a charged passage, Johnson permits his African characters to confront eighteenth-century imperial conquest directly. Ethiopian Christians, who constantly debate the logic of social and political institutions throughout *Rasselas*, dedicate their intellectual acumen to the question of why colonization seems to occur in one direction only. One should not underestimate the salutary shock, moreover, of the simple fact that Johnson's readers are thus placed in the position of registering the violent intersection of their world with that of characters with whom they have been encouraged to identify.

Imlac's musings on the global supremacy of northwestern Europe stress naval power and its economic basis: "'From Persia . . . I travelled through Syria, and for three years resided in Palestine, where I conversed with great numbers of the northern and western nations of Europe; the nations which are now in possession of all power and all knowledge; whose armies are irresistible, and whose fleets command the remotest parts of the globe'" (*Rasselas*, p. 46). Imlac's recognition of this current imbalance in power and knowledge led him, as he explains, to an inevitable contemplation of "difference":

> "When I compared these men with the natives of our own kingdom, they appeared almost another order of beings. In their countries it is difficult to wish for anything that may not be obtained: a thousand arts of which we have never heard are continually labouring for their convenience and pleasure; and whatever their own climate has denied them is supplied by their commerce." (p. 46)

It is worth noting the dispassionate tone with which Imlac registers this difference: he knows, and can calmly assess the value of, what he does not know.

To Imlac's description of Europe's apparent monopoly on wealth and power Rasselas replies with a question about the direction of world history: "'By what means . . . are the Europeans thus powerful? Or why, since they can so easily visit Asia and Africa for trade or conquest, cannot the Asiatics and Africans invade their coasts, plant colonies in their ports, and give laws to their natural princes? The same wind that carries them back would bring us thither'" (pp. 46–47). And Imlac then replies: "'They are more powerful, sir, than we . . . because they are wiser; knowledge will always predominate over ignorance, as man governs the other animals. But why their knowledge is more than ours, I know not what reason can be given but the unsearchable will of the Supreme Being'" (p. 47). It might seem in this last exchange that Johnson flirts with the hemispheric or "westering" understanding of the "progress" ideal. Both the animal reference and the phrase "almost another order of beings" suggests the well-known rearticulation of the Great Chain of Being in evolutionary terms.

It is crucial, however, to recognize the subtlety with which *Rasselas* addresses this most powerful of imperial themes. First of all, Imlac does say *"almost another order of beings"*; and the phrase itself is further deflated in a later passage, in which the superficial appearance of happiness in others – "such spritliness of air, and volatility of fancy, as might have suited beings of an higher order" (p. 66) – is revealed to be an illusion. Furthermore, the pointedly non-racial explanation given for the contemporary global imbalance of power – "the unsearchable will of the Supreme Being" – refuses any sort of racial essentialism by way of accounting for the imbalance. The supernatural reference introduces contingency rather than inevitability: a point, indeed, that Johnson reinforced some twenty years later to Boswell while pointing to this very passage of *Rasselas*. "This, Sir," Johnson said, "no man can explain otherwise" (*Life*, IV, 119).

Finally, one must note the deflating conclusion of this chapter, which fully acknowledges the material benefits of progress without assigning undue significance to their uneven distribution. After Rasselas rhapsodizes about those benefits, Imlac replies as follows: "The Europeans . . . are less unhappy than we, but they are not happy. Human life everywhere is a state in which much is to be endured, and little to be enjoyed" (*Rasselas*, p. 50). This illustrates that the belief in a universal human nature provides a crucial check on the ascription of a *racial* significance to uneven developments in the material infrastructure of cultures. The key point is that Johnson stubbornly refuses to link rationality – in his view, a universal, though also universally fragile and embattled, human characteristic – to any particular geographical site. So in *Rasselas*, and so throughout Johnson's *œuvre*.

Johnson's scrupulously minimalist universalism, as seen in *Rasselas*, is to be sharply distinguished from the false universalism inherent in the rhetoric that subtended imperial expansion. A study of Johnson's attitude toward empire, as Donald Greene, Thomas Curley, and Steven Scherwatzky have demonstrated, shows his systematic and lifelong loathing of imperialism.[11] Moreover, the basis of Johnson's anti-imperialism was precisely his profound antipathy to the sham universalism by which a racially exclusive notion of "progress" was ideologically deployed to underwrite exploitation abroad. Despite his own patriotism, Johnson had an acute awareness that modern nation-building was profoundly shaped by the brutal oppression of aboriginal populations. He often insisted on the legal, ethical, and political standing of aboriginal rights to annexed land, Johnson's abhorrence of colonialism is so systematic that it leaks into the quotations he selected for his *Dictionary*. Under *native*, for example, he quotes Francis Bacon: "Make no extermination of the natives under pretence of planting religion. God surely will no way be pleased with such sacrifices."

Johnson's critique of colonialism thoroughly exposes the contradictions and bad faith built into an ersatz universalism that denied full humanity to colonized peoples. In his Introduction to *The World Displayed* (1759), which deserves to be much better known than it is, Johnson performs an extraordinary delegitimation of such imperial civilization-mongering (*Works*, II, 208–34). Johnson uses the occasion of introducing a multi-volume assemblage of European voyage literature, as James Basker points out, to highlight the gratuitous violence, mass enslavement, bad faith, and sheer greed that accompanied such exploration.[12] Indeed, Johnson even remarks on the absence, in his historical sources, of any indignation toward this familiar pattern of colonial violence. Of one incident among many involving Portuguese violence against Africans, as recounted by Lafitau, Johnson writes the following:

> On what occasion, or for what purpose, cannons and muskets were discharged among a people harmless and secure, by strangers who without any right visited their coast, it is not thought necessary to inform us. The Portuguese could fear nothing from them, and had therefore no adequate provocation; nor is there any reason to believe but that they murdered the negroes in wanton merriment, perhaps only to try how many a volley would destroy, or what would be the consternation of those that should escape. (*Works*, II, 217–18)

The subsequent lines, in condemning the brutal attitude expressed in such violence, reverse the usual colonial ascription of "barbarity":

> We are openly told, that they had the less scruple concerning their treatment of the savage people, because they scarcely considered them as distinct from beasts; and indeed the practice of all the European nations, and among others of the English barbarians that cultivate the southern islands of America, proves, that this opinion, however absurd and foolish, however wicked and injurious, still continues to prevail. (II, 218)

This powerful paragraph then closes with a rather mournful reflection on the lethal combination of economic and psychological motives that serves to maintain racist ideology: "Interest and pride harden the heart, and it is in vain to dispute against avarice and power" (p. 218). Elsewhere the "vehemently anti-Columbus"[13] Johnson similarly debunked the much-fetishized date of 1492 as "hitherto disastrous to mankind," and noted that no part of the world had "reason to rejoice" that Columbus had eventually received the necessary financial backing for his venture (*Politics*, p. 421).

As his reference to "English barbarians" suggests, moreover, Johnson never relies on the infamy of Iberian colonial atrocities – on the "Black Legend" of the uniquely cruel Spanish conquistadors[14] – merely to legitimate by comparison a supposedly more benign British expansionism. In his *Introduction to the Political State of Great-Britain* (1756), published just as the Seven Years' War was heating up, Johnson uses the English phase of early European expansion to explain, and thus unmask, the militaristic political ethos of mid-eighteenth-century Britain. Of Jamaica Johnson remarks that it continues, even to this day, as "a place of great wealth, and dreadful wickedness, a den of tyrants, and a dungeon of slaves" (*Politics*, p. 137). And he describes the process by which English settlers colonized coastal North America as follows: "As we had, according to the *European* principles, which allow nothing to the natives of these regions, our choice of situation in this extensive country, we naturally fixed our habitations along the coast" (p. 147).

This remarkable indictment of British colonial aggression winds up by observing that the French settlers, having built somewhat better relations in North America with its indigenous inhabitants than did the British, may now enjoy a military advantage there. Johnson never forgets that the French are there as colonial robbers; but even so, as he observes drily, they threaten to outperform the British military because they do not add insult to injury by, for example, prohibiting intermarriage on racist grounds. The final sentence of this piece warns that "our traders hourly alienate the *Indians* by their tricks and oppressions, and we continue every day to show new proofs, that no people can be great who have ceased to be virtuous" (p. 150). Johnson goes even further in *Idler* 81, an attack on patriotic war-fever that was published some three years later. In this bold essay Johnson assumes the perspective of an "Indian" chief dispassionately hoping the competing French and British armies will decimate one another: "Let us look unconcerned upon the slaughter, and remember that the death of every European delivers the country from a tyrant and a robber" (*Idler*, p. 254).

What is crucial about Johnson's critique of imperial "progress," which would have otherwise been shared to some extent by several eighteenth-century British authors,[15] is that it was not articulated from an anti-modern perspective. Johnson, indeed, seems almost uniquely agile in his approach to negotiating with the Enlightenment's contradictions. He engages simultaneously with both its emancipatory potential at home and its potential abuse as an alibi for imperial domination abroad. Contrary to a widely held critical orthodoxy – and unlike his contemporary Edmund Burke – Johnson did not write from an "anti-Enlightenment" position. Burke, who in any case wanted to regulate rather than abolish empire, is best seen as a Romantic Orientalist. Johnson, however, utterly rejected the often sentimental resistance to progress found in pastoral and exoticizing genres. He was urban to the core, for one thing, and refused to scorn material progress under the bad-faith gestures of camping out in someone else's condition of undercapitalization.

Then again, in asserting his profound skepticism toward the imperial "gift" of progress abroad, Johnson did not in fact repudiate the forces of cultural progress at home. As a journalist, novelist, poet, critic, essayist, and biographer, he poured his creative energy into extending what Jürgen Habermas has called the bourgeois public sphere.[16] In his 1781 Preface of the *Lives of the Poets*, Johnson alludes in this vein to a "nation of readers."[17] However imperfect this public sphere undoubtedly was – however much it may have been historically constituted by the exclusion of various alternative publics – it should be noted that Johnson often and repeatedly embraced its anti-elitist potential. In "The Duty of a Journalist," for example, he asserted that it was the duty of a journalist "to consider himself not as writing to students or statesmen alone, but to women, shopkeepers, to artisans, who have little time to bestow upon mental attainments, but desire, upon easy terms, to know how the world goes" (Greene, p. 545). Johnson indeed refers frequently in his writings to the touchstone of the "common reader." Moreover, the anti-elitist significance of the marketplace is resoundingly affirmed in Johnson's famously exasperated rejection of Chesterfield's patronage in favor of the bookseller's hard cash.[18] This bourgeois public sphere arguably produced a more egalitarian sense of national identity, to which many of Johnson's major works – the Shakespeare edition, the *Dictionary*, the *Lives of the Poets* – are landmark contributions. It should be noted too that Johnson's wariness toward a rule-bound neo-classicism and his distaste for a too Frenchified literary language situate him, like many progressive nationalists of the era, as rejecting the inaccessible cultural capital of a Francophile elite in favor of more widely accessible cultural productions.[19]

What is often caricatured in Johnson as mere Tory politics is thus better seen as a specifically modern resistance to the emerging equation of the Enlightenment with "imperial progress." Johnson's minimalist universalism was heir to the legacy of the Enlightenment's emancipatory potential. Posterity, however, has too often chosen to deflect the challenge of Johnson's agile and selective negotiations with "progress" with a critical vocabulary that tends either to push his achievement into a distant past or to neutralize its critical force. It is our loss that Johnson's universalism has yet to be mined and reforged as a tool for contemporary critiques of imperialist and racist ideology.

The potential of Johnson's usefulness for the most critically advanced aspects of contemporary scholarship has surely been obscured by certain familiar gestures that confine him to the domain of the *passé*. For there is more than a coincidental link between Becky Sharpe's famous "junking Johnson" gesture – her throwing Johnson's *Dictionary* out of the carriage window in the first chapter of Thackeray's *Vanity Fair* – and Macaulay's notorious declaration, as the chief architect of an Anglicizing educational curriculum in India, that "a single shelf of a good European library [is] worth the whole native literature of India and Arabia."[20] In other words, nineteenth-century Anglicizing required a rewriting not only of the colonized, but also of the colonizer: a consignment to prehistory of awkward contradictions in Britain's own past. Macaulay thus produced a familiar narrative of literary history in which a caricature of Johnson figures as at best the inevitably doomed foil, something like the last of the Mohicans, over which later unfoldings of tradition must inevitably roll. He thus describes

Johnson as entering into London society as "the solitary specimen of a past age."[21] Macaulay also compares Johnson to Fielding's drolly retrograde Squire Western (p. 529). And he attacks Johnson's prose style as cumbersome and medieval: "Like those unfortunate chiefs of the middle ages who were suffocated by their own chain-mail," Macaulay writes of Johnson, "his maxims perish under that load of words which was designed for their defence and ornament" (p. 532). The full triumph of Macaulay's consignment of Johnson to prehistoric irrelevance is perhaps best illustrated by the disingenuous observation in 1924 by a British literary historian devoted to tracing the evolution of imperial literature: "One does not look to the universal wisdom of Dr. Johnson for much of note on matters of empire."[22]

Given that Macaulay refers us to James Bruce's *Travels* to learn what "a real company of Abyssinians" would have been like in Johnson's time, it is worth noting here that Macaulay's selective mobilization of Bruce's text also oversimplifies the complexity of the latter's account of eighteenth-century Ethiopian cultures. Bruce, for example, though burdened with no small imperial arrogance – and though explicitly not opposed to slavery in either the new world or the old – devotes only a page or so of his multi-volume work to the "live steak" incident that so exercises Macaulay.[23] And it is very doubtful that Macaulay would have endorsed Bruce's own historicist exercise in tracing civilization back to its supposed originators: according to his idiosyncratic philological reconstruction, the ancient Ethiopians (II, chapter 3).

It is Macaulay's strategic positioning of Johnson – as the epitome of the retrograde in a triumphalist narrative of "progress" – that has proved to be crucially influential for cultural history. For just as Johnson's thought failed to harmonize with imperial historiography, so it now proves to be a stumbling block for contemporary schools of thought that reverse Macaulay's judgments but fail to challenge, or even to recognize, his racialized version of history. It is not otherwise obvious why contemporary thinkers would persist in failing to recognize in Johnson a supreme example of the Enlightenment's capacity for self-critique.

Johnson's stringently modest universalism, despite the dismissive way it has repeatedly been positioned, could and should be an immensely relevant resource for a contemporary moment much preoccupied with the problem of cultural difference. Indeed, Johnson's contribution to thinking "difference" can be seen as more flexible and intelligent than many a contemporary theory in which the rhetorical courting of "difference" escalates quickly into absolute incommensurability. On the one hand, Johnson does not neglect the fact that human beings can be, and frequently are, divided by great discrepancies in their historical experiences. On the other, however, Johnson's analysis goes a step beyond the gesture of merely instituting a plurality of relativized perspectives: an inevitably ambiguous gesture that can as easily prescribe and fix oppressive differences as manifest neglected ones. It is indeed a crucial issue that Johnson pointedly refuses to freeze-dry such historically contingent categories of difference as "East" and "West" into self-explanatory and insular essences.

Johnson seems remarkably prescient, above all, in having anticipated the profound political disappointments that can now be tellingly summed up, in the convenient shorthand phrase of Max Horkheimer and Theodor Adorno, as the "dialectic of Enlightenment": the obscene complicity, that is, of a certain rationality with the most lethal and horrific systems of domination. Johnson, however, escapes precisely the traps into which Horkheimer and Adorno, and many thinkers after them, repeatedly fall in attempting to critique that rationality. For in their *Dialectic of Enlightenment* (1947), Horkheimer and Adorno undermine the critical force of their own argument by repeating, through mere inversion, the founding gesture of Romantic racialist historiography: they demonize a supposedly "Western" pathology, instrumental reason, by tracing this sinister faculty all the way back to its "origins" in Greek antiquity. Having failed to acknowledge the rupture produced by the rewriting of history in racialized terms, they lapse into the anachronism of extending a racially imagined "us" and "them" all the way back to the epoch of ancient civilizations. Johnson's thought, unhampered by the disabling racial logic of this anachronism, produces instead a thoroughly immanent critique of the Enlightenment. His eloquent critique insists on assuming at least a universal human faculty for practical and moral reflection, without which there can be little choice other than a banal and unhistorical relativism. Thus Johnson's anti-colonial writings, precisely because they remain stubbornly in and of the Enlightenment, provide almost uniquely supple and forceful examples of critical resistance to the hijacking of reason for purposes of domination.

NOTES

1 I am very grateful to Manuel Schonhorn, Mrinalini Sinha, and Greg Clingham for the benefit of their generously engaged responses to earlier versions of this essay.
2 Thomas Babington Macaulay, "Samuel Johnson" in *Selected Writings*, ed. John Clive and Thomas Pinney (University of Chicago Press, 1972), p. 145.
3 See Hannah Arendt, "Race-Thinking before Racism," in *Imperialism* (New York: Harvest and Harcourt, Brace, and Jovanovich, 1951), pp. 38–64. See also Kwame Anthony Appiah, "Race," in *Critical Terms for Literary Study*, ed. Frank Lentricchia and Thomas McLaughlin (University of Chicago Press, 1990), p. 282.
4 See Clement Hawes, "Leading History by the Nose: The Turn to the Eighteenth Century in *Midnight's Children*," *Modern Fiction Studies*, 39 (1993), 147–68.
5 See Vasant Kaiwar, "Racism and the Writing of History," *South Asia Bulletin*, 9 (1989), 32–56; and Gerald Newman, *The Rise of English Nationalism: A Cultural History 1740–1830* (New York: St. Martin's Press, 1987), pp. 114–22.
6 See Nigel Leask, *British Romantic Writers and the East: Anxieties of Empire* (Cambridge University Press, 1992).

7 This has been most forcefully argued by Martin Bernal in *Black Athena: The Afroasiatic Roots of Classical Civilization*, 2 vols. (New Brunswick: Rutgers University Press, 1987), I: *The Fabrication of Ancient Greece 1785–1985*, pp. 281–336.

8 For the origins of "Aryan," put into circulation in 1794 by the Sanskrit scholar and colonial judge William Jones, see Bernal, *Black Athena*, pp. 220, 478 (n. 113). For the most substantial analysis of the ideological impact of this racial anachronism on the reconstruction of the Indian past, see Romila Thapar, *Interpreting Early India* (New York: Oxford University Press, 1993). For the later impact of Jones's tendency to blur linguistic and "racial" categories, see Partha Mitter, "The Aryan Myth and British Writings on Indian Art and Culture," in *Literature and Imperialism,* ed. Bart Moore-Gilbert (Roehampton: Roehampton Institute, 1983), pp. 69–92. For the origins of "Caucasian," first put into print in 1795 by Johann Friedrich Blumenbach, see Stephen Jay Gould, "The Geometer of Race," *Discovery* (Nov. 1994), 65–69.

9 Among the earliest and most notorious anticipations of this imperial revisionism is a footnote added in 1753–54 to David Hume's essay, "Of National Characters" (1748), in which he denies that non-white peoples ever produced any glimmerings of civilization: "No ingenious manufactures amongst them, no arts, no sciences." See David Hume, *Essays: Moral, Political and Literary* (Oxford University Press, 1974), p. 213.

10 See S. P. Mohanty, "Us and Them: On the Philosophical Bases of Political Criticism," *Yale Journal of Criticism*, 2 (1989), 1–31.

11 See Donald Greene, *The Politics of Samuel Johnson*, 2nd edn. (Athens: University of Georgia Press, 1990); Thomas Curley, "Johnson and America," *AJ*, 6 (1994), 31–73; and Steven D. Scherwatzky, "Johnson, *Rasselas*, and the Politics of Empire, *ECL*, 16 (1992), 103–33.

12 James Basker, "Samuel Johnson and the African–American Reader," *The New Rambler* (1994/95), 47–57.

13 See Donald Greene, "Johnson and Columbus," *Johnsonian Newsletter* 52–53 (June 1992 – June 1993), 23.

14 See Roberto Fernández Retamar, "Against the Black Legend," in *Caliban and Other Essays*, trans. Edward Baker (Minneapolis: University of Minnesota Press, 1989), pp. 56–73.

15 See Clement Hawes, "Three Times Round the Globe: Gulliver and Colonial Discourse," *Cultural Critique*, 18 (1991), 187–214.

16 Jürgen Habermas, *The Structural Transformation of the Public Sphere: An Inquiry into a Category of Bourgeois Society*, trans. Thomas Burger, with the assistance of Frederick Lawrence (Cambridge, MA: MIT, 1989).

17 See John Cannon, *Samuel Johnson and the Politics of Hanoverian England* (Oxford: Clarendon Press, 1994), chapter 7, "Johnson and Nationalism."

18 See Alvin Kernan, *Samuel Johnson and the Impact of Print* (Princeton University Press, 1987), pp. 199–203.

19 See Michael Dobson, *The Making of a National Poet: Shakespeare, Adaptation and Authorship 1660–1769* (Oxford: Clarendon Press, 1992), pp. 185–222.

20 Macaulay, "Minute on Indian Education," in *Selected Writings*. p. 241.

21 Review of John Wilson Croker's edition of Boswell's *Life of Johnson* (1831), in *The Works of Lord Macaulay*, ed. Lady Trevelyan, 8 vols. (London: Longmans, Green, 1875), V, 524.

22 Edward Salmon, *The British Empire*, 12 vols., ed. Hugh Gunn (London: W. Collins, 1924), II: *The Literature of the Empire*, p. 83.

23 See James Bruce, *Travels to Discover the Source of the Nile in the Years 1768, 1769, 1770, 1771, 1772, & 1773*, 2nd edn., 8 vols. (Edinburgh: James Ballantyne, 1804). I am grateful to the John J. Burns Library, Boston College (Williams Collection), for access to Bruce's *Travels*.

9

FRED PARKER

The skepticism of Johnson's *Rasselas*

Rasselas was written and published in 1759, and immediately became a popular work, running to several editions in the course of Johnson's lifetime and being frequently reprinted thereafter. It is still the best known of any of Johnson's works, and is probably the best place to start for anyone coming to Johnson for the first time. It is short, for one thing, saying much in relatively few pages. It deals with a self-evidently large and interesting subject – Johnson thought of titling it "The Choice of Life" – and does so without reference to intellectual or historical matters now become obscure. It has the congenial form of a narrative fiction, and although it is unlike what the modern reader would think of as a novel, the narrative form remains essential to its effect: the unwinding line of the story and the contingency of event play against the discursive, intellectualizing impulse in a way that releases some of Johnson's best writing, here as in the *Lives of the Poets*. And, perhaps more unmistakably than any of his other works, *Rasselas* impresses with the power of Johnson's intelligence, the "strength of thought" which, as he says in the "Life of Cowley," is essential to any account of true wit (*Lives*, I, 20).

This quality of intelligence is more easily felt than defined; it conveys the sense of accumulated reflection upon experience being forcefully brought to bear upon a single point. It can manifest itself as a power of aphoristic compression: "Marriage has many pains, but celibacy has no pleasures" (p. 99). It regularly shows itself in Johnson's acuteness of logical distinction: "'Inconsistencies, answered Imlac, cannot both be right, but, imputed to man, they may both be true. Yet diversity is not inconsistency'" (p. 33). Sometimes it is to be felt in the penetration of Johnson's analysis of experience, especially internal experience:

> "No disease of the imagination," answered Imlac, "is so difficult of cure, as that which is complicated with the dread of guilt: fancy and conscience then act interchangeably upon us, and so often shift their places, that the illusions of one are not distinguished from the dictates of the other . . . For this reason the superstitious are often melancholy, and the melancholy almost always superstitious." (p. 162)

Most obviously, Johnson's intelligence appears in the discussions of particular subjects. Such are the "dissertation upon poetry," in chapter 10; the discussion of the motives for pilgrimage, in chapter 11; the advocacy and retraction of stoicism, in chapter 18; Imlac's account of the value of knowledge of the past, in chapter 30; the account of "the dangerous prevalence of imagination," triggered by the madness of the astronomer, in chapter 44; and the pervasive balancing of the evils against the advantages of society: this last topic is most explicitly discussed in the hermit's history (chapter 21), the debate on marriage (chapters 28–29), and the canvasing of monastic retirement (chapter 47). These passages are not only highly interesting in themselves, they also represent leading thoughts of Johnson's which frequently reappear, with altered emphasis or in other contexts, throughout his work. I would not wish to claim that *Rasselas* is in some sense the "key" to Johnson, but it does offer a point of vantage from which to appreciate the coherence and interconnectedness of his whole thought.

This is particularly true of the model of human psychology on which *Rasselas* depends: this rests upon the notion of the insatiability of the human mind. Rasselas has grown up in the Happy Valley, with every conceivable means of gratification at his beck and call, and finds himself, notwithstanding, a prey to ennui. Fundamental to all Johnson's thought is the proposition that to be filled by the present moment is not possible for any tolerably active and energetic mind, and Rasselas's restlessness forces him to be on the move, at first exclusively in imagination, in hopes and dreams about the outside world and the role he will play in it, and then in reality, as, under the guidance of the poet Imlac, a man of wide and long experience, he escapes to begin his survey of the living world. He undertakes this survey in order to make a rational "choice of life" and identify the form of life most conducive to happiness; his desire is thus for moral knowledge of a kind adequate to determine choice and justify action. But this proves to be a desire which cannot be fulfilled, despite the advantages of an apparently limitless budget and an all-knowing travel guide: partly because of the inherent difficulty of drawing general inferences from the many-sided complexity of life, but most fundamentally because that same radical restlessness which drives Rasselas on his quest ensures that not even the wisest of his interviewees can report themselves as happy or fulfilled

The understanding of the mind as insatiable can be traced through much of Johnson's other moral and critical writing. Several of the best of the *Rambler* essays deal with our inability to rest in the present moment, our need to live in the potentially unreal dimension of our memories, hopes, and fears; Johnson represents this restlessness as both essential and perilous to our humanity. The Preface to the *Dictionary* is largely offered as a meditation on the inevitable gap between design and performance; the desire to fix and define meaning, in particular, is one of those projects of the mind which can never be realized in actuality. Johnson's literary criticism rests on the conviction that we read in order to be delivered from "the common satiety of life," a deliverance which is, however, most readily achieved through "irregular combinations of fanciful invention" (*Shakespeare*, I, 61) whose novelty-value soon, in turn, wears out; enduring valuable work must therefore meet the paradoxical criterion of being "at once natural and new" ("Life of Cowley," *Lives*, I, 20). More generally, it is Johnson's sense of the disequilibrium between the vitality of our fantasies and the meager satisfactions offered by actuality that makes him so often represent experience according to the rhythm of expectation modified or subverted (e.g. in the *Journey to the Western Islands*), that makes him write so powerfully on the pull of the subjective imagination (e.g. the striking way he describes simple day-dreaming in *Rambler* 89: "this invisible riot of the mind, this secret prodigality of being" [IV, 106]), and that drives his recurrent emphasis on the need for the intellectual or the solitary to participate in the social world. Walter Jackson Bate has written well[1] on how the connections between Johnson's analysis of psychology and his moral thought are focused in Imlac's comment on the great pyramid:

> "It seems to have been erected only in compliance with that hunger of imagination which preys incessantly upon life, and must be always appeased by some employment. Those who have already all that they can enjoy, must enlarge their desires. He that has built for use, till use is supplied, must begin to build for vanity, and extend his plan to the utmost power of human performance, that he may not soon be reduced to form another wish."
>
> "I consider this mighty structure as a monument of the insufficiency of human enjoyments."
>
> (*Rasselas*, pp. 118–19)

Yet to lay too much emphasis on the interest of Johnson's thought as a "content" of *Rasselas* is to lose sight of *Rasselas* as a work of literature. It would be a mistake to take the kind of authoritative pronouncement by Imlac quoted above as the ground-note of *Rasselas*, or to think that the value of the work can be defined as a repository of Johnson's generalizations about human life. Such wise generalizations are, after all, precisely what Rasselas goes in search of, but under the pressure of experience finds continually to break down, or to point in bewilderingly different directions. A large source of Johnson's vitality as a writer and thinker is the paradoxical coexistence of two things: on the one hand, the impulse toward generalization and positive, weighty assertion – which is so memorably transmitted by Boswell that one rather too readily classifies it as quintessentially "Johnsonian" – and on the other hand, a no less fundamental skepticism with regard to all systematic theorizing and to the adequacy of all general formulations. In the *Dictionary* "enthusiasm" is defined as "1. A vain belief of private revelation; a vain confidence of divine favour or communication. 2. Heat of imagination; violence of passion; confidence of opinion." "Confidence of opinion" is not, it seems, distinguishable from "heat of imagination"; it is always likely to involve a knowingness that is the antithesis of true intelligence. The extreme case of knowingness is Soame Jenyns's attempt to demonstrate the harmony of the cosmos in *A Free Inquiry into the Nature and Origin of Evil* (1757), of which Johnson wrote:

> When this author presumes to speak of the universe, I would advise him a little to distrust his own faculties, however large and comprehensive . . . I do not mean to reproach this author for not knowing what is equally hidden from learning and from ignorance. The shame is to impose words for ideas upon ourselves or others. To imagine that we are going forward when we are only turning round.
>
> (Greene, pp. 531, 534)

The nearest approximation to this critique in *Rasselas* is Johnson's funny treatment of the philosopher who advocates living according to nature, in chapter 22. But it is not only the arguments of the vain and empty-headed that are infiltrated by Johnson's skepticism. Rasselas and Nekayah sit down in good faith to consider the relation of marriage to happiness, with a wealth of empirical data and the resources of Johnson's best logic at their disposal, but are still unable to come to a conclusion. "The more we enquire, the less we can resolve" (p. 99). Nekayah's explanation of this state of affairs rephrases what Johnson had already written in *Adventurer* 107, where the syntax reinforces the felt difficulty of coming to any comprehensive conclusion:

> As a question becomes more complicated and involved, and extends to a greater number of relations, disagreement of opinion will always be multiplied, not because we are irrational, but because we are finite beings, furnished with different kinds of knowledge, exerting different degrees of attention, one discovering consequences which escape another, none taking in the whole concatenation of causes and effects, and most comprehending but a very small part; each comparing what he observes with a different criterion, and each referring it to a different purpose.
>
> (p. 441)

Johnson's skeptical identification of a mismatch between the fluid complexities of experience and the rational categories of the mind, leads naturally to the conviction that no rational certainty is to be had with regard to the great questions of life. This conviction was something Johnson shared with many of the most vigorous minds of his age. Labels are always of limited use, but this period, which used once to be called the Age of Reason, might more plausibly have been labeled the Age of Skepticism. Gibbon recorded in his autobiography how "the belief and knowledge of the child are superseded by the more rational ignorance of the man."[2] Bolingbroke wrote to Pope that the root of all error "consists in the high opinion we are apt to entertain of the human mind. . . . The less men know, the more they believe that they know."[3] Pope made this thought central to his attack on "reasoning Pride" in the *Essay on Man*, and in the first part of the "Epistle to Cobham" vividly rendered the elusiveness of experience to rational categorization. Burke's attack, in the *Reflections on the Revolution in France* (1790), on the confident rationalism of the French Revolutionaries expressed a principle that was already explicit in his earliest writings. The foolish impotence of the attempt to theorize life is given extreme and unforgettable expression in Sterne's *Tristram Shandy* (1760–67). Many more such examples could be given.

The paradigm case is perhaps the conclusion to the first book of Hume's *Treatise of Human Nature* (1738–40), as Hume considers the implications of his argument that "the understanding, when it acts alone, and according to its most general principles, entirely subverts itself," and professes himself "ready to reject all belief and reasoning," utterly "confounded" by all the great ethical questions of life.[4] Hume had brought himself to this impasse by an elaboration of the empiricist philosophy of Locke, and one powerful influence on all these writers was the intellectual revolution effected by Locke's foregrounding of epistemology – the question of how we come to know what we know – as the primary philosophical issue. Somewhat against Locke's own declared intention, the *Essay concerning Human Understanding* (1690) had radically problematized the relation between the world of objective reality, on the one hand, and the ideas of the mind, on the other. Lockean empiricism needed only the smallest logical push to generate Hume's radical skepticism, and Locke's analysis of language in the *Essay* had much to do with the heightened awareness of the slippery, fickle responsibility of words to their referents that one finds in many eighteenth-century writers: Swift, Pope, Sterne, and Johnson among them.

Yet these developments in philosophy were only part of the story, as much concomitant as cause. The great underground root feeding eighteenth-century skepticism, and attitudes to skepticism, was most probably the erosion of religious faith as the unquestionable foundation of one's life and being. It was increasingly understood that the truths of Christianity did not lend themselves to rational demonstration. Gibbon was one of many for whom the road to skepticism went through theology: converted in his youth from Anglicanism to Catholicism, and then back to Protestantism again, his familiarity with the arguments on both sides left him finally a disciple only of the skeptic Pierre Bayle. Bayle's critical dictionary, Gibbon wrote, "is a vast repository of facts and opinions; and he balances the *False* Religions in his skeptical scales, till the opposite quantities, (if I may use the language of Algebra) annihilate each other. . . . 'I am most truly (said Bayle) a protestant; for I protest indifferently against all Systems, and all Sects'" (*Memoirs*, p. 64).

Gibbon's statement is similar to how, in Hume's *Dialogues concerning Natural Religion*, the Christian and the Deist cut one another's positions to pieces while the skeptic looks smiling on. Johnson, of course, detested such skepticism in the area of religion, but we can see a distinctly similar movement of mind in Nekayah's cogent arguments both for and against marriage, as Rasselas glosses them: "Thus it happens when wrong opinions are entertained, that they mutually destroy each other, and leave the mind open to truth" (p. 104). This last phrase has a hopeful ring, but even it is immediately modified by Nekayah – the opinions are not positively "wrong" but inevitably partial – so that all the truth Rasselas ends up with is that this hugely important life-choice, like others, has to be made without being sanctioned. Life is to be lived without sanctions, without the possibility of authoritative vindication: this is the urgent intuition which animates much of the most vital writing of the eighteenth century, writing which declines old certainties, on the one hand, and new rationalisms, on the other, while remaining committed to the exercise of, in Johnson's phrase, "an obstinate rationality" (*Life*, IV, 289). Not, of course, that Johnson's intuition is always of the same kind, or treated in the same way. The matrix of comedy, anxiety, melancholy, enlightenment, and exhilaration which it generates in *Tale of a Tub* is very different from *Tristram Shandy*, and both works are very different again from *Decline and Fall of the Roman Empire*. But there is a core of skeptical intelligence which they have in common, and in which *Rasselas* too participates.

To recognize this larger context is not only interesting in itself – radical skepticism is not, after all, the invention of the late twentieth-century academy – but is also helpful in establishing a clear distance between *Rasselas* and the gravitational pull exerted by our knowledge of Johnson the man. The perennial problem in dealing with Johnson is to do justice to the rich continuities between the works and the life without letting what is achieved in the writing be absorbed into the immense but often distinct interest of Johnson's character and personality. It is, for example, a remarkable fact that *Rasselas* was written in the evenings of a single week in order that Johnson might earn money to send to his dying mother. Yet there is no accent of personal distress to be felt in the episode of the philosopher's bereavement (chapter 18), any more than Johnson's personal fear of madness is evident in the account of the astronomer's insanity (chapters 40–44), or than the discussion of immortality (chapter 48) is illuminated by what we know of Johnson's own intense anxiety concerning the afterlife. These experiences must, no doubt, have gone into the work, but they have been transformed in the writing into something independent of biographical interest, so that we are likely to go wrong if we read *Rasselas* as the expression of what we know (or think we know) of Johnson's personal character and situation.

This point is particularly worth making as a corrective to one's impression of Johnson as the supreme authority-figure, the man who lays down the law, pronounces judgment, flattens opponents in debate. Johnsonian authoritativeness is certainly an important part of the subject-matter of *Rasselas*: but *Rasselas* is not itself authoritative in that way. Its attitude to its own generalizations is clearly distinguishable from the Johnsonian assertiveness familiar through biographical anecdote, as reported in the following instance in Mrs. Thrale's *Anecdotes*:

> Mr Johnson did not like any one who said they were happy, or who said any one else was so. "It is all *cant* (he would cry), the dog knows he is miserable all the time." A friend whom he loved exceedingly, told him on some occasion notwithstanding, that his wife's sister was *really* happy, and called upon the lady to confirm his assertion, which she did somewhat roundly as we say, and with an accent and manner capable of offending Mr. Johnson, if her position had not been sufficient, without any thing more, to put him in very ill humour. "If your sister-in-law is really the contented being she professes herself Sir (said he), her life gives the lie to every research of humanity; for she is happy without health, without beauty, without money, and without understanding."   (*JM*, I, 334–5)

There is "Doctor Johnson" in full cry: overbearing, aggressive, knowledgeable, unanswerable, explosive. The position he there asserted on human happiness might seem familiar from *Rasselas*, as in the much-quoted "Human life is every where a state in which much is to be endured, and little to be enjoyed" (p. 50). But in context that pronouncement does not sound so magisterial. Imlac has been expounding the tendency of knowledge to promote happiness and speaking of the very real advantages of life enjoyed by the relatively knowledgeable Europeans. Rasselas then jumps at the hope of a necessary inference from these acknowledged relative goods to the philosophical idea of *happiness* – "They are surely happy, said the prince, who have all these conveniences" – and it is the naive, rational certainty which obliges Imlac to insist that such happiness as can be met with in practice is not an absolute but a relative condition: "The Europeans, answered Imlac, are less unhappy than we, but they are not happy. Human life is every where . . ." According to Isobel Grundy, "The weightiness of Johnson's style, and his concision in phrase-making, constantly press the reader to make that pause at the end of a general statement which will disconnect it from the progress of the argument, and make it permanent: a stone, an aphorism. On the other hand the momentum of the argument converts the individual nuggets of truth into incomplete steps in the movement to comprehend complex questions."[5]

Rasselas does not, taken as a whole, tend toward the "finished" quality of aphorism, the note of authoritative, "Johnsonian" conclusiveness. The relationship which it dramatizes between question and answer, hypothesis and experiment, restless inquiry and disabused experience – typically but not invariably presented as the Rasselas–Imlac relationship – evolves from being one in which Imlac simply corrects Rasselas's naivety, rather as Michael corrects Adam in the final books of *Paradise Lost*, into a more mobile, dialogic rhythm. Emrys Jones has argued[6] that the forty-nine chapters of the work fall naturally into three sections of sixteen chapters each, with the last chapter as a "trailing coda"; in the first section Rasselas's discontent with the Happy Valley drives him out into the world; in the second, which ends with the visit to the great pyramid, the travelers' survey of the conditions of life signally fails to yield the data they had been confidently expecting for a rational choice of life; and in the third, containing Pekuah's abduction and the encounter with the astronomer, the formal quest is tacitly set aside as the travelers find themselves drawn by events into participation in life in ways which none of them (including Imlac) had chosen or foreseen. Whether or not one subscribes to Jones's precise numerical scheme, his identification of a dynamic progression helps one to see how the conclusive generalizations on "the insufficiency of human enjoyments" (quoted above) which close the thirty-second chapter, conclude one movement only to initiate another. These great general truths are also events in a journey, moments in a process, movements from one place to another. Imlac, the nominal authority-figure, functions in dialogue mostly as a counterer, a reactive voice, opening to Rasselas's earnest straightforwardness an unexpected field of qualifications and counter-assertions, but in a way that prompts him to move forward, to initiate further inquiries. For Imlac is not a cynic nor a pessimist nor a melancholic: he has nothing that he wants to teach Rasselas, not even (until Rasselas has found it out for himself) the unfeasibility of the aspiration to a single commanding truth or point of view. Imlac himself knows this aspiration from the inside; he is, after all, a poet; and when he rises to positive, definitive generalization on what it takes to be a poet, his pronouncements – however true – are not invulnerable to a certain irony, or necessary shift in perspective, as he himself wryly acknowledges:

> He must divest himself of the prejudices of his age and country; he must consider right and wrong in their abstracted and invariable state; he must disregard present laws and opinions, and rise to general and transcendental truths, which will always be the same . . .
>
> Imlac now felt the enthusiastic fit, and was proceeding to aggrandize his own profession, when the prince cried out, "Enough! thou hast convinced me that no human being can ever be a poet. Proceed with thy narration." "To be a poet," said Imlac, "is indeed very difficult." "So difficult," returned the prince, "that I will at present hear no more of his labours. Tell me whither you went when you had seen Persia." (pp. 44–46)

One feels very clearly in this well-known scene the function of the traveling, as that which is continually moving us on through particular perspectives and prospects, however impressive they may be, to the next, different, not predictable encounter. Even when the narrator, rather than Imlac, strikes the note of comprehensiveness and finality, the Voice of Disillusionment is sustained only with a rhetorical self-consciousness that attracts its own ironies: "Ye who listen with credulity to the whispers of fancy, and pursue with eagerness the phantoms of hope, who expect that age will perform the promises of youth, and that the deficiencies of the present day will be supplied by the morrow, attend to the history of Rasselas, Prince of Abyssinia" (p. 7). Or, more subtly: "The prince, whose humanity would not suffer him to insult misery with reproof, went away convinced of the emptiness of rhetorical sound, and the inefficacy of polished periods and studied sentences" (p. 76). Those final alliterations are just obtrusive enough to make one register that the disenchantment with rhetoric is (like Berowne's in *Love's Labour's Lost*) itself expressed as a polished period and a studied sentence. The complex turn of the irony here is characteristic of the work; it is in chapter 4, for example, when Rasselas "for a few hours, regretted his regret" (p. 20), or like the splendidly orotund rejoinder of Rasselas to Nekayah in chapter 28: "'Dear princess,' said Rasselas, 'you fall into the common errours of exaggeratory declamation, by producing, in a familiar disquisition, examples of national calamities'" (p. 102); or like that pointed up in the title of the final chapter, "The conclusion, in which nothing is concluded." What this play of irony confesses – and is unexpectedly at ease with – is the instability of disillusionment, the impossibility of summing up, of stepping outside the condition of humanity for long enough to draw any final conclusions, of rising to general truths which will always be the same. To be a poet is indeed very difficult.

The significance of Johnson's irony in *Rasselas* can be brought out through the contrast with the poem Johnson had written ten years before, *The Vanity of Human Wishes*, an imitation of Juvenal's Tenth Satire. As its title suggests, the subject-matter is loosely similar to that of parts of *Rasselas*, although there is also a significant difference: whereas in *Rasselas* life will not supply the wishes of the mind, in the poem people's wishes – for power, wealth, beauty, long life – *are* met, but to their downfall. People wish for their own wretchedness: this is the general truth about the stupidity of human aspiration. Unlike *Rasselas* and its conclusion in which nothing is concluded, in the poem we get answers; it *is* conclusive in its explicit and insistent comprehensiveness. The diction is markedly more generalized than in Juvenal's original or Dryden's translation of the same original, and Johnson's poem invests Juvenal's propositions with a double generality through the working of the imitation – the case of the classical Sejanus being duplicated by that of the modern Wolsey, Hannibal by Charles XII of Sweden, and so on. The confinement of generality to the realm of language was central to the agenda of skeptically oriented empiricism: Locke abolished "general natures" from the external world, and Hume seized with delight upon Berkeley's extension of this doubt into the realm of general ideas. But in the *Vanity* the generality of the diction marches resolutely in step with the law of life which it observes. The individual cases are felt to lead inexorably to the general truth which they exemplify, as inexorably as nemesis visits the characters' desires for distinction. In *Rasselas*, a work of endlessly shifting perspectives, the notion of a comprehensive and "extensive" view is offered only by the artist who builds the flying machine which belly-flops into the lake (chapter 6), but from the first lines of the *Vanity* we really are offered just such an "extensive view." The poem is in consequence a work of quasi-tragic force, partly because the supreme generalization that admits of no exceptions is that everything comes to an end, and partly because the poem's impulse to intellectual domination, to a power of comprehension which offers itself as comprehensive power, means that it knows itself to be inextricably implicated in its own satire on the nullity of aspiration. The passage on intellectual ambition (which has only a slim source in the original) was one that Johnson could not read out without breaking down; the scorn which plays upon human folly with such relieving ferocity in Juvenal is rendered self-suffocating here. It is the power of that scorn that permits Juvenal at the end simply to step outside the circle of folly, vice, and misery, and to give a vigorously positive ending to his poem:

> Still, if you must have something to pray for, if you
> Insist on offering up the entrails and consecrated
> Sausages from a white pigling in every shrine, then ask
> For a sound mind in a sound body, a valiant heart
> Without fear of death, that reckons longevity
> The least among Nature's gifts, that's strong to endure
> All kinds of toil, that's untainted by lust and anger . . .
> Fortune has no divinity, could we but see it: it's we,
> We ourselves, who make her a goddess, and set her in the heavens.[7]

Johnson's ending, with Christianity to help or to hinder him, is by comparison somewhat embarrassed in its formulation of positive values. There is a touch of bluster in "Enquirer, cease, Petitions yet remain, / Which Heav'n may hear, nor deem Religion vain" (349–50) and at the end an awkward and most un-Johnsonian vagueness about the idea of love, and the question of who is doing what for whom. For the poem is really a work of tragic or quasi-tragic power: and this is expressed, above all, by its conclusiveness.[8]

Concluding, that is to say, was for Johnson a fearful thing, always liable to be associated with the dread that he expressed in a famous note on *King Lear*: "I was many years ago so shocked by Cordelia's death, that I know not whether I ever endured to read again the last scenes of the play till I undertook to revise them as an editor" (*Shakespeare*, II, 704). (Congruently with this attitude to the finality of tragedy, the "lame and impotent conclusion" of what was probably his favorite play, *Henry IV*, took nothing away from his pleasure, and indeed seems almost to have enhanced it.) In the final *Idler* essay Johnson took as epigraph a line from Juvenal's satire, *Respicere ad longae jussit spatia ultima vitae*, which he had rendered in the *Vanity* as "caution'd to regard his End" (314), and wrote with striking force on what he called the "secret horror of the last":

> There are few things not purely evil, of which we can say, without some emotion of uneasiness, "this is the last." . . . This secret horrour of the last is inseparable from a thinking being whose life is limited, and to whom death is dreadful. We always make a secret comparison between a part and the whole; the termination of any period of life reminds us that life itself has likewise its termination; . . . I hope that when [my readers] . . . see this series of trifles brought to a conclusion, they will consider that by outliving the *Idler*, they have past weeks, months, and years which are now no longer in their power; that an end must in time be put to every thing great as to every thing little; that to life must come its last hour, and to this system of being its last day, the hour at which probation ceases, and repentance will be vain; the day in which every work of the hand, and imagination of the heart shall be brought to judgment, and an everlasting futurity shall be determined by the past.
>
> (*Idler*, pp. 314–16)

On the Day of Judgment there will be no room for irony, no appeal to a different point of view, no hope of traveling on. Mrs. Thrale tells how Johnson could never get to the end of a repetition of the *Dies Irae* "without bursting into a flood of tears" (*JM*, I, 284). The last *Idler* was written in Easter week, and allows us to see how any idea of coming to a conclusion could be colored by Johnson's attitude to death, in which his religious fear of the final judgement was balanced only by his dread that death might, after all, imply annihilation.

This argument helps, I hope, to suggest the importance of the open-endedness or inconclusiveness of *Rasselas*, which works upon the mind in a manner quite opposed to the tendency expressed in *The Vanity of Human Wishes* and elsewhere in Johnson's *œuvre*.[9] It is true that in the visit to the catacombs the travelers confront the fact of death, and that they there debate the nature of the soul and the probability of an afterlife. But Johnson's piety here operates rather differently: the emphasis falls on the fact that the soul does not seem likely to come to an end, no more than the philosophical argument is able to reach a conclusion. Religious feeling, which hangs in the air rather than being directly invoked as Christian doctrine, here supports, rather than puts an end to, indeterminacy:

> "Immateriality seems to imply a natural power of perpetual duration as a consequence of exemption from all causes of decay . . ."
>
> "But the Being," said Nekayah, "whom I fear to name, the Being which made the soul, can destroy it."
>
> "He surely can destroy it," answered Imlac, "since, however unperishable, it receives from a superior nature its power of duration. That it will not perish by any inherent cause of decay, or principle of corruption, may be shown by philosophy;

but philosophy can tell no more. That it will not be annihilated by Him that made it, we must humbly learn from higher authority."

The whole assembly stood a while silent and collected. "Let us return, said Rasselas, from this scene of mortality. How gloomy would be these mansions of the dead to him who did not know that he shall never die; that what now acts shall continue its agency, and what now thinks shall think on for ever."   (pp. 172–74)

Perhaps the most important aspect of Johnson's decision to set *Rasselas* in the east is the way in which this allowed the existence of Christian revelation in the world without the necessity of invoking it as the supreme authority.[10] Christianity was only partially and imperfectly established in Abyssinia, as Johnson knew from his translation of Father Lobo's *Voyage to Abyssinia*; Imlac speaks for the most part as a secular sage. The distinction between Christian faith and "natural religion," which is often treated in this period as a matter of the greatest moment, seems in *Rasselas* to be neither urgent nor absolute. The travelers are aware of Christianity; the visit to the catacombs puts them all into what might be called a religious frame of mind; but religion is felt to be only one part of life, and religious considerations determine neither the characters' actions nor how we think of them. Elsewhere in Johnson's writings Christian truth more often appears as a kind of on/off switch, that is capable, when activated, of simply trumping other considerations – as at the end of the *Vanity* ("Enquirer, cease"), or at the end of certain of the *Rambler*s (e.g. number 184), or in the discussion of religious poetry in the "Life of Waller" – but in *Rasselas* the invocation of a religious perspective finally determines nothing, and it is not a trivial point that this occurs in the *penultimate* chapter.

In the conclusion nothing is concluded. While the Nile is in flood and the travelers are confined to their house, Rasselas, Nekayah, and Pekuah "divert themselves" with various imaginary and impracticable schemes of happiness: Pekuah desires to be prioress of the convent of St. Anthony, Nekayah to found a college of learned women, Rasselas to act as the benevolent dictator of a small kingdom. "Of these wishes," we are told, "they well knew that none could be obtained" (p. 176). But the characters are not necessarily in thrall to the consolations of the unreal. Our feeling for the illusoriness of human expectations and wishes has changed since the beginning of the story. There we were naturally inclined to think of Rasselas, along with the other figures who live "only in idea" (Johnson's phrase in *Rambler* 2, a stimulating essay to read in connection with *Rasselas*), as comically naive, a foil for the corrective experience of real life. Such an expectation created by the sonorous opening sentence, and by the juxtaposition in the early chapters of Rasselas's naivety and Imlac's worldly wisdom. A pointed irony seems continually about to be released. Yet this expectation in the reader, like Rasselas's own expectations, has itself to be substantially modified in the light of experience. Even such obviously vulnerable flights of the mind as

Rasselas's expectation that the laws will deliver perfect justice, or the philosopher's profession of the power of stoicism, or even the engineer's expectations of his flying machine, are allowed a tenuous dignity that is not altogether overthrown when such theories, inevitably, collide with practice. (It is relevant to mention here Johnson's high opinion of *Don Quixote*, after the *Iliad* "the greatest in the world" [*JM*, I, 333].) The astronomer's more evidently insane delusion that he can control the weather is unfolded by Imlac with such sympathetic seriousness that we cannot distance ourselves from it as from an "abnormal" state of mind.

Nekayah's pretension to an everlasting grief at the loss of Pekuah, is treated by Johnson with a similarly complex irony; his touch here is at its finest:

> Nekayah, seeing that nothing was omitted for the recovery of her favorite, and having by her promise, set her intention of retirement at a distance, began imperceptibly to return to common cares and common pleasures. She rejoiced without her own consent at the suspension of her sorrows, and sometimes caught herself with indignation in the act of turning away her mind from the remembrance of her, whom yet she resolved never to forget.
>
> She then appointed a certain hour of the day for meditation on the merits and fondness of Pekuah, and for some weeks retired constantly at the time fixed, and returned with her eyes swollen and her countenance clouded. By degrees she grew less scrupulous, and suffered any important and pressing avocation to delay the tribute of daily tears. She then yielded to less occasions; sometimes forgot what she was indeed afraid to remember, and, at last, wholly released herself from the duty of periodical affliction.
>
> Her real love of Pekuah was yet not diminished. A thousand occurrences brought her back to memory. (pp. 128–29)

Nekayah believes that she will mourn for Pekuah with a perpetual and undiminishing grief; Imlac, and Johnson, know that she will not. But the irony that attends upon her endeavor to keep her grief going (rather like what we are told of Olivia at the start of *Twelfth Night*) is itself not conclusive. Our perception that this is a kind of foolishness interacts with our sense of something properly human in such endeavor. We are aware that to live only in the immediate moment, as do the uneducated young women Nekayah meets, would be something less than human: "Their grief, however, like their joy, was transient; every thing floated in their mind unconnected with past and future, so that one desire easily gave way to another, as a second stone cast into the water effaces and confounds the circles of the first" (p. 92). When Nekayah finally releases herself from the duty of periodical affliction, we see that this is partly because the pain of grief is wearing out with the passage of time, but also because the pain of grief is still, at moments, so sharp ("sometimes forgot what she was indeed afraid to remember"). Indeed, her grief survives her will to grieve: "her real love of Pekuah was yet not diminished." This open quality of the irony is epitomized in the double implication of "yet," which gives us two propositions in one: "Her real love of Pekuah was *as yet* not diminished (but would come to be in the course of time)," and "Her real love of Pekuah was *however* (despite time's erosion of her will to grieve) not diminished." "Yet not" suggests "not yet," which looks toward the end and time's final judgment on the permanence of love and grief and memory, ideas of the mind by which human beings invest their experience with the sense of significance and value. Simultaneously, "yet not" is felt also as a refusal to write "not yet," a cross-current of resistance to the narrative drift down the stream of time toward conclusion. These two (theoretically) opposed attitudes in practice interact with one another, without a final determination in either's favor.

Just so, at the end, the travelers' wishful thinking coexists with the realities of circumstance. It is significant that these wishes are openly exchanged and compared in conversation with each other: there is a clear contrast here with the reality-flouting daydreams to which they all three confessed in chapter 44, and which could be indulged only in secret and in solitude. The astronomer's insanity, we may remember, had been dissipated largely through the effect of company and conversation, and it is notable that all three of the fantasies that they now exchange concern communities. There is no longer anything here for Imlac to correct, and after we have heard the positive fantasies of Pekuah, Nekayah, and Rasselas, his own milder preference seems to be included within, as much as contradistinguished from, the list of impracticable wishes:

> Imlac and the astronomer were contented to be driven along the stream of life without directing their course to any particular port.
> Of these wishes that they had formed they well knew that none could be obtained. They deliberated awhile what was to be done, and resolved, when the inundation should cease, to return to Abissinia. (p. 176)

Imlac is here scarcely allowed more authority than any of the others. His wish to have no particular goal is included along with the fantasies of the others as wishes that cannot be obtained – as they all now well know, even while they indulge and cultivate those imaginations. This is a conclusion in which the position of wise disillusion, having done its utmost, is found after all to stand within, not outside, the human comedy. Imlac will after all have to direct his course to a particular port: in a powerfully and deliberately open ending to the narrative, they resolve to return to Abyssinia. What this return implies is that the quest for the choice of life has been recognized as simplistic, and outgrown. The party now recognizes that the answer to the question of how to live,? is not of a kind to be given by any conceivable encounter with the next moral celebrity. In that sense, at least, an illusion has been set aside. Returning to Abyssinia implies the impulse to deal in realities; returning to Abyssinia while building ideal kingdoms in imagination, and comparing them with one another, implies a complicated apprehension of what reality is for human beings; and the unstrenuous, constating tone of the final chapter suggests a genial tolerance of such complication.

Given the nature of my argument about *Rasselas*, conclusions are peculiarly dangerous. The temptation for the critic, which I fear I shall hardly resist, is to draw from the discussion some implication as to the "positive" or "negative" or "balanced" nature of Johnson's view of life in *Rasselas*, and so to risk reducing the work after all to a kind of statement, a view of life rather than imbued with life itself. Perhaps the point to hold onto is that Johnson's power of wit or irony is still commonly underappreciated, and that this power makes itself felt in the liveliness of mind that brings together discrepant considerations in a manner that is essentially sociable, like the important sociability of the travelers in his fable, and moves from one to another with a mobility and dynamism that is essentially vital, intelligently responsive to the vicissitudes – a word that stands for a large thought in Johnson's mind – of earthly life. "Do not suffer life to stagnate; it will grow muddy for want of motion: commit yourself again to the current of the world," advised Imlac (p. 127), administering one of the little pushes he gives to the travelers whenever they are in danger of getting stuck, as though the principle of life itself was to be found in such mobility. And it is the vitality of mind as conveyed in the writing that ensures that, although *the choice of life* remains an enigma, the notion of living well seems to be perfectly understood:

> "To him that lives well," answered the hermit, "every form of life is good." (p. 81)

> "It seems to me," said Imlac, "that while you are making the choice of life, you neglect to live."   (p. 111)

NOTES

1 *The Achievement of Samuel Johnson* (University of Chicago Press, 1955), chapters 2 and 3.
2 Edward Gibbon, *Memoirs of my Life*, ed. George A. Bonnard (London: Oxford University Press, 1966), p. 56.
3 "Letters or Essays Addressed to Alexander Pope," in *The Works of the Late Right Honorable Henry St. John, Lord Viscount Bolingbroke*, 5 vols. (London, 1754), III, 328, 330.
4 David Hume, *A Treatise of Human Nature*, ed. L. A. Selby-Bigge, rev. P. H. Nidditch (Oxford: Clarendon Press, 1978), pp. 267–69.
5 "Samuel Johnson: Man of Maxims?," in *Samuel Johnson: New Critical Essays*, ed. Isobel Grundy (London: Vision, and Barnes and Noble, 1984), pp. 28–29.
6 "The Artistic Form of *Rasselas*," *RES*, n.s. 18 (1967), 387–401.
7 *Juvenal: The Sixteen Satires*, trans. Peter Green (Harmondsworth: Penguin, 1974), p. 217.

8 See Ian White, "The Vanity of Human Wishes," *CQ*, 6 (1972), 115–25.

9 *Rambler*s 204–5, for example, which are often cited as a first sketch for *Rasselas*, recount the failure of the Emperor Seged's resolution to be happy, and they hammer home their piece of truth in just the way that *Rasselas* does not.

10 See also Arthur Weitzman, "The Oriental Tale in the Eighteenth Century: A Reconsideration," *Studies in Voltaire and the Eighteenth Century*, 58 (1967), 1839–55.

10

PHILIP SMALLWOOD

Shakespeare: Johnson's poet of nature

Johnson's first acquaintance with Shakespeare gave him a shock.[1] As a boy in Lichfield, and reading Shakespeare's *Hamlet* in the basement of his father's shop, he was frightened by the scene with the ghost and rushed upstairs "that he might see people about him."[2] Later, in the relatively unsuperstitious maturity of early middle age, Johnson published some sample notes for a planned edition of Shakespeare. In these, the *Miscellaneous Observations on the Tragedy of Macbeth* (1745), he lights on a passage that arouses but also scares him. Johnson compares the passage from Shakespeare with a famous passage from Dryden's *Conquest of Mexico* (1667):

> Night is described by two great poets, but one describes a night of quiet, the other of perturbation. In the night of Dryden, all the disturbers of the world are laid asleep; in that of Shakespeare, nothing but sorcery, lust and murder is awake. He that reads Dryden, finds himself lull'd with serenity, and disposed to solitude and contemplation. He that peruses Shakespeare, looks round alarmed, and starts to find himself alone. One is the night of a lover, the other that of a murderer.
>
> (pp. 19–20)

Johnson seems here to be registering the *force* of Shakespeare, the naked energy and fearful power in those passages from the plays which make their impact direct. And yet Johnson could not always feel unmixed pleasure in alarming experiences of this kind. There are times in Johnson's mature career when he found in Shakespeare scenes so deeply shocking that he could only face them with great reluctance and acute pain: "if my sensations could add anything to the general suffrage, I might relate, that I was many years ago so shocked by Cordelia's death, that I know not whether I ever endured to read over again the last scenes of the play till I undertook to revise them as an editor" (p. 704). "I am glad that I have ended my revisal of this dreadful scene," Johnson writes of Desdemona's murder: "It is not to be endured" (p. 1045).

But was Johnson also inhibited by this Shakespearean power? Many readers have thought so, concluding (for example) that Johnson preferred the happy ending of Nahum Tate's *Lear* (1681) to Shakespeare's, and that he wanted "poetical justice" to be done. One explanation for this and other judgments that is often put forward by critics of Johnson is that Johnson's emotions were hemmed in by the fixed critical structure of "neo-classicism," by implacably conservative tastes, and by an historical situation that places the restrained "Augustan" Johnson at a critical and cultural remove from the wild genius of Shakespeare. Critics of Johnson's Shakespearean statements such as F. R. Leavis[3] who have sought to explain Johnson's approach in terms of "Augustan" concepts have supposed that Johnson formed his critical notions on the "safe" ground of Dryden and Pope, and suggested that he brings standards set by these poets to bear when he comments upon Shakespeare. In this view, Johnson's disabling problem as a critic is his training and rule-bound habits of mind. He comes to Shakespeare with the wrong expectations and is *inevitably* disappointed.

This seems unlikely, however. First, the Shakespearean drama that shocked Johnson arguably is (or should be) a deeply distressing experience for any reader (two innocent women have died). The pain Johnson cannot endure at the end of *Lear*, and at the moment in *Othello* when Desdemona is murdered, reveals a capacity for deep feeling in this light. There is a human openness to the plays which is easily lost in the business of scholarship. Johnson's comments on *Lear* in particular are remarkable for combining detached impersonality with confessional intimacy ("I might relate . . ."). Personal testimony of this kind is totally alien to the practice of a standard modern edition of Shakespeare, where expressions of feeling are conventionally banned. But Johnson refuses to deny the emotional realities of following Shakespeare's text. At such moments, Shakespeare invaded the human subjectivity of Johnson. He seems to have penetrated to Johnson's emotional core. As an editor Johnson is living within the atmosphere of the plays.

As to the connections between Johnson's shocked reaction and his "training" as a critic, we can see that Johnson's commitment to the poetry and principles of Dryden and Pope was not unqualified. In the above comparison, Johnson draws attention to a distinction between the Shakespearean and the Augustan poet. But he obviously does not subordinate Shakespeare to Dryden. Nor does he suggest that the standards he is using for valuing the one are the only standards fit to apply to the other. No single standard is unambiguously present. When, as here, Johnson brings Shakespeare and Dryden together (and this is one of the rare occasions when he does), he does not take Dryden as the measure of Shakespeare. It would be in any case unwise to attach much weight to one isolated passage (albeit one carried forward into the complete edition). In Johnson's main statements on Dryden and main statements on Shakespeare, the latter *precedes* the former by approximately fifteen years (*Preface to Shakespeare*, 1765; *Lives of the Poets*, 1779–81).

But then most of Johnson's early published contacts with Shakespeare, like the above note, are somewhat slight. It is only when we take them together that they suggest the strength of Johnson's accumulating interest in Shakespeare over many years and his ambitions, from an early date, to place Shakespeare at the center of his critical concerns. Johnson seems to have had more time for Shakespeare in his early years than for any one poet (the *Miscellaneous Observations* was followed in 1753 by the Dedication to Charlotte Lennox's *Shakespear Illustrated*, and in 1756 by the *Proposals* for an edition). Until the complete edition in 1765, moreover, no single work of literature receives the sustained attention that Johnson gave to *Macbeth*. One important sign of the place of Shakespeare in Johnson's reading of the range of English poetry is the fact that in his *Dictionary* of 1755 Johnson drew many of the illustrative quotations from the plays.

But at this stage (prior to the *Preface*) Johnson's critical statement on Shakespeare remains largely unarticulated, as does his more general idea of the drama, and his sense of what the "dramatic" essentially is. As far as it is possible to tell, Johnson's concept of drama in the earlier phase of his critical life was more formalistic than it was later to become, and more technical in nature. The evidence for this view is sketchy, however. For example, only a few hints of how Johnson conceived of drama before the *Preface* appear in *The Rambler*. *Rambler* 156 (14 September 1751 [V, 65–70]) deals with the rules of tragedy, and the grounds for permitting drama to be "tragi-comic." (This is an issue I return to later.) In *Rambler* 168 (26 October 1751 [V, 125–29]) Johnson takes the case of another famous speech from *Macbeth*:

> Come, thick night!
> And pall thee in the dunnest smoke of hell,
> That my keen knife see not the wound it makes;
> Nor heav'n peep through the blanket of the dark,
> To cry, hold, hold!   (I.v.48–52)

and questions Shakespeare's use of the words "dun", "knife," and "blanket" as diction that is unacceptably "low." One common view is that Johnson regards these words, insofar as they refer to everday objects, as too mean for the occasion of such a dramatically crucial speech. If Johnson intends a serious negative criticism of Shakespeare here, and this is symptomatic of a more general response, it would also echo "neo-classic" inhibitions regarding the linguistic decorum of poetry. And this would strengthen the case for saying that Johnson approached the task of criticizing Shakespeare with a kind of mental block, and with inappropriate rules. And yet in the context of Johnson's general criticism of Shakespeare it seems difficult to accord much importance to this one periodical paper: the topic of "low words" does not arise again in the later criticism of

Shakespeare in the *Preface*. There may have been a rule in Johnson's mind against low diction at the time of *The Rambler*, but it is not applied in 1765. There are criticisms of the language of Shakespeare in the *Preface*, but this is not one of them. If Johnson has reservations about the language of Shakespeare in the *Rambler* paper, he also writes in the same place with peculiar warmth of Shakespeare's genius in language: Shakespeare exerts "all the force of poetry, that force which calls new powers into being, which embodies sentiment and animates matter" (v, 127).

This is high praise – as Leavis himself has recognized. But overall, there is too little sustained criticism of any kind prior to the *Preface to Shakespeare* to give a clear idea of the rules (if any) that Johnson used in his main statement on Shakespeare, or from what poets (other than Shakespeare) he derived them. The early material seems too provisional to predetermine Johnson's response, or to generate advance conclusions about what direction the maturer work would take. In particular, the view that Johnson took his standards from Dryden and Pope and then applied them to Shakespeare seems inconsistent with even the most basic chronological facts of Johnson's career: Johnson's declarations on Shakespeare in the *Preface* are Johnson's first extended statements on any poet (the early biography of Richard Savage [1744] excepted). Comments in *The Rambler* and elsewhere may seem to prepare for them, and in part they do; but such comments are not interchangeable with the *Preface*. The standards which seem to matter in judging Johnson's achievement as a critic emerge as part of his main Shakespearean declarations. Whether these seem the right standards for considering the plays is something we can now examine.

I

We can begin with what was happening around the period of Johnson's main efforts as an editor and critic of Shakespeare. We have seen that Johnson's critical thinking on drama by the date of the *Preface* in 1765 yields little to suggest how Johnson was disabled as a critic in his response to Shakespeare. But Johnson was also a creative writer, and his creative career over this period suggests a change in perspective as relevant to his position on Shakespeare as any of the earlier critical remarks. At the time when he was spending long hours editing Shakespeare, and deep in the midst of these labors, a reorientation of Johnson's creative energies seems to have occurred. This was the time when Johnson virtually gave up trying to be a serious poet. And after the limited success of the poetic tragedy *Irene* (1749) he completely gave up writing drama. The consequence or corollary of this creative evolution seems to be that Johnson's experience of Shakespeare comes together with a new view of human experience. This finds its creative focus in the wisdom of *Rasselas* (1759), in its ease, its humanity, and its comedy. In both – the critical and the creative work – we can see how Johnson discovers a relationship with the disappointments of life that is neither tragic (in the manner of Johnson's own play *Irene*), nor merely satiric (like Johnson's imitations of Juvenal). It is a view less rooted in the turbulent irritations of Johnson's personal history, or external biography, than either the somewhat abrasive *London* (1738) or the pessimistic *Vanity of Human Wishes* (1749); and it implies as the latter poem cannot an unregretful comprehension of the inevitable failure of human beings to live in the present.

Such a shift in Johnson's creative viewpoint (to the view Johnson realized creatively in *Rasselas*) inevitably affects how we understand the central critical term of the Shakespeare criticism – "general nature". The ramifications of the term can be directly appreciated from an early and famous passage in the *Preface*:

> Nothing can please many, and please long, but just representations of general nature. Particular manners can be known to few, and therefore few only can know how nearly they are copied. The irregular combinations of fanciful invention may delight a-while, by that novelty which the common satiety of life sends us all in quest; but the pleasures of sudden wonder are soon exhausted, and the mind can only repose on the stability of truth.
>
> Shakespeare is above all writers, at least above all modern writers, the poet of nature; the poet that holds up to his readers a faithful mirrour of manners and of life.   (pp. 61–62)

Johnson used the phrase "general nature" for the first time in the *Preface*, and though the term can seem very empty of meaning for readers today, it is the crux of the critical problem of Johnson's Shakespeare and of Johnson's value as a critic of Shakespeare today. That it has been possible to misunderstand this term, and to interpret it loosely, is apparent, for example, from the number of occasions when it is said that in appealing to "general nature" Johnson means, simply, the platitudes of "human nature." Johnson does say that Shakespeare has "human sentiments in human language" and that his plays contain the language "of men" (pp. 65, 84). But Johnson also praised Shakespeare as "an exact surveyor of the inanimate world," and he is clearly including inanimate alongside human nature in his epithet "general" (p. 89). As the above passage will help to suggest, a sense of the complex which is "general nature" comes out clearly in the form of the relations between "nature" and what Johnson called in the *Preface* "particular manners." For Johnson, in the criticism of Shakespeare we find in the *Preface to Shakespeare*, there is *both* a necessary apartness of "manners" and "nature" *and* a necessary link.

The "apartness" first. Modern and eighteenth-century critics alike have associated the power of Shakespeare with the features of an Elizabethan world picture, or the qualities inhering in the spirit of Renaissance England. So Shakespeare's language, for example, draws with exceptional range and variety

– as critics generally have acknowledged – on the linguistic resources of his time. For Johnson (who had a detailed – a lexicographer's and textual editor's – knowledge of the relations between Shakespeare and the contemporary resources of the English language) the important things in Shakespeare owe little to his time. He stands, finally, independent of the mass of contemporary ideas, fashionable humor, and his political and personal situation. As we see above, the central paragraphs of the *Preface* drive this distinction home with the full weight of Johnson's prose cadences.

We can understand the "manners" Johnson refers to in these paragraphs first of all in their contrast with nature – as free-floating, independent entities. The "manners," in this conception, consist of socially determined and personally cultivated habits, gestures, mannerisms, speech-features, eccentricities, nervous tics and so on. These mark particular people out and make them "of their time" or "of their place" or just make them the people they are. Johnson was later to write of Cowley's poems, the *Anacreontics*, that "Men have been wise in very different modes; but they have always laughed the same way," and he compared Dryden and Pope in the "Life of Pope" on the grounds that "Dryden knew more of man in his general nature, and Pope in his local manners" (*Lives*, I, 39–40; III, 222). Johnson established the groundwork for many of these future critical distinctions when he contrasted "manners" and "nature" in the *Preface*. The distinction that he draws there has several aspects to it. It is in part a distinction between surface and depths – how things and people appear to us and how they really are when we look deeper (the "manners" reflect how they appear). But it is also a division between things temporary and things permanent. Johnson seems to be thinking how law, language, customs, society all alter with the passage of time and belong to the "manners" in that sense. Finally, Johnson has in mind the large scope of the plays, and the proportion of human experience they embrace – the sense of "God's plenty." But here he seems to be pointing to how the achievement is analytic as well as inclusive or collective. Johnson finds Shakespeare working in an exploratory or experimental way to uncover a principle concealed behind all the mere everyday "manners" which makes them "particular" to their time and place, or to the individual exhibiting them.

There is however a sense in which the "manners" also express "nature." Shakespeare may be the "poet of nature" but the "nature" in question is revealed in and through the "manners," that is, through direct experience of the particular life and society of the world around us and a knowledge of the people we find there. When Johnson writes of the "manners," he seems to be saying that a poet cannot represent "nature" without this immediate contact with life. The "manners" (as this would suggest) do not therefore have to be specific to Shakespeare's own society (brutish uncouth Elizabethans in contrast to cultivated, polished, Augustans – Shakespeare has the complete range). The "manners," in this sense, are rather the habits, details of behavior, gesture, and speech found in the dead-and-gone society which remain atemporally human and therefore visible today. They are accessible now. These "manners" are spread out across time and are not culturally specific. In the words Johnson was later to use in the "Life of Butler," they are "co-extended with the race of man" (*Lives*, I, 214).

In copying "nature," Johnson thought Shakespeare made a selection from the "manners" in this sense. Little contextual scholarship of the "age" was necessary to bring the characters of Shakespeare alive to the contemporary reader because the reader could know them from life. But to understand Johnson's position on the question of character-drawing in drama more fully (and to see it in the light of the Johnsonian principle of "general nature"), we have to go back to *The Rambler*. In *Rambler* 156, we can recall, Johnson had said that plays must have "heroes" in order to qualify as tragedies. By the 1750s, the "hero" of a tragedy was only a "hero" if the author of the play had constructed an appropriately dignified character for him. Such a character had to be noble. The Johnson of the *Preface* owes no allegiance to this rule. He was not only in no doubt that the ennobling of heroes was at odds with Shakespeare's practice; he shows no sign of saying that obeying the rule, for all its conventional authority in professional criticism, would have made the plays better than they are: "Shakespeare has no heroes. . . . His story requires Romans or kings, but he thinks only on men" (pp. 64–65).

Johnson is here renouncing a standard neo-classical formula for the creation of character. According to this formula, authors of tragic drama were obliged to portray their heroes in line with a code of social decorum (a doctrine of verisimilitude based on the illusion of universal "good manners"). Such "good manners" required Romans to be noble and kings to act and be treated in a kingly fashion. Johnson thus answers once and for all the criticisms of Shakespearean character-drawing made by Voltaire among the French and by Rymer and Dennis among the English critics. Johnson noted in his *Preface* that Rymer had thought Shakespeare's heroes "not sufficiently Roman" and in his detailed notes to *Julius Caesar*, the play which is the occasion for Rymer's remarks, he took a view diametrically opposed to Rymer's. He stands the criticism on its head: it is precisely the Roman qualities, Johnson complains, which obstruct nature: "[Shakespeare's] adherence to the real story, and to Roman manners, seems to have impeded the natural vigour of his genius" (p. 836).

In comments such as this, Johnson is affirming the importance of Shakespeare's characters as representations of "general nature" rather than of "manners." It does not matter if kings or Romans are dramatically presented by Shakespeare with the imperfections of character common in the rest of the human race; if they are, say, weak or indecisive. If Shakespeare is the "poet of nature," they have to be presented in this way. The characters, ultimately, for all their individual life, are "a species." In this, Johnson rejects the demand that plays incorporate the incidentals of profession or rank as they appear from one historical and social perspective. But he does not wish to jettison particularity of character in all its forms; nor is his attachment to generality fatuous or naive. Johnson is not thinking of Shakespeare's characters as "morality play" types, or empty ciphers for an explicit authorial message. If Shakespeare's characters are not merely exceptional "heroic" beings, they do not lack the precise definition we expect in a poet of Shakespeare's extraordinary powers of individual human analysis. Johnson states clearly that "perhaps no poet ever kept his personages more distinct from one another." Such a comment conflates the notes to several plays where Johnson explicitly praises the distinctness of character – in *The Tempest*, for example:

> But whatever might be Shakespeare's intention in forming or adopting the plot, he has made it instrumental to the production of many characters, diversified with boundless invention, and preserved with profound skill in nature, extensive knowledge of opinions, and accurate observation of life. In a single drama are here exhibited princes, courtiers, and sailors, all speaking in their real characters.   (p. 135)

In the end-note on *Troilus and Cressida*, it is again strong individual character-drawing which comes to mind:

> As the story abounded with materials, he has exerted little invention; but he has diversified his characters with great variety, and preserved them with great exactness. His vicious characters sometimes disgust, but cannot corrupt, for both Cressida and Pandarus are detested and contemned. The comick characters seem to have been the favourites of the writer, they are of the superficial kind, and exhibit more of manners than nature, but they are copiously filled and powerfully impressed.   (p. 938)

while Johnson also notices distinctness of character in one or another form in notes to *King Lear* ("the striking opposition of contrary characters," p. 703) and *Henry IV Part 2* ("characters diversified with the utmost nicety of discernment," p. 523). In long notes on Polonius and Falstaff meanwhile, Johnson praises Shakespeare for creating some of the most dramatically realized, unheroic individuals in English literature (pp. 973–74, 523). This is not to say that Johnson thought Shakespeare *always* individualized his characters to this extent: Polonius is described as "a mixed character of nature and of manners." Most of the characters are less fully drawn.

II

It follows from Johnson's defense of the Shakespearean pursuit of "life" at the level of "nature" rather than "manners" that he should be duly skeptical – in the

Preface of 1765 if not in *The Rambler* of 1751 – about the modes of dramatic representation specific to the concept of "tragedy." We have seen how this skepticism helped him to defend Shakespeare's treatment of character against hostile critics. But it also has a bearing on two further (connected) aspects of Johnson's criticism of Shakespeare which we can now explore: how to apply the concept of "tragedy" validly to Shakespeare (and whether we can), and, finally, how to do justice to the sense in which Shakespearean drama is "moral." Many critics of Johnson's criticism have accused him of serious errors on both these counts. Both are areas in which Johnsonian criticism of Shakespeare has appeared eccentric or odd, remote from our own view and unable to affect it. This is one of the reasons why Johnson has been seen as a critic of largely historical importance, but of little direct use in understanding Shakespeare today.

How then does Johnson, by the time of the *Preface*, regard the concept of "tragedy" as relevant to Shakespeare? (We have already observed the shift in Johnson's work as a creator from *Irene* and the *Vanity of Human Wishes* to *Rasselas*.) The answer seems to be that just as Johnson could set aside the concept of tragic "heroes" by that date, so he could abandon "tragedy" whenever he needed to do justice to the *whole* of Shakespeare, or the appeal of *whole* plays. The relevant passage from the *Preface* contains the following famous statement: "Shakespeare's plays are not in the rigorous and critical sense either tragedies or comedies, but compositions of a distinct kind; exhibiting the real state of sublunary nature, which partakes of good and evil, joy and sorrow, mingled with endless variety of proportion and innumerable modes of combination; and expressing the course of the world" (p. 66).

Johnson does not develop a theory for the notion that Shakespeare's plays are "compositions of a distinct kind" and neither tragedies nor (their opposite) comedies. And yet our own experience of reading Shakespeare's plays may suggest quite adequately what Johnson means by "mingled drama" and how this idea is more important than the plays being tragedies or comedies. Neither Johnson's earlier comments on drama, nor the earlier creative works of "tragic" import such as the *Vanity* or *Irene* (Johnson's one experiment in noble and correct tragedy) anticipate the collapse in formalistic concepts of "tragedy" and "comedy" that takes place here. But there is in *Rasselas* one moment in Johnson's creative *œuvre* where "nature" includes the stability of both optimistic and pessimistic positions but inclines finally toward neither. Passages in this work look forward to the definition of "mingled drama," and they reflect the conception of "nature" that appears in the *Preface* and from which the particular judgments flow. In this respect *Rasselas* is a part of Johnson's "training" as a critic of Shakespeare as *Irene*, the *Vanity*, and *The Rambler* are not. One such passage is this representative statement of the central philosophy of *Rasselas*: "The causes of good and evil . . . [said Imlac] are so various and uncertain, so often entangled with each other, so diversified by various relations, and so much subject to accidents which cannot be foreseen, that he who would fix his condition upon incontestable reasons of preference, must live and die enquiring and deliberating" (*Rasselas*, p. 44).

Johnson's critical affinities have evolved markedly in the direction of this conception of "general nature" by the time of the *Preface*. Comparing the *Preface* with *The Rambler* can again serve to confirm this. In *Rambler* 156 (as mentioned above), Johnson had defended the concept of "tragi-comedy." But at this earlier stage he retained a sense of the generic distinctness of "tragedy" and "comedy" and an apparent commitment to the idea of "tragedy" and "comedy." The arguments of *Rambler* 156 and the *Preface* are only superficially similar, however. Johnson did not write of "tragi-comedy" in the *Preface*, nor, apparently, are "tragi-comedy" and "mingled drama" there employed as synonymous terms, as they had been in *The Rambler*. If "tragi-comedy" is an alternation of serious and comic *scenes*, "mingled drama" is a mixing *within* any scene – comic speeches, lines, and nuances in desperate, bitter, wretched, or terrible contexts, and cruel or solemn ones in otherwise comic plays or those having "happy" endings. In identifying Shakespeare's plays as "mingled drama" Johnson opens himself to more of Shakespeare as Shakespeare really affects his readers, and as he might affect us (regardless of the particular critical affinities of our time). Johnson has now broadened his standard from one adequate to describe alternating settings of courtly propriety and tavern jocularity, such as we find in *Henry IV*, to one able to account for the mix of elements in a play like *Hamlet*, where gravediggers joke over skulls and where "tragedy" and "comedy" are not isolated from each other in watertight compartments defined by the limits of scenes. Johnson puts himself at a distance from the terms the professional critics of his day used to describe the formal properties of art. In turn he values more highly the way that Shakespeare brings drama close to the texture of life.

But facing this fact about the direction of Johnson's development entails abandoning the idea common amongst critics of Johnson that he preferred Shakespeare's comedies (in the generically defined sense of the term) to his tragedies (defined in the identical sense), and that, in so doing, his criticism of Shakespeare is characteristically perverse (and thus lacks value). Johnson says of Shakespeare (in the *Preface*) that "In his tragick scenes there is always something wanting, but his comedy often surpasses expectation or desire." He also writes that Shakespeare's "tragedy seems to be skill, his comedy to be instinct" (p. 69). But in the former of these statements Johnson is writing about "scenes" rather than whole plays. This does not conflict with the relatively full attention that Johnson gives to *King Lear*, *Macbeth*, *Hamlet*, and *Othello* in his notes to those plays. Nor is this a preference for comed*ies*, since Johnson has just that minute praised (and we have just discussed) the Shakespearean "mingled drama." To understand the second statement we need to know what Johnson meant by "skill." The information we want is in the notes to the plays: *Othello* shows "such proofs of Shakespeare's skill in human nature, as . . . it is vain to seek in any modern writer" (p. 1047). "Skill," for Johnson, meant something closer to "knowledge" than our modern restricted significance of "technical expertise." The term describes the means used by Shakespeare to produce tragedy. It cannot be taken to reflect adversely on trage*dies*.

The key statement, that Shakespeare's "disposition . . . led him to comedy," tends to be missed in the theory of relative valuation; but it suggests that Johnson may not *in the main* be weighing Shakespeare's types of drama, comedies on the one hand *versus* tragedies on the other. Johnson is, rather, analyzing the source of all that Shakespeare wrote (tragedies, comedies, histories), and diagnosing the effect of Shakespeare working at times *pro* and at times *con* the natural disposition which led him to "repose, or to luxuriate" in comedy. One of Johnson's most important services to the modern reader, whenever he is writing about tragedy and comedy, is to remind us how hard Shakespeare found it to resist comedy, and how he delighted in it up to and beyond the point where it warranted praise – hence the indulgence in quibbles, or "fatal Cleopatra[s] for which he lost the world, and was content to lose it" (p. 74).

Johnson praises comedy, and he criticizes tragedy. But the scene, not the play, is the unit of evaluation in which he thinks. Accordingly, the main difference between Johnson and most of the Shakespearean criticism in the world not written by him (and in this sense the origin of his so-called "perversity" as a critic) is the very high value that Johnson accords to Shakespeare's comic *scenes*. As the plays as wholes are in any case "mingled dramas," it does not matter whether such scenes come in plays officially designated as comedies or as tragedies. But the praise of the comic scenes in the *Preface* is exceptionally full. Plays of all kinds are covered by it:

> The force of his comick scenes has suffered little diminution from the changes made by a century and a half, in manners or in words. As his personages act upon principles arising from genuine passion, very little modified by particular forms, their pleasures and vexations are communicable to all times and to all places; they are natural, and therefore durable; the adventitious peculiarities of personal habits, are only superficial dies, bright and pleasing for a little while, yet soon fading to a dim tinct, without any remains of former lustre; but the discriminations of true passion are the colours of nature; they pervade the whole mass, and can only perish with the body that exhibits them. (p. 70)

As this passage reinforces, it is in his comic *scenes* that Shakespeare approaches nearest to "general nature." And, as we have seen, "just representations of general nature" characterized the main value of his writings for Johnson. It is in comedy that Johnson thought Shakespeare had most fully transcended the "manners."

The faults of the tragedy, the declamatory speeches and the swollen language, are correspondingly faults in the work of much more ordinary dramatists than Shakespeare. They resemble what Johnson was later to criticize in the tragedies of Thomson or of Young. Shakespeare's disposition led him to comedy. From this fact it follows that his tragedy is flawed according to the visible effort (the non-instinctual labor) Shakespeare seems to have expended upon it. In tragedy, Shakespeare works against the grain of his natural disposition, and it is then that "his performance seems constantly to be worse, as his labour is more" (pp. 72–73). But again the point is made by reference to how an ordinary reader of the tragic scenes and passages would be likely to take them, and how we might take them ourselves. Johnson is not engaged in marking down Shakespeare against some standard of "Augustan" or neo-classical tragic purity. Nor is he deploying some personal theory of tragedy the terms of which Shakespeare does not meet. In fact, where Johnson praises the tragedy of Shakespeare, as he does in a later passage of the *Preface,* it is because Shakespeare is in general profoundly unlike the kind of tragedy that he (Johnson) had once tried to write. The important point is that Johnson had *abandoned* all ambitions as a tragedian by the time of his major criticism of Shakespeare. In the *Preface* Johnson can momentarily switch the commentary into the first person plural and appear to include himself in the criticism: "we still find that on our stage something must be done as well as said, and inactive declamation is very coldly heard, however musical or elegant, passionate or sublime" (p. 84).

This difference between the failed author of *Irene* and the disinterested critic of Shakespeare is finally defined in Johnson's account of how Shakespeare's drama is moral. We have seen that Johnson had stressed the "mingled drama" of Shakespeare, and Shakespeare's "disposition" to comedy. He had lavished particular praise on the comic scenes. But this raises the question of whether Shakespearean drama can, for Johnson, comprehend the "seriousness" of tragedy. The power of tragedy to improve or to teach its audience was a considerable part of the value attached to the tragic form by critics of Johnson's immediate age. Johnson himself sees the dramas as neither deadened by an overemphatic moral didacticism (like *Irene*) nor wanting in morals. What he says (somewhat controversially) is that Shakespeare "sacrifices virtue to convenience and is so much more careful to please than to instruct, that he seems to write without any moral purpose" (p. 71). "Seems" is the operative word in this sentence: there are many occasions in the notes where Johnson shows that Shakespeare points an extremely purposeful moral. In *Macbeth*, for example, "The passions are directed to their true end. Lady Macbeth is merely detested; and though the courage of Macbeth preserves some esteem, yet every reader rejoices at his fall" (p. 795). The difference here between what Johnson says and what might be said of *Macbeth* by readers nowadays is not that Johnson does not feel or see moral purpose; it is that he makes so much of it. (We do not normally say we "rejoice" at Macbeth's fall.)

Johnson is thus sharply alive to the variety of ways in which Shakespeare incorporates moral truth in dramatic form. And whatever the spirit of his negative remarks, Johnson does not assert that Shakespeare, in order to make these points, adheres only to stated morals. This has been suggested, and it is true that Johnson appreciates the quantity and importance of Shakespearean moral statement: "From his writings indeed a system of social duty may be selected, for he that thinks reasonably must think morally" (p. 71). Johnson's point is, however, that Shakespeare does not *always* think morally. Because Shakespeare is "so much more careful to please than to instruct," "his precepts and axioms drop casually from him." And rather than aim his criticism at one kind of morality, Johnson suggests that Shakespeare is not as consistent as he should be in his concern about morals in general. Johnson highlights in the notes times when it suited Shakespeare to leave moral questions aside – because it was convenient to do so:

> I do not see why Falstaff is carried to the Fleet. We have never lost sight of him since his dismission from the king; he has committed no new fault, and therefore incurred no punishment; but the different agitations of fear, anger, and surprise in him and his company, made a good scene to the eye; and our authour, who wanted them no longer on the stage, was glad to find this method of sweeping them away. (p. 522)

Shakespeare "seems" to write without any moral purpose here because he is being more careful to please than to instruct. That is a fault, and it is the first and most serious that Johnson lists in his "faults and defects" section of the *Preface*. But Johnson qualifies the criticism in two important ways. First, it does not damn Shakespeare altogether: "Nothing can please many and please long but just representations of general nature." We have seen from this earlier statement how enthusiastically Johnson celebrated the power of Shakespearean drama to please. And pleasure in the Johnsonian system has priority over instruction. This is appreciable wherever Johnson considers moral purpose in the *Lives*, as in his essays on Pope, say, or on Addison or Matthew Prior. In all such cases, Johnson always metes out the harshest treatment to work that tries to instruct without pleasing. Johnson was one of the most easily bored of literary critics, and an overconscious morality bored him most.

The second qualification is that Johnson sees Shakespeare as setting the standard by which he is judged. Shakespeare's (seeming) tendency to sacrifice virtue to convenience is a serious fault only by Shakespeare's own moral ideal. Johnson strikes a balance on the issue of moral purpose that is typical of the juxtaposition of praise and blame in the *Preface* as a whole. This is at once a judgment of Shakespeare as a whole. Though the overall verdict is overwhelmingly positive, he is holding the good and the bad in the scales. The more strained, declamatory passages, and the overt moralizing Johnson does not want (in tragedy or wherever) are hard for any reader to take because Shakespeare's "real power," his dramatically realized hold over questions of right and wrong, lies quite elsewhere: "It is from this wide extension of design that so much instruction is derived. It is this which fills the plays of Shakespeare with practical axioms and domestick wisdom . . . Yet his real power is not shown in the splendour of particular passages, but by the progress of his fable and the tenour of his dialogue" (p. 62). Nowhere, of course, in the discussion of Shakespeare's dramatic power, does Johnson demand that "poetical justice" be done.

To recapitulate: the *Preface to Shakespeare* is the focus of Johnson's Shakespearean criticism, and is Johnson's earliest extended critical treatment of any writer. We have little unambiguous confirmation of Johnson's critical commitments before 1765 and little evidence of the Johnsonian "training" (other than the fact of his striking developments in the creative grasp of "nature" at around the time of his work on Shakespeare, his intimate knowledge of the plays and some enthusiastic thinking upon them). Second, it is in the *Preface* that Johnson's mature critical terminology emerges for the first time. "Nature" and "mingled drama" replace "tragedy" and "tragi-comedy." These and other concepts applicable to the criticism of drama (such as the concept of the tragic "hero") are abandoned or critiqued by Johnson at this point. Third, we have seen that Johnson is well able to appreciate the moral power of Shakespearean drama and the source of this power in Shakespeare's human ambitiousness as writer, his "wide extension of design." But for Johnson the sense of right and wrong in Shakespeare must always be dramatically realized. Johnson's appreciation does not stop short at approving the didactic statement of a preexisting ethical code. Johnson the critic of Shakespeare is not the author of *Irene*. The moral import of the plays must be part of their life. Only when Shakespeare deviates from a portrayal of life (as Shakespeare's own dramas have created it and as Johnson finds it created convincingly in them) do Johnson's negative criticisms tell.

III

Perhaps the most striking single feature of Johnson's criticism of Shakespeare, from the viewpoint of the modern reader, is not, however, connected with any positive or negative aspect of the content of the criticism, nor with any difficulty in critical language or controlling concepts. It lies with the method – Johnson's unusual confidence as a critic of the whole of Shakespeare and his judgment in the *Preface* of so much detailed and diverse material in exceptionally general terms. "Great thoughts are always general," Johnson was later to write in his "Life of Cowley," "and consist in positions not limited by exceptions, and in descriptions not descending to minuteness" (*Lives*, I, 21). Johnson explains with some precision in the *Preface* what it means to write criticism of this general kind:

> These observations are to be considered not as unexceptionably constant, but as containing general and predominant truth. Shakespeare's familiar dialogue is affirmed to be smooth and clear, yet not wholly without ruggedness or difficulty; as a country may be eminently fruitful, though it has spots unfit for cultivation: His characters are praised as natural, though their sentiments are sometimes forced, and their actions improbable; as the earth upon the whole is spherical, though its surface is varied with protuberances and cavities.   (pp. 70–71)

Johnson is here establishing the grounds for an evaluative estimate of the whole of Shakespeare. In so doing, the prefatory mode of utterance in which he shapes his most important propositions may seem somewhat remote and unbodied compared with the sort of expositional monograph on Shakespeare current today, or a modern ("Arden"-style) introduction to individual plays; but it is one which makes his criticism's relation both to the reader and to the plays useful in different and perhaps more challenging ways. It has always been easy to exaggerate the shallowness of this method or to miss its purpose. The global statements of the *Preface to Shakespeare* do not pointlessly distance the reader or critic from the experience of the plays, nor do they suggest that Johnson lacked the resources of a modern and sophisticated apparatus of practical criticism, or textual, linguistic, and structural analysis. Their function is to complete and to release the congregate mass of local, regional, and subordinate judging, appreciating, interpreting, commenting, glossing, responding, and so forth that go on all the time when editing and mediating Shakespeare for readers. The generalizations subsume several prior and inferior levels of the dramatic and critical text; they are an act of "comprehending" in more than one sense.

Johnson's detailed reactions to Shakespeare, word by word, line by line, speech by speech, and play by play, arise as notes. There are notes at the foot of the page, and there are "General Observations" drawing the notes on each play to a close. If some of the latter are brief in the extreme, others seem consciously developed as miniature essays. They record the mix of arguments, definitions, affirmations of taste, and personal testimony that we found, for example, in the "Observation" on *King Lear*. As the foregoing commentary has suggested, hardly a play escapes without criticism of some kind, and this is sometimes surprisingly harsh, cryptic, or liable to strike the reader from an unexpected angle, or with an unusual "edge." A throwaway brevity is occasionally present, as if Johnson, like Shakespeare before him when the end of a play drew near, had shortened the labour to snatch the profit. Praise takes every possible form, and no two "General Observations" are exactly alike. There is no standard pattern or critical template.

As indicated above, the "General Observations" most likely to interest readers today are those on the conventionally regarded "great tragedies" – on *Othello*, for example, where Johnson writes with unrestrained enthusiasm that "The beauties of this play impress themselves so strongly upon the attention of the reader, that they can draw no aid from critical illustration" and remarks on "The fiery openness of Othello . . . the cool malignity of Iago" and "the soft simplicity of Desdemona" (p. 1047). On *Hamlet*, which inspires a fairly structured account of merits and flaws (echoing, as do other local judgments, the rhetorical equipoise of the general *Preface*) Johnson writes that the "particular excellence" is "the praise of variety." At this level – one stage removed from the detailed glosses and explanatory comments of the incidental notes – Johnson's approach is judicial rather than interpretive: "The incidents are so numerous, that the argument of the play would make a long tale. The scenes are interchangeably diversified with merriment and solemnity. . . . The conduct is perhaps not wholly secure against objections. The action is indeed for the most part in continual progression, but there are some scenes which neither forward nor retard it" (pp. 1010–11). But interesting and extended commentary of an evaluative or interpretive nature can also appear at any point in the run of notes to a play – on important individuals such as Polonius or Falstaff, for example, whose character sketches we have touched on above. Comments in response to the dramatic significance of a scene, a habit of language or moment of acute tension, humor, pity, or delight are too various to tie down to single examples.

It would be wrong, however, to overstate the importance that Johnson attaches to weighing the merits, or fixing the defects of whole individual plays (whether in "General Observations" or by inferences drawn together from different notes). In valuing Shakespeare's achievement as one, Johnson is appreciating a larger unit than that of the play. This is a focus that blurs the success or failure of achievements within the Shakespearean *œuvre* at levels which include the level of the unitary "work" and any *particular* "mingled drama", so that, compared with most modern critics of Shakespeare, Johnson's sense of the quintessence of the play as "the thing" is secondary to his apprehension of the sustained commitment of an active and varied total dramatic career. The best of plays and the worst of plays, great tragedies or run-of-the-mill comedies, are almost all accorded a comment; but their boundaries are ultimately dissolved in this larger view. Johnson's criticism has the holistic completeness that only distance from the object allows. And that, of course, is the key to the visibility – to Johnson's eyes – of the Shakespearean "general nature." This is the combining quality of the manifold that is all the plays. For "The Works of Shakespeare" Johnson might have substituted the singular concept "Work": his "poet of nature" is in one sense the author of a single "poem."

That Shakespeare is for such reasons at the center of Johnson's achievement and development as a critic will surprise no one used to finding affinities between the *Preface* and the *Lives of the Poets*. What may be surprising is how wonderfully Shakespeare had concentrated Johnson's mind. We have seen that in reading and responding to Shakespeare, Johnson enjoyed above all the "progress of [Shakespeare's] fable and the tenour of [his] dialogue." This sense of the "dramatic" quality to be found when good drama alerts the attention with its reality and life, when it seizes or "fills" the mind, or even when it shocks, became part of the whole body of thinking that distinguishes Johnson's criticism. Johnson ultimately appreciates Shakespearean drama as drama rather than as poetry. In this way Shakespeare imposed on Johnson a demand that he wanted satisfied, but mostly found unsatisfied, in almost every kind of poet or dramatist he later went on to discuss. At one time, for example, Johnson had admired the formal model of tragic perfection he found in Addison's *Cato* (*Idler* 77, p. 241). But he mentions *Cato* in cool terms in the *Preface* (p. 84) and is no more enthusiastic about it when he comes to discuss it in his "Life of Addison" fifteen years later as "rather a poem in dialogue than a drama" (*Lives*, II, 132). Still more striking, perhaps, is the way that the imaginative appeal of the Shakespearean "dramatic," with its requirement for the progress of the fable and a reality of dialogue drawn from life, can be felt even when Johnson is not talking about the drama necessary to plays, but has turned to the subject of narrative poetry: Butler's *Hudibras*, for example, is less interesting than it might be, according to the "Life of Butler," because it requires "a nearer approach to dramatick spriteliness" without which "fictitious speeches will always tire, however sparkling with sentences and however variegated with allusions" (*Lives*, I, 212).

Shakespeare's impact on Johnson was something more than a temporary shock from which it was possible to recover one's Augustan composure and then read on, unchanged by the experience. Shakespeare contributed to the sum of the criteria that formed the amalgam of literary and personal human experience present in the critical thinking of the *Lives*. He reformulated the existing language of Johnson's criticism such as it was. In many ways Shakespeare set the standards for the later work and his value to Johnson lies behind many of the negative as well as the positive judgments in the *Lives*. The effect of this Shakespearean presence in Johnson's criticism may be to diminish somewhat the sense in which the poets treated in the *Lives* are significant in defining the critical ideas and ideals of Johnson, how he formed his taste or experienced a "training." This includes the place of the poetry of Dryden and Pope in that training, and more broadly the "Augustan" dramatic and poetical model. But that is one way that Johnson's criticism of Shakespeare (and his criticism more generally perhaps) secures its continuity with the future. The same is true when Stendhal later called Johnson "le père du romanticisme."[4] Or, to apply T. S. Eliot's words on the life of dead poets to the life of a dead critic, it is one way that Johnson "asserts[s] [his] immortality most vigorously."[5]

NOTES

1 I am grateful to Dr. Tom Mason of Bristol University for the conversations over the years which have helped to develop thoughts appearing in this essay. All citations included in the text are from the Yale edition of Johnson's *Shakespeare* (see List of short titles and abbreviations), unless otherwise stated.

2 See Hester Lynch Piozzi, "Anecdotes of the Late Samuel Johnson, LL.D.," *JM*, I, 158.

3 See F. R. Leavis, "Johnson and Augustanism," in *The Common Pursuit* (Harmondsworth: Penguin, 1969), pp. 97–115.

4 See Henri Beyle (Stendhal) "Du romanticisme dans les beaux arts" (1819), in *Racine et Shakspeare* (1823), 2 vols., in *Oeuvres complètes de Stendhal*, 31 vols. (1913–34), II, 119.

5 "Tradition and the Individual Talent" (1919), in *Selected Essays* (London: Faber and Faber, 1932), p. 14.

11

GREG CLINGHAM

Life and literature in Johnson's
Lives of the Poets

When Matthew Arnold formulated his ideal of liberal education, he turned not to Coleridge or Hazlitt or De Quincey, or even to Keats or Wordsworth or Tennyson, but to Johnson's *Lives of the Poets*. In his *Six Chief Lives from Johnson's "Lives of the Poets"* (1878) Arnold designated Johnson's lives of Milton, Dryden, Pope, Addison, Swift, and Gray as *points de repère* – "points which stand as so many natural centres, and by returning to which we can always find our way again."[1] These critical biographies covered the period from the birth of Milton in 1608 to the death of Gray in 1771, a crucial century and a half in English literature; and although there were significant critical disagreements of judgment between Arnold and Johnson, when it came to an education in literary history, biography, and criticism Arnold saw the *Lives of the Poets* as offering a "compendious story of a whole important age in English literature, told by a great man, and in a performance which is itself a piece of English literature of the first class" (p. 362).

I

Like almost everything Johnson wrote, the *Lives of the Poets* was an occasional work. Johnson's career as a biographer had begun in 1740 with brief lives of Blake, Drake, and Barretier, had included the *Life of Richard Savage* (1744) – republished as one of the *Lives* – and had involved Johnson in many other biographical projects. In 1777 a group of London booksellers planned to publish an edition of the works of the English poets, in competition with an Edinburgh edition of 1773, and Johnson, as a celebrity, was asked to provide brief introductions to the poems. "I am engaged to write little Lives, and little Prefaces, to a little edition of the English Poets," he wrote to Boswell (*Letters*, III, 20), and noted in the author's advertisement that "my purpose was only to have allotted to every Poet an Advertisement, like those which we find in the French Miscellannies, containing a few dates and a general character" (*Lives*, I, xxvi). However, as Johnson engaged with the lives and the works of his subjects his imagination caught fire, and "through the honest intention of giving pleasure" (as he noted in the Preface to the edition of 1783), Johnson wrote a work of complex and far-reaching critical, biographical, and historical substance. This was *Prefaces, Biographical and Critical to the Works of the English Poets*, published as the first ten volumes of the sixty-volume edition of the English Poets. Volumes I–IV appeared in 1779, and volumes V–X in 1781.[2] The publishers soon realized that they had a best-seller on their hands and issued Johnson's fifty-two prefaces separately in 1781 as *The Lives of the English Poets*, since when the work has appeared under that title (or simply as *Lives of the Poets*), as an autonomous text, separate from the poetry that it was initially designed to introduce.

The diversity, range, and depth of Johnson's *Lives* resist any easy conceptualization and introduction. Not only does Johnson's work respond to a great range of personal and historical experience as represented by the lives of the fifty-two poets under consideration, but the writing of Cowley, Donne, Milton, Dryden, Pope, Swift, and Gray – to mention only the major writers covered – stimulated Johnson to articulate *several* critical discourses in order to accommodate the specificity of the works and lives under discussion. A partial list of the different topics covered suggests the *Lives*'s multiplicity: metaphysical poetry, the pindaric ode, pastoral, epic poetry, heroic drama, blank verse, translation, imitation, satire, devotional verse, theological discourse, epitaphs, metaphor and simile, the refinement of diction in English poetry, the development of English prose, familiar correspondence, French neo-classicism, the Greek and Roman classics, Renaissance scholarship, and contemporary eighteenth-century literary criticism. The topics in criticism covered in the *Lives* read like a list of most of the important issues in literary history during the years 1600–1781. To this list, moreover, might be added the following, equally important historical, biographical, and philosophical topics: literary history of the seventeenth and eighteenth centuries, the relation of politics to literature, Puritanism, the English Civil War, the Restoration, Jacobitism, literature and the Hanoverians, regicide, literary friendship, literary warfare, literary values, publishing, painting, changing social forms, gardens, travel, money, madness, artistic ambition and failure, and death. Diverse as the contents, narratives, and critiques of the *Lives* might be, the above topics are all contained within one capacious work whose general themes might be said to be the effect of time on human endeavor, and the relation between the finite human being and the continuing experiences and pleasures offered by literature. Holding together all of these disparate materials, and suffusing them with its own distinctive humane imagination, is Johnson's commemorative intelligence.

II

Johnson's intelligence is informed by two interlinked paradigms that govern both specific judgments and the larger structure of the *Lives of the Poets*: the first concerns the theoretical and artistic possibilities of biography as a genre; the second concerns the function of what Johnson's calls "nature" in his critical and biographical writing.

The fictional nature of biography – the use of tropes and figurative language in "constituting" a life in writing – is generally accepted today.[3] Johnson, by contrast, is usually assumed to work within positivistic ideas of verisimilitude emphasizing the direct relation between the biographer's words and the documentary truth of the life of his subject. This commonplace, however, does not do justice to Johnson's idea or practice of biography, which are much more imaginatively inflected. For instance, *Rambler* 60 proposes that the essence of biography is no different from that of "imaginative" literature. Johnson says that biography succeeds in proportion to its appeal to common human experiences, and the imagery he uses to describe this process links biography with poetry and drama:

> All joy or sorrow for the happiness or calamities of others is produced by an act of imagination, that realises the event however fictitious, or approximates it however remote, by placing us, for a time, in the condition of him whose fortune we contemplate; so that we feel, while the deception lasts, whatever motions would be excited by the same good or evil happening to ourselves. Our passions are therefore more strongly moved, in proportion as we can more readily adopt the pains and the pleasures proposed to our minds, by recognising them as at once our own, or considering them as naturally incident to our state of life. (III, 318–19)

The sympathetic experience described in this essay is no different in kind from that described in the passage on dramatic illusion in the *Preface to Shakespeare* (I, 60), or in the following passage from the "Life of Cowley" in which Johnson registers what he feels to be *absent* from the poetry of Donne and Cowley: "They were not successful in representing or moving the affections. As they were wholly employed on something unexpected and surprising they had no regard to that uniformity of sentiment, which enables us to conceive and to excite the pains and the pleasures of other minds" (*Lives*, I, 20).

Good literature for Johnson – whether drama, poetry, or biography – appeals to and represents human "passions" (joy, sorrow, happiness, calamities), and *Rambler* 60 assumes that a biographer fulfills his purpose *in proportion to* the creativity of the writing. The biographer must not only "conceive the pains and the pleasures of other minds," but must also "excite" them. Many biographers, Johnson notes, "imagine themselves writing a life when they exhibit a chronological series of actions and preferments," while only a few can "portray a living acquaintance, except by his most prominent and observable particularities, and the grosser features of his mind" (*Idler* 84, p. 262).

The portrayal of a "living acquaintance" through the biographer's narrative is connected to the moral purpose of biography. In *Idler* 84 Johnson discusses the prudential nature of the genre, which designates "not how any man became great, but how he was made happy" – how, to paraphrase Johnson, knowledge manifests itself in action in a person's life. That is, biography is prudential both in manner and subject: it establishes the relation between, first, particular moments in time and human conduct, and, second, the ends of action – "ends" here being multiple and ambiguous, and comprehending the sense of "end" as consequences, "end" as aim or objective, "end" as achievement, and "end" as end, terminus, death. For the subjects of the *Lives* are, of course, authors who have employed their energies in representing some truth – whatever it might be – about their lives, through the crystallization of their experiences in literature. Johnsonian biography might therefore be said to detect whatever truth a person has realized in the ends of his or her activity – that is, in literature, but also at the end of that individual's life.

This link between action and literature in Johnson's idea of biography suggests a complex and active structure for the *Lives*. In general, all the individual lives follow a similar pattern: a biographical and chronological sketch of the author's life and writings is followed by a critical dissertation on the works. However, the larger lives of Cowley, Milton, Dryden, Pope, and Addison split the difference between biography and work with an intermediate section on the author's intellectual or poetic character that addresses his specific intellectual behavior. While the smaller lives (e.g., Halifax, Dorset, Yalden, Duke, Garth, and Hammond) encompass biography and criticism in just a few pages, in the large lives each of the three sections are substantial, and the intellectual portrait consciously and skillfully mediates between biography and criticism, constituting an organizing principle and structure in the whole life. Many of the middle-size *Lives* (e.g., Waller, Butler, Rochester, Congreve, Otway, and Gay) have the tripartite structure on a reduced scale. It has been argued that the structure of individual lives reflects Johnson's intention of separating life from work as belonging to two quite different realities (a division supposedly reflected in the title of *Prefaces, Critical and Biographical*); but this discontinuous structure, and the correspondingly formalistic divisions between genres that it implies (i.e., poetry is different in kind from biography), ignores Johnson's writing about biography, as well as the obvious fact that the *Lives* deliberately *bring together* literature and experiences supposedly "outside" literature in one coherent form. Indeed, what interests Johnson are the various continuities and discontinuities between literature and life.

Years before Boswell wrote his *Life of Johnson* (1791), now reputed to be the first modern, self-reflexive biography, Johnson understood that biographical truth is relative, and that the truths, whether factual or critical, are dependent on the biographer's story, his narrative.[4] As Richard Holmes remarks, "The inventive, shaping instinct of the story-teller struggles with the ideal of a permanent, historical, and objective document."[5] Certainly, Johnson knows that biography cannot *reproduce* a life that has been lived and is over, yet his biographies confer a *fictional* presence on the fragmented realities of the author's life and works. That is, Johnson's theory and practice of biography entail a representation implying consciousness of artifice and of differences between art and life. There is no literal correspondence of living and writing, because it is not in the nature of language to provide such correspondence; and because "it may be shewn much easier to design than to perform . . . It is the condition of our present state to see more than we can attain" (*Rambler* 14, III, 75, 76). However, Johnson's prudential approach to biography registers a *fictional* correspondence and hence a *continuity* of life and work that anticipates modern critics in focusing on the transformative power of life-writing. As Frederick Karl notes of Conrad: "In biography, we must edge up to that meeting point between mind and work, to areas where the figure who has created something must be related to the work he has created; so that we have a model of his mind. . . . [B]iography is at all times the reconstruction of a human model who seems suitable for the work created. Our goal is to understand the transformations that occur when life becomes work, and when work pre-empts life."[6]

Those transformations in Johnson's writing are difficult to unravel, since he does not overtly discuss the psychological origins of specific works or the process of literary creation. But he is interested in the "reconstruction of a human model who seems suitable for the work created," and these efforts encounter the ubiquitous presence of failure and death, identifying the individual's inadequacy to the political and historical events in which he is involved as signs of human division. This perception is a version of the vanity of human wishes ("Delusive Fortune hears th'incessant Call, / They mount, they shine, evaporate, and fall" [*Vanity of Human Wishes*, 75–76]). The biographer's retrospective glance (for all of Johnson's subjects are dead and gone) distinguishes the irony in the discrepancy between their intentions and achievements, and ruefully turns that scrutiny upon his own efforts:

> History may be formed from permanent monuments and records; but Lives can only be written from personal knowledge, which is growing every day less, and in a short time is lost for ever. What is known can seldom be immediately told; and when it might be told, it is no longer known. The delicate features of the mind, the nice discriminations of character, and the minute peculiarities of conduct, are soon obliterated.
>
> ("Life of Addison," *Lives*, II, 116)

The interaction between the individual and his or her historical moment, constantly slipping from the biographer's understanding because of the gap between the present and the past, is analogous to the discrepancy between human will and action with which Johnson's moral essays are concerned. Both are indications of the limits of reason; Johnson's treatment of limits and the resultant suffering from self-division are usually identified as tragic ("Fate wings with ev'ry Wish th' afflictive Dart" [*Vanity*, 15]).[7] But notwithstanding Johnson's ironic consideration of human destinies (as witness the careers of Wolsey and Swedish Charles in the *Vanity*), of which his rueful biographical treatment of literary failure is part, Johnson's proto-tragic view is transformed in the *Lives*. For the acknowledged deficiencies of historical evidence are repaired by Johnson's seeing a person's life and work in the light of each other and of a larger continuum. In Lawrence Lipking's words, Johnson discovers how poetry "can constitute the experience of a life," and how a great poet "makes his own destiny; makes it, precisely, with poems."[8] In the *Lives* the distinctive combinations of criticism and biography discover not only some of the lost delicacies of mind and discriminations of character in the *works* of the authors dealt with, but they also mitigate the otherwise inevitable vanity of human wishes. Johnson thereby imparts to the structures of the *Lives* a value and a function not present in any one part of a life by itself. He discovers in human limitations and the historical realm a dignity and grace which moves his writing from proto-tragedy into a "mingled" mode, becoming, like Shakespeare's drama, "compositions of a distinct kind; exhibiting the real state of sublunary nature, which partakes of good and evil, joy and sorrow, mingled with endless variety of proportion and innumerable modes of combination; and expressing the course of the world" (*Shakespeare*, 1, 66). This transformation is achieved in the *Lives* as it is in Shakespeare, through what Johnson called nature.

Although "nature" is *the* crucial critical touchstone for Johnson, it is the least easily explicated of Johnson's major terms. G. F. Parker has suggestively explained how Johnson inherited (through the mediation of Pope) and developed certain intuitions about art, truth, and language from the seventeenth-century French writers Boileau and Bouhours, and how these ideas were themselves distinguished from a more formalistic and rule-bound aesthetics of French and English neo-classicism.[9] Johnson discovered in the French (as Addison put it in *Spectator* 62 when discussing Bouhours) the idea that "it is impossible for any Thought to be beautiful which is not just, and has not its Foundation in the nature of things";[10] and, in addition, the "belief in the validity of affective rather than intellectual awareness."[11] Like the French, Johnson believed that literature could release the human mind from its everyday, empirical constrictions, but that the truth and the reality to be found in such literature is inherent in – and not beyond – everyday experience.

While the *Lives* draw on the works of Boileau and Bouhours, they also share Johnson's earlier principles formulated in his engagement with Shakespeare. Shakespeare is a real though implicit presence in the *Lives*, his drama operating as a general touchstone by which to read such works as *Paradise Lost*, the plays of Milton, Dryden, Congreve, Addison, and Rowe, the poems of Donne and Cowley, and Dryden's translations. There is, however, a significant difference between Johnson's use of the term "nature" in the essays of the 1740s and 1750s – for example, his relatively narrow and moralistic use of the term in *Rambler* 4 to discuss the proprieties and moral dangers of the new realistic fiction of the 1740s (the novels of Richardson and Fielding) – and his use of the term in the Shakespeare criticism and the *Lives*. While the realistic novel imitates the details of common and domestic life (what Johnson calls "manners") with a life like accuracy, the power of Shakespeare's drama lies in its generality and its capacity to generate pleasure for Johnson: "Shakespeare is above all writers . . . the poet of nature. . . . His persons act and speak by the influence of those general passions and principles by which all minds are agitated, and the whole system of life continued in motion" (*Shakespeare*, I, 62). Novelists like Richardson and Fielding are "engaged in portraits of which every one knows the original, and can detect any deviation from exactness of resemblance" (*Rambler* 4, III, 20); Shakespeare's drama, by contrast, "approximates the remote and familiarises the wonderful," and has the power to rectify confused imagination (*Shakespeare*, I, 65). Johnson's admiration for Shakespeare emphasizes the felt life in a drama that exhibits "the real state of sublunary nature" in all its diversity (I, 66); but this quality is contained within and is at one with the generality of Shakespeare's drama: "Nothing can please many and please long, but just representations of general nature. . . . In the writings of other poets a character is too often an individual; in those of Shakespeare it is commonly a species" (I, 61–62).

The running distinction in Johnson's criticism between the literature of "manners" and that of "nature" (both admired by Johnson, but differently) has not prevented many critics from confusing the two. The apparent contradiction between the general and the particular, however, touches upon a paradox of "nature" that vanishes when it is realized that "general nature" and "sublunary nature" are different ways of saying the same thing that are made one in Shakespeare's drama.[12] For Johnson, it is inaccurate to assume that our observations of the world are immediate and empirical, or that our consciousness is fully possessed in daily experiences. Quite the contrary. The *Rambler* essays testify to the essential emptiness of human consciousness and to the discrepancy between the will and human action that underlies Johnson's thinking about the mind: "The mind of man is never satisfied with the objects immediately before it" (*Rambler* 2, III, 9); "almost all that we can be said to enjoy is past or future; the present is in perpetual motion: (*Rambler* 41, III, 223). The vanity of human wishes and the "striking and manifest contrariety between the life of an author and his writings" (*Rambler* 14, III, 74) are two versions of Johnson's skeptical belief that the human mind, language, and the things of the world are disjunct. So, "general nature" is not part of empirical experience for Johnson, but it becomes accessible through literature, implying the momentary and fictional bringing together of mind and world that Johnson finds deeply pleasurable and existentially grounding: "Nothing can please many, and please long, but just representations of general nature . . . the pleasures of sudden wonder are soon exhausted, and the mind can only repose on the stability of truth" (*Shakespeare*, I, 61).

Johnson's formulation of general nature develops both Dryden's understanding of wit as a "propriety of thoughts and words – or, in other terms, thoughts and words elegantly adapted to the subject"[13] – and Pope's well-known lines in the *Essay on Criticism*:

> True *Wit* is *Nature* to Advantage drest,
> What oft was *Thought*, but ne'er so well *Exprest*,
> *Something*, whose Truth convinc'd at Sight we find,
> That gives us back the Image of our Mind. (297–300)

Pope's lines sound very Johnsonian, and Johnson, who thought the *Essay* "one of [Pope's] greatest . . . works" ("Life of Pope," III, 228), is sometimes taken as simply echoing Pope in his discussions of wit and poetry in the "Life of Cowley" and elsewhere. One version of this assumption is that because Johnson's poetic taste was formed by the couplet art of Dryden and Pope, his conception of wit (i.e. poetry) is necessarily theirs. Pope's wit is certainly impressive. In the *Essay on Criticism* wit depends upon the transforming yet transparent function of language to waken an immanent knowledge within the mind in such a way that the mind takes cognizance of that knowledge as if it were a phenomenal object (a "thing" in Pope's word). This imaginative engagement is a means of knowing the self more fully, and of knowing more fully the self's integration into the world. In these lines Pope was assimilating an impressive body of thought about poetry from Aristotle, Horace, and Longinus to Boileau, Dryden, and Walsh. These were some of the qualities that prompted Johnson to note that the poem "displays such extent of comprehension, such nicety of distinction, such acquaintance with mankind, and such knowledge both of ancient and modern learning as is not often attained by the maturest age and longest experience" (III, 94).

In the "Life of Cowley," however, Johnson thought that "Pope's account of wit is undoubtedly erroneous; he depresses it below its natural dignity, and reduces it from strength of thought to happiness of language" (I, 19). This statement comes as part of Johnson's dissertation on the metaphysical poets. The "Life of Cowley" was the first to be written (1777), and it stood first in the *Prefaces*

(1779). According to Boswell, Johnson considered this to be the best of the *Lives* "on account of the dissertation which it contains on the *Metaphysical Poets*" (*Life*, IV, 38), and, according to Sir John Hawkins, because of its "investigation and discrimination of the characteristics of wit" (Hawkins, p. 482). The function of the famous section on the metaphysical poets is complex. It consists of just fourteen paragraphs (49–63 in G. B. Hill's edition) in a text that totals 200; it is preceded by a chronological sketch of Cowley's life, and followed by two sections of detailed commentary and quotation, the first offering specific examples from Donne and Cowley to exemplify Johnson's remarks, the second concentrating on Cowley's main poems, from the *Miscellanies* to the *Davideis*. The central section on the metaphysical poets represents Johnson's statement about Cowley's poetic character, and as with other Lives, this section addresses important critical and historical issues. Johnson casts his net widely in this life not only by offering a revaluation of Cowley's works (after long critical neglect), but also by formulating a mini critical tradition (Aristotle to Johnson himself), implying a mini literary history (Jacobean Age to the Georgian), all in the process of defining a specific poetic style – the metaphysical. While never actually offering the section on the metaphysicals as a manifesto ("To circumscribe poetry by a definition will only shew the narrowness of the definer" ["Life of Pope," III, 251]), it makes a powerful statement of principles and exemplifies Johnson's criticism in the *Lives*.

Johnson's principles and *practice* are related to his sense that Pope's wit falls below the dignity of natural poetry, and he incorporates the reference to Pope into the discussion of the metaphysicals. Even though nature for Pope (as for Johnson) is "At once the *Source*, and *End*, and *Test of Art*" (*Essay on Criticism*, 73), there is the sense that the reader's experience with which Pope's passage begins is no different from that with which it ends. The circle is too small so that the reader is left with the impression that nature is only embellishment ("well *Exprest*"), and with a corresponding sense that Pope's words do not quite engage with the thought, as the passage declares it *does* ("*True Wit* is *Nature* to Advantage drest, / What oft was *Thought*, but ne'er so well *Exprest*"). In Johnson's terms the passage does not discover general nature in sublunary nature. Notwithstanding Pope's talk of "things" (true wit is "*Something*" whose truth convinces us once we see it), the passage's delicate refinement has the effect of dissolving the world it aims to mirror into the image of the mind suggesting Pope's proximity to Marvell's "Mind, that Ocean where each kind / Does streight its own resemblance find" ("The Garden," 43–44). In the "Life of Pope" Johnson is responsive to the social grace and nuances of Pope's poetry, but in the "Life of Cowley" he registers its limited consciousness, commensurate with Pope's skill for "particular manners" rather than "general nature."

Johnson is interested in the "representations of general nature" and the "grandeur of generality," which he associates with literature that "finds the passes of the mind" and "awakens those ideas that slumber in the heart" (*Lives*, III, 227; I, 459). Johnson's judgments on metaphysical poetry all rest on criteria that support that general experience of reading, and inform his formulation about wit: "If by a more noble and more adequate conception that be considered as Wit which is at once natural and new, that which though not obvious is, upon its first production, acknowledged to be just; if it be that, which he that never found it, wonders how he missed; to wit of this kind the metaphysical poets have seldom risen" (*Lives*, I, 19–20).

This line of thought began with a historical observation as part of a historical process ("Wit . . . has its changes and fashions" [I, 18]), and concludes various ideas of wit and poetry, including Aristotle's (poetry as an imitative art), Dryden's (wit as distinguished from poetry), and Pope's (true wit is nature to advantage dressed) (I, 18–19). Johnson's idea about wit has two distinctive components: it stresses the reader's experience of reading, and it perceives wit as simultaneously combining qualities (naturalness and originality) that *seem* to be mutually exclusive. Johnson's judgments from this point in the "Life of Cowley" exemplify *several* applications of his sense of true wit as being "*at once* natural and new," and how the metaphysicals (especially Donne, Cowley, and Cleveland) are felt *not* to fulfill those criteria. That perception means that for Johnson the metaphysicals are unable to evoke deep human feeling (I, 20) and to fill and expand the mind (I, 20–21).

These judgments (paras. 57–58 in Hill's edition), on the absence of pathos and sublimity in most metaphysical poems, are central to how Johnson works as a critic. Johnson clearly valued Donne's poetry highly: he admired its learning and subtlety ("their learning instructs, and their subtlety surprises" [I, 20]), its great labor and great abilities, its capacity to stimulate the reader to "recollection or inquiry," and its originality ("to write on their plan it was at least necessary to read and to think. No man could be born a metaphysical poet" [I, 21]). That is, Johnson identifies Donne as having *risen above* all the mediocre and merely traditional poets in the *Lives*. He belongs in the company of Milton, Dryden, Pope, and Cowley.

Yet for Johnson, Donne's impressive qualities are at one with the conceited inflection of his wit that makes for the violent yoking together of "heterogeneous ideas" (para. 58), becoming hyperbolical (para. 59), and leading Johnson to exclude Donne from his notion of wit as at once natural and new (para. 55).

> On a round ball
> A workman that hath copies by, can lay
> An Europe, Afric, and an Asia,
> And quickly make that, which was nothing, all,
> So doth each tear,

Which thee doth wear,
A globe, yea world by that impression grow,
Till thy tears mixed with mine do overflow
This world, by waters sent from thee, my heaven dissolved so.

Johnson quotes this stanza (para. 77) from "A Valediction: Of Weeping" as an example of the far-fetched and perplexing nature of the "heterogeneous ideas" of the metaphysicals. T. S. Eliot praised this passage for its agility and its rapid metaphoric movement;[14] but while Johnson notices the metaphoric cast of the lines ("The tears of the lovers are always of great poetical account, but Donne has extended them into worlds" [para. 77]), he also registers their effect and implication: "Their attempts were always analytick: they broke every image into fragments" (para. 58). This is one reason why Donne "was not successful in representing or moving the affections" (para. 57), for the poem's linguistic triumph and its intellectual self-consciousness evade the opportunity of exploring or presenting either what it feels like to weep for the parting of one's lover, or what it might mean. This is perhaps why Johnson remarks that as the metaphysical poets "were wholly employed on something unexpected and surprising they had no regard to that uniformity of sentiment, which enables us to conceive and to excite the pains and the pleasures of other minds" (para. 57). The Johnsonian reader is, as it were, kept on the outside of the poem, admiring its dexterity ("their learning instructs, and their subtlety surprises") but unable to feel the connection with the lovers' actual drama of the senses and of the soul ("the reader commonly thinks his improvement dearly bought, and, though he sometimes admires, is seldom pleased" [para. 56]).

The failure to move the feelings of the reader is, for Johnson, a failure to represent them, which points to a failure of imagination and of art. This perception is similar to his statement that in Milton's "Lycidas" "there is no nature, for there is no truth; there is no art, for there is nothing new" ("Life of Milton," I, 163) – where Johnson's complaint is *not* mainly about the poem's pastoral form or Johnson's supposed expressive theory, but rather about the effect the poem has on Johnson as reader. It is the *effect* of Donne's wit that prompts Johnson's metaphoric idea that the metaphysicals "wrote rather as beholders than partakers of human nature; . . . as Epicurean deities making remarks on the actions of men and the vicissitudes of life" (para. 57), linking this poetry with Soame Jenyns's remote rationality (attacked by Johnson in his review of *A Free Inquiry* [1757]) and distinguishing it from the epicureanism of Cowley's *Anacreontiques*, songs "dedicated to festivity and gaiety, in which even the morality is voluptuous, and which teach nothing but the enjoyment of the present day" (I, 39) – qualities which Johnson greatly enjoyed.

Donne's poetry moves Johnson to formulate a wholly special kind of wit: "But Wit, abstracted from its effects upon the hearer, may be more rigorously and philosophically considered as a kind of *discordia concors*; a combination of dissimilar images, or discovery of occult resemblances in things apparently unlike" (1, 20; para. 56). That is, defining the particular effect Donne has on the reader necessitates a degree of *abstraction*, a separation of the reader from experience ("Wit, abstracted from its effects upon the hearer"). Although Johnson is able to *imagine* the poem "philosophically" in this way, and to formulate its unrelatedness, he clearly does not like or value the *accompanying feeling*. It is that feeling of absence or frustrated human expectation that Johnson designates when remarking the *discordance* of the metaphysical style ("*discordia concors*"), just as it is when he describes "Lycidas" as "harsh" ("Life of Milton," 1, 163).

The idea of "harmony" as a poetic standard can confuse the reader into thinking that what Johnson refers to is the mere sound of the Augustan heroic couplet, and the ordered world of much of that verse. However, Johnson responds from his sense of the "grandeur of generality" that is lost when "all the power of description is destroyed by a scrupulous enumeration . . . and the force of metaphors is lost" (para. 133), and this perception, we must remember, is informed by his reading of Shakespeare's drama, as well as by his reading of Milton's blank verse. In *Rambler*s 86, 88, 90, 92, and 94 (on prosody and poetic experience) it is Milton and Homer who are designated as the great "harmonious" poets for Johnson – not any writer of couplets. They are so designated, not on the basis of the *sound* of their verse, but due to their particular "force of poetry:" "it is certain that without this petty knowledge ['deliberation upon accents and pauses'] no man can be a poet; and that from the proper disposition of single sounds results that harmony that adds force to reason, and gives grace to sublimity; that shackles attention, and governs passion" (*Rambler* 88, IV, 99). It is Milton who, according to Johnson, comes closest to replicating Homer's "force of imagination . . . [and] flexibility of language" that "gave him full possession of every object" (*Rambler* 92, IV, 124–25). These *Rambler* essays, together with Johnson's discussion of *Paradise Lost* and the *Iliad* in the *Lives*, confirm the idea that harmony arises when literary art is able to establish continuity (not identity) between different realms of experience, such as "musick" and "reason" and "intellect and body"[15] so as to create a wit that is *at once* natural and new.

Jean Hagstrum finds Johnson's criticism governed by three discourses – the beautiful, the pathetic, and the sublime – and each of these qualities to be exemplified by a different writer (Pope is beautiful, Shakespeare is pathetic, Milton is sublime).[16] But the point of Johnson's observations on the absence of pathos, sublimity, and harmony in metaphysical poetry lies in his discovering *various* poetic experiences in one composition that are thought of as mutually exclusive. He finds astonishment along with rational admiration, naturalness along with originality. Pathos and sublimity are not, then, characteristics of different poems – just as, in Shakespeare, tragedy and comedy are not formally exclusive genres

– but different ways in which the *same* poem might be experienced as a "just representation of general nature."

Johnson's critical prose is similarly ambiguous: it is equally sensitive to that which Johnson approves and to that which he disapproves. For example, when Johnson writes, "Their attempts were always analytick: they broke every image into fragments, and could no more represent by their slender conceits and laboured particularities the prospects of nature or the scenes of life, than he who dissects a sun-beam with a prism can exhibit the wide effulgence of a summer noon" (1, 20–21; para. 58) – the metaphoric form of this statement is both a joke at Donne's expense, as well as a sensitive echo of Donne's wit:

> And as no chemic yet the elixir got,
>   But glorifies his pregnant pot,
>   If by the way to him befall
> Some odoriferous thing, or medicinal,
> So, lovers dream a rich and long delight,
> But get a winter-seeming summer's night.
>   ("Love's Alchemy," 7–12)

As the above stanza shows, splitting a sunbeam with a prism in order to demonstrate the beauty of a summer's day, and then to make *that* a metaphor for "the scenes of life," is quite typical of Donne's wit!

When Johnson writes, however, that the metaphysicals "were wholly employed on something unexpected and surprising [and] had no regard to that uniformity of sentiment, which enables us to conceive and to excite the pains and the pleasures of other minds" (1, 20; para. 57), the measured deliberateness and the eloquence of the sentence enlarges and opens the mind of the reader, creating (I would suggest) something of an *equivalence* to the experience Johnson does *not* find in the poetry itself. The parallel clauses, the internal rhymes, and the rhythm ("enables us to conceive and to excite the pains and the pleasures") expand the reader's sense and suggest some feeling beneath the level of conscious thought ("awakening," as Johnson says of the poetry of nature, "those ideas that slumber in the heart" ["Life of Dryden," 1, 459]) which gesture toward the general nature that Johnson finds absent in the poetry. One might add that, as Johnson remarks on the absence of feeling in the poetry, his prose at the same time manifests a sadness, a pathos mirrored by the particular choice and disposition of words ("Their courtship was void of fondness and their lamentation of sorrow. Their wish was only to say what they hoped had never been said before" [1, 20]).

The general nature by which metaphysical poetry is implicitly tested, then, is a composite experience (not a simple proposition or cognitive idea) toward which Johnson's prose moves; it is neither entirely part of his given experience,

nor entirely outside it. His critical position here might be said to enlist the anti-
thetical wit of the metaphysicals in its own imaginative statement about poetry.
In this critical yet serendipitous relationship with his subject-matter, typical of
Johnson's criticism in the *Lives*, his prose is as he describes Dryden's: "the criticism of a poet; . . . a gay and vigorous dissertation, where delight is mingled with
instruction, and where the author proves his right to judgment by his power of
performance" ("Life of Dryden," 1, 412).

III

Johnson's literary biography is governed by a rooted self-possession and an open
responsiveness that comes under the heading of "nature." Johnson's "general
nature" is, as Christopher Ricks explains, a set of *principles* that is applied in
flexible and particular ways depending upon the context: "'The task of criticism'
was, for Johnson, to 'establish principles' (*Rambler*, No. 92), and he everywhere
made clear that his refusal to elaborate and concatenate the needed concepts
beyond a certain point (a point reached early) was not a refusal to continue to
think, but a decision to think thereafter about the application of the principles
and not to elaborate principles into theory."[17] These are principles operating in
Johnson's discussions of the lives as well as the works of the poets, and they
condition the distinct "mingled" quality of the *Lives*. Johnson is aware of the
historical and relative nature of language ("*words are the daughters of earth,
and . . . things are the sons of heaven*. Language is only the instrument of science,
and words are but the signs of ideas" [Preface to *Dictionary*, Greene, p. 310]),
yet he does not hold an aesthetic view of literature, as Coleridge does. Literature,
for Johnson, does not occupy its own separate realm, but is part of the ordinary
experiences of life, offering potentially transforming pleasures to the reader, but
essentially no different from the other pleasures of life.

In the *Lives* Johnson is additionally interested in the ways in which literature
manifests the powers and the qualities of mind and sensibility of the authors
themselves. This is not an expressive or naively biographical view of literature –
one that imagines a correlation between the good person and the good work –
but a sophisticated understanding that, in the words of Henry James, "There is
one point at which the moral sense and the artistic sense lie very near together;
that is in the light of the very obvious truth that the deepest quality of a work of
art will always be the quality of mind of the producer. In proportion as that intelligence is fine will the novel, the picture, the statue partake of the substance of
beauty and truth."[18] It is a similar thought to that of James, grounded in the
commonality of "nature," that underlies Johnson's interest in the continuities
and discontinuities of the lives and the works of the poets.

Johnson's way of writing Cowley's life, as Lawrence Lipking remarks, is to subordinate the biographical questions to the poetic, because Johnson felt that Cowley's life had been more fully treated (by Sprat, for example) than his poetry and because Bishop Hurd's 1772 selection of Cowley's works was prejudicial.[19] In all the major lives Johnson records how poetic genius transforms the personal into the impersonal, the temporal into the eternal, and the individual's personality into the poet's character. While critics have tended to see Johnson's idea of poetic character as governed by rules that privilege the sublime and the heroic,[20] the *Lives* actually trace *different* ways in which poets give shape and value to their experience. Just as Shakespeare's drama is not exclusively natural,[21] so not all the poets in the *Lives* are poets of nature. While Donne is metaphysical, Milton is sublime, and Pope is idealist, only Dryden (and, in some degree, Cowley) is natural. Our sense of the differences between these writers is conveyed by the manner and engagement of Johnson's particular lives. Whereas the "Life of Milton" is monolithic and intellectual, and the "Life of Pope" is subtle and minutely discriminatory, the "Life of Dryden" is easy, comfortable, and capacious, as if Johnson were relaxing in the company of a friend with whom he felt an inner kinship, and where the "repose" he associates with nature in the *Preface to Shakespeare* is felt, despite the many criticisms he makes of Dryden. The style of each of these lives is directly responsive to, and (in some way) imitative of, the qualities of mind of the poets discussed. Johnson is, as he says of Dryden, "always 'another and the same'; he does not exhibit a second time the same elegances in the same form" ("Life of Dryden," I, 418).

IV

The lives of Dryden, Pope, Milton, Swift, and Addison all register how poets "realize" their characters or "genius" in literature. For Johnson, making a character is tantamount to *re-member-ing* or making a self out of the unconscious, the past or a general human nature. This is not the absolute, hegemonic attitude often identified as Johnsonian by readers who have only a superficial knowledge of Johnson's texts and the flexibility and sophistication of eighteenth-century thinking. In one of the finest essays on the *Lives*, James Battersby discusses how "our conceptual grasp of character [in the *Lives*] depends upon Johnson's conjectures and surmises . . . from the available facts and especially from the writings."[22] It is important here to notice that the process is from text to character and not from biography to text: Johnson is not making interpretations of the author's text from what he knows about the author's life, but rather working toward a conception of poetic character and literary text that recognizes their differential yet unified structure.[23] Although Milton's sublimity, Pope's idealizing aspiration, and Dryden's numinous energy all testify, as Johnson says in the "Life of Gay" (II, 282), to the "*mens divinior*," the divine soul in the poet,[24] Johnson does not reify reason or any other intellectual aspect that goes to the making of poetry; each poet and *œuvre* is circumstantially contingent, and each poet realizes his character through his work differently.

The "Life of Milton," for example, depicts the dynamic relationship between man and poet more starkly and paradoxically than the other lives. The work of Lawrence Lipking, Stephen Fix, and Isobel Grundy has made it possible to appreciate that, despite Johnson's oppositional treatment of Milton in the biographic part of the life, he establishes continuities between Milton's life and work that have a different meaning when considered in association with *Paradise Lost*, a poem that Johnson considers as second only to Homer's *Iliad* in Western literature. Johnson detects human qualities common to Milton the man and Milton's poetry, but however much he disapproves of Milton's egotism, aloofness, and radical republicanism, he also recognizes that those qualities nurtured a mind peculiarly apt for writing *Paradise Lost*. Milton's "character" is actually not a given in this life, but created by the confluence of the personal and the poetic as traced by Johnson's text.

The biographical part of the text records Johnson's hostility to Milton's politics but it also registers a bafflement at the way a transcendent imagination enslaves itself to a political program whose fancied good entails the destruction of the political, social, and religious orders of English civilization. For Johnson, Milton's republicanism is more serious than Edmund Waller's support of Cromwell, which, by comparison, is the mere weakness of a superficial man.[25] Unlike Waller's political allegiances, obsequiously bending in the winds of change, Milton's republicanism is deep-rooted, founded on principle, and supported by his "envious hatred of greatness . . . sullen desire of independence . . . and pride disdainful of authority" (1, 157). At the same time this aloofness and pride fed Milton's poetic genius: "He had accustomed his imagination to unrestrained indulgence, and his conceptions therefore were extensive. The characteristic quality of his poem is sublimity" (1, 177). Johnson's treatment of Milton's personal characteristics and politics suggests that what starts out as childish distrust of the world issues into a poem of great and beautiful splendor. The qualities of mind exemplified by Milton's politics cease to be obnoxious to Johnson when they are enlisted in a poetic enterprise such as *Paradise Lost*.

This paradox also characterizes Milton's religious opinions. Johnson gives much weight to the fact that Milton distanced himself from all churches, both Protestant and Catholic ("he loves himself rather than truth" [1, 106]; see also 154–56). How does a man, Johnson seems to be asking, who has the "profoundest veneration" for the Holy Scriptures, and a "confirmed belief of the immediate and occasional agency of Providence" (1, 155–56) live without visible worship? Johnson never answers this implied question, but, once he brings Milton's poetry into play, the paradox ceases to be problematic and becomes, instead, expressive of the complexity of Milton's character, for "Prayer certainly was not thought superfluous by him, who represents our first parents [i.e. Adam and Eve] as praying acceptably in the state of innocence, and efficaciously after their fall. That he lived without prayer can hardly be affirmed; his studies and meditations were an habitual prayer" (I, 156). Johnson does not say that because Adam and Eve are represented as praying in *Paradise Lost* therefore Milton himself must have prayed. Instead, he says that the intelligence in the poetry is so clearly imbued with spirituality that, given Milton's belief in the truths of Christianity, it is inconceivable that he did not also, *somewhere*, acknowledge his human status through prayer.

It is in a "fictional" realm, then, between life and text, in which Johnson creates a representation of Milton's character, that the above discrepancy vanishes. "In Milton every line breathes sanctity of thought and purity of manners" (I, 179). This suggests that the obstinacy which prevented Milton from accepting his own ordinariness, dissolves in the seriousness which comes upon his mind when filled by the "*mens divinior*:" "The heat of Milton's mind might be said to sublimate his learning, to throw off into his work the spirit of science, unmingled with its grosser parts" (I, 177). The movement of the "Life of Milton" from Milton's personal characteristics to the manifestation of qualities of mind in poetry is marked in Johnson's writing by the evaporation of personalized and ironic treatment. In *Paradise Lost* Milton's mind seems to come free, legitimately encounters no opposition from the world, and is able to expand to the limits of conception, and therefore Johnson registers Milton's ability to "realize fiction" (I, 170): "To display the motives and actions of beings thus superior, so far as human reason can examine them or human imagination represent them, is the task this mighty poet has undertaken *and performed*" (I, 172). The poetic success of *Paradise Lost* in Johnson's estimation might be gauged by comparing his qualified response to the religious poems of Waller, Watts, and Cowley with his unqualified admiration for Milton's poem. Not only does the poem satisfy the demands of the epic ("the first praise of genius is due to the writer of an epick poem, as it requires an assemblage of all the powers which are singly sufficient for other compositions" [I, 170]), but it also overrides the imaginative and moral reservations Johnson usually has toward religious verse: "[*Paradise Lost*] contains the history of a miracle, of Creation and Redemption; it displays the power and the mercy of the Supreme Being: the probable therefore is marvellous, and the marvellous is probable" (I, 174).

The sublimity of *Paradise Lost* and the heroic aspect of Milton's character are not, however, the mode of being with which Johnson is most comfortable, nor the reality he found in Shakespeare's mingled drama. Milton, in contrast to Shakespeare, "would not have excelled in dramatick writing; he knew human nature only in the gross, and had never studied shades of character, nor the combinations of concurring or the perplexity of contending passions. He had read much and knew what books could teach; but he had mingled little in the world, and was deficient in the knowledge which experience must offer" (I, 189). Johnson's terminology recognizes the impersonality of the poetic activity, tracing the path from the individual personality to the poetic character, but it also delimits the distance between Milton and himself. This distance might be thought of as a space in which Milton manifests himself, and his manifestation is dialectically related to Johnson's action of confronting and parrying Milton's otherness. The most polemical and strategic use of Socrates in Johnson's work occurs in this life, when Johnson aligns himself with Socrates against Milton's educational views, for it was Socrates's "labour to turn philosophy from the study of nature [by "nature" here Johnson means natural science] to specula-tions upon life, but the innovators whom I oppose [i.e. Milton and others] are turning off attention from life to nature" (I, 100). In keeping with this distancing of Milton, the words most remembered by readers of Johnson's critique of *Paradise Lost* are that "we desert our master, and seek for companions" (I, 184). This sentiment locates Milton's grandeur at a distance from Johnson the common reader, and – insofar as Johnson possesses and manifests the authority he claims for his positions – from nature and humanity. Significantly, however, Johnson does not express this view through criticism or irony, but by demanding a *bond* with Milton in order to mitigate the loneliness revealed in and induced by the heroic and sublime imagination – Milton's loneliness and the loneliness Johnson feels as a reader.

In this respect the "Life of Pope" identifies Pope as a Miltonic poet who strives for the heroic and is similarly distanced from the common reader, while the "Life of Dryden" discovers what might be called a Shakespearean diversity, a conge-nial intimacy and insight into the human mind in the works of Dryden that should remind modern readers of the error of coupling Dryden and Pope as exemplars of a uniform Augustanism.

The "Life of Pope" also develops an argument about the relations between person and text. What distinguishes the "Life of Pope" as a profound and cre-ative example of literary biography is the delicacy and insight with which it maintains the sense of difference-in-continuity between the moral and the liter-ary aspects of Pope's life, and marks the psychological complexity and the arti-fice of Pope's poetry in Johnson's own sensitive representation.

Johnson's portrait of Pope's poetic and intellectual character, forming the imaginative center of the text (paras. 255–311 in Hill's edition), articulates the interrelationships between Pope's behavior, mind, body, and poetry governing Johnson's earlier biographical discussion of the main events in Pope's life (paras. 1–254) and his subsequent criticism of particular poems by Pope (paras. 312–86). In appreciating the seriousness of these passages consideration needs to be given to the detail and care of Johnson's depiction of Pope and his poetry.[26] Johnson writes suggestively (paras. 255–63) about Pope's physical appearance, sensitivities and deformity, his behavioral eccentricities, and his delight in artifice ("In all his intercourse with mankind he had great delight in artifice and endeavoured to attain all his purposes by indirect and unsuspected methods" [III, 200]). From these aspects of Pope's life arise Johnson's consideration of his intercourse with others and the ways he represented himself. Paragraphs 264–91 deal with Pope's conversation, sense of humor, frugality, hospitality, social qualities, letters and their rhetorical self-constructions, attitudes toward his own poetry, contemptuousness of others and public opinion, friends and attitudes to friendship, self-importance, religion, and learning. Johnson's narrative then takes up these topics in the closing paragraphs of this central section of the life to treat Pope's intellectual character (paras. 293–96), his methods of poetic composition (paras. 297–302), and, in a famous comparison with Dryden, Pope's poetic character (paras. 303–11).

The formal comparison with Dryden stands in a line of similar set pieces in the history of criticism;[27] in it Johnson encapsulates all the tension and the force of Pope's poetry and Pope's life. When read with a lively remembrance of Pope's poetry (not only the *Imitations of Horace* and the *Moral Essays* but also the *Essay on Criticism*, *The Rape of the Lock*, and the translation of Homer's *Iliad*, which Johnson considered the greatest of Pope's poems) Johnson's portrait of Pope is recognized as being of a mind elevated to grandeur and dignity, and at the same time painfully *unable* to embody the knowledge for which it strives: "Pope had likewise genius; a mind active, ambitious, and adventurous, always investigating, always aspiring; in its widest searches still longing to go forward, in its highest flights still wishing to be higher; always imaging something greater than it knows, always endeavouring more than it can do" (III, 217).

It is not immediately clear how this energy of mind can be construed as weakness, especially since "It is the proper ambition of the heroes in literature to enlarge the boundaries of knowledge by discovering and conquering new regions of the intellectual world" (*Rambler* 137, II, 362). But whereas Milton was able to conquer and *contain* within the imaginative structure of *Paradise Lost* those new regions, Pope's poetry is registered as partially unrealized, only *striving toward* a vision that is never quite brought into focus and never quite embodied.

The metaphor of the body in the above statement about Pope's imagination is apt for Johnson's text since he gives much weight to Pope's physiognomy and bodily experiences. He sees Pope's crippled and hunchbacked body, with great tact and seriousness, as the material basis for Pope's particular imagination, and as a metaphor for his poetry. As with Milton's blindness, which Johnson invokes as a pure factual component to the extraordinary inner light of Milton's poetry – as if in compensation for his outer darkness – so Johnson's references to Pope's twisted body are offered entirely without irony and with deep insight into the connectedness of different sides of our being at the deepest levels:

> He was then so weak as to stand in perpetual need of female attendance; extremely sensible of cold, so that he wore a kind of fur doublet under a shirt of very coarse warm linen with fine sleeves. When he rose he was invested in boddice made of stiff canvas, being scarce able to hold himself erect till they were laced, and he then put on a flannel waistcoat. One side was contracted. His legs were so slender that he enlarged their bulk with three pair of stockings, which were drawn on and off by the maid; for he was not able to dress or undress himself, and neither went to bed nor rose without help. His weakness made it very difficult for him to be clean.
>
> (III, 197)

This important passage forms part of Johnson's extended exploration of the pain and inconvenience under which Pope labored, and its poignancy is perhaps sharpened by Johnson's personal experience of physical awkwardness and suffering (so fully treated by Boswell in the *Life*). Pope's physique was important to himself and to his contemporaries: he writes about his body frequently, and others attack him for it. Given Johnson's awareness of the disparity between intellectual gestures and physical actions, and given the readiness with which he criticizes Pope's rhetorical pretentiousness (e.g. para. 280), it is remarkable that Johnson presents Pope's physical being without any tonal inflection. The dignity of the above passage lies, partly, in the recognition of the possibility of making crushing satire on Pope, and choosing *not* to do so in the name of a larger vision. Close to the surface of the passage lies a parody along the lines of *The Rape of the Lock*: Pope being "invested" in armor by the domestic deities before going out to do battle with the world. There is also the implicit contrast between Pope's weakness and dependence on others and his intellectual (and financial) independence, and the imaginative heights of his poetry. Johnson's vision here sensitively connects and contrasts Pope's human weakness – the physical weakness shown up repeatedly in the perpetual striving for transcendence of the earthly in the poetry – with a cool rootedness that seems to lie outside life itself.[28]

While Johnson dwells on the particulars of Pope's person and activities, he unobtrusively links them with their effect on the world. In Johnson's text Pope is not allowed to slip into the privacy of his materiality or to escape through his imagination. Hence, the range of Johnson's references become more and more inclusive, from the observation that "He is said to have been beautiful in his infancy; but he was of a constitution originally feeble and weak" (para. 255), to the recognition that "The indulgence and accommodation which his sickness required had taught him all the unpleasing and unsocial qualities of a valetudinary man" (para. 259), to the idea that as "He was fretful and easily displeased, [so he] allowed himself to be capriciously resentful" (para. 265). From the perception of the shaping power of Pope's physical nature, Johnson moves into a discussion of Pope's social qualities as presented through his letters (paras. 273–88), and then on to the articulation of Pope's intellectual qualities and poetic genius (paras. 293–311).

That intellectual portrait connects Pope's striving, disembodied genius with other aspects of intellectual skill: with good sense ("a prompt and intuitive perception of consonance and propriety"), a quality that Johnson identifies as the "constituent and fundamental principle" of Pope's mind (para. 293), as well as with Pope's strong memory and "incessant and unwearied diligence" (paras. 295–96). These qualities, combined with Pope's genius, clearly make for a very high degree of imaginative excellence and poetic finish of the kind that made *The Rape of the Lock* for Johnson the "most airy, the most ingenious, and the most delightful of all his compositions" (III, 101). Unlike Shakespeare or Dryden, who "seldom struggled after supreme excellence, but snatched in haste what was within his reach" ("Life of Dryden," I, 464), Pope "was never content with mediocrity when excellence could be attained" (III, 217). But Pope's excellence also raises in Johnson's mind the idea of the compulsive and unresolved drive of Pope's efforts, registered by the frequently repeated words "always" and "still": Pope is "always investigating . . . always aspiring . . . still longing . . . still wishing . . . always imagining . . . always endeavouring." Recognizing that critical judgment required the contextualization of Pope's linguistic purity and finish in terms *other* than itself, Johnson (within a few paragraphs) invokes Dryden as a standard of a *different* and evidently more encompassing form of genius by which to measure Pope: "Of genius, that power which constitutes a poet; that quality without which judgement is cold and knowledge is inert; that energy which collects, combines, amplifies, and animates – the superiority must, with some hesitation, be allowed to Dryden" (III, 222; para. 310).

Since the "Life of Pope" was the last of the lives to be written (completed 5 March 1781) and the "Life of Dryden" was one of the first (completed between 21 July and early August 1778), this comparison between Pope and Dryden draws upon Johnson's earlier discussion of Dryden in developing the critical discriminations under consideration. The reader is clearly expected to recall those earlier arguments. The essential point about the "Life of Dryden" for the comparison is that it had traced out a natural rather than a heroic character for Dryden most typically exemplified in his translations of Horace and Lucretius (in *Sylvae* [1685]) and of Homer, Boccaccio, Chaucer, and Ovid (in *Fables* [1700]).[29] While Johnson does not hesitate to criticize Dryden's temporizing ("in the meanness and servility of hyperbolical adulation I know not whether, since the days in which the Roman emperors were deified, he has been ever equalled" [I, 399]), his moral judgment is modified by the power of Dryden's writing.

This poetic power, as it were, redeems the baseness of Dryden's flattery ("he had all forms of excellence, intellectual and moral, combined in his mind, with

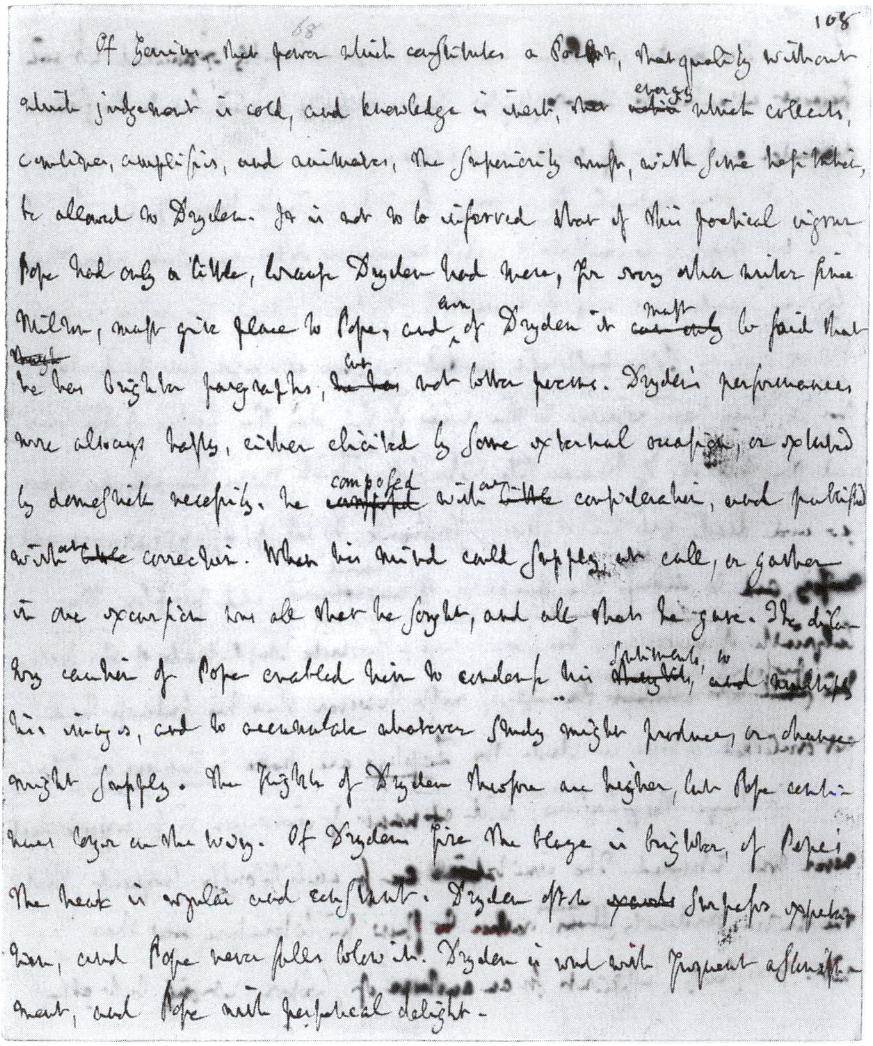

Of Genius, that power which constitutes a Poet, that quality without which judgement is cold, and knowledge is inert, that energy which collects, combines, amplifies, and animates, the superiority must, with some hesitation, be allowed to Dryden. It is not to be inferred that of this poetical vigour Pope had only a little, because Dryden had more, for every other writer since Milton, must give place to Pope, and of Dryden it must be said that he has brighter paragraphs, but not better poems. Dryden's performances were always hasty, either excited by some external occasion, or extorted by domestick necessity. he composed without any consideration, and published without any correction. What his mind could supply at call, or gather in one excursion was all that he sought, and all that he gave. The dilatory caution of Pope enabled him to condense his sentiments, to multiply his images, and to accumulate whatever study might produce, or chance might supply. The flights of Dryden therefore are higher, but Pope continues longer on the wing. Of Dryden's fire the blaze is brighter, of Pope's the heat is more regular and constant. Dryden often surpasses expectation, and Pope never falls below it. Dryden is read with frequent astonishment, and Pope with perpetual delight.

Plate 6 Samuel Johnson, holograph manuscript of "The Life of Pope"

endless variation" [I, 399]), it administers to the pleasure that Johnson finds necessary to all reading ("Works of imagination excell by their allurement and delight; by their power of attracting and detaining the attention" [I, 454]), and it issues into the paradoxical qualities that define the essence of all Dryden's writing for Johnson, both prose and verse:

> none of his prefaces were ever thought tedious. They have not the formality of a settled style, in which the first half of the sentence betrays the other. The clauses are never balanced, nor the periods modelled; every word seems to drop by chance,

though it falls into its proper place. Nothing is cold or languid; the whole is airy, animated, and vigorous; what is little is gay; what is great, is splendid . . . Though all is easy, nothing is feeble; though all seems careless, there is nothing harsh; and though since his earlier works more than a century has passed they have nothing yet uncouth or obsolete.

He who writes much will not easily escape a manner, such a recurrence of particular modes as may be easily noted. Dryden is always "another and the same"; he does not exhibit a second time the same elegances in the same form, nor appears to have any art other than that of expressing with clearness what he thinks with vigour. (I, 418)

This passage may start by considering Dryden's critical prose; it quickly becomes clear that Johnson is responding to a deep imaginative dimension of Dryden's poetic mind. What distinguishes Dryden's genius for Johnson is its being "another and the same"; this quality marks a continuity and not a discreteness of self and world in Dryden's writings; he uses his art as a means of registering and embodying the materiality of the world and of experience while also, apparently, circumventing the demands of the ego, expatiating confidently and pleasurably in his own poetic creations. These complex qualities of Dryden's writing are registered and *recreated* in Johnson's own descriptive prose as it traces the movement and clarity of Dryden's mind in its articulation of positions clearly felt by Johnson to be general and pleasurable.

Dryden's genius is, as the comparison in the "Life of Pope" observes, one that "collects, combines, amplifies, and animates," and its "nature" locates the self firmly in the world of differential experiences. Pope's genius, by comparison, is one that strives relentlessly to transcend that world of nature and commonality, although the tension that Johnson detects in that effort also indicates that Pope cannot wholly leave the world behind. Certainly, the consequences of Pope's drive take a toll on his moral being:

With such faculties and such dispositions he excelled every other writer in *poetical prudence*; he wrote in such a manner as might expose him to few hazards. He used almost always the same fabrick of verse . . .

Pope was not content to satisfy; he desired to excel, and therefore always endeavoured to do his best: he did not court the candour, but dared the judgement of his reader, and, expecting no indulgence from others, he shewed none to himself. He examined lines and words with minute and punctilious observation, and retouched every part with indefatigable diligence, till he had left nothing to be forgiven. (III, 219, 221)

The literary qualities of this description have, as with Dryden and Milton, moral and psychic ramifications, and reflect the relation of reader to poems and reader to poet. Pope's urgency ("desire to excel") has two direct consequences: it diminishes the poet's engagement with the world ("expose him to few hazards"), and it establishes an aloofness ("he did not court the candour but dared the judgement of the reader"); both have the effect of cutting him off from the reader *and from himself* ("he had left nothing to be forgiven"). To have nothing to be forgiven exempts the human being from redemption and frustrates the human contact and the self-forgiveness that comes with the movement of self toward the other.

The stance described by Johnson identifies a poetic consciousness that took the form of opposition between Pope and the world:

> Ask you what Provocation I had?
> The strong Antipathy of Good to Bad.
> (*Epilogue to the Satires*, II. 197–98)

and a discreteness of consciousness that Johnson finds even in such great poems as *The Rape of the Lock* when, notwithstanding the praise and pleasure the poem occasions, he pursues John Dennis's observation of a flaw in the poem: "It is remarked by Dennis . . . that the machinery is superfluous; that by all the bustle of preternatural operation the main event is neither hastened nor retarded" (III, 235).

Johnson, of course, refers here to that crucial point in Pope's poem in which Ariel, one of Belinda's mock-heroic superintending deities, is unable to help her when she is "threatened" by a suitor who intends to cut off a lock of her hair. Ariel's helplessness (III.143–46) is significant in various ways. It is a mark of the necessary separation of the real from the fantasy world in which Belinda lives that conditions her growth in the poem as she deals with the expectation of compromise in social and personal relationships. For all of their brilliance in dramatizing Belinda's beauty, the sylphs are disembodied and beyond real human passions. In this sense the sylphs (the poem's "machinery") function in the poem as the gods do in Homer's *Iliad*, who, as Felicity Rosslyn has beautifully demonstrated, draw attention to human limits (gods are immortal while people are mortal), and therefore shed grace and dignity on human aspirations as well as on the pure pity the gods feel for mortals on the other side of an insuperable divide:

> Zeus is the machine by which the imagination can grasp what humanity is from the outside . . . When the poet tells us that gods and men are alike, he helps our imaginations conceive of ourselves on the grandest scale; and when he says in the same breath that we have nothing in common worth mentioning, for gods are immortal, he helps us take all our actions more seriously, for human actions are taken under the sentence of death.[30]

Pope has appropriated Homer's divine machinery in an ironic and comic manner as a "divine shadow-play of the humanly possible" (Rosslyn, "Of Gods and Men," p. 17), and Johnson recognizes that the invention and deployment of the sylphs is a stroke of original genius animating the poem: "In this work are exhibited in a very high degree the two most engaging powers of an author: *new things are made familiar, and familiar things are made new*. A race of arial people never heard of before is presented to us in a manner so clear and easy, that the reader seeks for no further information" (III, 233 – my emphasis).

Yet Johnson's description of the sylphs suggests another way of understanding their function in the poem. For Pope's conception of the sylphs is different from Homer's gods in one crucial aspect, for in the *Iliad* the heroes are *aware of* the presence of the gods and experience their power in their very actions and encounters, whereas Pope's Belinda is aware of nothing but herself in her refined, artificial world. Johnson therefore notes that "The sylphs cannot be said to help or to oppose, and it must be allowed to imply *some want of art* that their power has not been sufficiently intermingled with the action" (III, 235). That Johnson observes that the sylphs have "powers and passions proportionate to their operation" (III, 232) simply draws attention to their circumscribed function. Clarissa's choral speech (V.9–34), designed, as Pope himself says in a note, to open the moral of the poem, goes unheeded by all in the poem:

> But since, alas! frail beauty must decay,
> Curled or uncurled, since locks will turn to grey;
> Since painted, or not painted, all shall fade,
> And she who scorns a man, must die a maid;
> What then remains but well our power to use,
> And keep good-humour still whate'er we lose.
>
> (V.25–30)

Johnson's qualifications, then, prompt the reader to reflect on the precise terms of his strong praise of the poem. One notices, for example, that Johnson's description of the poetic powers of the poem use the words "new" and "familiar" rather than "new" and "natural," as he does in the "Life of Cowley" when articulating his conception of true wit: "In this work are exhibited in a very high degree the two most engaging powers of an author: new things are made familiar, and familiar things are made new" (III, 233). "Familiarity" does not carry the same powerful poetic appeal in Johnson's thought as "nature." If, as I have argued above, Johnson thought of the deepest poetry as being "at once natural and new," then his syntax in the passage on the *Rape* suggests that the making of one thing into another in that poem is somehow divided and incomplete. Newness and familiarity in the *Rape* are kept separate, and, furthermore, the two terms are kept scrupulously apart in the two paragraphs Johnson gives to elaborating these qualities in the *Rape* (paras. 338–39). Johnson's syntax, prose structure, and thought, therefore, reflect the divided and double consciousness in the *Rape*, played out in its imaginative structure, that is of a piece with the particular type of genius that he finds in all of Pope's writing, and that is echoed, in a different register, in Pope's life. These are the qualities in Pope to which Johnson responds when he finds that, in comparing Dryden's *Alexander's Feast* with Pope's *Song for St. Cecilia's Day*, "Pope is read with calm acquiescence, Dryden with turbulent delight; Pope hangs upon the ear, and Dryden finds the passes of the mind" (III, 227).[31] This too is why Johnson identifies the specific *limits* of Pope's type of wit in the "Life of Cowley," at the beginning of the *Lives of the Poets*: "But Pope's account of wit is undoubtedly erroneous; he depresses it below its natural dignity, and reduces it from strength of thought to happiness of language" (I, 19).

Nonetheless, Johnson's complex response to Pope maintains throughout a fine awareness of the complexity of the poet himself and of his poetry. The "Life of Pope" asks for Pope's qualities to be taken in two always coexistent ways: Pope's heroically aspiring genius is perfectly at home in an insubstantial form, mirrored in the great dexterity of his couplet verse; at the same time, this perfection has serious human consequences, both for the man in his relations with the world, but also as replicated in the experiential range and consciousness of the poetry. Pope "was not content to satisfy . . . [he] left nothing to be forgiven."

V

Not all poets rise to such levels as Milton, Dryden, and Pope; the lives of these poets strike a more clearly memorializing or redemptive tone. The "redemptive-ness" of the *Lives* is a delicate notion. Although the term "redemptive" is the right word for Johnson's work, it is not meant to convey any theological or strictly religious meaning. The *Lives* are among the first biographies in English literature to have stripped themselves of medieval hagiographic overtones. The "Life of Rochester," for example, is a good example of how Johnson, notwith-standing his deeply religious nature, declines the opportunity to make a Christian interpretation out of a person's life and work. Johnson admires Bishop Gilbert Burnet's *Some Passages in the Life and Death of John, Earl of Rochester* (1680) for its elegance, argument, and piety, and recognizes the change of behav-ior and belief at the end of Rochester's libertine life documented by Burnet ("Life of Rochester," I, 222). At the same time, the "Life of Rochester" bears no resem-blance to the hagiographic structure of Burnet's work. For the clergyman, Rochester's late conversion is exemplary and evidence of providential interven-tion in human affairs. Johnson, however, internalizes hope; it manifests itself – or does not – in life and action. Though Johnson may be happy that Rochester *may* have saved his soul, the weight of his life of Rochester falls on his deeds and works: "every where [in his works] may be found tokens of a mind which study might have carried to excellence" (I, 226).

Johnson's biographical method is, therefore, not providential, but it does register the moral and spiritual power of a person's life with regard to the quality and influence of his work. In the case of Joseph Addison, Johnson is quite aware that "to write and to live are very different" (II, 125), and that a degree of skepticism is necessary in assessing Addison's moral professions. Yet, notwithstanding Johnson's reluctance to place Addison in the highest category of *writers*, his treatment of Addison's writing emphasizes the moral and redeeming power of the writer's life:

> It is justly observed by Tickell that [Addison] employed wit on the side of virtue and religion. He not only made the proper use of wit himself, but taught it to others; and from his time it has been generally subservient to the cause of reason and of truth. . . . This is an elevation of literary character, "above all Greek, above all Roman fame."
> (II, 125–26)

Yet, "Addison is to pass through futurity protected only by his genius" (II, 126), and Johnson's assessment of Addison's contributions to English literature in the form of the familiar essay perfectly capture the strengths and weaknesses of that "genius." *The Spectator* was instrumental in transforming middle-class sensibility in the early eighteenth century by "regulat[ing] the practice of daily conversation" (II, 92); yet notwithstanding this powerful cultural intervention, Johnson also registers the particular limitation of Addison's writing:

> His prose is the model of the middle style; on grave subjects not formal, on light occasions not groveling; pure without scrupulosity, and exact without elaboration; always equable, and always easy, without glowing words or pointed sentences. Addison never deviates from his track to snatch a grace; he seeks no ambitious ornaments, and tries no hazardous innovations. His page is always luminous, but never blazes in unexpected splendor.
> (II, 149)

The weaknesses of these apparently strong qualities are evident in the modesty and mediocrity (in the eighteenth-century sense of politeness, delicacy, and moderation) that Johnson's words carefully seek to delineate, and they become clearer when compared with Johnson's passages on Dryden's energetic prose ("Life of Dryden," I, 411–13) and with Johnson's own prose. Equally important, however, is that alongside the *literary* judgement of Addison's prose – of his literary character – is the sense that the purity of Addison's life and thought is what redeems his work and makes for a "literary character, 'above all Greek, above all Roman fame.'"

This "redemption" is less equivocal in the case of Isaac Watts, one of the poets added to the *Lives* at Johnson's request. Watts's religious poetry is registered as being good but not great: Johnson did not feel that Christian devotion was a suitable subject for poetry, because, as he writes in the "Life of Waller," "Contemplative piety, or the intercourse between God and the human soul, cannot be poetic. Man admitted to implore the mercy of his Creator and plead the merits of his Redeemer is already in a higher state than poetry can confer" (I, 291). He rates Watts as having "done better what no man has done well" (III, 310). But Watts's piety penetrated whatever he touched ("As piety predominated in his mind, it is diffused over his works" [III, 309]), so that Johnson's focus in this life does not linger on the works as literary creations, but focuses on the piety and innocence of this selfless man. Significantly, the very last word of the "Life of Watts" is "God" (III, 311).

Rochester, Addison, and Watts are all writers who, in one way or another, have some substance. Johnson's secular redemptiveness works differently for writers who have less substance, who are more absent from the historical imagination. The "Life of Halifax" is a case in point. This is a very short text (fifteen paragraphs in Hill's edition) of a small poet who had extensive political influence and extended significant patronage to other poets of the Restoration. Yet this life proposes a complicated relation between Halifax's power as a patron and the quality of his own poetry, and recognizes (though does not judge) that Halifax's poetry was, inevitably, overvalued because of his political influence. The moral complexities of this situation, however, are dissolved by the fact of Halifax's death, which makes possible the recognition of the diminishing attractions of his poetic output. Johnson's manner of handling the movement from Halifax's life to his memory, after death, is most illuminating:

> Many a blandishment was practised upon Halifax which he would never have known, had he no other attractions than those of his poetry, of which a short time has withered the beauties. It would now be esteemed no honour, by a contributor to the monthly bundles of verses, to be told that, in strains either familiar or solemn, he sings like Montague. (II, 47)

These are the last words of the text. The fading beauties of Halifax's poetry are implicitly connected to his death. The movement from power to mortality is the movement from "Halifax" to "Montague," Charles Montague being the given name and Halifax the earldom acquired as he came of age, and which was associated with political power. Johnson's thought moves in two directions at once: away from Halifax's political world as death comes, and toward the private world of Montague, whose presence and reality are remembered in the text even though his poems have been forgotten. Without invoking a religious dimension, Johnson's paragraph simply registers some reality about the *difference* between the business of the world and the realities of death and time, and in registering that difference casts a kind of grace on the life of Charles Montague that it would otherwise not have had.

The symbolic and metaphoric commemorativeness of the *Lives* might be summed up in a short passage from the "Life of Parnell." At the opening of this Life Johnson remembers his dead friend Goldsmith:

a man of such variety of powers and such felicity of performance that he always seemed to do best that which he was doing . . . I have . . . this gratification from my attempt that it gives me an opportunity of paying due tribute to the memory of Goldsmith.

ho gar geras esti thanonton

(II, 49)

Johnson's Greek quotation comes from the *Odyssey* Book 24, where the spirit of Amphimedon addresses the spirit of Agamemnon: "Thus we perished, Agamemnon, and even now our bodies still lie uncared-for in the halls of Odysseus; for our friends in each man's home know naught as yet – our friends who might wash the black blood from our wounds and lay our bodies out with wailing; *for that is the due of the dead*" (186–190).[32]

"Paying tribute to the memory" of Goldsmith is metaphorically and metonymically seen as washing the dead body, a narrative act whereby the absent spirits of the dead poets are released through memory and ritual so that they may find their way from the past into the present. Not only is the washing of the dead body what the dead need, it is also what the living need for their fulfillment. Memory here touches both those who are gone and those who remain. Johnson's prose inculcates that fulfillment, and gives it an authority. Such commemoration is religious in a non-doctrinal sense; it is also an act of witnessing, and therefore political in nature, because it shifts the locus of authority from the material and temporal to the eternally embodied, by giving voice to others, empowering them to manifest themselves.

Commemorativeness, therefore, suggests that Johnson's skeptical exploration of human division and failure is not, as they are habitually interpreted, necessarily tragic. Death, indeed, always comes as a blow, and, in an obvious sense, is always final. But both the structure and the style of the *Lives*, by taking into themselves the fractured nature of human endeavor and the distance between the past of the poets and the present of the reader, imitate and enunciate a triumph in time not unlike what we find in Shakespeare's comedy. In this sense the *Lives of the Poets* is a comic work. It is comic too insofar as it dramatizes and transforms an important Christian theme, one shared by Chaucer's *Canterbury Tales*, Montaigne's Essays, and Erasmus's *In Praise of Folly* – that *because* humankind is divided and foolish, *therefore* are we susceptible of grace. But this is a grace which manifests itself, and keeps the consciousness in the *present world*, while enlarging that world with human difference normally beyond experience. Paradoxically, grace reveals itself at the point in the *Lives* where different discourses meet; where the impermanent, imperfect details of a person's life touch the potentially permanent, immortal realm of art. Johnson's art as a biographer – which is also his art as a literary critic – bridges the gap between the two, making grace the best effect of his writing.

NOTES

1 *Selected Criticism of Matthew Arnold*, ed. Christopher Ricks (New York: Signet, 1972), p. 351.

2 For the genesis of the *Lives* see T. F. Bonnell, "John Bell's *Poets of Great Britain*: The 'Little Trifling Edition' Revisited," *MP*, 85 (1987), 128–52.

3 See, for example, Ira Bruce Nadel, *Biography: Fact, Fiction and Form* (New York: St. Martin's Press, 1984), chapter 5; and essays by Frederick Karl and Paul Mariani in *The Craft of Literary Biography*, ed. Jeffrey Meyers (London: Macmillan, 1985).

4 For Boswell's biographical self-reflexivity, see, for example, William R. Siebenshuh, *Fictional Techniques and Factual Works* (Athens: University of Georgia Press, 1983), and Greg Clingham, *James Boswell: The Life of Johnson* (Cambridge University Press, 1992).

5 "Biography: Inventing the Truth," in *The Art of Literary Biography*, ed. John Batchelor (Oxford: Clarendon Press, 1995), p. 20.

6 "Joseph Conrad," in *The Craft of Literary Biography*, p. 72; see also Karl Miller, *Authors* (Oxford: Clarendon Press, 1989), p. 182.

7 The tragic implications of Johnson's view of human failure are argued by (among others) W. J. Bate, *The Achievement of Samuel Johnson* (University of Chicago Press, 1955), Leopold Damrosch, Jr., *Samuel Johnson and the Tragic Sense* (Princeton University Press, 1972), and Robert Folkenflik, *Samuel Johnson, Biographer* (Ithaca: Cornell University Press, 1978).

8 *The Life of the Poet: Beginning and Ending Poetic Careers* (University of Chicago Press, 1981), p. ix.

9 See G. F. Parker, *Johnson's Shakespeare* (Oxford: Clarendon Press, 1989), pp. 28–42.

10 *The Spectator*, ed. Donald F. Bond, 5 vols. (Oxford: Clarendon Press, 1965), I, 268.

11 E. B. O. Borgerhoff, *The Freedom of French Classicism* (Princeton University Press, 1950), p. 238.

12 For differences between "manners" and "nature," and between "general nature" and "sublunary nature" in Johnson's writing, see Parker, *Johnson's Shakespeare*, pp. 15–28, and the essay by Philip Smallwood in this volume.

13 "The Author's Apology for Heroic Poetry" (1677), in *Of Dramatic Poesy and Other Critical Essays*, ed. George Watson, 2 vols. (London: Everyman, 1971), I, 207.

14 "The Metaphysical Poets," in *Selected Essays* (London: Faber and Faber, 1972), pp. 282–83.

15 In praising the simile of the angel in Addison's *The Campaign*, Johnson writes that "the mind is impressed with the resemblance of things generally unlike, as unlike as intellect and body" ("Life of Addison," II, 130).

16 *Samuel Johnson's Literary Criticism* (University of Chicago Press, 1952), chapter 7.

17 Christopher Ricks, "Literary Principles as Against Theory," in *Essays in Appreciation* (Oxford: Clarendon Press, 1996), pp. 322–23.

18 *The Art of Fiction* (New York: Oxford University Press, 1948), p. 21.

19 *The Ordering of the Arts in Eighteenth-Century England* (Princeton University Press, 1970), pp. 428–34.

20 See, for example, Robert Folkenflik, "Johnson's Heroes," in *The English Hero, 1680–1800*, ed. Robert Folkenflik (Newark: University of Delaware Press, 1983), pp. 143–67.

21 On how tragedy violates Johnson's conception of nature, see Parker, *Johnson's*

Shakespeare, chapter 4; and Frank Kermode, "The Survival of the Classic," in *Renaissance Essays* (London: Collins, 1973), p. 170.

22 "Life, Art, and the *Lives of the Poets*," in *Domestick Privacies: Samuel Johnson and the Art of Biography*, ed. David Wheeler (Lexington: University Press of Kentucky, 1987), pp. 32, 33.

23 Johnson's thought here has much in common with Foucault's and Barthes's arguments with regard to the author's relation to text. See Michel Foucault, "What is an Author?," in *The Foucault Reader*, ed. Paul Rabinow (New York: Pantheon 1984), pp. 101–20; Roland Barthes, "The Death of the Author," in *Image Music Text*, trans. Stephen Heath (New York: Hill and Wang, 1977), pp. 142–48.

24 The phrase comes from Horace Satires I.iv.43.

25 "Of his [Waller's] behaviour in this part of his life it is not necessary to direct the reader's opinion. 'Let us not,' says his last ingenious biographer [i.e. Percival Stockdale], 'condemn him with untempered severity, because he was not the poet, the orator, and the hero'" ("Life of Waller," *Lives*, I, 267; see also 266–67, 281).

26 Full consideration is offered in my forthcoming *Writing Memory: Textuality, Authority, and Johnson's "Lives of the Poets."*

27 For example, Dryden compares Jonson with Shakespeare in "Of Dramatic Poesy" (1668) and Juvenal with Horace in "A Discourse Concerning . . . Satire" (1693). Johnson, however, may be most indebted to Pope's own comparison of Homer with Virgil in the Preface to his translation of the *Iliad* (1715); see P. J. Smallwood, "Johnson's Life of Pope and Pope's Preface to the *Iliad*," *NQ*, n.s. 225 (1980), 50.

28 For the continuities between Pope's body and poetry as seen by Johnson, cf. Helen Deutsch, *Resemblance and Disgrace: Alexander Pope and the Deformation of Culture* (Cambridge, MA: Harvard University Press, 1996), pp. 33–35 and *passim*.

29 See Greg Clingham, "Another and the Same: Johnson's Dryden," in *Literary Transmission and Authority: Dryden and Other Writers*, ed. Jennifer Brady and Earl Miner (Cambridge University Press, 1993), pp. 121–59.

30 Felicity Rosslyn, "Of Gods and Men," *CQ*, 13 (1984), 6–7.

31 See Greg Clingham, "Johnson's Criticism of Dryden's Odes in Praise of St. Cecilia," *MLS*, 18 (1988), 165–80; and "Johnson, Homeric Scholarship, and 'the passes of the mind,'" *AJ*, 3 (1990), 113–70.

32 *The Odyssey*, trans. A. T. Murray, 2 vols. (London: Heinemann, 1924), p. 415 (Loeb Classical Library).

12

MICHAEL F. SUAREZ, SJ

Johnson's Christian thought

I

It is impossible adequately to understand or appreciate Johnson the author without seriously considering Johnson the Christian believer and theological thinker. From the time Johnson first read William Law's *Serious Call* at the age of twenty, Boswell tells us, "religion was the predominant object of his thoughts" (*Life*, I, 69–70). Another early biographer, Sir John Hawkins, examined the plan of study Johnson composed at Pembroke College, Oxford, and concluded: "his favourite subjects were classical literature, ethics, and theology" (Hawkins, p. 11). Johnson's first book, a translation of a French edition of the Portuguese Jesuit Jerome Lobo's *A Voyage to Abyssinia* (1735), reveals his willingness to engage with the theological and religious debates of the seventeenth century.

A further sign of Johnson's early theological inclination is the fact that the second project he ever proposed to Edward Cave, editor of the *Gentleman's Magazine*, was a new translation of a long, complex, and heavily annotated theological work: Paolo Sarpi's *History of the Council of Trent* (*Letters*, I, 12–13). This work immersed him in the most contentious theological issues of the Reformation and Counter-Reformation: sacramental theology, ecclesiastical polity, apostolic succession, and justification by faith alone. Because of competition from another translator, Johnson eventually abandoned the project in April 1739, though not until he had already produced between 400 and 800 quarto pages of translation and commentary over the course of nine months.[1]

Johnson's theological concerns are also evident in "The Vision of Theodore, Hermit of Teneriffe," written for Robert Dodsley's *Preceptor* (1748). The theme of this brief allegorical fiction is that the best exercise of reason leads us to the higher truths of religion, a motif that also runs through the illustrative quotations Johnson selected for his *Dictionary*. In the final number of the *Rambler*, Johnson tells readers that his intention has been to produce a series of essays "exactly conformable to the precepts of Christianity, without any accommodation to the licentiousness and the levity of the present age" (*Rambler*, V, 320).

This kind of Christian didacticism persists throughout his writings from "The Life of Dr Herman Boerhaave" (1739), which portrays the Dutch physician as a model of piety and learning, to the *Lives of the Poets* (1779–81), in which the reader is led to consider the brevity of life and the transience of earthly glory.

"Learning," wrote Johnson in sermon 6, "is of use to display the greatness, and vindicate the justice, of the Almighty; to explain the difficulties, and enforce the proofs, of religion" (*Sermons*, p. 71). Convinced that "One of the great duties of man . . . is . . . to propagate goodness and enforce truth" (*Sermons*, p. 147), Johnson devoted his writing life to fostering Christian virtue and championing the eternal verities of revealed religion, which he believed were essential to the happiness of humankind (*Sermons*, p. 15). In Johnson's "PRAYER ON THE RAMBLER" he petitions "the giver of all good things" for the Holy Spirit, "that I may promote thy glory, and the Salvation both of myself and others"; the "PRAYER ON THE STUDY OF RELIGION" asks God to "invigorate my studies . . . that I may by due diligence and right discernment establish myself and others in thy holy Faith" (*Diaries*, pp. 42, 62).

During a period of at least thirty-two years Johnson "composed about forty sermons" (*Life*, V, 67) for clergymen friends. Many of the twenty-seven sermons that still survive reveal his close familiarity with works by seventeenth-century divines frequently cited in the *Dictionary*, including Jeremy Taylor, Henry Hammond, Richard Allestree, John Wilkins, Robert South, Edward Stillingfleet, and John Tillotson. Richard Baxter, William Law, and Samuel Clarke were particularly important homiletic models for Johnson, though he excluded Clarke from the *Dictionary* because of his unorthodox beliefs regarding the Trinity (*Life*, IV, 416, n. 2).[2]

Hawkins tells us that "Johnson owed his excellence as a writer" to his study of "the divines and others of the last century" and remarks that he was "completely skilled in the writings of the fathers [the theologians of the early church], yet was he more conversant with those of the great English church-men, namely [Richard] Hooker, [James] Us[s]her, [Joseph] Mede, [Henry] Hammond, [Robert] Sanderson, [Joseph] Hall, and others of that class" (Hawkins, pp. 271, 542). In the catalogue of the Harleian Library he compiled with William Oldys from November 1742 to January 1744, Johnson displays a comprehensive knowledge of English church history and formidable theological erudition in the entries for such categories as "Controversies with the Papists," "Theologica Ascetica," "Deists," and the "Trinitarian Controversy."[3]

Incessant references to God and Providence in the *Dictionary*'s illustrative quotations have led Robert DeMaria to conclude that "Religion is the most important subject in Johnson's curriculum."[4] Moreover, when he revised the *Dictionary* for the fourth edition (1773), Johnson added a considerable body of religious poetry and material from orthodox Anglican controversialists, leading

Allen Reddick to note "the remarkable infusion of theological passages . . . into the revised work."[5] Johnson's genius imparts a religious and theological program even to a dictionary.

When Johnson and Boswell were on their tour of the Hebrides, they fantasized about creating a new college at the University of St. Andrews, staffed exclusively with members of the Club, the informal gathering of great men of learning who, since 1764, had met every week for purposes of conversation. "I'll trust theology to no one but myself," Johnson asserted. When he considered that Thomas Percy was a clergyman, however, he respectfully decided to split the job with him, giving Percy "practical divinity" and appropriating "metaphysics and scholastick divinity" for himself (*Life*, v, 108–9). Johnson's claim here is telling; he gives the practicing minister responsibility for applied theology, while asserting his own competence in the more academic aspects of the discipline. By "scholastic" he does not mean "pertaining to the medieval school-men" – there is no such definition of the word in the *Dictionary* and the only medieval theologians in Johnson's library were Anselm and Aquinas. Instead, Johnson simply refers to what we today would call systematic theology, theological writing on the fundamental beliefs of Christianity: the Trinity, Revelation, redemption, nature versus grace, the Incarnation.

Between 1755 and 1781, Johnson made many resolutions "to study Theology" or Divinity (e.g., *Diaries*, p. 57) and some twenty determinations to read the Bible. He wrote to Boswell in Utrecht in 1763: "You will, perhaps, wish to ask, what Study I would recommend. I shall not speak of Theology, because it ought not to be considered as a question whether you shall endeavour to know the will of God" (*Letters*, I, 238). Ten years later, when Boswell suggests that Johnson "should write expressly in support of Christianity," he replies, "I hope I shall" (*Life*, v, 89). On another occasion, he specifically resolves "To gather the arguments for Christianity" (*Diaries*, p. 268). It seems that Boswell's assertion that "religion was the predominant object of his thoughts" was no pious exaggeration.

Johnson's reputation as a Christian moralist and advocate of religion led one of London's leading booksellers to offer him "a large sum of money" for a book of "Devotional Exercises."[6] Hawkins tells us that among the works Johnson himself had projected were a "small book of precepts and directions for piety," translations of Aristotle's *Nicomachean Ethics* and Cicero's *De natura deorum*, a "Dictionary to the [Book of] Common Prayer," and a "Comparison of Philosophical and Christian Morality by sentences collected from the moralists and [church] fathers" (Hawkins, pp. 81–84). Upon his death, he was hailed by his contemporaries as a great moral teacher and proponent of Christian truths.[7]

In light of the religious and moral background of Johnson's periodical essays, fiction, poetry, lexicography, and biographical writing, it is hardly surprising that Pat Rogers sees "Johnson the religious being" as the "core of his creative self."[8] But how are we to understand Johnson as a Christian writer? Most attempts by modern critics, focusing either upon Johnson's inner psychology or his religious practices, have fallen far short of the mark because of their own neglect of theological knowledge. If we wish to understand "Johnson the religious being," then we must recognize that he was not only a serious Christian believer, but also an equally serious Christian *thinker* very well read in patristic and seventeenth-century theology and in classical and contemporary ethics. Although Johnson's Christian convictions and theological thinking are more richly complex than is generally recognized by present-day readers, suffice it to say that the key to this vital aspect of Johnson's life and writings lies in his understanding of three crucial ideas: religious authority, conditional salvation, and Christian morality.

II

Johnson regarded the Bible, the "sacred and inscrutable word, which will shew . . . the inefficacy of all other knowledge," as the revealed word of God whereby we are "taught to know the will of our Maker . . . by messengers inspired by himself" (*Sermons*, pp. 95, 40). As a Protestant, he believed that the Scriptures contained everything necessary for salvation and that doctrines not established by the sacred page could not be required (*Sermons*, p. 20). In Johnson's view, the light of revelation made clear those truths every soul needed to know (*Sermons*, pp. 29, 40); yet, at the same time he argued that the Bible was the "most difficult book in the world" (*Life*, III, 298), a complicated canon of texts whose meaning beyond the essential truths of salvation, immortality, heaven, and hell was far from apparent. Tradition, especially the legacy of the early church as handed down by the Fathers, was therefore an essential secondary authority for fostering Christian understanding in matters of church polity and doctrine. "With regard to the order and government of the primitive church," says Johnson of the Fathers,

> we may doubtless follow their authority with perfect security. . . . From their writings we are to vindicate the establishment of our church, and by the same writings are those who differ from us, in these particulars, to defend their conduct. Nor is this the only, though perhaps the chief use of these writers, for, in matters of faith, and points of doctrine, those, at least, who lived in the ages nearest to the times of the apostles undoubtedly deserve to be consulted.　　　(*Sermons*, pp. 82–83)

Johnson is proposing a theological methodology that uniquely privileges early patristic writings as the most reliable and legitimate non-biblical source for the right conduct of theological inquiry: "Thus, by consulting first the holy

Scriptures, and next the writers of the primitive church, we shall make ourselves acquainted with the will of God; thus shall we discover the good way, and find that rest for our souls which will amply recompense our studies and enquiries" (*Sermons*, p. 83).

But why the church Fathers? Were the Anglican divines of the seventeenth and eighteenth centuries not enough for a layman who seldom went to church? Johnson announces his reasons for turning to patristic theology in his own sermon 7. He begins by stating the problem: "The prevailing spirit of the present age seems to be the spirit of scepticism and captiousness, of suspicion and distrust, a contempt of all authority, and a presumptuous confidence in private judgement; a dislike of all established forms, merely because they are established, and of old paths, because they are old" (*Sermons*, p. 77). Subsequently, he explains why this is so: the age is beset with "an overfondness for novelty . . . and a neglect of . . . asking for the old paths, where is the good way, and walking therein" (*Sermons*, p. 78). For Johnson, "walking therein" amounts to "searching into antiquity" (*Sermons*, p. 79) or studying the church Fathers. This view is succinctly reiterated in his spiritual diary when he lists the causes of skepticism; immediately following "Complaint of the obscurity of Scripture" is "Contempt of Fathers and of authority" (*Diaries*, p. 414).

Johnson thoroughly embraced the Anglican orthodoxy of his time, a *via media* between what he regarded as the fideism and superstition of Roman Catholicism and the dangerously traditionless and personality-oriented characteristics of Dissent. Although Johnson was less vehemently opposed to Roman Catholicism than most of his fellow Englishmen, and even once told Boswell, "I would be a Papist if I could" (*Life*, IV, 289), he nevertheless clearly rejected much Roman doctrine and practice (*Life*, III, 407). In the *Dictionary*, his definitions and examples for "reformation," "transubstantiation," and "pope" and its variants leave no doubt about the strength and sincerity of his animus against the Roman church. His life of Paolo Sarpi (1738) and his translation of Lobo's *A Voyage to Abyssinia* (1735) further document his hostility to Roman Catholicism. Nevertheless, because of his belief in the importance of the apostolic or "primitive church" and the authority of the Fathers, Johnson was far more sympathetic to Catholicism than he was to many forms of Dissent, which he regarded as modern innovations lacking legitimizing contact with the past. His personal belief in Purgatory and, hence, in the efficacy of prayers for the dead (*Life*, I, 240; II, 104–5, 162–63) – doctrines associated with Catholicism – was based largely upon the teachings of the Fathers (*Life*, V, 356; Hawkins, p. 449). Yet Johnson was so thoroughly a Church of England man that he prayed for the soul of his deceased wife "conditionally" and for his dead relatives "so far as it might be lawful" (*Diaries*, pp. 50, 79).

"Johnson's profound reverence for the [Church of England's] Hierarchy"

(*Life*, IV, 75, 197–98), the emblem of ecclesiastical authority and order, helps to explain why he held the seventeenth-century Puritans in particular disdain. His "Life of Butler" voices his contempt for "the sour solemnity, the sullen superstition, the gloomy moroseness, and the stubborn scruples of the ancient Puritans"; he laments the instability of the mid-seventeenth century when "the tumult of absurdity and clamour of contradiction . . . perplexed doctrine, disordered practice, and disturbed both publick and private quiet" (*Lives*, I, 214). Most damaging was the loss of authority, for the Puritan ascendancy inaugurated an age "when subordination was broken and hissed away; when any unsettled innovator who could hatch a half-formed notion produced it to the publick; when every man might become a preacher, and . . . collect a congregation" (*Lives*, I, 214–15). "The destruction of order, and the abolition of stated regulations," wrote Johnson, "must fill the world with uncertainty, distraction, and sollicitude" (*Sermons*, p. 245).

In similar vein, Johnson's "Life of Milton" brims with contempt for the Puritan assault upon the stabilizing forces of monarchy and episcopacy, which in Milton's case Johnson ascribed to "not so much the love of liberty as repugnance to authority" (*Lives*, I, 157). That Milton, a believing Christian, "was of no church" Johnson found "dangerous" (*Lives*, I, 155). He considered the Calvinist doctrines of election and predestination to be especially problematic and unacceptable, maintaining that predestination was included in the Thirty-Nine Articles merely because of "the clamour of the times" (*Life*, II, 104). Deeply distrustful of private revelation and of the assurance of being saved, Johnson repeatedly stresses the unreliability of human fancy and the enormous capacity we possess for self-deception (*Rambler*, IV, 33ff.).

He sincerely commended the Methodists, who had not yet seceded from the Church of England, for their plain style of preaching that made the gospel message intelligible to the common folk (*Life*, I, 458–59; II, 123; V, 392). Yet he was deeply distrustful of the emotionalism associated with the Methodists, and helped to popularize Joseph Trapp's sermons against religious "enthusiasm," abridging them for the *Gentleman's Magazine* in 1739. As with the Calvinists, Johnson regarded the Methodist notion of "inward light" as "a principle utterly incompatible with social or civil security" because it was a private principle of action without recourse to any external authority (*Life*, II, 126). A "presumptuous confidence in private judgement" (*Sermons*, p. 77) should not supplant publicly established forms of religious and moral authority.

Because of his firm conviction that episcopal government was uniquely consonant with the practice of the primitive church, Johnson rejected the legitimacy of all other forms of ecclesiastical polity. Although he was willing to accept that Presbyterianism should be the state religion of Scotland, he refused even to enter a Presbyterian church when he was traveling with Boswell (*Life*, V, 121): he would not sanction Presbyterians' worship by his presence because they "have no church, no apostolical ordination" and "no form of [public] prayer," such as the *Roman Missal* and the *Book of Common Prayer* (*Life*, II, 103, 104; *Journey*, pp. 104–5). His brief biography of the Presbyterian controversialist Francis Cheynell (1608–65), perhaps Johnson's most mordantly ironic production, reveals his antipathies: Presbyterian preaching is "noisy and unmeaning," and defenders of that denomination are confounded by a group of simple soldiers (*Early Lives*, pp. 396, 397–98).

Johnson advocated a moderate form of Erastianism, the right of the state to establish a church and to regulate the ecclesiastical life of its citizens. The governor's trust, he believed, "includes, not only the care of the property, but of the morals of the people," and that "deficiencies in civil life can be supplied only by religion"; therefore, "The first duty of a governour is to diffuse through the community a spirit of religion" (*Sermons*, pp. 252, 256). The state is obliged to exercise its powers to create a climate promoting public worship and fostering Christian virtue: "That religion may be invigorated and diffused, it is necessary that the external order of religion be diligently maintained, that the solemnities of worship be duly observed, and a proper reverence preserved for the times and places appropriated to piety" (*Sermons*, p. 257).

At the same time, however, Johnson deeply resented any state abridgment of ecclesiastical power or prerogative, and told David Hume that he "would stand before a battery of cannon, to restore the Convocation [a clerical assembly for the government of the Church of England] to its full powers" (*Life*, I, 464). When, in 1773, the Dissenters Bill sought to remove mandatory subscription to the Thirty-Nine Articles by all holders of political office, Johnson was vehemently opposed (*Letters*, II, 13, n. 8). He was unwilling to countenance any measure he thought might diminish the stature of the established church. Clergy, he insisted, should have the "right of censure and rebuke" of their spiritual charges, making his case yet again upon "the practice of the primitive church" (*Life*, III, 59). In short, Johnson was "a sincere and zealous Christian, of high Church-of-England and monarchical principles, which he would not tamely suffer to be questioned" (*Life*, IV, 426).

When Johnson himself was enduring a personal crisis (*Diaries*, pp. 44–47, 59–60) or when he was engaged in that awkward and difficult business of sending condolences to the recently bereaved, he almost invariably turned to *The Book of Common Prayer* and composed a kind of liturgical collect informed by the rhythms and language of the prayer book. Writing to his stepdaughter Lucy Porter on the death of her aunt, for example, Johnson echoes the language of the Collect for the Fourth Sunday after Easter: "There is always this consolation, that we have one Protector who can never be lost but by our own fault, and every new experience of the uncertainty of all other comforts should determine us to fix our hearts where true joys are to be found" (*Letters*, I, 301). His letters to Hester Thrale on the death of her son and husband (*Letters*, II, 312; III, 330), his funeral sermon for his wife (*Sermons*, pp. 261, 271), and his last two letters to his dying mother (*Letters*, I, 174, 176) all reveal Johnson's reliance on both the style and the substance of the prayer book. Johnson was a man of enormous reading, but the text he knew best was *The Book of Common Prayer*.

Johnson sought refuge in the Anglican service book not merely because he found there "the sublimest truths, conveyed in the most chaste and exalted language" (*JM*, II, 319), but also because it symbolized for him the distinctive qualities of the Anglican church: the purity of its doctrine and its use of ritual untainted by Popery. Respect for the preeminence of the primitive church helps to explain Johnson's great love for *The Book of Common Prayer* and his admiration for its special authority. From Anthony Sparrow's *Rationale upon the Book of Common Prayer of the Church of England* (1655) to Thomas Comber's *A Companion to the Temple* (rev. edn. 1734), several prominent Anglican theologians had emphasized the service book's conformity with the early church by frequent quotations from Scripture and the Fathers, especially the Greek Fathers of the undivided church, to establish the soundness of Anglican doctrine and ritual. Similarly, Johnson treasured Robert Nelson's *A Companion for the Festivals and Fasts of the Church of England* (1704) as an aid to his devotions (*Diaries*, pp. 91–92, 100). Though less obviously learned than Sparrow or Comber, Nelson too is careful to appeal to the early Greek church and to emphasize the centrality of primitive Christianity in forming the calendar of Anglican liturgical worship. Thus, the *Book of Common Prayer* put Johnson in touch with an authorized mode of prayer, a Christian tradition going back not only to Thomas Cranmer and his contemporaries, but also to the early centuries of the church.

III

Johnson's understanding of Christian salvation was typical of Arminianism, a set of theological tenets that enjoyed wide currency in the eighteenth century. Against the determinism of Calvinism, Arminianism insists upon three principles: that divine sovereignty is compatible with real free will in humankind; that all theologies of predestination are without basis in Scripture; and that Christ died for all people, not only the elect. If Calvinism views salvation as a definitive and irreversible act of God, then Arminianism regards salvation as a provisional outcome dependent upon how humans accept and cooperate with the grace that God freely bestows. Opposing predestination and its implications, Arminianism emphasizes individual moral freedom and the conditional nature of salvation. The sinner seeking salvation must engage in constant self-examination, perform interior and exterior labors of repentance, and be strongly committed to charitable works. While Calvinists examined themselves to discover signs of God's favor and election, Arminians scrutinized the quality of their Christian living in order to determine whether or not they had done their duty and, thus, rendered their lives acceptable to God.

Johnson was thoroughly Arminian in his outlook. A great devotee of the Dutch jurist and theologian Hugo Grotius, Europe's most forceful and able exponent of Arminianism, Johnson rejected predestination (*Life*, II, 104) and emphasized free will (*Life*, II, 84; III, 291–93; IV, 329; V, 117). Most importantly, his public and private writings repeatedly and consistently underscore the centrality of *self-examination* (the "vital principle of religion") (*Sermons* 9, 10, 16, and 22; *Rambler* 155), of *repentance* (the "great duty") (*Sermons* 2 and 28; *Rambler* 110), and of *charitable works* ("the height of religious excellence" and "the great test by which we shall be judged") (*Sermons* 10, 17, 19, and 27; *Politics*, pp. 287–89).

In the ongoing debate as to whether faith alone was sufficient for salvation or whether works too were necessary, Johnson was an unswerving advocate of works. God will punish or reward "every man, according to his works," he believed (*Sermons*, p. 115). While acknowledging the importance of faith, "the foundation of all Christian virtue" (*Sermons*, p. 303), Johnson saw the judgment which immediately follows after death (*Idler*, p. 316) as the occasion "when men shall give account of their works" (*Sermons*, p. 115). This is why the parable of the talents (Matthew 25: 14–30) figures prominently in Johnson's religious imagination (*Sermons*, p. 212; *Diaries*, p. 50). Johnson's God wants to know what Samuel Johnson has *done* with what he has been given; the just Judge "compare[s] performance with ability" (*Sermons*, p. 268).

Faith is a condition of salvation (*Sermons*, pp. 104, 303), but for Johnson it was insufficient without works. His understanding of Christ's saving Passion reflects this view: "the blood of Christ was poured out upon the cross to make [sinners'] best endeavours acceptable to God" (*Sermons*, p. 72). Believing that charity is "inseparable from piety," Johnson even went so far as to associate our knowledge of charity with "the light of revelation" (*Idler*, pp. 12, 13). For all his emphasis on works, however, he is no Pelagian – someone who believes that humans can achieve righteousness on their own, without divine assistance. Never doubting the need for grace "without which no man can correct his own corruption" (*Sermons*, p. 114), Johnson was chiefly preoccupied by how thoroughly the believer accepts grace and lives by God's commands.

According to Johnson, faith, self-examination, repentance, and charitable works are the conditions of each individual's being saved. "The business of life," wrote Johnson, echoing Philippians 2: 12, "is to work out our salvation" (*Sermons*, p. 161); yet, "No man can be sure that his obedience and repentance will obtain salvation" (*Life*, III, 295). The faithful person can never know whether or not his or her attempts to live the Christian life will be sufficiently pleasing to "that awful and just God . . . by whose sentence all Eternity will be determined" (*Letters*, IV, 367). This is the difficulty of the believing and self-aware Arminian: salvation is always conditional and he can never be certain until his death whether those conditions have been fulfilled. Therefore, he must live in a state of radical indeterminacy as to his fate: either torment or bliss for all eternity.

Johnson's alleged psychological anguish over his own death and the issue of his own salvation has been badly mishandled by several commentators who have understood neither the theological content of his religious anxieties nor the spiritual context of his private diaries. In many of these confessional notes, Johnson is following the counsel of his Latin poem "Christianus Perfectus": the one who seeks holiness must "always be mindful of what is to come" ("semperque futuro / Instet") (*Poems*, p. 344). Johnson's much-discussed fear of death is primarily a fear of judgment, an anxiety over not measuring up to the pattern of righteousness God will demand for salvation (*Diaries*, p. 106). Sometimes, the effect of his spiritual vigilance is to despair of ever being worthy or to fall into "vain" and "needless scruples" (*Diaries*, pp. 64, 276). Knowing that he had been given a great deal, he believed much would be expected.

In his diaries and prayers, Johnson applies especially rigorous standards to his conduct because he considers himself "as acting under the eye of God"; continually "under the Eye of Omnipresence," he is seeking Christian perfection because he is uncertain whether anything less will suffice (*Letters*, I, 46; II, 134). Wishing to be saved on the Day of Judgment, he knows that spiritual stocktaking is no place for presumption, that "nothing is more dangerous than spiritual pride" (*Sermons*, pp. 175, 304). Self-examination – which he learned from reading William Law, Robert Nelson, Jeremy Taylor, and Richard Allestree – would be pointless if he did not measure himself against the highest requirements. "What can any man see, either within or without himself," he demands, "that does not afford him some reason to remark his own ignorance, imbecility and meanness?" (*Sermons*, p. 94).

One difficulty in Johnson's own spiritual life was that his capacious and active mind occasionally led him into theological speculation and uncertainty. Four months before he died, he penned an entry in his diary, "AGAINST INQUISITIVE AND PERPLEXING THOUGHTS," in which he prayed: "enable me to drive from me all such unquiet and perplexing thoughts as may mislead or hinder me . . . teach me by thy Holy Spirit to withdraw my Mind from unprofitable and dangerous enquiries, from difficulties vainly curious, and doubts impossible to be solved" (*Diaries*, pp. 383–84). Johnson's distrust of speculative theology is abundantly clear in his identifying "Raphael's reproof of Adam's curiosity [*Paradise Lost*, VIII. 167–87] . . . may be confidently opposed to any rule of life which any poet has delivered" (*Lives*, I, 177), in his conversations with Boswell (e.g., *Rambler* 180) and his reviews of *Four Letters from Sir Isaac Newton to Doctor Bentley, Containing Some Arguments in Proof of a Deity* (1756) and Soame Jenyns's *Free Inquiry* (1757). Nevertheless, his love of argument, his probing mind, and the habitual turning of his thoughts toward the spiritual meant that religious doubt and perplexity were part of his ongoing struggle to lead an authentic Christian life.

Johnson believed that both his understanding of salvation as conditional and his resultant fear that he might not have fulfilled the conditions necessary to be saved were rational (*Life*, IV, 278, 299). Such a "holy fear" quite reasonably should impel us "to a constant state of vigilance and caution, a perpetual distrust of our own hearts, a full conviction of our natural weakness, and an earnest solicitude for divine assistance" (*Sermons*, p. 30). Knowing that "the wisest man is not always wise, and the best man is not always good," Johnson strove to root out whatever folly and evil he found within himself (*Sermons*, p. 259). Often in the *Diaries* he is preparing his soul for the reception of Holy Communion, "the highest act of Christian worship," a "renewal of our broken vows" and a "renovation of that covenant by which we are adopted the followers of Jesus" (*Sermons*, pp. 306, 100, 102). His diaries and prayers are the private record of a man struggling with his own sinfulness and limitations before a God he had learned "to consider . . . as his Creator, and Governour, his Father and his Judge" (*Sermons*, p. 29).

The Christian pilgrimage, he knew, was never easy:

> To give the heart to God, and to give the whole heart, is very difficult; the last, the great effort of long labour, fervent prayer, and diligent meditation. – Many resolutions are made, and many relapses lamented, and many conflicts with our own desires, with the powers of this world, and the powers of darkness, must be sustained, before the will of man is made wholly obedient to the will of God.
>
> (*Sermons*, p. 143)

Could there be a better sketch of Johnson's own *Diaries*? Striving to make progress in his spiritual life, he records personal deficits so that he may address them; his assets he scarcely dares acknowledge. Reckoning the "provision to be made for eternity" (*Letters*, IV, 130), he follows the Pauline injunction to "work out your own salvation with fear and trembling" (Phil. 2: 12). What we see in the *Diaries*, then, is a man in the world laboring to make "the choice of eternity" (*Rasselas*, p. 175).

IV

Almost all the unhappiness in life, according to Johnson, stems from some defect in our obligations toward religion and virtue, "the neglect of those duties, which prudence and religion equally require" (*Sermons*, p. 7). Virtue is "the parent of felicity"; religion "the basis of happiness" (*Sermons*, pp. 13, 15). In contrast, "Misery is the effect of wickedness, and wickedness is the cause of misery" (*Sermons*, pp. 37–38). God is not responsible for our tribulations, for "if we suffer, we suffer by our own fault," since "physical and moral evil entered the world together" (*Sermons*, p. 55). Most of our miseries, therefore, are the consequence of our own transgressions or those of others; sin, not God, is the cause of human suffering (*Life*, v, 117). "We fail of being happy," says Johnson, "because we determine to obtain felicity by means different from those which God hath appointed," instead of "founding happiness on the solid basis of reason and reflection" (*Sermons*, pp. 58, 150). Like Locke before him, Johnson never questions the legitimacy of pleasure and its role in human happiness, though the pleasures of virtue and the rewards of religion must be seen as eclipsing all others. In one of the most resonant passages he ever penned, Johnson renders a picture of earthly happiness rooted in Christian virtue and integrity:

> He is happy that carries about with him in the world the temper of the cloister; and preserves the fear of doing evil, while he suffers himself to be impelled by the zeal of doing good; who uses the comforts and conveniences of his condition, as though he used them not, with that constant desire of a better state, which sinks the value of earthly things; who can be rich or poor, without pride in riches, or discontent in poverty; who can manage the business of life, with such indifference, as may shut out from his heart all incitements to fraud or injustice; who can partake the pleasures of sense with temperance, and enjoy the distinction of honour with moderation; who can pass undefiled through a polluted world; and, among all the vicissitudes of good and evil, have his heart fixed only where true joys are to be found. (*Sermons*, pp. 33–34).

This is no monastic asceticism, but a baptized version of Aristotle's "golden mean," another *via media*, a Christian philosophy of engagement with the world embracing prayer, charity, honesty, stewardship, moderation, humility, and the hope of salvation.

Knowing that "virtue is the consequence of choice" (*Sermons*, p. 56) and that choosing the good must therefore be made attractive (*Rambler*, IV, 98), Johnson imagines "a community, in which virtue should generally prevail, of which every member should fear God . . . and love his neighbour as himself . . . and endeavour . . . to imitate the divine justice, and benevolence" (*Sermons*, p. 60). In this community of Christian virtue – a kind of religious utopia – fear, poverty, and unhappiness are virtually unknown, while concord, charity, and justice predominate. "Such is the state," he observes, "at which any community may arrive by the general practice of the duties of religion" (*Sermons*, p. 62). Thus, Johnson's maxim, "while it is in our power to be virtuous, it is in our power to be happy," applies equally to the individual and to the commonweal (*Sermons*, p. 55; cf. *Idler*, p. 351).

Yet, Johnson is not so naive as to believe that moral excellence is a guarantee of felicity. He well understood that "we do not always suffer by our crimes; we are not always protected by our innocence" (*Idler*, p. 468). This aspect of our existence compromises neither the truth nor the value of Christianity, however, since "under the dispensation of the gospel we are no where taught, that the good shall have any exemption from the accidents of life, or that natural and civil evil shall not be equally shared by the righteous and the wicked" (*Sermons*, p. 168). Indeed, Johnson confidently assails the simplistic notion that temporal "happiness is the unfailing consequence of virtue" (*Idler*, p. 468; cf. *Letters*, I, 226). Instead, he argues that, for the virtuous Christian, affliction "prepares us for felicity" by pointing to a future state in which God's justice triumphs and "every man shall be happy and miserable according to his works" (*Idler*, pp. 470, 469). Although Johnson maintains that "We know little of the state of departed souls, because such knowledge is not necessary to a good life" (*Idler*, p. 130), he nevertheless, like Thomas Aquinas before him, surmises from the nature of humankind that the "happiness of heaven will be, that pleasure and virtue will be perfectly consistent" (*Life*, III, 292). Heaven will be "a state more constant and permanent, of which the objects may be more proportioned to our wishes, and the enjoyments to our capacities" (*Sermons*, p. 135). Meanwhile, "Affliction is inseparable from our present state" (*Idler*, p. 468).

The Christian who trusts in God's Providence recognizes that "his troubles are sent to awaken him to reflection, and that the evils of this life may be improved to his eternal advantage" by calling him to repentance (*Sermons*, p. 179). Sufferings are best seen, then, "as notices mercifully given us to prepare ourselves for another state" (*Letters*, IV, 167), as "calamities by which Providence gradually disengages us from the love of life" (*Idler*, p. 129). Our tribulations point the way toward heaven by directing our minds and hearts to an existence where there is "a more permanent and certain happiness" (*Sermons*, p. 270). "None would fix their attention on the future," argues Johnson, "but that they are discontented with the present" (*Idler*, p. 277).

Accordingly, Johnson maintains that suffering is a corrective for "hardness of heart," which he understands as the condition of being so taken up with present passions as to neglect our proper mindfulness of the future state, a "carelessness of the world to come" (*Sermons*, pp. 35, 37). He proposes that "Evil is not only the occasional but the efficient cause of charity," the "most excellent of all moral virtues" (*Idler*, p. 277). For Johnson, "physical evil may be therefore endured with patience, since it is the cause of moral good" (*Idler*, p. 278). In his Review of Jenyns's *Free Inquiry*, however, Johnson wholeheartedly rejects Jenyns's fatuous argument that evil is a consequence of the subordination and, hence, the imperfection, of creatures necessary for the overall felicity of the creation. Dismissing Jenyns's moral and theological determinism, his trivialization of human suffering, and his highly speculative theodicy, Johnson instead advocates a position of humility: "The only reason why we should contemplate evil," he suggests, "is that we may bear it better" (Greene, p. 536).

With Richard Baxter, Johnson believed that "man is not afflicted but for good purposes" (*Sermons*, p. 166); the suffering of the virtuous in this life demonstrates the inadequacy of a purely philosophical ethics and highlights the necessity of a morality grounded in religion. "Human wisdom has . . . exhausted its power in giving rules for the conduct of life," he observed, "but those rules are themselves but vanities" (*Sermons*, p. 131). They neither address the injustices of our present suffering, nor consider the ultimate end of humanity: "Philosophy may infuse stubbornness, but religion only can give patience" (*Idler*, p. 131). From religion, "we shall find that comfort which philosophy cannot supply," since "it was reserved for the preachers of Christianity to bring life and immortality to light" (*Sermons*, pp. 268, 109; cf. 2 Tim. 1: 10). Christian revelation vouchsafed to humankind what all the reason of secular philosophy could not: the immortality of the human soul and its destiny to endure in a state of eternal rewards or punishments. "To bring life and immortality to light," he believed, "is the peculiar excellence of the gospel of Christ" (*Sermons*, p. 265).

Johnson repeatedly emphasizes the idea that everything necessary for salvation is given to humankind in the Bible; revelation liberates us from the realm of philosophical speculation by giving us "certain knowledge of a future state, and of the rewards and punishments, that await us after death, . . . adjusted according to our conduct in this world" (*Sermons*, p. 107). Therefore, Christians "have no need to perplex themselves with difficult speculations, to deduce their duty from remote principles . . . The Bible tells us, in plain and authoritative terms, that there is a way to life, and a way to death" and so we "may spare ourselves the labour of tedious enquiries. The holy Scriptures are in our hands" (*Sermons*, pp. 29, 40). Similarly, important theological truths which could be derived from learned investigations are "evidently revealed to us in the Scriptures" to assist "those that are incapable of philosophical enquiries, who make far the greatest part of mankind" (*Sermons*, p. 17). The two fundamental truths we are to learn from revealed religion are, first, humankind's "dependence on the Supreme Being . . . his Creator, and Governour, his Father and his Judge" (*Sermons*, p. 29), and, second, that "this changeable and uncertain life is only the passage to an immutable state, and endless duration of happiness or misery" (*Sermons*, p. 161).

For Johnson, religion invariably leads the believer to a life of morality, and morality just as surely leads to eschatology – the theology of "the four last things:" death, judgment, heaven, and hell. Johnson's eschatological perspective, his habit of regarding all human actions by the light of eternity,

allowed him to face the problem of seemingly unjust suffering with some fortitude, since, he hoped, all spiritual accounts would be balanced in the next life
and God's justice would triumph. More important still, his emphasis on eternal
rewards and punishments enabled him to explain how people, whom he
regarded as no more naturally good than a wolf (*Life*, v, 211), could live surrounded by sin and temptation and nevertheless accept the salvation won for
humankind by Christ.

No person either "performs, [or] forbears any thing upon any other motive
than the prospect, either of an immediate gratification, or a distant reward," he
argued (*Sermons*, p. 149). Christianity teaches us "the vanity of all terrestrial
advantages" when compared with "a more permanent and certain happiness" in
the life hereafter, and thus gives us a compelling motive for goodness (*Sermons*,
p. 270). Revealed religion alone can effectively direct humankind to lead a moral
existence in the midst of sin and difficulty because it uniquely teaches people
how to regulate their lives "by a constant reference of [their] actions to [their]
eternal interest," the very spiritual exercise Johnson repeatedly performs in his
spiritual diary (e.g., *Diaries*, pp. 56–57, 78–79). "To subdue passion, and regulate desire," wrote Johnson, "is the great task of man as a moral agent; a task
for which natural reason . . . has been found insufficient, and which cannot be
performed but by the help of religion" (*Sermons*, p. 193).

Johnson the moral writer regularly advances a prudential argument of theo-
logically enlightened self-interest: the temporary indulgences of life must be
considered very slight indeed when compared with either the pain of everlasting
punishment or eternal bliss. God has providentially ordained that this should be
so, since "it is not possible for a being, necessitous and insufficient as man, to act
wholly without regard to his interest" (*Sermons*, p. 238). If Johnson seems to
focus too often on death, "the day in which . . . an everlasting futurity shall be
determined by the past" (*Idler*, p. 316), he is attempting to impress upon the
reader that eschatological perspective which makes manifest the unreasonable-
ness of sin and the advantages of moral goodness. "Religion," said Johnson, "is
the highest Exercise of Reason."[9]

Yet, as noted earlier, Johnson in no way believes that reason without revealed
religion is sufficient for happiness. "Reason has no authority over us, but by its
power to warn us against evil," he argues (*Idler*, p. 277). What is needed,
Johnson suggests in *The Vanity of Human Wishes*, is "celestial wisdom,"
understanding rooted in the higher truths of revelation and religious tradition.
It might be argued that the trajectory of *Rasselas* also lends itself (as Boswell
believed [*Life*, 1, 341–44]) to the interpretation that it is only in the hereafter
that our hopes for fulfillment can be satisfied. The prince, who is possessed of
all earthly comforts and plagued by none of the concerns that commonly afflict
humanity, is discontented nonetheless. "Give me something to desire" is the dis-

satisfied plea of Rasselas, who "wants nothing"; having everything, his longing is for something greater than himself, something beyond this world (*Rasselas*, pp. 16, 14). As the work draws to a close, the discussion with the old man leaves an impression of the shortness of life on the young people, a notion echoed by the visit to the Egyptian catacombs and amplified by Imlac's discourse on the nature of the soul and the prospect of immortality. "The highest honour, and most constant pleasure this life can afford," wrote Johnson to Miss Hester Maria Thrale in July 1784, "must be obtained by passing it with attention fixed upon Eternity" (*Letters*, IV, 339). Thus, Rasselas's search for true happiness cannot be fulfilled until he understands that "There is but one solid basis of happiness; and that is, the reasonable hope of a happy futurity. This may be had every where" (*Letters*, III, 119).[10] All is vanity, "but we must still prosecute our business, confess our imbecility, and turn our eyes upon [God]" (*Sermons*, p. 132).

V

"We cannot make truth," said Johnson; "it is our business only to find it" (*Sermons*, p. 223). In the revealed religion of Christianity, Johnson encountered and made his own the truths he considered essential to human happiness in this world and to eternal felicity in the next. As he told Boswell, to study theology is to "endeavour to know the will of God" (*Life*, I, 474). Although we may say of Johnson the religious thinker what Johnson said of his wife; that he "had a just diffidence of [his] own reason, and desired to practise rather than dispute" (*Sermons*, p. 269), he nevertheless believed that "it is the duty of every man to publish, profess, and defend any important truth," most especially "the truths of religion" (*Sermons*, pp. 78, 147). Accordingly, Johnson's unswerving conviction that "Christianity is the highest perfection of humanity" informs and enriches almost everything he ever wrote (*Letters*, I, 269).

NOTES

1 Thomas Kaminski, *The Early Career of Samuel Johnson* (Oxford University Press, 1987), p. 74.
2 Robert DeMaria, *The Life of Samuel Johnson* (Oxford: Blackwell, 1993), p. 169.
3 Samuel Johnson and William Oldys, *Catologus Bibliotecae Harleianae*, 5 vols. (London, 1743–45).
4 Robert DeMaria, *Johnson's Dictionary and the Language of Learning* (Chapel Hill: University of North Carolina Press, 1986), p. 222.
5 Allen Reddick, *The Making of Johnson's Dictionary, 1746–1773* (Cambridge University Press, 1990), p. 121.
6 John Nichols, *Literary Anecdotes of the Eighteenth Century*, 9 vols. (London, 1812–16), II, 552.

7 See *Early Biographies*, pp. 7, 11, 21, 27, 42, 134–35, 186, 220.
8 Pat Rogers, *Samuel Johnson* (Oxford University Press, 1993), p. 21.
9 Hester Lynch Piozzi, *Thraliana*, ed. Katherine C. Balderstone, 2 vols. (Oxford: Clarendon Press, 1942), I, 183.
10 Cf., however, Greg Clingham, *Boswell: The Life of Johnson* (Cambridge University Press, 1992), pp. 86–88, and Charles H. Hinnant, *Samuel Johnson: An Analysis* (New York: St. Martin's Press, 1988), pp. 101–2.

13

JOHN WILTSHIRE

"From China to Peru": Johnson in the traveled world

"When a man is tired of London, he is tired of life, for there is in London all that life can afford." Johnson made this famous declaration in 1777, but he had already said something similar to James Boswell on 11 October 1773 whilst they were both temporarily marooned on the island of Coll in the Hebrides. Boswell had commented that until their joint expedition, "You yourself, sir, had never seen, till now, any thing but your native island," to which Johnson replied "But, Sir, by seeing London, I have seen as much of life as the world can shew." It seems clear that "life" in these pronouncements cannot mean whatever it was that Johnson had come to the Hebrides to see. London could encapsulate "life" because life everywhere – that is to say human character – is the same. London's social and cultural diversity, the richness of its human resources, means that it is the perfect laboratory for the study of human nature. Johnson's remarks can be read as testimony not only to his love of the city, but to his conviction that human beings are alike everywhere, the same, in fact, in London as (to use his phrase at the opening of *The Vanity of Human Wishes*) "from China to Peru." What then had taken him to the highlands of Scotland?

Boswell was correct, of course: for most of his life Johnson had lived only in one city. What these comments conceal is that for long he had perforce to be content with the life that London could afford. He left Lichfield for the metropolis in 1737, when he was twenty-eight, and, as far as is known, scarcely left London at all for the next twenty-odd years. Confined there by his literary toils and penury, Johnson would often, in those decades, mock the idea that one would necessarily be better off, or feel better, if you could travel somewhere else. Most memorably in *Rambler* 6, he compares the desire for a change of place with the struggles of a dog maddened with rabies. "It is common for a man, who feels pain, to fancy that he could bear it better in any other part," the Rambler tells his readers (and no doubt himself) ridiculing "the persuasion that content was the inhabitant of particular regions" (III, 35). Similarly, *Rambler* 135 (2 July 1751) is a sardonic commentary on "this time of universal migration" when

London is emptied for the countryside. The happiness supposedly found in rural retreat is a myth, Johnson declares:

> Should any man pursue his aquaintances to their retreats, he would find few of them listening to Philomel, loitering in woods, or plucking daisies. . . . Some will be discovered at a window by the road side, rejoicing when a new cloud of dust gathers towards them, as at the approach of a momentary supply of conversation, and a short relief from the tediousness of unideal vacancy.   (IV, 353)

Envious or not, this contempt for the supposed happiness of country life is a theme that runs through Johnson's writings from the satire on the pastoral in *Rasselas* (chapters 19–21), to the discussion of Cowley's dreams of retirement (*Lives*, I, 15–17). Residence in another place, Johnson insists, will not, of itself, help your moral life or state of mind: it is no therapy. The idea that you might assuage your discontent, or fulfill your desires by travel is a constant target for the stern moralist who insists that "the fountain of content must spring up in the mind" (*Rambler* 6, III, 35) that reformation must come from within. But on this topic he seems later to have had second thoughts.

At the same time as Johnson frequently derided those who imagined they could change themselves by changing their place, he shared his age's conviction of the therapeutic virtues of journeying. The essays are full of metaphors of inertia and stagnation, but, in contrast, movement and activity are equated with vigor and health (sorrow, *Rambler* 47 declares, "is the putrifaction of stagnant life, and is remedied by exercise and motion" [III, 258]). Johnson shared his contemporaries' belief that traveling, whether on horseback, as Dr. Thomas Sydenham had recommended, or in a coach, was good for both body and mind. "Dr. Horse" was widely – and perhaps perfectly reasonably – thought to be of more benefit than the attentions of the medical man; David Garrick, for example, attributed his own recovery on one occasion to "that excellent *physician*, a *horse*."[1] Motion in itself, underwritten by a conception of the body as a system of tubes and vessels that become hardened and blocked in sickness, is understood to perform the therapeutic function. And so in 1782, towards the end of his life, Johnson wrote to John Perkins, the Thrales' clerk, "I am very much pleased that You are going on a very long Journey, which may by proper conduct restore your health and prolong your life," adding that he should "get a smart seasickness if you can" and that only by casting away anxiety can the benefits of travel be attained (*Letters*, IV, 63–64). In his later life, too, Johnson seems to have attained a more nuanced view of the possible benefits to be attained from a change of place. Whilst reaffirming that "no man can run away from himself," as an old one of seventy-four he goes on to declare to Mrs. Thrale that in traveling "he may yet escape from many causes of useless uneasiness. That the *mind is its own place* is the boast of a fallen angel, that had learned to lie. External locality has great effects, at least upon all embodied beings. I hope this little journey will afford me at least some suspence of melancholy" (*Letters*, IV, 191).

This, then, may be one of the routes by which Johnson came to be in the Hebrides. But in fact he was deeply and passionately interested in travel, and in travel narratives, throughout his life. Those remarks about London's sufficiency also conceal the urgency of his wanderlust; even, so it was reported, in his early days as a student at Oxford he declared "I'll go and visit the other Universities abroad" (*Life*, I, 73). At various times he expressed wishes, or made plans, to travel to Iceland, to India, to Sweden, to the shores of the Mediterranean. He even – if momentarily – thought of joining Joseph Banks and Daniel Solander on their proposed expedition to the South Seas in 1772 (*Life*, II, 148). He was fascinated by travel books, which he reviewed and read voraciously, only lamenting, in *Idler* 97, in 1760, how little they satisfied the desires and curiosity of their reader. After 1762, when Johnson was granted a pension, he left London at least once a year, sometimes for several months. In 1773 he was traveling, mostly on horseback and in boats, but occasionally on foot, across the highlands and western islands of Scotland, with Boswell, thirty years his junior, fit and agile, as Johnson, who passed his sixty-fourth birthday at Dunvegan, was not. In the next two years he went with the Thrales on a tour to north Wales, and then to Paris. When he was sixty-six he wrote to Mrs. Thrale that "Perhaps, if you and Master did not hold me I might go to Cairo, and down the Red Sea to Bengal, and take a ramble in India. Half fourteen thousand [the profits of Thrale's brewery that year] would send me out to see other forms of existence and bring me back to describe them" (*Letters*, II, 243).

It was "forms of existence," rather than "life," then, that he was out to see. Johnson's restless desire to travel, his eager curiosity "to examine the laws and customs of foreign nations" (*Life*, I, 89) might seem at odds with the conviction of the stability of truth, the universality of human life, and the penchant for the grandeur of generality that distinguishes his work. Johnson was both a man of his time and very modern, both convinced that "wherever human nature is to be found, there is a mixture of Vice and Virtue, a contest of Passion and Reason" (as he put it in his Preface to his first published work – the translation of a travel book, Father Lobo's *Voyage to Abyssinia* in 1735), and eager to discover and record the different species of human existence, as his being drawn to Lobo in the first place, of course, proclaims.

The History of Rasselas, The Prince of Abissinia, a Tale, its settings evidently prompted by his earlier interest in Father Jerome Lobo's *A Voyage to Abyssinia* (1735), indicates something of its author's passionate interest in foreign cultures. But it is easy to forget that *Rasselas* is set in exotic locations, in Abyssinia, Cairo, and the Egyptian desert, that it tells the story of a journey, and is indeed a kind of travel narrative. Few readers think of it this way because *Rasselas*, like most of Johnson's work, insists not on variety of experience and culture, but on the homogeneity of human nature whatever its local setting or circumstances. His hero's mentor, Imlac, may be born near the fountains of the Nile, and travel through India and Persia before living three years in Palestine, but the book in which Imlac speaks calls attention continually to the premise that human nature is the same the world over, indeed, that "Human life is every where a state in which much is to be endured, and little to be enjoyed." Yet Imlac – perhaps he is a vehicle for the author's longings here – tells his listener that when he saw the shores of the Red Sea his "heart bounded like that of a prisoner escaped. I felt an unextinquishable curiosity kindle in my mind, and resolved to snatch this opportunity of seeing the manners of other nations" (*Rasselas*, p. 34). His impulse in traveling seems to be to see how *different* customs and cultures are in other parts of the world.

Between *Rasselas* as travel narrative – drawing on the idiosyncrasies, the differences, of exotic cultures – and *Rasselas* as moral fable, in which Cairo is just any big city, in which young men are drunken and thoughtless and philosophers betray their precepts, just like anywhere else, there is an odd disparity. "Their way lay through fields, where shepherds tended their flocks, and the lambs were playing upon the pasture": it scarcely matters that this very English landscape is supposedly to be found "near the lowest cataract of the Nile" (*Rasselas*, p. 76) because one recognizes implicitly that Johnson's shepherds, like his hermit and philosopher, are representative, lay, figures. Though Johnson certainly makes use of his oriental locale, and includes scenes set near the great pyramid (of which Rasselas's party, interestingly, "measured all its dimensions") the monument is most memorably used as a text for Imlac to dilate upon "the insufficiency of human enjoyments." The moralist whose reflections upon human life the tale contains and illustrates is in creative tension with the incipient, perhaps more novelistic, desire to capture particularities of culture and location. Imlac, the reader is told, "was diverted with the admiration which his companions expressed at the diversity of manners, stations and employments" on their journey from the valley: yet the prose that points to this diversity is itself abstract, general, and notional. There is thus a tension between the writer's professed interest in diversity and specificity, and the controlled form and style through which he views them.

Imlac is eager not only to see the manners of other nations, but also "to learn sciences unknown in Abissinia." Johnson, too, partook of his age's intense curiosity about the natural and physical worlds, as his reviews of books on scientific experiments and medicinal innovations, as well as on travel, suggest. He was himself touched, in a small way, by that drive for knowledge which became so intimately connected with exploration. In 1755, on behalf of his ailing friend Zachariah Williams, he wrote a pamphlet called *An Account of an Attempt to*

Ascertain the Longitude at Sea. Williams had been trying for the large prize that, since 1714, had been offered by parliament for a more accurate way of determining longitude, since the difficulty of doing so was a major impediment to exploration by sea and the development of overseas trade. For this was, of course, the period of British imperial expansion, of the colonization of North America, India, and the Pacific. Imperial and commercial ambitions came together with scientific curiosity and research to jointly promote the exploration of previously unknown regions of the globe.

Foremost among such endeavors were those which surveyed the world (even if a largely watery world) that stretches from China to Peru. Captain James Cook's three voyages to the South Seas (1768–71, 1772–75, 1776–79), in particular, undertaken in the first place for scientific and navigational reasons, came upon many new and isolated island cultures, and contributed much material toward what Johnson describes, in his *Preface to Shakespeare*, as the current "contest about the original benevolence or malignity of man." Whether, as followers of Shaftesbury and others were claiming, the native people were innocent and happy, or, being bereft of education and learning, sinful, and vicious, became a major controversy. Johnson's work inevitably reflects, and reflects on, these initiatives, discoveries and arguments.

"The business of a poet," says Imlac, famously, "is to examine, not the individual, but the species; to remark general properties and large appearances: he does not number the streaks of the tulip" (*Rasselas*, p. 43). While Johnson is not identified with Imlac's ideals of Enlightenment criticism, the voyages to unknown regions also tested those ideals in an unforeseen way. When the Admiralty and the Royal Society sent out artists to sail with Cook and Joseph Banks in the *Endeavour*, their instructions were precisely the reverse: they were to number the streaks of the tulip, they were to draw the details of the botanical specimens Banks found on remote islands, to render the forms and colors of exotic life with exact precision. But as Bernard Smith argues in his famous study *European Vision and the South Pacific* (1959), the artists, when confronted with the need to depict native life, fell back upon the topoi, the poses, the compositional structures bequeathed to them by Enlightenment practices. They rendered the distinct scenes before them as versions of universal human images. A similar tension or ambiguity can be found in Johnson's own work. When Johnson himself began to travel, and to record his experience in the *Journey to the Western Islands of Scotland* (1775), the scientific and anti-romantic imperative – the drive to depict only what he saw and to recount only what he could be sure of – coexisted within a mind and imagination imbued with literary classics and with the desire to see the general within the instance, the need to enhance the particular with the aura of the universal. On the island of Armadale, Boswell discovered a monument to Sir James Macdonald with an eloquent tribute in

English. "Dr Johnson said," he reports, "the inscription should have been in Latin, as every thing intended to be universal and permanent, should be" (*Life*, V, 154). Accordingly, Johnson bestowed on his Odes commemorating the particular qualities of the isle of Skye the dignity of that classical language.

European colonial expansion occupied Johnson's thinking a good deal, and in his commentaries on this subject, he is especially arresting. The same Preface to Lobo that praises him for recognizing the uniformity of human nature also excoriates the hypocrisy of colonizers who "preach the gospel with swords in their hands, and propagate by desolation and slaughter the true worship of the God of peace." The European exploration of the world should always, Johnson insisted, be accompanied by an ethical and civilizing mandate, though it was a mandate that in practice, he found, was almost always disregarded. Excited by the prospect of travel and by foreign cultures, he also consistently applied a universalistic Christian moral view to the topic of imperial expansion – whether it was in Africa, America, India, or in Scotland. One recurrent theme in all his travel writings, as Clement Hawes discusses above, concerns what we should now call the rights of indigenous peoples.

His Introduction to "A Collection of Voyages and Travels" called *The World Displayed*, written in the same year as *Rasselas* (1759), is an ironic, and at times caustic, history of European (mostly Portuguese) exploration of the African coast in the fifteenth century, and culminating in Columbus's discovery of America. The narrative treats the Europeans as invaders, and devotes a good deal of sarcasm to the civilizing and missionary pretensions of those who are seen to be motivated only by the hope of gain and dominion. The historians Johnson is summarizing describe the amazement of the African natives at Portuguese firepower, and in terms reminiscent of his trenchant criticism of Soame Jenyns's rationalistic theodicy, he comments as follows:

> On what occasion, or for what purpose, cannons and muskets were discharged among a people harmless and secure, by strangers who without any right visited their coast, it is not thought necessary to inform us. The Portuguese could fear nothing from them, and had therefore no adequate provocation; nor is there any reason to believe but that they murdered the negroes in wanton merriment, perhaps only to try how many a volley would destroy, or what would be the consternation of those that should escape. (*Works*, II, 217–18).[2]

Johnson is certainly a Christian moralist, but he can hardly, in his many pieces that touch on imperial expansion, be called Eurocentric: the Europeans treated native peoples so badly, Johnson continues, "because they scarcely considered them as distinct from beasts" (II, 218). Here, as in his "Introduction to the Political State of Great Britain" of 1756, "European" is used as an ironic, or even derisory, term. It is apparent that Johnson's thought about the expansion of

European horizons, trade, and culture, which was taking place with great energy in his time, turned upon this question of moral values. In his *Dictionary* of the previous year the words "savage" and "barbarian" are more or less interchangeable, used to define each other, but in this passage, touched with the same mingled indignation and fear at random violence as his review of Soame Jenyns's *A Free Inquiry*, Johnson discriminates between "savage people," who are the innocent occupants of their land, and "barbarians," the European, and British, whose cruelty is the main thing that distinguishes them from the natives. Boswell claimed that "the truth is, like the ancient Greeks and Romans, he allowed himself to look upon all nations but his own as barbarians" (*Life*, V, 20), but this possibly quite accurate reflection of Johnson's casual talk quite fails to appreciate his attitude in the introduction to *The World Displayed*. If "the power of Europe has been extended to the remotest parts of the world," Johnson insists, that is not to be seen as the conquest of civilization. "The Europeans have scarcely visited any coast," he declares, "but to gratify avarice, and extend corruption; to arrogate dominion without right, and practise cruelty without incentive" (*Works*, II, 220).

Yet like the imperialist designs that sent Cook across the South Seas, Johnson's interest in foreign places and civilizations was partly utilitarian or centripetal. He was motivated – as were many travelers to India, the Far East, the Pacific, and Australasia – by the possibility of the discovery of "useful arts," and the hope of finding new medicinal substances; in other words of bringing back useful information to the metropolis. Confessing how much he himself longed to travel in India, he wrote to its Governor-General, Warren Hastings, in 1774 of

> how much may be added by your attention and patronage to experimental knowledge and natural history. There are arts of manufacture practised in the countries in which you preside which are yet very imperfectly known here either to artificers or philosophers. Of the natural productions animate and inanimate we yet have so little intelligence that our books are filled, I fear, with conjectures about things which an Indian Peasant knows by his senses. (*Letters*, II, 136–37)

At the same time, the apprehension that colonies might be merely exploited never left him. When in 1773 Johnson was "imprisoned" in Skye by the weather, he wrote to bid farewell to his friend and protegé, Robert Chambers, who was soon to depart for Calcutta. "You are going where there will be many opportunities of profitable wickedness," he declared, adding the hope that Chambers would return "but with fortune encreased, and Virtue grown more resolute by contest" (*Letters*, II, 86).

In December 1774, Johnson, hearing of the departure of a ship to Bengal, sent Hastings a prepublication copy of his *Journey to the Western Islands of Scotland*. "A region less remote and less illustrious than India," Scotland had yet afforded him "some occasions for speculation" (*Letters*, II, 160). The *Journey*, the fruit of his tour with Boswell, is Johnson's only strict contribution to the literature of travel, and in it his universalism and his absorbed interest in local conditions and specific cultures meet and intertwine. Imlac had spoken of "the manners of other nations"; writing to Mrs. Thrale, Johnson speaks of "forms of existence." There is a subtle difference between these phrases, since "manners" suggests merely styles, cultural idiosyncrasies that decorate or clothe an unchanging moral core. Other "forms of existence" tend to collapse the distinction between nature and culture, implying that the entire human life – its moral as well as its cultural dimensions – may be distinct in different civilizations, that culture, so to speak, goes all the way down. In the *Journey*, an accurate picture of the distinctiveness of highland life is framed by an encompassing narrative form that holds firm to a reflective or "speculative" standpoint.

In many respects, Johnson's book is a work of early sociology or ethnography. The fruit of much impatience with the vagueness of travel writers, and spurred by the desire to emulate, in however minor a way, the travels that others were undertaking all around him (thus Boswell called it his "transit of the Caledonian hemisphere") the *Journey* is filled with the distinctively modern concern of the scientific observer to obtain reliable reports and valid evidence. Both Johnson's devotion to literature and his scrupulousness about evidence contrast, sometimes implicitly and sometimes explicitly, with the culture that he is studying and presenting. The highlanders are "an illiterate people, whose whole time is a series of distress." In Johnson's estimation, they can have no interest in accurate history. Even among the better-off Scots, stories, myths, and false information are continually circulated. They are credulous and uninquiring. This is a largely premodern society in which orality predominates, and which notably lacks a concern with the accuracy and permanence of record. As scholar, and as observer and reporter, Johnson personates a culture very different from the world he is passing through.

But this is not the only way in which the attitude, or sensibility, of the narrator is incommensurate with the cultural landscape he depicts. Johnson's *Journey* is both episodic and contingent – reflecting the incidents, the vicissitudes, of the journey – and carefully structured and organized. It is a hybrid form whose basic shape is that of a diary, or record of temporal events, yet it contains, in its lengthy middle section, under "Ostig in Sky" (pp. 78–120), a broad sociological overview of all aspects of the culture of the highlands in which narrative momentum is forgotten. The text is also hybrid in that whilst it is committed to a broadly episodic format, picking topics as they are thrown up in the course of the journey, certain questions seem to recur continually. In the event, they are thematized, and come to resemble a structured or coherent meditation. Johnson is concerned, from the first sentence, with questions that occupy the field marked out by his

From the Isle of Raasay looking Westward

Plate 7 View of Skye from Raasay, by William Daniell (1820), from Richard Ayton, *Voyage Round Great Britain* (1814–25). "The general air of festivity, which predominated in this place, so far remote from all those regions which the mind has been used to contemplate as the mansions of pleasure, struck the imagination with a delightful surprise, analogous to that which is felt at an unexpected emersion from darkness into light" (*Journey*, p. 59).

recurrent terms – "civil," "elegant," "polished" – and by "savage," "primitive,"
"barbarian." This is a traveler's tale, a journey, but it is also the tale of a traveler whose mind is full of questions about civilization, what it is, and what conditions make it possible. A third set of terms – "monuments," memorials, "letters"
– cumulatively become key markers in this pondering of the various meanings of
civil and agricultural "cultivation" when confronted by this uncongenial landscape and the primitive hardships of life in the Hebrides.

The culture of the narrator of the *Journey* is "polished," ironic, allusive,
scholarly; his narrative ranges over times and places. He spans the globe. The
stone heads of arrows on Raasay resemble those that "Mr Banks has lately
brought from the savage countries in the Pacifick Ocean" (p. 63). He compares
the wildness to "the desarts of America" and Col to the Czar of Muscovy. He
recalls Roman road builders and Greek poetry. The women of the Macraes "like
the Sythian ladies of old, married their servants." But the terrain before him is
isolated, hemmed in by mountains and the sea, an intensely specific and local
culture, whose inhabitants are constrained by their circumstances. Their eyes,
through barrenness and isolation, are bent on the immediate tasks before them.
Johnson, on the other hand, sees beyond the local and the present. He is both a
scientific observer, verifying detail with his own eyes ("No man should travel
unprovided with instruments for taking heights and distances," he writes), and
the learned scholar, seeing through the spectacles of books, remarking, for
instance, that the road to Fores "to an Englishman is classic ground" (p. 25) or
comparing his stay at Raasay with Odysseus at Phaeacia. The presence of both
the local, scientific interest and the broad, classical, reflective quality of the text
gives the *Journey* its inner dialectic.

Johnson's qualities as a reporter are best illustrated by the famous passage
devoted to his first sight of a highland hut. (He has just compared the highland
goats to ones described by Plutarch.) This dwelling place is described at first, as
by an ethnographer, in generic terms. "The wall, which is commonly about six
feet high, declines from the perpendicular a little inward," Johnson writes, with
typical exactness of mesuration. Yet this careful and specific description passes
into the wry reflection that "Huts however are not more uniform than palaces;
and this which we were inspecting was very far from one of the meanest, for it
was divided into several apartments; and its inhabitants possessed such property
as a pastoral poet might exalt into riches" (p. 32). Through the ironic or laconic
comparison the reader senses that the speaker is possessed of the civilization, the
amenity, that the family he contemplates lacks. The passage continues in a spare
prose that is at least as common in Johnson as his more pompous manner:

> When we entered, we found an old woman boiling goat's-flesh in a kettle. She spoke
> little English, but we had interpreters at hand; and she was willing enough to
> display her whole system of economy. She has five children, of which none are yet

gone from her. The eldest, a boy of thirteen, and her husband, who is eighty years old, were at work in the wood. Her two next sons were gone to Inverness to buy "meal," by which oatmeal is always meant. Meal she considered as expensive food, and told us, that in spring, when the goats gave milk, the children could live without it. She is mistress of sixty goats, and I saw many kids in an enclosure at the end of her house. She had also some poultry. By the lake we saw a potatoe-garden, and a small spot of ground on which stood four shucks, containing each twelve sheaves of barley. She has all this from the labour of their own hands, and for what is necessary to be bought, her kids and her chickens are sent to market.   (p. 33)

This passage is remarkable for its borrowing of the peasant woman's own voice. Like the other old woman whom Johnson finds living in the vault of the ruined cathedral at St. Andrews, her own speech, in the present tense, comes directly into the narrative.[3] The phrase "She has all this from the labour of their own hands" captures even the cadence of her personal pride. By this technique Johnson conveys his subject's stature, and his respect for her, even whilst his material defines the narrowness of her circumstances. Hers is a functioning "system of economy," a successful wresting from harsh conditions of the rudiments of civilized existence. Johnson specifically relates that, though the kirk is a long way off, "she goes thither every Sunday."

His account concludes "she begged snuff; for snuff is the luxury of a Highland cottage." Thus this description is specific, factual, and infused with pathos – the pathos that is brought to the material facts by their association with the broader prospects, the richer resonances, of the narrator's own ironic references to the "pastoral poet," and to "luxury." The combination, as exemplified in the episode under consideration, of a reflective, sophisticated sensibility and the starkness and resistance of the life recorded contributes to make the *Journey* uniquely moving among Johnson's works.

He begins his travels, as many commentators have noticed, with ideas that he is later forced to revise.[4] He hopes or expects "to hear old traditions and see antiquated manners," but he comes too late, for the clans have been reformed by their English conquerors. He discovers as he travels through the barren and inhospitable landscape that "the fictions of the Gothick romances are not so remote from credibility as they are now thought." At first he harshly criticizes the highlanders for their neglect in planting trees. Later, when he understands more about the highland environment, he perceives that his earlier expectations are the result of an unthinking imposition on this culture of ideas and opinions appropriate only to another. "It may soon be discovered, why in a place, which hardly supplies the cravings of necessity, there has been little attention to the delights of fancy" (pp. 139–40) – soon discovered, that is, by an imaginative observer, able now to participate by proxy in the life before him.

Johnson's earlier notion that "manners" are separate from other aspects of life, that manners may be different but nature is the same, starts to break down. In his section on "The Highlands" he deduces the "savagery" of highland "manners" from the highlanders' geographical situation, each clan cut off by the terrain from each other. The "manners of mountaineers are commonly savage, but they are rather produced by their situation than derived from their ancestors" – an account that derives cultural formations from geographical and economic circumstances. Yet it seems here that "manners" may be indistinguishable from "forms of life": "such were the qualities of the highlanders," Johnson concludes, "while their rocks secluded them from the rest of mankind, and kept them an unaltered and discriminated race" (p. 47). This "discriminated race," filled with enmity "against the wicked inhabitants of the next valley" seems to belie the earlier confidence in the undifferentiation of humankind from "China to Peru."

Johnson's own broad view – his capacity to survey humankind, and to look back to the Greeks and Romans — is a flower of more genial soil than the highlands provide. In this environment, the records of human struggle over adversity, over time and the elements, acquire a special importance. This is why Johnson is so indignant about the depredations of Calvinism: it has "blasted ceremony and decency together," obliterating and effacing the records that are the only testimony to man's power to transcend the here and now, and thus to escape from mere "naked existence." The peasantry of the highlands and the islands have no time nor energy to spare to think about anything but providing for the day that passes over them. Rather than condemning the highlanders for their lack of interest in history, their failure to provide for posterity, he comments now that "we soon found what memorials were to be expected from an illiterate people, whose whole time is a series of distress." Johnson becomes, in effect, a spokesperson for the highlanders, an advocate for them against the lowland Scots, to whom "the state of the mountains and the islands is equally unknown with that of Borneo or Sumatra." "Every one is busy for himself, without any arts by which the pleasure of others may be increased; if to the daily burden of distress any additional weight be added, nothing remains but to despair and die" (p. 133). The terms "primitive," and even "barbarian," come to evoke not so much savagery, as deprivation.

These are people whose energies are utterly absorbed in the struggle to survive in a bleak, unyielding landscape. Evidence of human life not so absorbed – of the power to reflect on the past and plan for the future – thus acquires a peculiar poignancy. "We did not perceive that this tract was possessed by human beings, except that once we saw a corn-field, in which a lady was walking with some gentlemen," he writes, and the casual, fleeting glimpse of leisure and cultivation has a epiphanic quality, inscribing value by its rarity. Another such moment is on Mull, inflected more sardonically. "We travelled many hours through a tract,

Plate 8 Dunvegan Castle, from Francis Grose, *The Antiquities of Scotland* (1797). "Here the violence of the weather confined us for some time, not at all to our discontent or inconvenience" (*Journey*, p. 69).

black and barren, in which, however, there were the reliques of humanity: for we found a ruined chapel in our way" (p. 139). "Romance does not often exhibit a scene that strikes the imagination more," Johnson writes of Inch Kenneth, than ladies and gentlemen practicing "all the kindness of hospitality, and refinement of courtesy" in "these depths of western obscurity" (pp. 142–43).

It is such graphic contrasts as these that make the *Journey* a testimony to the preciousness of civilized life (see plate 8). Against this remote and harsh background the values that Johnson's own reflective, learned narrative style incorporates are understood and celebrated. "More notions than facts," as Johnson described his writing to Boswell (*Letters*, II, 145), the *Journey* amounts to a powerful meditation on the crucial role that "letters" play in such a life. What defines savagery and barbarianism, in fact, is the absence of literature, of records, and of the capacity to reflect that these denote. The culmination of such thoughts, is Johnson's famous meditation about the ruins of Iona.

"Truth," declares Imlac, sternly, "is always found where it is honestly sought." Yet even in *Rasselas*, it is allowed that since we are embodied and imaginative, rather than wholly rational beings, pilgrimage to sacred places may have its efficacy. "He who supposes that his vices may be more successfully combated in

Palestine, will, perhaps, find himself mistaken, yet he may go thither without folly," declares the sage (*Rasselas*, p. 48). On Iona, Johnson expresses a sense of the imaginative power of place more fully and genially, and yet with a new moral force drawn from his recent study and understanding of a culture absorbed by the immediate struggle for existence, without reflection and without learning. The speaker, for a moment avowedly confessional, draws together the themes that he has contemplated through the journey from the first sights of ruined cathedrals in St. Andrews and Aberbrothick:

> We were now treading that illustrious island, which was once the luminary of the Caledonian regions, whence savage clans and roving barbarians derived the bene-fits of knowledge and the blessings of religion. To abstract the mind from all local emotion would be impossible, if it were endeavoured, and would be foolish, if it were possible. Whatever withdraws us from the power of our senses; whatever makes the past, the distant, or the future predominate over the present, advances us in the dignity of thinking beings. Far from me and from my friends, be such frigid philosophy as may conduct us indifferent and unmoved over any ground that has been dignified by wisdom, bravery, or virtue. That man is little to be envied, whose patriotism would not gain force upon the plain of Marathon, or whose piety would not grow warmer among the ruins of Iona? (p. 148)

With its references to the past and the classics, this writing exemplifies a form of that transcendence over time and immediate contingency that the cathedral itself once instantiated. This is both a representative and a particular place. Like the passage in which Johnson describes the bank surrounded by "unknown and untravelled wilderness" in which he first conceived the thought of writing his book (pp. 40–41), the setting is the necessary adjunct to, part of, the thought, necessary to the thought's full flowering. Yet the thought transcends its moment, its occasion. Iona, in being a particular place, is an exemplar of all such places, and being there prompts Johnson's meditations to rise into their accustomed expansive and generalizing form. Thus in this passage Johnson brings about a *rapprochement* between his moralizing, universalizing bent and his newly acquired sense of the power and authority of particular landscapes, the spirit of particular places.

Johnson ends the *Journey* with a modest remark about his having passed his time "almost wholly in cities" (p. 164). His appetite for exploration, at last acted upon, was an expression of that modern, progressive side of his temperament which shared his age's curiosity about the natural world. In his writings on travel there is a creative tension between Johnson the classicist and moralist, insisting on the uniformity of the moral world, and Johnson the modern, the progressive, delighting in the diversity, variousness, and promise of the natural and experi-ential world. Johnson's thought on the subject of travel is thus caught between the ancient idea of universality and the modern interest in distinctness, between essentialism and ethnography. He is a scientific traveler, observing and measuring, a seeker after facts, yet he admits, especially later in his life, that places cast a spell, and that imagination may legitimately flourish in the presence of the Egyptian pyramids or the ruins of Iona. The central struggles of Johnson's temperament, between the stern rebukes of reason and the solicitations of an irrepressible imagination, are perhaps, then, nowhere more strikingly illustrated than in his thinking about the traveled world.

NOTES

1 Roy Porter, *Doctor of Society: Thomas Beddoes and the Sick Trade in Late Enlightenment England* (New York: Routledge, 1991), p. 123.

2 See Hawes's discussion of this passage, above, pp. 120–21. Compare Johnson's depiction of European cruelty in the *World Displayed* with the inhumanity of Soame Jenyns's rationalistic theodicy in *A Free Inquiry* (Greene, pp. 535–36).

3 "One of the vaults [of the religious buildings in St. Andrews] was inhabited by an old woman, who claimed the right of abode there, as the widow of a man whose ancestors had possessed the same gloomy mansion for no less than four generations. The right, however it began, was considered established by legal prescription, and the old woman lives undisturbed. She thinks however that she has a claim to something more than sufferance; for as her husband's name was Bruce, she is allied to royalty, and told Mr. Boswell that when there were persons of quality in the place, she was distinguished by some notice; that indeed she is now neglected, but she spins a thread, has the company of her cat and is troublesome to nobody" (*Journey*, pp. 8–9).

4 See, for example, John B. Radner, "The Significance of Johnson's Changing Views of the Hebrides," in *The Unknown Samuel Johnson*, ed. John J. Burke, Jr. and Donald Kay (Madison: University of Wisconsin Press, 1983), pp. 131–49.

14

TOM KEYMER

"Letters about nothing": Johnson and epistolary writing

I

Cicero describes a poet who, undeterred by losing his audience, continues his recitation to the end: "Plato alone is as good as a hundred thousand," the poet declares. It is no surprise that this tale of merit's endurance in a hostile age should have lodged in Johnson's mind. "The Lecturer was surely in the right, who, though he saw his audience slinking away, refused to quit the Chair, while Plato staid," he tells John Wesley (6 February 1776; *Letters*, II, 290 and n.). He later acknowledges a compliment from Hester Thrale with quieter reference to the tale: "There is some comfort in writing, when such praise is to be had. Plato is a multitude" (18 March 1779; III, 157).

To value a lone connoisseur as highly as a mass readership was not only to salvage pride in an overlooked work, nor was it simply to claim kinship with such other addressees of "fit audience . . . though few" as Milton.[1] In the context of his correspondence with Hester Thrale (who elicited from Johnson no fewer than 373 surviving letters, including many of his finest), it was also to suggest that private genres like the letter itself could count for as much as literature printed and bound. Coterie poets of the seventeenth century had addressed specialized verse to like-minded readers through scribal publication, and the practice still flourished among women poets of Johnson's circle like Elizabeth Carter and Hester Mulso. The same advantages of restricted address could persuade such virtuosos of the familiar letter as Horace Walpole and Lady Mary Wortley Montagu to lavish their energies on a primary audience of one, or on the limited secondary audience with which their writing would often be shared. Posthumous publication might be envisaged or even prepared, but more important at first were the special freedoms and opportunities to be gained by playing in private to an audience that was both known and knowing. Here styles of writing could flourish which the forms and decorums of published literature would otherwise cramp – among them the intimate shorthand allusiveness with which Johnson goes on to ridicule the minor playwright now best known as Sheridan's model for Sir Fretful Plagiary in *The Critic*. Ironically consoling Hester Thrale on the tedium of Brighton society, he multiplies to absurdity the hyperbole of Cicero's poet: "The want of company is an inconvenience, but Mr. Cumberland is a Million, make the most of what you have" (21 October 1779; III, 195). She would not have missed this fleeting further glance at Cicero's tale, with its ludicrous implicit view of Georgian Brighton as a cut-price, mock-heroic Athens in which the father of philosophy is replaced by a strutting hack.

We have been slow to recognize the brilliance of Johnson's epistolary output, and slower still to develop approaches adequate to it. R. W. Chapman's edition of 1952 did little to stimulate critical interest, and the few critics to tackle the letters in his wake read them as unmediated acts of disclosure from which the complicating aspects of epistolary self-portraiture discerned by Johnson himself seemed magically erased. The letters were "not essentially 'literary' creations," as Philip B. Daghlian put it, but transparent sources in which "the reader curious to see Dr. Johnson without any intervening elements" might find "a view of him as he was."[2] Subtler accounts have been written of rhetorical style, literary allusion, and didactic strategy in famous individual letters, but the myth of Johnson's epistolary artlessness has proved tenacious. Only lately has the notion of epistolarity – "the use of the letter's formal properties to create meaning"[3] – modified the tendency of scholars to relegate the correspondence as a whole to the status of mere biographical source. Bruce Redford has recently insisted "that Johnson's letters richly merit, and abundantly repay, the kind of close scrutiny we automatically accord the 'major' works,"[4] and other recent accounts of their intensive techniques of allusion and parody and their development of a flexible, playful, and generically specific style lend significant weight to his claim. It is now possible to see the correspondence as a central yet intriguingly anomalous part of the Johnson canon, which moves beyond the normal styles and procedures of his published output and demands to be read instead on terms of its own. In these letters is heard a private voice – or voices – markedly distinct from that of the public Johnson, yet no less complex, artful, or impressive.

Public/private, formal/informal, ceremonious/familiar: distinctions of this kind have underpinned the theory of letter-writing in English since the earliest efforts to fashion a native aesthetic distinct from the preciosity of French models. Two governing metaphors reach back to the seventeenth century, each locating the letter within a domestic sphere of intimate sociability. The first likens the language of letters to the measured spontaneity of conversation. "All Letters mee thinks should bee free and Easy as ones discourse, not studdyed, as an Oration, nor made up of hard words like a Charme," as Dorothy Osborne put it in 1653; she goes on to censure those who "labour to finde out term's that may Obscure a plaine sence, like a gentleman I knew, whose would never say the weather grew cold, but that Winter began to salute us."[5] With this insistence on colloquial simplicity went a licensing of expressive frankness, often articulated in terms of undressing the soul or heart. Praising the correspondence in which Abraham Cowley "always express'd the Native tenderness and Innocent gayety of his Mind," Thomas Sprat ruled in 1668 that letters "should have a Native clearness and shortness, a Domestical plaines, and a peculiar kind of Familiarity, which can only affect the humour of those to whom they were intended." Intimate in both style and substance, they retained meaning and decency only within the limited realm in which they were first composed and received. "In such Letters the Souls of Men should appear undress'd," Sprat concludes: "And in that negligent habit they may be fit to be seen by one or two in a Chamber, but not to go abroad into the Streets."[6]

To writers like Osborne and Sprat, metaphorical touchstones of this kind did not imply a sanctioning of artless abandon. One addressee of Osborne's wrote that she would improve her correspondence "by making it less ceremonious & using me with a freedom, that may give me more access into your heart,"[7] and this mingling of informality and circumspection in her letters reminds us that the conversation to which she looked was itself seen as an art, and one in which the appearance of spontaneity was far from meaning casual chat or unguarded confession. The conversational letter was to cultivate stylistic plainness and expressive frankness, to be sure; but it was not to lapse into undisciplined babble or unchecked emotional outpour. Even Sprat's image of the undressed soul did not imply nakedness or total exposure – undress meaning simply "a loose or negligent dress" (*Dictionary*). Here was a style in which outdoor standards of propriety were relaxed, not wholly suspended.

This sense of familiar letters as a mode in which candor and informality were simultaneously prized and kept in check began to fade, however, as the language of Osborne and Sprat turned into cliché. When defining "letter" in the *Dictionary* Johnson cites William Walsh's *Letters and Poems, Amorous and Gallant* (1692), with its dictum that "the stile of *letters* ought to be free, easy, and natural; as near approaching to familiar conversation as possible," but here the analogy led only to meandering inconsequence or – as Johnson elsewhere judges Walsh's practice – "pages of inanity" (*Rambler* 152, V, 44). A more knowing exponent of the traditional language of epistolary intimacy was Walsh's protégé Alexander Pope, but in Pope's hands the usual terms are carefully stripped of any sense of artfulness or reserve. Now the letter stands in unqualified opposition to published genres, supremely immediate in the access it gives to the writer's heart, the authenticity of its reports at once achieved and guaranteed by a distinguishing spontaneity of style. "You see my letters are scribbled with all the carelessness and inattention imaginable," Pope assures one reader: "my style, like my soul, appears in its natural undress before my friend." In the paradoxical act of publishing revised versions of these supremely private texts, Pope defines his letters as "by no means Efforts of the Genius but Emanations of the Heart." They seem almost his literary lifeblood – "a proof what were his real Sentiments, as they flow'd warm from the heart, and fresh from the occasion."[8]

II

Johnson's earliest letters share this sense of an unguarded, conversational mode in which stylistic elegance and confessional authenticity stand in inverse relation. In 1735 he rebukes Richard Congreve for an "Excess of Ceremony . . . which . . . portended no great Sincerity to our future Correspondence," urging instead a mode of "frank and unreserv'd communication:" to "converse" in this way would be to recover their childhood intimacy, "embarrass'd with no forms, and . . . such as well became our rural Retreats, shades unpolluted by Flattery and falsehood, thickets where Interest and Artifice never lay conceal'd!" (25 June 1735; I, 9). In a famous letter written four decades later to Hester Thrale, however, Johnson puts idealizing clichés of this kind under severe ironic strain:

> In a Man's Letters you know, Madam, his soul lies naked, his letters are only the mirrour of his breast, whatever passes within him is shown undisguised in its natural process. Nothing is inverted, nothing distorted, you see systems in their elements, you discover actions in their motives.
>
> Of this great truth sounded by the knowing to the ignorant, and so echoed by the ignorant to the knowing, what evidence have you now before you. Is not my soul laid open in these veracious pages? do not you see me reduced to my first principles? . . . The original Idea is laid down in its simple purity, and all the supervenient conceptions, are spread over it stratum super stratum, as they happen to be formed.
>
> (27 October 1777; III, 89–90)

By pushing to absurdity the claims implicit in the conventional language of undress, the po-faced pseudo-scientisms of Johnson's letter expose the fragility of the unexamined "great truth" to which they explicitly seem committed. The *coup de grâce* comes with a willfully inept geological metaphor, in which (like an exhibit from that favorite source of the *Dictionary*, John Woodward's *Natural History of Fossils*) the epistolary subject seems not so much brought glittering to the surface as buried beneath layer upon layer of verbal sludge.

Johnson's doubts about the representational status of epistolary discourse find their most telling expression in the "Life of Pope" (1781). The ideal of pastoral intimacy voiced in his early letter to Congreve is now revoked. Dismissing expectations "that the true characters of men may be found in their letters" as belonging only to some mythical "*Golden Age*," he finds in the form a crippling mixture of self-deception and self-promotion, with Pope the most brilliant culprit: "Very few can boast of hearts which they dare lay open to themselves, and of which, by whatever accident exposed, they do not shun a distinct and continued view; and certainly what we hide from ourselves we do not shew to our friends. There is, indeed, no transaction which offers stronger temptations to fallacy and sophistication than epistolary intercourse." Analogies with the spontaneity of conversation are void, Johnson adds, the letter being instead "a calm and deliberate performance in the cool of leisure." Void too is the usual distinction between epistolary and published discourse, which he turns on its head to insist that "in writing to the world . . . the author is not confronted with his reader, and takes his chance of approbation among the different dispositions of mankind; but a letter is addressed to a single mind of which the prejudices and partialities are known." Now the very privacy of the form, so long held to guarantee its representational fidelity, ensures only its lurch into fiction (*Lives*, III, 206–7).

The paradox here is that, even in denying the letter its representational claims, Johnson also elevates it as a creative art in which the writer's self is not so much naively reflected as constructed or willfully shaped. A similar sense of high possibilities and high demands distinguishes his earlier discussion in *Rambler* 152 (31 August 1751), which targets the bland enthusiasm for epistolary negligence of Walsh and his imitators. Here Johnson does allow the form a representational field of its own: "much of life must be passed in affairs considerable only by their frequent occurrence," and it is in familiar letters that this mundane yet highly nuanced continuum is most appropriately traced. He seems more interested, however, in the letter as a realm of exciting semantic inconsequence, free of those extensive views, general properties, and large appearances which the poet is charged to record – a realm in which one does not write about anything in particular so much as simply *write*. When he speaks here of "the art of decorating insignificance," he seems to envisage – if not exactly the playful *écriture* of poststructuralism – an epistolarity otherwise void of significant content, in which the rigors of describing the world give way to a gratuitous excess of writing over meaning and the pursuit of sheer style. Johnson's conclusion hovers ambiguously between this tempting sense that style is all and a residual commitment to signification: "The pebble must be polished with care, which hopes to be valued as a diamond; and words ought surely to be laboured when they are intended to stand for things" (*Rambler* 152, V, 44–47).

Though separated by decades, *Rambler* 152 and the "Life of Pope" share a single key assumption: that traditional models of spontaneity and transparency at once vitiate the practice of the form and mislead its reception. Limiting the letter first to minor phenomena unworthy of note in higher forms, Johnson then denies it the one remaining subject – authentic representation of the writing self – in which it had traditionally been held to excel. Letters, it would seem, could have nothing to say. Yet to diminish or deny this representational function was not to dismiss the form, for it was the very groundlessness of epistolary meaning that made it so demanding an art – an art of creative self-fashioning, and an art in which attention and effort shift ineluctably from signification to style. "To sit down so often with nothing to say, to say something so often, almost without consciousness of saying, and without any remembrance of having said," he tells Hester Thrale, "is a power of which I will not violate my modesty by boasting, but I do not believe that every body has it" (27 October 1777; III, 89).

III

Johnson's sense of the letter-form as an arena of conspicuous style and theatrical self-fashioning is nowhere better displayed than in his famous attack on the Earl of Chesterfield (7 February 1755; I, 94–97), who after years of indifference was now attempting to win prestige as patron of the *Dictionary*. Casting himself as "a retired and uncourtly Scholar," one "overpowered . . . by the enchantment of your adress," Johnson at first seems wholly innocent of rhetorical skill. Yet the letter he writes is at the same time a brilliant rhetorical display, not so much a polished gem as a lethally accurate missile. "The notice which you have been pleased to take of my Labours . . . has been delayed till I am indifferent and cannot enjoy it, till I am solitary and cannot impart it, till I am known and do not want it": it is the spat-out closing monosyllables that do the damage here, delivering a sting unheralded by the more innocuous parallel terms that come before. Another resounding triplet ("without one Act of assistance, one word of encouragement, or one smile of favour") goes uncluttered by any mention of the small payment that Johnson had in fact received (a payment which, he told Bennet Langton, "could not properly find place in a Letter of the kind that this was": I, 96n.). Mere facts, it would seem, must run second to style, and be shaped by rhetorical need. Johnson later denied rumors that he had cooled his heels in an antechamber while Chesterfield entertained Colley Cibber, and it is not known whether his complaint that "seven years . . . have now past since I waited in your outward Rooms or was repulsed from your Door" is literally true. What matters is the way in which these words tacitly align Johnson's case with ancient and modern precedent. Not only is there an implicit contrast here with Horatian satire;[9] also in play is a work posthumously published only weeks before Johnson's letter was written, *The Journal of a Voyage to Lisbon*, which opens with the ailing Henry Fielding summoned from his sickbed by his arrogant and negligent "patron" the Duke of Newcastle. In a punitive assertion of power, Newcastle then finds himself too busy for an audience, and sends Fielding away unseen.[10]

Letters like Johnson's to Chesterfield and his similarly famous challenge of 20 January 1775 to James "Ossian" Macpherson, of course, are neither familiar nor even private. Written not least as displays of rhetorical prowess, they soon began to enter the public domain: "You may print this if you will," Johnson told Macpherson (II, 169), while manuscript texts of both letters were circulating well before their publication in Boswell's *Life*. The status of the Chesterfield letter as both public document and Johnsonian masterpiece was tacitly recognized by both writer and addressee. Johnson could dictate it from memory twenty-seven years later, and was careful to specify from which of several copies it should be printed. With provocative insouciance, Chesterfield displayed the original on his desk, read it to visitors, "pointed out the severest passages, and observed how well they were expressed" (*Life*, I, 265). Far from quietly pursuing the converse of the pen, the two antagonists were engaged in a stylized and highly visible ritual of mutual defiance.

These are exceptional cases, but there are other ways too in which Johnson's epistolary writing can seem far from discontinuous with his published output. The quality of the many letters of advice, instruction, and consolation produced throughout his life has long been recognized, largely because of their obvious closeness to his published work on similar themes. These are Ramblers on particular occasions, Ramblers in the second person, Ramblers in the imperative: "Do not . . . hope wholly to reason away your troubles; do not feed them with attention, and they will die imperceptibly away," he counsels Boswell (5 March 1776; II, 299). Given urgency and specificity by the varying afflictions of their addressees, these letters also share the didactic structure and truth-telling sonority of the Johnson essay. When he tells James Elphinston on 25 September 1750 that "the business of life summons us away from useless grief, and calls us to the exercise of those virtues of which we are lamenting our deprivation" (I, 45), it is not only the warning against excessive mourning but the orotund diction and measured phrasing that recall the mode of the *Rambler*.

For the rhetorician Hugh Blair, letters of this kind were not epistolary in any meaningful sense, being modeled on the prior forms and styles of divinity or ethics.[11] Yet in Johnson's hands the distinguishing particularity of epistolary condolence does nonetheless manage to make its stylistic mark. On the death decades later of Elphinston's wife, he shifts into a plainer mode, a pared-down Ramblerism, or oscillates from one to the other. Elphinston's loss "leaves a dismal vacuity in life, which affords nothing on which the affections can fix, or to which endeavour may be directed," he writes, typically enough, before abandoning the resonantly general for a plain and personal yet residually cadenced style: "All this I have known, and it is now, in the vicissitude of things, your turn to know it" (27 July 1778; III, 121). On the death of Hester Thrale's infant son, the effect is yet more marked. "He is gone, and we are going. We could not have enjoyed him long, and shall not long be separated from him" (25 March 1776; II, 311): here parallel phrases strike a studied balance between mourning and consolation, gently linking lament at the gulf between dead and living with affirmations of their shared condition. A second letter progressively eradicates its philosophic words, as though only the simplest of statements will finally do: "I know that such a loss is a laceration of the mind. I know that a whole system of hopes, and designs, and expectations is swept away at once, and nothing left but bottomless vacuity. What you feel, I have felt" (30 March 1776; II, 313). These are masterpieces of companionate mourning, in which the usual structures of Johnsonian parallelism are stripped to their starkest form.

If private letters could familiarize the public mode, they could also help to construct it. Another link between the epistolary and the published was seen by Macaulay, who thought Johnson's letters from Scotland "the original of that work of which the Journey to the Hebrides is the translation."[12] It is not simply that letters could be testing-grounds in which to draft A Journey to the Western Islands of Scotland (1775); they could also accommodate an enthusiasm which, for all its importance in motivating the voyage, could find little room in the published work of a pensioner of George III. In a typical example, the Journey's anodyne "gentleman of Raasay" (Journey, p. 58) is originally "a Gentleman who conducted Prince Charles through the mountains in his distresses" (21 September 1773; II, 80). A second letter notes the disaffection of the islanders in an approving telegraphese: "You may guess at the opinions that prevail in this country, they are however content with fighting for their king, they do not drink for him, we had no foolish healths" (24 September 1773; II, 83). In political terms the Journey is not so much a translation, indeed, as a work of self-censorship. Perhaps that is why Johnson thought his original letters of such importance: "I hope my mistress keeps all my very long letters," he tells Hester Thrale from Mull, "longer than I ever wrote before" (15 October 1773; II, 100).

IV

Yet it was not only on extraordinary occasions – a quarrel, a bereavement, a voyage – that letters were needed, and much of Johnson's epistolary output enacts his theoretical sense of the form as writing with nothing to say. "The purpose for which letters are written when no intelligence is communicated . . . is to preserve in the minds of the absent either love or esteem" (Rambler 152, V, 47): this essentially phatic purpose was one he felt with urgency all his life, and it dominates the private, intimate, familiar letters that make up the bulk of his surviving correspondence. Not so much a vehicle of meaning as a perpetuating gesture of friendship, the letter-exchange was a central means of transcending his sense of being "broken off from mankind . . . a gloomy gazer on a World to which I have little relation" (21 December 1754; I, 90). To read a letter was to feel such relation restored, and in Johnson's case the need was acute enough for him to tell his physician Richard Brocklesby that "none of your prescription[s] operate . . . more certainly than your letters operate as cordials" (21 August 1784; IV, 377–78). "There is this use in the most useless letter, that it shows one not to be forgotten," he writes elsewhere (31 July 1756; I, 139), and throughout his correspondence one hears variations on the desperate cry that he most plainly utters to Bennet Langton: "Do not forget me, You see that I do not forget You" (20 March 1782; IV, 23).

In order to receive, however, it was also necessary to send. At one stage Johnson is writing to Hester Thrale by every post to elicit the same rate of return (26 June 1775; II, 235), and he later addresses Richard Brocklesby "not so much because I have any thing to say, as because, I hope for an answer" (26 August 1784; IV, 381). Here was Johnson's dilemma, and here was the special nature of the letter's demand: post-day might come with nothing to be said, yet something would have to be written. To Joseph Baretti in Italy he laments "that he who continues the same course of life in the same place, will have little to tell . . . The silent changes made by time are not always perceived; and if they are not perceived, cannot be recounted" (10 June 1761; I, 196–97). While Baretti had voyaged across Europe, Johnson himself had merely "risen and lain down, talked and mused," and so had nothing to write. Nor could he simply return to the letter's traditional function of self-portraiture, his need being instead "to escape from myself" (I, 199). The underlying dilemma – an absence of external events, and a fear of confronting the internal – returns when he complains that the sociable Hester Thrale enjoys "all the ingredients that are necessary to the composition of a Letter," while he himself has nothing to describe "but my own solitary individuality" (26 July 1775; II, 256). Nowhere is it more acute than in a letter to Lucy Porter which combines an almost Richardsonian sense of writing as present-tense crisis with a stylishness all Johnson's own. "It is again Midnight, and I am again alone," he opens, going on to lament that "if I turn my thoughts upon myself what do [I] perceive but a poor helpless being reduced by a blast of wind to weakness and misery" (30 December 1755; I, 117).

The trouble is, of course, that this unbearable subjectivity can nowhere be set aside. Even among the rich materials of his Hebridean journey Johnson feels the same magnetic pull of solipsism, digressing to review "a life diversified by misery, spent part in the sluggishness of penury, and part under the violence of pain" (21 September 1773; II, 75). Reluctantly, he half-resembles "the Doge of Genoa who being asked what struck him most at the French Court, answered, 'Myself'" (30 September 1773; II, 94).

Johnson's overwhelming need, in consequence, was to find a way of writing what he memorably calls "letters about nothing" (c. 3 July 1775; II, 237) – letters in which relation with the world might be sustained despite absence of matter; letters in which the self, the one intractable, painful subject that was always to hand, might be displaced, dodged, or at the very least constructed in tolerable form. The difficulty of the task is one he often stresses, writing disparagingly to Boswell of "topicks with which those letters are commonly filled which are written only for the sake of writing" (8 December 1763; I, 238). But in his more highly charged exchanges with Hill Boothby or Hester Thrale, to sustain writing "when by the confession of both there is nothing to be said" (4 November 1772; I, 405) becomes at once a challenge and a high achievement, an exacting process in which the undiscriminating rehearsal of mere trivia is never enough. As he reminds Hester Thrale (with more than a hint put in play of Tristram Shandy's famous dilemma), "an intemperate attention to slight circumstances . . . is to be avoided, lest a great part of life be spent in writing the history of the rest" (6 September 1777; III, 61).[13] It was only through sheer force of style that letters about nothing could keep going. The point is nicely demonstrated by the closing flourish with which, even in describing the emptiness of a letter, Johnson also contrives its saving virtuosity: "I am willing enough to write though I have no thing to say, because . . . I would not have you forget that there is in the world such a poor Being as, Madam, your most humble servant, / SAM. JOHNSON" (7 November 1779; III, 210).

To write these letters about nothing, then, was an opportunity as well as a problem, and one to which Johnson's theoretical conviction that the form of the familiar letter could neither license negligence nor guarantee confession presented no obstacle. Here was a form which, far from dictating artlessness, focused unusual effort on its own surface while providing a risk-free zone in which stylistic experiments might be privately made. Here was a form that gave release, moreover, from the daily maintenance of formal identity, and which, far from enshrining some definitive self, established a realm in which public reputation might be discarded or challenged and alternative senses of self brought into play. In this peculiarly provisional and flexible form, in short, Johnson could seek escape from the official burdens and responsibilities of being "Dr Johnson." Celebrated above all as the moralist and truth-teller of the *Rambler*, or as the upholder, in the *Dictionary*, of linguistic purity and rigor, he could temporarily shed the duties of weighty signification and exemplary style that went with these formal roles. He could throw off, or at least suspend, the identity as a public writer and public figure which otherwise dominates his literary output; the sage and literary colossus could take a break.

That is not to say, once again, that Johnson's epistolary style is wholly at odds with the amplitude of his published prose. His characteristic precision is a vital resource in the struggle to assert linguistic control over the pain and decay of his dying years. Redundancy is never an issue, however, in letters which fix the shifting crisis of sickness with startling economy and lexical rigor. Insomniacs might relish the modulated succinctness with which he finds himself "condemned to the torture of sleepyness without the power to sleep" (19 April 1783; IV, 125). No less memorable is the unflinching lexical bullseye with which he concludes his account of a testicular growth: "I now no longer feel its weight; and the skin of the scrotum which glistened with tension is now lax and corrugated" (9 October 1783; IV, 223). Not only the lexicographer is on agonized duty here; the essayist is heard in the openings into generality with which Boswell is told that "every hour takes away part of the things that please us, and perhaps part of our disposition to be pleased" (1 September 1777; III, 57), or Thrale that "the time has run away, as most time runs, without account, without use, and without memorial" (6 September 1777; III, 60). Yet here again the charge of redundancy can never be leveled, the occasional verbosity of Ramblerism falling away as it undergoes its distinctive epistolary mutation.

If, on the one hand, the letter-form worked to pare down the characteristic flourishes of Johnsonian style, it also gave an opportunity for kinds of linguistic experiment, transgression, and play with which his prose is rarely associated. One recurrent feature is the wry reflexiveness with which Johnson insistently comments on his own locutions even as he puts them to work. "My *Arthritical* complaints, there's a nice word, rather encrease, but are not yet, as the Scotch say, *ferious*," he explains, his playful language sharply at odds with the sickness it seeks to describe (30 March 1783; IV, 119). Elsewhere he revels in dialects, registers, and jargons of the kind he would elsewhere proscribe, juggling Welsh adverbs ("Mrs. Williams wrote me word, that you . . . *behaved lovely*" [1 August 1775; II, 259]), cockney wisdom ("in the phrase of Hockley in the Hole, it is pity he has not a better bottom" [13 September 1777; III, 66]), midland vernacular ("I am glad Master huspelled you, and run you all on rucks" [6 October 1777; III, 81]). Calculated vulgarisms run riot: "his Book must be a Porters load" (21 October 1779; III, 196), "did You quite down her?" (11 April 1780; III, 236), "I do not love them since that *skrimage*" (6 June 1780; III, 266), "a good rabble trick" (10 June 1780; III, 271), "none of the giddy gabblers" (27 July 1780; III, 289). It would overstate the case to find here some Bakhtinian carnival of language, in which the monological authority of Johnsonian English is split apart. Yet it is striking to see how far, having labored in public "to refine our language to grammatical purity, and to clear it from colloquial barbarisms, licentious idioms, and irregular combinations" (*Rambler* 208, V, 318–19), the Johnson of the letters takes an exuberant holiday from linguistic rectitude, playing havoc with language in ways licensed by the potentially anarchic context of epistolary exchange. Here he could happily violate criteria he would otherwise uphold. Advising Garrick on Hogarth's epitaph, he insists that "*Feeling* for *tenderness* or *sensibility* is a word merely colloquial of late introduction, not yet [confident] enough of its own existence to claim a place upon a stone" (12 December 1771; I, 384); to Thrale he writes of a sentimental acquaintance that "if she be a feeler, I can bear a feeler as well as You"

(8 November 1779; III, 211). Marmoreal and epistolary language were worlds apart.

Nor is this almost Shandean waywardness in Johnson's letters a matter of lexical choice alone. When Sterne himself boasts that he "never yet knew what it was to say or write one premeditated word in my life," and would never send "a fine set Essay in the Stile of your female Epistolizers, cut and trim'd at all points," his claims chime oddly with Johnson's own practice.[14] Just as the form could license that lexical abandon in which Johnson so clearly delights, so also it was a lawless area of discontinuous logic and structural disorder in which even a letter of consolation could end: "I know not how I have fallen upon this, I had no thought of it, when I began the letter" (18 November 1756; I, 149). Randomness becomes a virtue, enabling him to contest Hester Thrale's view of herself as "the first Writer in the world for a letter about nothing" with applause instead for the vagaries of his own writing – "so miscellaneous, with such noble disdain of regularity" (11 April 1780; III, 237).

Not content with loosening the usual styles and structures that contain his prose, Johnson even uses the letter as a medium of self-parody, misdirecting his characteristic sagacity toward mere trivia with playful extravagance. The letters are marked, of course, by a genuine commitment to the ordinary, and everyday matters are often treated to striking effect as appropriate objects of solemn attention. "We deal in nicer things / Than routing armies, and dethroning Kings" (19 June 1775; II, 229), as he puts it to Hester Thrale, and throughout the letters he finds no anomaly in lavishing the truth-telling mode of his essays on the finer points of domestic life. The moral that "Power is nothing but as it is felt, and the delight of superiority is proportionate to the resistance overcome" is fixed to no greater case, for example, than the motivation of a nanny (21 October 1779; III, 194–95). Equally often, however, Johnson subjects his moralizing mode to the kind of deliberate bathos with which he earlier reflects on foreknowledge: "Beyond to morrow where is the wonder that all is uncertainty; yet I look beyond to morrow, and form schemes for tuesday" (2 April 1773; II, 26). More often still he settles into a mock-heroic mode which hovers uneasily between asserting the importance of the domestic and deriding its hollowness. His long-standing feud with Boswell's wife becomes a Trojan war in which an irenic jar of marmalade puts him in mind of Greeks bearing gifts (3 May 1777; III, 19); the squabbling of his household companions finds comparable treatment when "Mr. Levet who thinks his ancient rights invaded, stands at bay, *fierce as ten furies*" (9 November 1778; III, 139, echoing *Paradise Lost*, II.671). The levity is more mixed and the tone more ambivalent when the death of a cat prompts him to reflect that "generations, as Homer says, are but like leaves" (2 November 1772; I, 404) or when he observes, on returning to Lichfield: "Many families that paid the parish rates are now extinct like the race of Hercules. Pulvis et umbra sumus. What is nearest us, touches us most" (11 July 1770; I, 345). In his final months, this strain in Johnson's letters takes on the desperate plangency of his famous valediction to Hester Thrale, which amplifies its lament at the severance of the two through complex double analogy with Virgilian epic and Scottish history (8 July 1784; IV, 343–44).

Elsewhere an underlying melancholy is only uneasily kept at bay by self-mocking forms of role-play. Most striking here is a sustained Falstaffian pose which, beginning as mere comic displacement of self, finally assumes a grim appropriateness. With teasing deference to Falstaff as a model of commonplace wisdom ("Life, says Falstaff, is a shuttle" [3 November 1777; III, 92]) or laughable self-pity ("I am old, I am old, says Sir John Falstaff" [27 September 1777; III, 77]), Johnson wittily defines his relations with Hester Thrale or Charlotte Lennox in terms of Falstaff's spats with Prince Hal or Mistress Quickly (III, 212; V, 11). He finds in Shakespeare's character – a source of fascination throughout his career – a ludicrous *alter ego* whose gluttonous, vainglorious buffoonery could be mimicked to witty effect. ("I am not grown fat," he implausibly insists: "I did thrive a little, but I checked the pernicious growth, and am now small as before" [9 May 1780; III, 255.]) At the same time, Falstaff's possession of "the most pleasing of all qualities, perpetual gaiety" (*Shakespeare*, p. 523) could seem to supply the very quality of which Johnson most painfully felt the lack. Yet in the end his identification with Falstaff seems to have assumed a more unwelcome life of its own. Rejected by his Prince (in a textual crux to which Johnson as editor paid fine attention), the dying Falstaff is famously reported to have "babled of green fields" (*Shakespeare*, p. 541). It is hard not to suspect a morbid self-consciousness in play – if not indeed anticipation of his equally crushing breach with Hester Thrale – as his letters repeat this last pathetic act of a broken man. "I hardly saw a green field, but staid in town to work, without working much," he laments of one lost summer (17 October 1780; III, 317). A childhood haunt is revisited with gloom: "we went with Mrs. Cobb to Greenhill Bower. I had not seen it perhaps for fifty years. It is much degenerated. Every thing grows old" (29 May 1779; III, 166).

V

Perhaps in the end even these remarkable letters could offer no truly adequate escape from the pain of self-consciousness. Even as death nears, however, they continue to try. Margaret Doody has written of "the weight of life" as a pre-occupation of Johnson's letters, a "sense of being shackled, becalmed, of being gigantically stuck."[15] Nowhere is this more true than in his later years, in which the relentless deterioration of his swollen, earthbound body coexists bizarrely in his writing with fantasies of unshackling and flight. Crippled by gout, he seems literally "a very poor creeper upon the earth, catching at any thing with my hands to spare my feet" (5 June 1776; II, 341); breathless with asthma and swollen with dropsy, he finds himself trapped in "an unwieldy, bloated half drowned body" (22 March 1784; IV, 300). Yet all the while he dreams of soaring away – "of kicking the Moon" (6 June 1776; II, 342), of having "a brush at the cobwebs in the sky" (8 May 1783; IV, 137), even (with wonderful implausibility) of being "carried away – just like Ganymede of Troy" (30 April 1778; III, 116). It becomes his obsessive physical ambition to "grow light and airy" (28 October 1779; III, 202); he literally seeks "to try another air" by leaving town (1 June 1784; IV, 330).

"All our views are directed to the air," wrote Horace Walpole in 1783, the year the Montgolfier brothers had achieved their first successful ascension above Paris: "*Balloons* occupy senators, philosophers, ladies, everybody."[16] Asked to explain the enabling technology, Johnson's first reaction was to scoff that Thrale had "leisure to want intelligence of air ballons" (22 September 1783; IV, 203–4). But as Montgolfier-mania took hold in London, his letters show increasing absorption in the general craze. Early in 1784 he subscribes "to a new ballon which is [to] sustain five hundred weight, and by which, I suppose, some Americo Vespucci . . . will bring us what intelligence he can gather in the clouds" (31 January 1784; IV, 279). A few days later he mingles complaint at being "confined to the house . . . the eighth week of my incarceration" with enthusiasm for the plans "with which some daring adventurer is expected to mount, and bring down the state of regions yet unexplored" (3 February 1784; IV, 280–81). Increasingly, and with increasing deliberateness, Johnson's fixation with ballooning becomes not only a grotesque echo of his bloated physical state but also a magnificent fantasy of transcendence which lets him imagine, with fascinated horror, "the earth a mile below me" (31 January 1784; IV, 279).

By autumn, however, the inaugural London flights have left Johnson unconvinced of ballooning's potential to advance either transport or science. Like the flying machine imagined in *Rasselas*, his newer fantasy comes down to earth: "I had rather now find a medicine that can ease an asthma," he tells Brocklesby (6 October 1784; IV, 416). Already his own lungs will not inflate sufficiently to let him ascend so much as the Bodleian library staircase (13 October 1784; IV, 418–19), and by 17 November his residual interest in ascending balloons can carry on only by proxy: "I sent Francis to see the Ballon fly, but could not go myself" (IV, 438). Deprived of his last inspiration, Johnson is thrown back for the final weeks of his life on his habitual, brilliant, desperate activity of writing letters about nothing. "You may always have something to tell," he laments to Francesco Sastres: "You see some ballons succeed and some miscarry, and a thousand strange and a thousand foolish things. But I see nothing; I must make my letter from what I feel, and what I feel with so little delight, that I cannot love to talk of it" (1 November 1784; IV, 432–33).

Plate 9 Pierre Montgolfier and *The Balloon at Versailles near to Capsizing, 1783.* "You see some ballons succeed and some miscarry, and a thousand strange and a thousand foolish things. But I see nothing" (*Letters*, IV, 432–33).

NOTES

1 *Paradise Lost*, VII.31.
2 "Dr. Johnson in his Letters: The Public Guise of Private Matter," in *The Familiar Letter in the Eighteenth Century*, ed. Howard Anderson, Philip B. Daghlian, and Irvin Ehrenpreis (Lawrence: University Press of Kansas, 1966), pp. 128, 108.
3 Janet Gurkin Altman, *Epistolarity: Approaches to the Form* (Columbus: Ohio State University Press, 1982), p. 4.
4 "Hearing Epistolick Voices: Teaching Johnson's Letters," in *Approaches to Teaching the Works of Samuel Johnson*, ed. David R. Anderson and Gwin J. Kolb (New York: MLA, 1993), p. 78.
5 *Letters to Sir William Temple*, ed. Kenneth Parker (Harmondsworth: Penguin, 1987), p. 131.
6 "An Account of the Life and Writings of Mr. Abraham Cowley," in *Critical Essays of the Seventeenth Century*, ed. J. E. Spingarn, 3 vols. (London: Oxford University Press, 1957), II, 137.
7 *The Collected Works of Katherine Philips*, ed. Patrick Thomas *et al.*, 3 vols. (Stump Cross: Stump Cross Books, 1990–93), II, 138.
8 *The Correspondence of Alexander Pope*, ed. George Sherburn, 5 vols. (Oxford: Clarendon Press, 1956), I, 155; I, xxxvii; I, xxxviii–ix.
9 *Satires*, II.vi; see Redford, "Hearing Epistolick Voices," p. 82.
10 *The Journal of a Voyage to Lisbon*, ed. Tom Keymer (Harmondsworth: Penguin, 1996), p. 12.
11 *Lectures on Rhetoric and Belles-Lettres*, 2 vols. (London, 1783), II, 297.
12 Quoted by W. K. Wimsatt, Jr., *The Prose Style of Samuel Johnson* (New Haven: Yale University Press, 1941), p. 78.
13 See Laurence Sterne, *The Life and Opinions of Tristram Shandy, Gentleman*, ed. Melvyn New and Joan New (Gainesville: University of Florida Press, 1978), pp. 340–43 (IV, chapter xiii).
14 *Letters of Laurence Sterne*, ed. L. P. Curtis (Oxford: Clarendon Press, 1935), p. 120.
15 Review of *Letters*, LRB (5 Nov. 1992), p. 10.
16 To Sir Horace Mann, 2 December 1783, quoted in *Letters*, IV, 204n.

STEVEN LYNN

Johnson's critical reception

What James Clifford and Donald Greene observed in 1970 is still true: "The history of Johnson's reputation since his own lifetime is in fact complex and needs even more study than it has received." Their introduction to *Samuel Johnson: A Survey and Bibliography of Critical Studies* (*Survey* hereafter) is essential reading for anyone interested in Johnson and his reception. I could, in fact, recommend their survey to my readers and end my essay at this point, except for three considerations: their discussion goes only to 1969 (Greene and John Vance's update, *A Bibliography of Johnsonian Studies, 1970–1985*, does not include a survey); they offer perhaps more detail than the reader who seeks an introduction might desire; and their discussion considers only indirectly the methods used in Johnson's critical reception.

Two other valuable resources should be mentioned at the outset. Edward Tomarken's *History of the Commentary on Selected Writings of Samuel Johnson* (1994) contains much that is useful and enlightening, but his "interpretive history" aims for "a new kind of literary method," which he calls "New Humanism." Thus Tomarken examines the critical record according to his ambitious goal. In addition, James Boulton's *Johnson: The Critical Heritage* very conveniently collects and excerpts eighty-one documents related to Johnson's reception from the period 1738–1832.

By the time Johnson died in 1784, he had become much more than a well-known writer and scholar. A few years earlier he reportedly remarked to Boswell, "I believe there is hardly a day in which there is not something about me in the newspapers." Helen McGuffie's patient search of the London and Edinburgh newspapers (from 1749 to 1784) revealed in 1976 that Johnson "was closer to the truth than he may have realized."[1] The press apparently tracked his every move, reporting on 27 August 1784, for instance, that he had returned from Oxford; on the 28th, that he was visiting Lichfield; on 1 September, that he was visiting John Taylor at Ashbourne; on 21 September, that he had visited the Duke of Devonshire and would be returning to London soon; and on 4 October (stretching even to travel wishes), that he wanted to visit Mrs. Piozzi. Johnson's health was similarly scrutinized with reports on 27 August 1784 that he was ill, the next day that he was improving, a week later that he was feeling worse, and then two days later that he was better again. When there were no sightings or symptoms to report, the papers made things up, recycled anecdotes, quoted excerpts from his works, or focused on someone somehow related to Johnson (Richard Russell, for instance, who was the subject of some twenty newspaper articles from 4 October to 13 November, 1784: he had left money in his will to Johnson and then changed his mind [McGuffie, *Samuel Johnson*, pp. 321–28]).

Why was Johnson such a celebrity? And how has that status affected his critical reception? Charlotte Lennox was not alone in determining as early as 1752 that "the Author of the Rambler" was "the greatest Genius in the present Age," as she puts it in the penultimate chapter of *The Female Quixote*. By 1764, the *Biographia Dramatica* could refer to Johnson as "no less the glory of the present age and nation, than he will be the admiration of all succeeding ones" (*Survey*, p. 4) – before Johnson's Shakespeare (1765), *Journey to the Western Islands* (1775), or *Lives of the Poets* (1779–81). Such prophetic praise hardly seems excessive today: Johnson societies flourish around the world; eight volumes (so far) have appeared in *The Age of Johnson*, an impressive annual edited by Paul J. Korshin, and a wide range of important books and essays focusing on Johnson continue steadily to appear. But interest in Johnson is by no means limited to academic specialists. His wider cultural importance can perhaps be suggested simply by noting the ten pages occupied by his words in the *Oxford Dictionary of Quotations*; or the tourist draw of the Johnson Birthplace Museum; or his recurrent appearance in cartoons, political speeches, newspaper editorials, and scientific articles.

Johnson's literary achievements only begin to explain why he captivated the public imagination. As Johnson reportedly put it: "It is advantageous to an authour, that his book should be attacked as well as praised. Fame is a shuttlecock. If it be struck only at one end of the room, it will soon fall to the ground. To keep it up, it must be struck at both ends" (*Life*, v, 400). Johnson's works certainly were struck passionately at both ends, during his lifetime and afterward. As Vicesimus Knox put it in 1788: "Few men could stand so fiery a trial as he has done. His gold has been put into the furnace, and really, considering the violence of the fire, and the frequent repetition of the process, the quantity of dross and alloy is inconsiderable" (*CH*, p. 1).

The critical purification of Johnson and his work referred to by Knox began in earnest in the 1760s with such performances as Charles Churchill's caustic portrait of "Pomposo" in *The Ghost* (1762); William Kenrick's smoldering reviews of the Shakespeare edition (1765); and Archibald Campbell's *Lexiphanes* (1767), which lambasted Johnson's style. Johnson did what was no doubt most infuriating to his critics: he ignored them. Johnson's pension (in 1762), his political pamphlets (the 1770s), his reflections on Scotland (1775), all activated new enemies.

When the *Prefaces, Critical and Biographical* appeared (1779, 1781), the immediate critical response suggested that Johnson had, once more, created a work that people loved, or loved to hate. An unsigned review in the *Annual Register* for 1782 offers us a representative sample of the praise:

> Perhaps no age or country has ever produced a species of criticism more perfect in its kind, or better calculated for general instruction, than the publication before us: for whether we consider it in a literary, philosophical, or moral view, we are at a loss whether to admire most the author's variety and copiousness of learning, the soundness of his judgment, or the purity and excellence of his character as a man. (*CH*, p. 293)

The reviewer's praise, we may notice, is not limited to the virtues of Johnson's work, but focuses upon the "purity and excellence of his character as a man," his learning, his judgment.

When Johnson's work is received negatively, it also tends to be examined in these same terms. In 1783, while acknowledging that "the present age owes much to the vigorous and manly understanding of Dr. Johnson," Robert Potter also worries that "the public has so long been habituated to receive and submit to his decisions, that they are now by many considered as infallible" (*CH*, p. 295). To attack Johnson's authority, Potter notes his excessive attention to trivia ("Can it be of any importance to us to be told how many pairs of stockings the author of *Essay on Man* wore?" [*CH*, p. 297]) and his erratic judgments, especially regarding Gray. Johnson simply had, Potter asserts, "no portion nor sense of that *vivida vis animi* ['lively energy of mind'], that etherial flame which animates the poet," and lacking this poetic fire, Johnson "is therefore as little qualified to judge of these works of imagination, as the shivering inhabitant of the caverns of the North to form an idea of the glowing sun that flames over the plains of Chili" (*CH*, p. 302). Similarly, Johnson's friend, Sir John Hawkins, contended in his 1787 biography that the *Lives* provide "the most judicious examen of the effusions of poetic genius, that any country, not excepting France, has to shew"; but Hawkins also asserted, like Potter, that Johnson was "totally devoid" of "the poetic faculty" himself, and therefore ill-equipped to judge poetry, especially descriptive poetry. Hawkins provides a different explanation for Johnson's deficiency: his eyesight was so poor that "all his conceptions of the grandeur and magnificence of external objects, or beautiful scenes, and extensive prospects, were derived from the reports of others, and consequently were but the feeble impressions of their archetypes" (*CH*, p. 304).

While Hawkins and Potter seem to assume that Johnson would see poetic achievement if he could (for Hawkins he lacks a mirror; for Potter, a lamp), other readers complained of his critical views more severely: for Anna Seward, writing in 1789, for instance, Johnson's "unjust" and "dispicable" treatment of Gray and Milton is the result of his own failed bid for poetic fame, his "rival-hating envy" (*CH*, p. 311). Although William Cowper thought Johnson for the most part had "acquitted himself with his usual good sense and sufficiency," he also found the treatment of Milton "unmerciful to the last degree," and based on a personal animus: "A pensioner is not likely to spare a republican," Cowper famously said (*CH*, p. 273).

Whatever aspect of Johnson's work is being examined (style, audience effect, referential accuracy), these elements seem to be referred back to Johnson himself: they reveal Johnson the man, and they are explained by Johnson the man. Johnson's early critics thus seem to employ a Great Man theory of literature, a paradigm that sees the text as a reflection of the writer: we read great literature and great judgments of literature so that we may share momentarily the insights of great minds. But the Great Man theory is a Romantic conception; Johnson and his immediate critics should be inhabiting, according to standard critical history, a mimetic paradigm that evaluates a work's ability to instruct and delight – to please an audience in order to convey an accurate and useful account of reality. The thing that Johnson's early critical reception most wants to receive (or reject), however, is clearly Johnson himself. Johnson thus appears to be an early stimulus to the Romantics' Great Man theories (more on this below), and to serve in literary history (as in many other things) as a grand and revealing challenge to our norms.

Like other larger-than-life figures, Johnson did nothing to quell public demand for him by dying. Boswell's *Life of Johnson* (1791) was simply the most spectacular and creative of many works addressing this demand, which included a desire for Johnson's works. In 1787 Sir John Hawkins's edition of Johnson's works appeared in eleven volumes (supplementary volumes XII–XV supplied by Percival Stockdale and others). In 1792 an edition of Johnson's works, edited by Arthur Murphy in twelve volumes, emerged, and it was reprinted in 1793, 1796, 1801, 1806, 1809, 1810, 1816, 1818, 1823, and dated 1824. In 1825, no fewer than four new impressions appeared. And then, for over 150 years no subsequent editions were needed. As a *TLS* essay on "Johnson's Reputation" put it in 1921 (1 September), "there are more copies [of Johnson's collected works] in the second-hand shops than there are patrons of literature willing to spare Johnson two feet of shelf-room" (p. 553).

One way to think about what happened to Johnson's reception in the nineteenth century would be to compare George Gleig's thoughtfully appreciative essay on Johnson in the 1797 *Encyclopedia Britannica*, to Thomas Babington Macaulay's in the 1856 *Britannica*. Gleig acknowledges, for instance, that some detractors have found Johnson's style excessively difficult and pompous, while others have thought it both energetic and elegant. He suggests that the *Rambler*'s style is indeed fatiguing for anyone who "reads *half a volume*" at a time, while "he who reads only one paper in the day will experience nothing of this weariness." Gleig also understands that Johnson's style varies with his purpose. In the *Rambler* Johnson's goal was to *remind* his readers of "known truths," and so his style is designed to "rouse the attention." But in the *Lives of the Poets*, "a great part consists of the narration of facts; and such a narration in the style of the *Rambler* would be ridiculous." Gleig also answers those who have ridiculed Johnson's use of triplets by asserting that "the triplet is unquestionably the most energetic form of which an English sentence is susceptible," and so it "*should* frequently occur in detached essays, of which the object is to inculcate moral truths."

In his *Britannica* entry, on the other hand, Macaulay sees Johnson's style quite differently: "his diction was too monotonous, too obviously artificial, and now and then turgid even to absurdity."[2] Macaulay does say of the *Life of Savage* that "No finer specimen of literary biography exists in any language, living or dead" (p. 796). He concedes that the criticisms in the *Lives of the Poets* "even when grossly and provokingly unjust, well deserve to be studied" (p. 802), and that the *Dictionary*'s definitions are so good "that a leisure hour may always be very agreeably spent in turning over the pages" (p. 797). But overall, Macaulay leaves his reader with a sense of Johnson as a spectacle, not a writer, "blinking, puffing, rolling his head, drumming with his fingers, tearing his meat like a tiger, and swallowing his tea in oceans" (p. 802).

Macaulay's *Britannica* piece is actually much kinder to Johnson than his earlier and more influential review in 1831 of Croker's edition of Boswell's *Life*. This review, frequently reprinted in textbook anthologies, introduced generations of students to Johnson – or rather, to Macaulay's vividly memorable version of the main character in Boswell's *Life*. Macaulay's thesis thoroughly discredits this "Johnson:" "The characteristic peculiarity of his intellect was the union of great powers with low prejudices" (*CH*, p. 423). He attacks the philosophical basis of Johnson's criticism: "His whole code of criticism rested on pure assumption," and not the "nature of things" (p. 424). Johnson's "systematically vicious" style, exhibits an unreal language, and therefore "the knowledge of life which he possessed in an eminent degree is very imperfectly exhibited" (p. 426). Johnson's defects of style, substance, and effect reveal that he simply lacked a sufficiently great mind to appreciate "the works of those great minds which 'yield homage only to eternal laws'" (p. 425) – thus reversing precisely the characteristic earlier praise of the *Annual Register* reviewer.

Although Johnson's conversation deserves attention, what is important for Macaulay is not so much what Johnson says as who is saying it: "the gigantic body, the huge massy face, seamed with the scars of disease, the brown coat, the black worsted stockings, the grey wig with the scorched foretop, the dirty hands, the nails bitten and pared to the quick" (p. 431). Macaulay's Johnson appears to be more of an *idiot savant* than a great intellect, a portrait that was supported by other early nineteenth-century detractors, such as Blake, Wordsworth, Coleridge, and De Quincey. For Hazlitt, for instance, Johnson's mind was narrowly gloomy to the point of deformity: *Rasselas* displayed "the most melancholy and debilitating moral speculation that ever was put forth."[3] For Arthur Murphy, Sir John Hawkins, James Boswell, and others, Johnson's troubled mind was something over which he triumphed, and the skepticism regarding things temporal simply urged his readers to confront his underlying religious message. But the Romantics generally did not read the effects of original sin the way Johnson did: his gloom and skepticism they saw as reflections of his prejudice and even meanness.

The Romantics were in fact especially bothered by Johnson's treatment of Milton, although his supposed failure to appreciate the genius of Shakespeare and Gray as they did bothered them too. Milton, as J. A. Wittreich puts it, was "the quintessence of everything the Romantics most admired."[4] Repeatedly the Romantics define themselves by embracing an anti-Johnsonian Milton, rejecting the previous century by deposing its great critical arbiter. When Coleridge gave a public lecture in 1812 on Milton, to pick just one example, he apparently became so worked up attacking Johnson that he used vulgarity, for which he was "hissed." His response, according to Henry Crabb Robinson's diary, was to say "it was the nature of evil to beget evil and that he had therefore in censuring Johnson fallen into the same fault" (Wittreich, *Romantics on Milton*, p. 204).

There were, to be sure, some supporters of Johnson's work in the nineteenth century, people who actually read his work (including his multivalent criticism of Milton). G. Birkbeck Hill, for instance, recommended that the centenary of Johnson's death be celebrated "by destroying the grotesque figure which Macaulay set up" (*Survey*, p. 8). That project has meant collecting the materials needed to examine more closely Boswell's and everyone else's version of Johnson. Many men and women – R. B. Adam, Edward Newton, Chauncey Tinker, Herman Liebert, James Osborne, Donald and Mary Hyde – began in the late nineteenth and early twentieth centuries to uncover and gather manuscripts and materials related to Johnson. Hill himself worked heroically, bringing out from 1887 to 1905 scholarly editions of Boswell's *Life* and *Tour to the Hebrides*, plus Johnson's *Letters*, *Miscellanies*, and *Lives of the Poets*, thus providing a foundation for the present and forthcoming standard scholarly editions (including Bruce Redford's recent Hyde edition of the letters).

An important early landmark in this still-ongoing turn to Johnson's work, is Walter Raleigh's *Six Essays on Johnson*, which in 1910 looked carefully at Johnson's criticism and editing. But T. S. Eliot, who acknowledges Raleigh in his later essays on Johnson, plays perhaps the most crucial role in Johnson's modern critical reception. Eliot of course also played a crucial role in forming the critical paradigm that displaced the Great Man theory and has dominated most of the twentieth century – the so-called "New Criticism." His pivotal essay, "Tradition and the Individual Talent" (1917), argued that "Honest criticism and sensitive appreciation are directed not upon the poet but upon the poetry,"[5] a principle Eliot later applied to that part of Johnson's canon the Romantics had found most lacking, his poetry, in a classic 1930 essay celebrating *London* and *The Vanity of Human Wishes*. Eliot undermined the idea that great poetry and great prose are fundamentally different, and he identified in Johnson the "precision" and force of thought that marks great poetry, noting "the certainty, the ease with which he hits the bull's-eye every time."[6] Eliot maintained, echoing Johnson on Pope, that if the *Vanity of Human Wishes* is not poetry, then he did not know what poetry is.

Elsewhere Eliot directs favorable attention to Johnson's criticism: his 1921 essay on "The Metaphysical Poets" takes Johnson's "shrewd and sensitive" analysis very seriously (Johnson is "a dangerous person to disagree with," Eliot says[7]), and he delivers an influential lecture on "Johnson as Critic and Poet" in 1944, the same year that F. R. Leavis writes appreciatively on "Johnson as Critic" in *Scrutiny* – "an indubitable real critic, first-hand and forceful."[8] Also in 1944, Bertrand Bronson draws on the growing wealth of materials related to Johnson (A. L. Reade's discoveries about Johnson's early life, Mrs. Thrale's diaries and letters, for instance) and provides the twentieth century's first full-length biography of Johnson, *Johnson Agonistes*, that, as Clifford and Greene say, "would have startled and amused Victorian readers" because its "chief strength . . . lies in the critical analyses of Johnson's own works" (p. 14). Allen Tate's 1949 essay on "Johnson and the Metaphysical Poets" disagreed with some of Johnson's particular judgments but admired his critical acumen. Obviously Johnson studies gained considerable momentum in the 1940s with attention from two major poets like Eliot and Tate, and from a critic of Leavis's stature, not to mention the lively, imaginative, careful scholarship of Krutch and many others.

And so, in the 1950s, with substantial private support, the Yale Edition of the Works of Samuel Johnson was launched. As the edition has crawled toward completion, the editorial decisions have not always pleased all scholars, but the edition has helped further energize Johnson studies by making standard texts more readily available (and sparking discussion). While Johnson's recent scholars have certainly focused more attention on these works themselves, they have generally still been unwilling to ignore Johnson himself, accept the New Critical axioms of the intentional and affective fallacies, and admire his works as well-wrought urns. Johnsonians have also been unwilling to follow the Romantics in seeing the work as an expression of the Great Man's inner self. And they have generally been less willing to see Johnson's texts as free-floating signifiers in a sea of language. Instead, Johnson's modern critics have generally preferred to think of his texts as rhetorical performances, with the public *ethos* of "Johnson" (created by the historical Johnson) as a crucial part of his rhetoric. The dominant paradigm of Johnson's modern critical reception has been neither the formalism of New Criticism nor the expressionism of the Great Man theory. It has been instead, in a word, *Johnsonian*, fascinated and enriched by what Johnson loved most "the biographical part of literature" (*Life*, I, 425), striving to connect the author and his work, but also alert to the "manifest and striking contrariety between the life of an author and his writings" (*Rambler*, III, 74).

Thus, after Krutch's *Samuel Johnson* (1944), outstanding biographical studies that illuminate Johnson's works have continued to supplement and correct Boswell and company. James Clifford unfolds Johnson's early life with *Young Sam Johnson* (1955) and *Dictionary Johnson* (1979); John Wain offers an engagingly readable survey for general readers (1974); Walter Jackson Bate's *Samuel Johnson* (1977) eloquently blends biography, psychological analysis, and stimulating criticism; Thomas Kaminski adds an impressive mass of details to our knowledge of *The Early Career of Samuel Johnson* (1987); and Robert DeMaria invokes a new context for *The Life of Samuel Johnson* (1993) in the international world of scholarship to which Johnson belonged.

Our desire to recover the "real" Johnson, whose representation is part of his works' rhetorical force, has naturally led scholars to reexamine vigorously Boswell's great *Life*. Excellent samples of this work are collected in *Boswell's "Life of Johnson": New Questions, New Answers*, edited by John Vance, and in *New Light on Boswell: Critical and Historical Essays on the Occasion of the Bicentenary of "The Life of Johnson,"* edited by Greg Clingham. The positions taken range from Donald Greene's suggestion that Boswell's *Life* be ignored as a biography, given Boswell's unreliability, to John Burke's point that Boswell's Johnson is not really *Boswell's* Johnson, since so much of the *Life* consists of material from others, including Johnson himself, to Frederic Bogel's discussion of the "presence" of Johnson as a textual construct, thus setting aside the question of whether Boswell's *Life* is a biography or a novel, because both "generate this illusion of presence."[9]

The effort to relate Johnson to his work has naturally also encouraged projects of intellectual history. In an essay called "'Johnson and . . .': Conceptions of Literary Relationship," Paul Korshin explores this tendency to study Samuel Johnson in relation to someone else: Johnson and William Law, Johnson and Voltaire, even *Dr. Johnson and the Ladies of the Lichfield Amicable Society*.[10] In recent years Johnson has also often been studied in more expansive contexts: Johnson and politics, in J. C. D. Clark's *Samuel Johnson: Literature, Religion, and English Cultural Politics from the Restoration to Romanticism*, and in

Donald Greene's *The Politics of Samuel Johnson*; Johnson and the history of ideas, as in Nicholas Hudson's *Samuel Johnson and Eighteenth-Century Thought*; Johnson and medicine, as in John Wiltshire's *Samuel Johnson in the Medical World*; Johnson and history, as in John Vance's *Samuel Johnson and the Sense of History*; Johnson and the arts, as in Morris Brownell's *Samuel Johnson's Attitude towards the Arts*; Johnson and the impact of printing, as in Alvin Kernan's *Printing Technology, Letters, and Samuel Johnson*; Johnson and travel, as in Thomas Curley's *Samuel Johnson and the Age of Travel*; Johnson and the heroic, as in Isobel Grundy's *Samuel Johnson and the Scale of Greatness*; Johnson and moral philosophy, as in Paul Alkon's *Samuel Johnson and Moral Discipline*; Johnson and Newtonian science, as in Richard Schwartz's *Samuel Johnson and the New Science* and Charles Hinnant's *Samuel Johnson: An Analysis*.

Johnsonians (like eighteenth-century scholars generally) have also begun increasingly in recent years to employ or at least engage the diversity of critical methods that have emerged in the last few decades. In closing this review, then, I will attempt to give some sense of the current critical reception of Johnson's major works, including the use of other theoretical orientations.

Johnson's early biographies (including the *Life of Savage*) have gained considerable respect in the twentieth century. John Burke, for instance, has shown how in these early lives Johnson evolves the theory of biography articulated later in *Rambler* 60 and *Idler* 84. And Charles Batten, Richard Wendorf, O M Brack, Jr., and others have revealed Johnson's artistry and his commitment to truth in these lives.[11] But Johnson's artistry has not been the most energizing issue for modern critics of these early lives, as Robert Folkenflik makes clear in *Samuel Johnson, Biographer*: rather, critics have been especially interested in the relationship between life and art, between biography and literature – which is, of course, what Johnson seems most interested in himself. Catherine Parke in *Samuel Johnson and Biographical Thinking* does bring a new perspective to the old interest in Johnson's conversation by drawing on Richard Rorty's notion of *conversation* as the ultimate context for understanding knowledge. Parke sees *Savage* as the crucial point in Johnson's career because he discovers that biography, as part of an evolving conversation, is the main way that we learn.

Johnson's play, *Irene*, has received some modern attention, principally for what it can tell us about its genre. No matter what critical approach has been used, Johnson's own judgment in 1780 ("Sir, I thought it had been better" [*Life*, IV, 5]) had not been contested until Kathleen Kemmerer's new contextualization of the play in terms of Johnson's sexual politics in *"A Neutral Being Between the Sexes": Samuel Johnson's Sexual Politics*.

Although *London* is a powerful and interesting poem, most recent critics seem to have accepted Howard Weinbrot's assertion in 1969 that it suffers from certain rhetorical flaws. Regarding Johnson's poetic masterpiece, *The Vanity of Human Wishes*, the central critical issue has concerned not its effectiveness, which is generally affirmed, but rather just what effect it makes: specifically, critics have argued over the relationship of the religious conclusion to the rest of the poem (logical entailment, disjunction, contradiction, satire?). For instance, Patrick O'Flaherty argued that the consolation of the ending is overwhelmed by the preceding gloom,[12] while at the same time Donald Greene thought the ending conveys the potentially comforting insight that happiness is made, not found.[13]

Efforts to resolve such alternative visions of the relationship between the ending and the rest of the poem have usually involved turning to Johnson's mind, considering what he intends the reader to feel. But in *This Invisible Riot of the Mind*, Gloria Sybil Gross uses the psychological turn to set aside the question: the ending of the *Vanity* is not a rhetorical construct but a "psychological event," brought about by an agency, "celestial wisdom," that is not far from "the function of the superego."[14]

Johnson's essays, especially *The Rambler*, have been particularly celebrated in our time. R. M. Wiles's investigation in the late 1960s into the distribution of the *Rambler* found that it was more popular than previously thought, since many issues were widely stolen and reprinted.[15] Since these essays were supposedly written at the last minute, they arguably offer an opportunity to see how Johnson's mind worked – again using the work to reveal the great mind. While some critics have thought that Johnson's title pretty much describes the movement of his essays, others have noted certain recurrent rhetorical strategies in the *Rambler*. James Boyd White in *When Words Lose Their Meaning* draws attention to the way that the reader is drawn through a process that corrects and complicates the "truisms and cliches," and the "uncertainty or doubt" that the reader inhabits at the beginning of an essay. In *Samuel Johnson after Deconstruction*, Steven Lynn uses a variety of critical strategies – Bloom's anxiety of influence (showing how Johnson persistently deals with his precursor, the *Spectator*), feminist criticism, reader-response, and deconstruction (which Johnson both anticipates and sees through) – to show how Johnson's masterful rhetoric recurrently moves the reader toward hope and faith.

Some remarkable work has been done on Johnson's great *Dictionary*, primarily focusing on what James Sledd and Gwin Kolb called its "biography." Their important 1955 work (*Dr. Johnson's Dictionary*) has been substantially advanced by Allen Reddick's fascinating reconstruction of *The Making of Johnson's "Dictionary,"* including the strategies that he abandoned. Robert DeMaria, Jr., in *Johnson's "Dictionary" and the Language of Learning*, relates the *Dictionary* to Johnson's era by showing how it can be read as an encyclopedia, a survey of knowledge in the tradition of Renaissance humanism. Anne McDermott's Cambridge University Press CD-ROM version of the *Dictionary* promises to spark even more study of this work and its relationships, allowing for rapid searching of both the 1755 and the extensively revised 1773 editions, presenting digitized images of the original pages.

Rasselas has occasioned a greater variety of readings than any other of Johnson's works.[16] George Sherburn had a large impact on criticism by observing what seems obvious in retrospect, that the travelers do not return to the Happy Valley but to Abyssinia – thus undermining any arguments that the tale is clearly circular.[17] Howard Weinbrot pointed out what again would seem to be obvious from a New Critical perspective, namely that a character in a work is not the same thing as the author, and that Imlac's views in his dissertation on poetry cannot be taken as Johnson's.[18]

As critics have examined *Rasselas* and its purpose closely, they have generally moved beyond seeing it as a prose version of the *Vanity*, and have focused on three issues: Is it a religious work (which has often been addressed by considering the book's tone)? Is it effective – how, for instance, do the comic and exotic elements work? What is its genre? Irvin Ehrenpreis provided yet another instance of the desire in eighteenth-century studies to keep the author and the work together by arguing that the concept of "structure" is useless unless it is "a design conceptually prior to the completion of the work under examination, and established in such a way that both the author and the reader may know it."[19]

Alan Liu's use of Derridean deconstruction and Lacanian psychoanalysis clearly inhabits a different universe: situated after poststructuralism, Liu assumes the impossibility of demonstrating what an author knows, or how a particular design precedes a work, which means that the reader is free to locate whatever structures can be persuasively identified; and Liu argues, intelligently, that the mummy in the catacombs, who stands in for Johnson's recently dead mother, is an "embalmed signifier," "the central structure of Johnson's thought."[20] Similarly, issues of gender have informed discussions by Lynn, for instance, who shows how Johnson positions himself between male and female, and questions the essence of each; and by Parke (*Samuel Johnson and Biographical Thinking*), who looks at the way Nekayah subverts Rasselas's drive toward a masculine mastery.

Although some Romantics frequently found it strategically useful to attack Johnson's Shakespeare, modern criticism has often admired his work. Assertions such as Joseph Ritson's, that Johnson did not collate the folios, are now known to be false. In fact, Arthur Eastman in 1950 estimated that Johnson made between 14,000 and 15,000 textual changes, vastly improving the clarity of Shakespeare's texts.[21] Although Arthur Sherbo concluded there was little real Shakespeare criticism in the notes, he later completed an edition of Johnson's *Notes to Shakespeare* and changed his mind, asserting that Johnson's greatest contribution is in the notes.[22] In *Johnson's Shakespeare*, G. F. Parker has elegantly related these notes to the great *Preface to Shakespeare*, placing Johnson in relation to French neo-classicism and German and English transcendentalism, and finding that Johnson's controlling idea is his vision of Shakespeare as "the poet of nature"; Parker uses this platitude of mimetic theory to show how Johnson continues to offer us radical criticism of Shakespeare. And in 1991, Edward Tomarken's *Samuel Johnson on Shakespeare: The Discipline of Criticism* concentrates on Johnson's notes *as interpretations* of specific plays of Shakespeare.

In the 1960s critics began to look beyond the question of whether Johnson is fair toward the Scots in his *Journey to the Western Islands of Scotland*, and to direct more attention to its themes and artistry. Jeffrey Hart's essay in 1960 was pivotal, seeing the *Journey* as a tragedy in prose.[23] Hart's controversial thesis displaced the biographical/historical focus, and opened the way for considerations of the *Journey* as travel book, as philosophy, as psychological evidence, as political exhortation, and as romance.[24] Johnson's avowedly political works, however, have tended to resist displacement into other contexts – in part, perhaps, because the question of Johnson's political views is so complex and still unsettled. Johnson's relationship to Jacobitism, for instance, remains a substantially disputed issue (see Robert Folkenflik's essay in this volume, and especially his first note, which points to ten essays in volumes 7 [1996] and 8 [1997] of *The Age of Johnson* addressing the question of Johnson's supposed Jacobitism).

It is no wonder that Johnson's *Lives of the Poets* has continued to fascinate modern critics, since it combines, as Lawrence Lipking observes in *The Ordering of the Arts in Eighteenth-Century England*, biography, prefaces to an anthology, literary criticism, intellectual history, literary history, moral philosophy, psychology, and a biographical encyclopedia. Much of the modern critical attention has been divided between analyzing formal elements of the *Lives* and considering its more controversial judgments. Paul Korshin, for instance, explains how Johnson's "unwillingness to open his mind to Swift's obvious merits" stems from "what he construed as a great offense to mankind," namely Swift's depiction of human nature in Part 4 of *Gulliver's Travels*, and how additional prejudices culminated "in an unfair treatment which Johnson could neither help nor avoid."[25] Leopold Damrosch's *The Uses of Johnson's Criticism* finds the greatness of Johnson's *Lives* in his "broad conception of literary history as a branch of human history," and in this vision we feel Johnson's presence: "the *Lives* succeed because they reflect Johnson's own powerful individuality, combining intellectual energy, moral authority, and rhetorical wit."[26]

How more recent theory departs from such traditional approaches can once more be seen in Annette Wheeler Cafarelli's assertion that, in reading Johnson's *Lives*, "we must accustom ourselves to thinking of biographical narrative as a symbolic structure."[27] While we might wonder what Johnson, reading of such a necessity, would think, the power of such assumptions can be seen nonetheless in Cafarelli's persuasive demonstration that the Romantics, "even as they anathematized him," actually imitated Johnson's symbolic structures.

Johnson's critics, as this brief overview has suggested, have tended to operate from within a critical paradigm that Johnson himself would recognize, seeking to connect the man and his work. The early critics looked at Johnson's substance, style, and effect in order to find the inner man in his works, to celebrate his genius or denigrate his deformity. Modern critics in looking closely and carefully at his works have also resisted giving up the historical Johnson, as they have tried to suppress the fictional Johnson, even as recent theories have questioned whether there is any difference. If we recognize that his works construct a "Johnson" with a potentially complex relationship to the man, Johnsonians have nonetheless labored with incredible energy, intelligence, imagination, and even passion to understand them both. For his critics, Johnson has indeed (as Gerard Hamilton said) "made a chasm, which not only nothing can fill up, but which nothing has a tendency to fill up" (*Life*, IV, 420).

NOTES

1 *Samuel Johnson and the British Press, 1749–84: A Chronological Checklist* (New York: Garland, 1976), p. 5.
2 8th edn. vol. XII (1856), p. 797.
3 William Hazlitt, *Lectures on the Comic Writers* (London, 1819), p. 201.
4 *The Romantics on Milton: Formal Essays and Critical Asides*, ed. Joseph Wittreich (Cleveland: Case Western Reserve University Press, 1970), p. 11.
5 *Selected Essays* (New York: Harcourt, 1960), p. 11.
6 Quoted in Donald Greene, *Samuel Johnson* (Boston: Twayne, 1989), pp. 26–27.
7 *Selected Essays*, p. 250.
8 "Samuel Johnson," in *The Importance of Scrutiny*, ed. Eric Bentley (New York: George Stewart, 1948), p. 59.
9 *Boswell's "Life of Johnson": New Questions, New Answers*, ed. John Vance (Athens: University of Georgia Press, 1985), p. 89.
10 "'Johnson and . . .': Conceptions of Literary Relationship," in *Greene Centennial Studies*, ed. Paul J. Korshin and Robert R. Allen (Charlottesville: University Press of Virginia, 1984), pp. 288–306.
11 Charles Batten, "Samuel Johnson's Sources for the 'Life of Roscommon,'" *MP*, 72 (1974), 185–89; O M Brack, Jr., "*The Gentleman's Magazine*, Concealed Printing, and the Texts of Samuel Johnson's *Lives of Admiral Robert Blake* and *Sir Francis Drake*," *Studies in Bibliography*, 40 (1987), 140–46; Richard Wendorf, "The Making of Johnson's 'Life of Collins,'"*Publications of the Bibliographical Society of America*, 74 (1980), 95–115.
12 "Dr. Johnson as Equivocator: The Meaning of *Rasselas*," *MLQ*, 31 (1970), 195–208.
13 Donald Greene, *Samuel Johnson* (updated edition) (Boston: Twayne, 1989), p. 36.
14 Gloria Sybil Gross, *This Invisible Riot of the Mind* (Philadelphia: University of Pennsylvania Press, 1992), p. 66.

15 R. M. Wiles, "The Contemporary Distribution of Johnson's *Rambler*," *ECS*, 2 (1968), 155–71.

16 For a survey see Edward Tomarken, *Johnson, "Rasselas," and the Choice of Criticism* (Lexington: University Press of Kentucky, 1989).

17 "Rasselas Returns – to What?," *PQ*, 38 (1959), 383–84.

18 "The Reader, the General and the Particular," *ECS*, 5 (1971), 80–96.

19 "*Rasselas* and Some Meanings of 'Structure' in Literary Criticism," *Novel*, 14 (1981), 108.

20 "Toward a Theory of Common Sense: Beckford's *Vathek* and Johnson's *Rasselas*," *Texas Studies in Language and Literature*, 26 (1984), 202, 205.

21 "Johnson's Shakespeare and the Laity," *PMLA*, 65 (1950), 1114.

22 *Samuel Johnson, Editor of Shakespeare* (Urbana: University of Illinois Press, 1956), and *Johnson's Notes to Shakespeare*, ed. with introductions by Arthur Sherbo (Los Angeles: Augustan Reprint Societ,. nos. 59–60 [1956], nos. 65–66 [1957], nos. 71–73 [1958].

23 "Johnson as Philosophic Traveler: The Perfecting of an Idea," *ELH*, 36 (1969), 679–95.

24 See, for example, Thomas M. Curley, *Samuel Johnson and the Age of Travel* (Athens: University of Georgia Press, 1976), Hart, "Johnson as Philosophic Traveler," Curt Hartog, "Johnson's Journey and the Theatre of the Mind," *Enlightenment Essays*, 7 (1976), 3–16, Thomas Preston, "Homeric Allusion in *A Journey to the Western Islands of Scotland*," *ECS*, 5 (1972), 545–58, and Eithne Henson, "*The Fictions of Romantick Chivalry*": *Samuel Johnson and Romance* (Rutherford: Fairleigh Dickinson University Press, 1992).

25 "Johnson and Swift: A Study in the Genesis of Literary Opinion," *PQ*, 48 (1969), 478.

26 Leopold Damrosch, Jr., *The Uses of Johnson's Criticism* (Charlottesville: University Press of Virginia, 1976), pp. 160, 164.

27 *Prose in the Age of Poets: Romanticism and Biographical Narrative from Johnson to De Quincey* (Philadelphia: University of Pennsylvania Press, 1990), p. 191.

FURTHER READING

This bibliography should be used in conjunction with Steven Lynn's essay on "Johnson's Critical Reception." It does not repeat the information in Lynn's essay, which offers a survey of Johnson criticism since 1784 (although in some respects they overlap), nor does it necessarily list all references in the individual essays in this volume. The aim of this guide is limited to registering some of the main critical studies of Johnson and his works, and to include some that are considered by this editor as the *best* work on Johnson. The general reader and the non-specialist will thereby have a relatively manageable and informative entrance to the works and the life of Johnson, while the specialist's perspective will be challenged by the particular selection.

For greater comprehensiveness the reader should consult *Samuel Johnson: A Survey and Bibliography of Critical Studies*, ed. James L. Clifford and Donald J. Greene (Minneapolis: University of Minnesota Press, 1970), *A Bibliography of Johnsonian Studies, 1970–1985*, ed. Donald Greene and John A. Vance, in the English Literary Studies series of the University of Victoria (Victoria, BC, 1987), and the continually updated and up-to-date bibliography by Jack Lynch on the World Wide Web: <http://www.english.upenn.edu/~jlynch/Johnson/ sjbib.html>. Useful book reviews and bibliographies pertaining to Johnson are also to be found in The *Johnsonian News Letter* (founded by James L. Clifford and now edited by Stuart Sherman), and in *The Age of Johnson: A Scholarly Annual*, edited by Paul J. Korshin, now in its ninth volume and continuing to publish some of the best criticism and scholarship on Johnson, his contemporaries, and eighteenth-century culture.

PRIMARY WORKS

The standard text is *The Yale Edition of the Works of Samuel Johnson*, general editor Allen T. Hazen, later John H. Middendorf, which presently has thirteen volumes (see list of short titles and abbreviations). Forthcoming volumes include the *Debates in Parliament* (vols. XI–XIII), ed. Benjamin Hoover; *Annotations to Crousaz's Commentary of Pope's "Essay on Man"* (vol. XVII), ed. O M Brack, Jr.; *Philological Writings* (vol. XVIII), ed. Gwin J. Kolb and Robert DeMaria, Jr.; *Biographical Writings* (vol. XIX), ed. O M Brack, Jr.; *Lives of the Poets* (vols. XX–XXII), ed. John H. Middendorf; *Shorter Prose* (vol. XXIII), ed. O M Brack, Jr., and the Inclusive Index (vol. XXIV).

The standard edition of the *Lives of the Poets* is that in three volumes by G. B. Hill (Oxford: Clarendon Press, 1905). Johnson's earlier biographies are accessible in *Early Biographical Writings of Dr Johnson*, ed. J. D. Fleeman (Farnborough: Gregg International, 1973), and the *Life of Savage* in an edition by Clarence Tracy (Oxford: Clarendon Press, 1971).

In addition to the Yale edition of the poems, there are excellent alternate editions by David Nichol Smith and E. L. McAdam, Jr. (Oxford: Clarendon Press, 2nd edn. 1974) and by J. D. Fleeman (Harmondsworth: Penguin and New Haven: Yale University Press, 1971). Niall Rudd provides a useful annotated parallel-text edition of Johnson's *Vanity of Human Wishes* and *London* with Juvenal's third and tenth satires (Bristol Classical Press, 1981 and 1988); and the same press has published (1985) an introductory, annotated facsimile-edition of Johnson's *Preface to Shakespeare* by P. J. Smallwood that helpfully facilitates connections between Johnson's specific notes and the plays, his general comments in the *Preface*, and the broader context of eighteenth-century critical writing.

J. D. Fleeman is the editor of the exhaustive Clarendon Press edition of *A Journey to the Western Islands of Scotland* (Oxford, 1985), excellent as a scholarly supplement to the Yale edition; but more accessible than either – and with a good introduction – is the Penguin edition (Harmondsworth, 1984), edited by Peter Levi, of Johnson's and Boswell's different accounts of their journey.

Johnson's letters are now available in the beautiful five-volume Hyde edition, edited by Bruce Redford, and published by Princeton University Press and the Clarendon Press (Princeton and Oxford: 1992–94), but the three-volume edition by R. W. Chapman (Oxford: Clarendon Press, 1952) is still valuable (unlike the Hyde edition, it prints Mrs. Thrale's letters to Johnson).

Rasselas is available in many editions, the standard one (after the Yale text) being that by Geoffrey Tillotson and Brian Jenkins (Oxford University Press, 1971), and the most convenient (and helpful by way of introduction and annotation) being the Oxford World Classics edition by John Hardy (1968, repr. 1988).

The Dictionary of the English Language, 2 vols. (1755, substantially revised for the 4th edn., 1773) has been available in a series of facsimile reprints (1967, 1968, 1979, and 1980), but the texts of both the first and the fourth editions are now available in a Cambridge University Press CD-ROM (ed. Anne McDermott) that facilitates comparison between the two editions and makes for an efficient electronic browsing of all 80,000 entries in both editions.

Other important writing by Johnson includes an edition of his prefaces and dedications, edited by Allen T. Hazen (New Haven: Yale University Press, 1937), and Johnson's contributions to the Vinerian law lectures at Oxford, in Sir Robert Chambers, *A Course of Lectures on the English Law, 1767–1773*, ed. Thomas M. Curley, 2 vols. (Madison: University of Wisconsin Press and Oxford: Clarendon Press, 1986).

For works not presently included in the Yale edition, the reader might consult the edition of Johnson's works by Sir John Hawkins (13 vols., London, 1787) or by Arthur Murphy (12 vols., London, 1792, 1806, and 1823; and 15 vols., Edinburgh [1806]), although these editions are textually unreliable. Of the many general anthologies of Johnson's writings, one of the best is Bertrand H. Bronson's Rinehart selection *Samuel Johnson: Rasselas, Poems, and Selected Prose* (1952 and 1971), while Donald Greene's Oxford Authors *Samuel Johnson* (Oxford University Press 1984) contains a wide sampling of different works, including some not easily available in a modern text.

SECONDARY WORKS

Biographies

The most influential early biographies of Johnson are James Boswell's *Life of Samuel Johnson, LL.D.* (1791, 2nd edn. 1793) and *Journal of a Tour to the Hebrides with Samuel*

Johnson, LL.D. (1785) (these two works published together in the edition of the *Life* by G. B. Hill, revised L. F. Powell, 6 vols. [Oxford: Clarendon Press, 1934–64]), Sir John Hawkins's *Life of Samuel Johnson* (London, 1787) and Hester Lynch [Thrale] Piozzi's *Anecdotes of the Late Samuel Johnson* (London, 1786). Additional biographical reflections on Johnson by Mrs. Thrale can be found in *Thraliana*, ed. Katherine C. Balderstone, 2 vols. (Oxford: Clarendon Press, 1942). Piozzi's *Anecdotes* and Arthur Murphy's *Essay on the Life and Genius of Samuel Johnson* [1792], together with excepts from Hawkins, and many other early biographical texts can be found in the *Johnsonian Miscellanies*, ed. G. B. Hill, 2 vols. (Oxford: Clarendon Press, 1897). Of great interest, and containing additional early biographies, is *The Early Biographies of Samuel Johnson*, ed. O M Brack, Jr. and Robert E. Kelley (University of Iowa Press, 1974).

Although wrong-headed, the two articles by Thomas Babington Macaulay – the review of John Wilson Croker's edition of Boswell's *Life* (1831) and the life of Johnson for the *Encyclopedia Britannica* (1856) – have deeply influenced how Johnson is read.

Among modern biographies, "factual" contextualizations are offered by James L. Clifford's *Young Sam Johnson* (New York: McGraw-Hill, 1955) and *Dictionary Johnson* (New York: McGraw-Hill, 1979), and by Thomas Kaminski's *The Early career of Samuel Johnson* (Oxford University Press, 1987); but W. J. Bate's *Samuel Johnson* (New York: Harcourt, Brace, Jovanovich, and London: Chatto and Windus, 1977) challenges the reader to think psychoanalytically about Johnson, and John Wain's *Samuel Johnson: A Biography* (London: Macmillan, 1974) engages in Johnson's inner and outer life with a writer's sympathy.

Critical works

Alkon, Paul K., *Samuel Johnson and Moral Discipline* (Evanston: Northwestern University Press, 1967).

Basker, James G., "Dancing Dogs, Women Preachers and the Myth of Johnson's Misogyny," *AJ*, 3 (1990), 63–90.

    "Samuel Johnson and the African–American Reader," *The New Rambler* (1994/95), 47–57.

    "Radical Affinities: Mary Wollstonecraft and Samuel Johnson," in *Tradition in Transition: Women Writers, Marginal Texts, and the Eighteenth-Century Canon*, ed. Alvaro Ribeiro, SJ, and James G. Basker (Oxford: Clarendon Press, 1996), 41–55.

Bate, W. J., *The Achievement of Samuel Johnson* (University of Chicago Press, 1955).

Battersby, James L., "Life, Art, and the *Lives of the Poets*," in *Domestick Privacies: Samuel Johnson and the Art of Biography*, ed. David Wheeler (Lexington: University of Kentucky Press, 1987), pp. 26–56.

    Rational Praise and Natural Lamentation: Johnson, Lycidas, and the Principles of Criticism (Rutherford: Fairleigh Dickinson University Press, 1980).

Bogel, Fredric V., *The Dream of My Brother: An Essay on Johnson's Authority*. English Literary Studies, 47, (Victoria, BC: University of Victoria, 1990).

Boulton, James T. (ed.), *Johnson: The Critical Heritage* (London: Routledge and Kegan Paul, 1971).

Bronson, Bertrand H., *Johnson Agonistes and Other Essays* (Berkeley: University of California Press, 1946).

Brownell, Morris R., *Samuel Johnson's Attitude to the Arts* (Oxford: Clarendon Press, 1989).

Burke, John J. and Donald Kay (eds.), *The Unknown Samuel Johnson* (Madison: University of Wisconsin Press, 1983).

Cafarelli, Annette Wheeler, "Johnson and Women: Demasculinizing Literary History," *AJ*, 5 (1992), 61–114.

Cannon, John, *Samuel Johnson and the Politics of Hanoverian England* (Oxford: Clarendon Press, 1994).

Chapin, Chester, *The Religious Thought of Samuel Johnson* (Ann Arbor: University of Michigan Press, 1968).

Clark, J. C. D., *Samuel Johnson: Literature, Religion and English Cultural Politics from the Restoration to Romanticism* (Cambridge University Press, 1994).

Clingham, Greg, *Boswell: The Life of Johnson* (Cambridge University Press, 1992).
    "Another and the Same: Johnson's Dryden," in *Literary Transmission and Authority: Dryden and Other Writers*, ed. Jennifer Brady and Earl Miner (Cambridge University Press, 1993), pp. 121–59.
    "Johnson, Homeric Scholarship, and the 'passes of the mind,'" *AJ*, 3 (1990), 113–70.
    Writing Memory: Authority, Textuality, and Johnson's "Lives of the Poets" (forthcoming).

Curley Thomas M., *Samuel Johnson and the Age of Travel* (Athens: University of Georgia Press, 1976).

Damrosch, Leopold, *Fictions of Reality in the Age of Hume and Johnson* (Madison: University of Wisconsin Press, 1989).
    "Johnson's *Rasselas*: Limits of Wisdom, Limits of Art," in *Augustan Studies: Essays in Honor of Irvin Ehrenpreis*, ed. Douglas Lane Patey and Timothy Keegan (Newark: University of Delaware Press, 1985), pp. 205–14.
    The Uses of Johnson's Criticism (Charlottesville: University of Virginia Press, 1976).

Davis, Philip, *In Mind of Johnson: A Study of Johnson the Rambler* (Athens: University of Georgia Press, 1989).

DeMaria, Robert, Jr., *Johnson's "Dictionary" and the Language of Learning* (Chapel Hill: University of North Carolina Press, 1986).

Eliot, T. S., "Johnson as Critic and Poet," *On Poets and Poetry* (London: Faber and Faber, 1971), pp. 162–92.

Engel, James (ed.), *Johnson and his Age*. Harvard English Studies, 12. (Cambridge, MA: Harvard University Press, 1984).

Fix, Stephen, "The Contexts and Motive of Johnson's *Life of Milton*," in *Domestick Privacies: Samuel Johnson and the Art of Biography*, ed. David Wheeler (Lexington: University of Kentucky Press, 1987), pp. 107–32.
    "Johnson and the 'Duty' of Reading *Paradise Lost*," *ELH*, 52 (1985), 649–71.
    "Distant Genius: Johnson and the Art of Milton's Life," *MP*, 81 (1984), 244–64.

Folkenflik, Robert, *Samuel Johnson, Biographer* (Ithaca: Cornell University Press, 1978).

Fussell, Paul, *Samuel Johnson and the Life of Writing* (London: Chatto and Windus, 1972).

Greene, Donald J., *The Politics of Samuel Johnson* (New Haven: Yale University Press, 1960; 2nd edn. revised 1990).

Grundy, Isobel, *Samuel Johnson and the Scale of Greatness* (Leicester University Press, 1986).
    (ed.), *Samuel Johnson: New Critical Essays* (London: Vision, and Barnes and Noble, 1984).
    "Samuel Johnson as Patron of Women," *AJ*, 1 (1987), 59–77.

"Samuel Johnson: A Writer of Lives looks at Death," *MLR*, 79 (1984), 257–65.

Hagstrum, Jean H., *Samuel Johnson's Literary Criticism* (Minneapolis: University of Minnesota Press, 1952; 2nd edn. University of Chicago Press, 1967).

Hinnant, Charles H., *Samuel Johnson: An Analysis* (New York: St. Martin's Press, 1988).

Hudson, Nicholas, *Samuel Johnson and Eighteenth-Century Thought* (Oxford: Clarendon Press, 1988).

Jones, Emrys, "The Artistic Form of *Rasselas*," *RES*, n.s. 18 (1967), 387–401.

Keast, William R., "The Theoretical Foundations of Johnson's Criticism," in *Criticism and Criticism*, ed. R. S. Crane (University of Chicago Press, 1957), pp. 169–87.

"Johnson's Criticism of the Metaphysical Poets," *ELH*, 17 (1950), 59–70.

Kemmerer, Kathleen, *"A Neutral Being Between the Sexes": Samuel Johnson's Sexual Politics* (Lewisburg: Bucknell University Press, 1998).

Kermode, Frank, "The Survival of the Classic," in *Renaissance Essays: Shakespeare, Spenser, Donne* (London: Routledge and Kegan Paul, 1971), pp. 164–80.

Kernan, Alvin, *Printing Technology, Letters and Samuel Johnson* (Princeton University Press, 1987).

Korshin, Paul J. (ed.), *Johnson after Two Hundred Years* (Philadelphia: University of Pennsylvania Press, 1986).

Leavis, F. R., "Johnson as Critic," in *"Anna Karenina" and Other Essays* (London: Chatto and Windus, 1973), pp. 197–218.

"Johnson and Augustanism," in *The Common Pursuit* (Harmondsworth: Penguin, 1969), pp. 97–115.

Lipking, Lawrence, *The Ordering of the Arts in Eighteenth-Century England* (Princeton University Press, 1970).

Lynn, Steven, *Samuel Johnson after Deconstruction: Rhetoric and "The Rambler"* (Carbondale: Southern Illinois University Press, 1992).

"Sexual Difference and Johnson's Brain," in *Fresh Reflections on Samuel Johnson: Essays in Criticism*, ed. Prem Nath (Troy, NY: Whitston, 1987), pp. 123–49.

McGilchrist, Iain, "Johnson," in *Against Criticism* (London: Faber and Faber, 1982), pp. 77–130.

Morris, John, "Samuel Johnson and the Artist's Work," *Hudson Review*, 26 (1973), 441–61.

Parke, Catherine N., *Samuel Johnson and Biographical Thinking* (Columbia: University of Missouri Press, 1991).

Parker, G. F., *Johnson's Shakespeare* (Oxford: Clarendon Press, 1989).

Quinlan, Maurice, *Samuel Johnson: A Layman's Religion* (Madison: University of Wisconsin Press, 1964).

Raleigh, Walter, *Six Essays on Johnson* (Oxford: Clarendon Press, 1910).

Reddick, Allen, *The Making of Johnson's Dictionary 1746–1773* (Cambridge University Press, 1990; revised paperback edn., 1996).

Ricks, Christopher, "Literary Principles as Agianst theory," in *Essays in Appreciation* (Oxford: Clarendon Press, 1996), pp. 311–32.

"Samuel Johnson: Dead Metaphors and 'Impending Death,'" in *The Force of Poetry* (Oxford University Press, 1987), pp. 80–88.

(ed.), Introduction to *Poems and Critics* (London: Fontana, 1972).

Scherwatzky, Steven, "Johnson, Rasselas, and the Politics of Empire," *ECL*, 16 (1992), 103–13.

"Samuel Johnson and Eighteenth-Century Politics," *ECL*, 15 (1991), 113–24.

Schwartz, Richard B., *Samuel Johnson and the New Science* (Madison: University of Wisconsin Press, 1971).

    Samuel Johnson and the Problem of Evil (Madison: University of Wisconsin Press, 1975).

South Central Review. Special Issue: *Johnson and Gender*, ed. Charles H. Hinnant, vol. 9, no. 4 (1992).

Tomarken, Edward, *Samuel Johnson on Shakespeare: The Discipline of Criticism* (Athens: University of Georgia Press, 1991).

Vance, John A., *Samuel Johnson and the Sense of History* (Athens: University of Georgia Press, 1985).

Voitle, Robert, *Samuel Johnson the Moralist* (Cambridge, MA: Harvard University Press, 1961).

Wechselblatt, Martin, *Bad Behavior: Samuel Johnson and Modern Cultural Authority* (Lewisburg: Bucknell University Press, 1998).

Weinbrot, Howard D., "The Reader, the General, and the Particular: Johnson and Imlac in Chapter Ten of *Rasselas*," *ECS*, 5 (1971), 80–96.

    The Formal Strain: Studies in Augustan Imitation and Satire (University of Chicago Press, 1969), chapters. 7 and 8.

White, Ian, "On Rasselas," *CQ*, 6 (1972), 6–31.

Wiltshire, John, *Samuel Johnson in the Medical World: The Doctor and the Patient* (Cambridge University Press, 1991).

Wimsatt, William K., *The Prose Style of Samuel Johnson* (New Haven: Yale University Press, 1941).

INDEX